ZEN
AND THE ART OF
RACING
MOTORCYCLES

Archway Publishing books may be ordered through booksellers or by contacting:

Archway Publishing
1663 Liberty Drive
Bloomington, IN 47403
www.archwaypublishing.com
1-(888)-242-5904

Because of the dynamic nature of the Internet, any web addresses or links contained in
this book may have changed since publication and may no longer be valid. The views
expressed in this work are solely those of the author and do not necessarily reflect the
views of the publisher, and the publisher hereby disclaims any responsibility for them.

Any people depicted in stock imagery provided by Thinkstock are models,
and such images are being used for illustrative purposes only.
Certain stock imagery © Thinkstock.

ISBN: 978-1-4808-1198-0 (sc)
ISBN: 978-1-4808-1199-7 (e)

Library of Congress Control Number: 2014917967

Printed in the United States of America.

Archway Publishing rev. date: 11/17/14

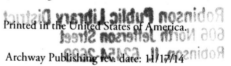

DEDICATION

For Vicky,
my patient wife
and partner in life,
who loves me enough
to put up will all that comes with
buying, building, restoring and racing
vintage motorcycles and
tolerates my compulsion
to be an equal opportunity
exasperator.

You deserved diamond earrings, but you got
to volunteer and score the races
instead

Table of Contents

Preface

I AM A MOTORCYCLE racer of the first order – that is to say I found my true self in racing motorcycles like I never found myself anywhere else in life. I began riding in the early sixties and took up racing as soon as there was another bike on the road. I was already a racer of other things, many other things, so it was a natural enough transition. I had ambitioned to be an Indy car driver but seeing Dave McDonald and Eddie Sachs burned to death in 1964 took that notion right out of my head.

I still had the desire to go fast, a competitive nature, and an inquisitive mind to apply to my life's work. The story of those things in play with the vagaries of chance and a nothing to lose attitude comprise what follows. They are stories, to be sure, but they are my stories.

This work searches for a useful link between concrete and abstract knowledge. I know things in both realms. I can juggle abstractions all day and still drive home from the office afterward while singing along with Steppenwolf on the radio. The chasm between the two realms is immense yet we hop back and forth across it all the time. There is a truth to this that I think matters and I believe that some insight into that truth can be found in what we do and how we do it. I call that 'Zen' because it speaks of discipline and meditative purposeful action intended to reveal useful truths. If you don't think that interests you then I suggest you are living a timid life.

There are people out there, right now, who are challenging everything about the world around them and are trying with all their resources to come to some understanding of what it all means before their opportunity to do so is gone.

Some of them race motorcycles. I am one of them. There are others no doubt, in many other fields of endeavor doing many different things and thinking all the while about what they do and how they do it and what meaning it brings to their life. I do not suggest that their path is any less productive than what I show here. I do point out that all of us share the journey and perhaps even the destination.

If you are dogmatic, then chew on this. If you are looking for the truth in things then look with us.

Gregg Bonelli
Summer 2014

1970 500 cc H-1 Kawasaki of Dave Crussel, same model as that ridden by Ron Muir at Indianapolis Photo by the author

1.

The Duality Of Existence

WE LIVE ON A planet that is two worlds. These worlds touch here and there, sometimes in peace, sometimes in conflict. The occupants of these worlds can see one another and can communicate on some levels, but they are as alien to one another as if they were from different planets.

In one of these worlds, the population is concerned with safety and the preservation of life. They love life and think it precious. They believe they understand its scientific underpinnings and operations. They see it as a societal duty to prolong it in each of us as long as productively possible for the greater good of all. They are fundamentally opposed to activities and behaviors that put life at risk and where allowed, will do all they can to minimize those risks or curb those behaviors.

There is another world where the population only cares about speed. Not the kind you take as a drug or the type you feel artificially from being on top of a mountain or at the end of a particularly well done performance of the minute waltz. They are not adrenaline junkies looking for another thrill. They care about movement through space on a motorcycle in competition with others of their kind.

They are a breed apart from other men, and there are some women too, but this narrative is not intentionally about them, for which I make no apology but give them their proper deference and admit that I do not understand women and would not presume to

1

attempt to explain why they do anything, let alone why they might race motorcycles. I will let them tell me, and I will listen.

As for the men I know, the ones from this other planet that walk among us, I know they carry a brain in their heads that has been programmed to react to certain things in certain ways that all have to do with being a motorcycle racer. They will organize and arrange their lives in such a way as to put themselves in a leather suit on a grid somewhere, some day, with a running racing motorcycle beneath them that is as well prepared as they can manage and as fast as they can afford and put out of their minds all that went before and focus just on that moment as they wait for the flag to send them off into a separate reality.

They recognize that there are risks and costs associated with this practice, and have taken steps to do what they can in light of those factors but believe sincerely, that it is their choice and even their right to do as they wish and even die in the process if that is the outcome. Some do that as well, but none would have thought it would be them if you asked.

In that other mundane world, the one that is populated by everyone else, they do not really approve of such behavior and think it dangerous and addictive. On one level they understand that tradition has allowed some measure of freedom to ride and even race motorcycles but they would really rather they did not exist or had air bags and seat belts and could be crash tested in some manner that would make them safe enough for those who were in crashes to be certain to survive. They appreciate that the normal appeals to reason and informational honesty that have been made to the operators as to the terminal effects of such life threatening behavior seem to be to no avail.

Being the majority, they have imposed liability and sanctions upon the practice so that now the perception of madness and daredevil behaviors have been eliminated so far as possible and computer assisted machines make calculations and apply brakes within the limits that the program tells the lever the tires can accommodate under current conditions. Meanwhile the throttle is modulated to only allow as much power to be called upon relative to what the rear wheel spin sensor says is sufficient to avoid a loss of traction.

I do not write about these modern machines made to placate the mundane world or the men who ride them, although I assume in my naiveté that there may be some distant relation between them and myself. If there is, it is so attenuated that it can be transmitted over electronic pathways and produce performances less connected to the brain of the rider than those connected to mine by a piece of wire running through a housing designed two centuries ago.

. . .

SCENE: A generic television studio with a public person shuffling pieces of blue paper while the producer gives him a signal that they are off the air. He looks up and a door opens off to one side and I am shown in to a seat facing him uncomfortably and a technician attaches a microphone to my lapel as another powders my face even though a moment ago I had asked her not to. There is a picture window on one wall that reveals a control room full of people wearing headphones and worried looks. One of the two signs on the wall is lit, the one that says "OFF AIR". The one above it, says "ON AIR" and I wonder to myself why it was necessary to leave 'the' out.

The man stops shuffling the papers, underlines a few things and then looks up at me like a fish might look out at you from a tank in a seafood restaurant. A camera on a dolly comes a bit closer and its movement brings it to my attention. A man appears from the shadows into the cone of light in which we sit. He holds up a hand with his fingers spread and says, "In Five, Four, …" and stops speaking as his fingers go ahead and count down and then points at us and the signs switch from "OFF AIR" to 'On Air.'

The man opposite me begins speaking in a sing song baritone that is the professional voice of an on air commentator. It is pleasant but rapid and has a sense of urgency that I do not feel or share at the moment. I hear him but he hasn't gotten to the end of what he is saying yet so it's not my turn to say anything and he skipped over the cursory social greetings so there was no early opportunity to be polite or show that I am not an animal of some kind on display. He pauses, and so I figure my introduction is over.

COMMENTATOR: "So, You're the national champion?"

ME: I have been, and I may be again, it's a transitory state.

COMMENTATOR:(snidely): Pretty big words for a motorcycle racer.

Now my brain begins its two step dance wherein it entertains itself with what it would like to say while giving my mouth words that are thought more socially acceptable to say instead.

BRAIN: Fuck you, Bob. (Everyone is 'Bob' to this brain)

MOUTH: It's a common misconception, Tom, that people who race motorcycles are all idiots to some degree. Actually that is not true at all, and neither are we all daredevils nor do we have a death wish.

COMMENTATOR:, (speaking over my answer before I finish) But isn't it true that hundreds of motorcycle racers die every year?

BRAIN: Note to self: Warning! This is a set up with some statistical bullshit in the follow up to come

MOUTH: That is not true at all; you are safer racing a motorcycle than as a passenger in an airplane. (I'm excluding the Isle of Man from my computation, pretending it is of a different order, which it is and for which I have no explanation, and thinking instead of trying to fly over Russian armed separatists in the Ukraine on Air Malaysia, or just flying anywhere on Air Malaysia and disappearing off the map).

COMMENTATOR:, holding up a blue sheet of paper, it says here that since 1908 two hundred and thirty six motorcycle racers have been killed while racing.

BRAIN: I see a Wikipedia tag line on the sheet and know from where he speaks.

ME: Well, I don't generally do math in public but 1908 was over a hundred years ago, which negates any possibility that your earlier statement was correct. But, while I am here, wouldn't you like to know why we race motorcycles?

COMMENTATOR: (not reacting, shuffling through two more pages of blue paper and marking through some of it, before looking back at the camera) That's all the time we have for now, stay tuned for an on the scene interview with a woman whose dog sleeps with her cat.

A guy with headphones steps out from behind a camera and makes a cut your throat gesture with his hand and it's over and the lights go back to 'Off Air'. I am largely ignored as I un-mike myself and stand up, leaving it in the too low barrel chair that was not designed for humans. Tom sticks his hand out and says something about being nice to have me but I wave him off and know it's just part of his other world behavior that doesn't really care to understand anything about racing or those who do it, but just wants something, anything, that will get people to watch his TV spots.

I think as I wipe the powder off my face and head back through the blue room where I had waited for three hours for this that I had wasted my time being here. A woman with a clipboard stops me in the hallway and hands me a check, I don't look at it and have an urge to give it back to her.

"They'd like to have you back next Tuesday," she says, and then holds her hand up to her face with her thumb out and her pinky finger sticking down by her mouth which is moving and mouthing the words, "*Call me*" then she winks and hands me a slip of paper with a number on it which I assume is hers and I nod and put it and the check in my pocket. She can have her fantasy for now, I am that kind at least, but I won't be calling her.

"What about Tuesday?" she asks out loud to my back as I walk away. I give her a 'thumbs up' sign without looking back. Hours later, I have finally calmed down a bit once I am back in my workshop and remind myself while surrounded by the artifacts of speed that what matters to me means nothing to them. I will make the effort to help them understand. I know they can and will eliminate mine if someone doesn't get through to them. I have no conflict with going back and I don't have to check my calendar. We don't race on Tuesdays.

SCENE: Next Tuesday, same set, same players, no powder on my face this time and I am wearing a black tee shirt with Old English block letters that say,
"Faster Than You"
and showing the Axes and Hammers logo Inspired by Adrian's mother. (She's the one who put Laura Ashely curtains in her son's caravan to make it homey while he was at the races. Taking his friends' derision was the price for that, but he paid it).

The lights go on and off, the man points, we are back on the air. The commentator gives an intro and it is pleasantly delivered and the national champion part is tucked in nicely like any descriptor of a person who should be listened to on the subject about to be considered.

COMMENTATOR: Thank you for taking the time to come back and give our viewers more of an insight into your sport -Many called in.

ME: You're welcome, Tom, some insight might be useful.

BRAIN: His tit's in a wringer over blowing me off last time and he's giving me the cursory courtesy treatment without being interested himself.

COMMENTATOR: Why do you race motorcycles?

BRAIN: Because tricycles are too slow, Bob…

ME: It is a question I have asked myself. Some people are born to race, that's the best answer I can give you. I have come to understand myself well enough to know that doing it reveals an essential truth to me about what matters and what doesn't that nothing else does.

COMMENTATOR: So it's the adrenalin rush you're after?

BRAIN: He didn't listen to my answer at all, just skipped on to the next talking point on his list - Points for being polite; no points for being stupid.

ME: No, it's not a drug and I am not an addict.

COMMENTATOR: So you could stop?

ME: I'm not racing now, am I? Apparently I can stop and do other things anytime I want for as long as I feel like it.

(I hear myself sounding irritated and moderate my tone).

COMMENTATOR: You seem to be an intelligent man - why would you do something so dangerous for so little reward?

BRAIN: Seem to be? Left handed compliments are never right.

ME: Living is dangerous and we all die sometime. In the meantime, I race exactly because it is so difficult and dangerous and because it is definitive in its conclusions.

COMMENTATOR: I don't understand.

BRAIN: Talk about an understatement! What can I tell this guy?

ME: There is a winner, and there are lots of others who raced to win but didn't. At the same time there is a transcendent moment available to all of us that has nothing to do with winning but more to do with ourselves individually.

COMMENTATOR: So it's about winning?

BRAIN: Give up; say something he wants to hear before you lose him.

ME: No, it is about speed. We all want to go fast and then go faster than anyone else. Winning is just the temporal acknowledgement that at a given track on a given day one of us finished the race before the others.

COMMENTATOR: So the winner is the fastest rider?

ME: Not necessarily, because he is riding 'something' and that 'something' may have abilities that the other bikes in the race didn't have that day. The fastest bike wins more often than the fastest rider.

BRAIN: I think he heard me.

Tom nods, thoughtfully, digesting what has been said and looking for an insightful wrap up. He's not quick enough and a signal is given from the darkness and he looks genuinely disappointed. The lights go on and off and we're done. He sticks out his hand, "Thank you," he says, and he sounds sincere. I shake it and feel the handshake of a man who knows what a handshake should be.

"You're welcome," I say and I see on the monitor that they are playing some clip of a race I was in somewhere and the faces illuminated by the screens before them in the control room look up and see me in front of them and then back down at the clip on their screens as I leave them.

Their expressions stay with me. They are incredulous. They are troubled. The things they believe important are of no use when faced with people like myself who see things differently. They realize that we are from different worlds. 'It is a beginning,' I think to myself.

In the hallway the "Call me" girl appears and blocks me over into one wall. "You didn't call," she says, pouting mouthed, showing me that she can make her false eyelashes go up and down. "Top dead center," I say.

She had already signaled her face to look pleased if I responded in any way but it caught her mid-coo that she wasn't sure if it was a 'yeah' or a 'nay' to her innuendo. As I begin to move away she figures out that the 'nays' have it and the meeting has been adjourned. Roberts' rules.

Her façade of sophistication breaks down completely. "Huh?" she blurts, dissembling. "Indeed," I answer and move around her and on my way, happy to have her behind me.

I pivot and walk backwards with an afterthought, not wanting ambiguity to linger. Facing her, I wag the deaf sign "Y" at her with both hands as I shake my head. (Ain't playin').

I turn again and go on my way.

(Exit stage door left. Curtain.)

2.

Arrivals And Departures

It is a hot sunny day and I am leaving Daytona after a week of sleeping with sand in everything and am back on the interstate heading home. It was just my third trip and it already feels like part of my life's routine which shakes me a little since my first trip was just a few years ago and since then everything, and I mean everything, has become totally unlike anything I had ever known.

For one thing it was the end of February, which had always been winter in my life but after driving up and down Mont Eagle in a little Ford Econoline van its tiny motor screaming away in the box between the front seats I had stepped out into the humid warm Florida night and asked the gas station attendant where the ocean was.

He was an all-night guy and I had worked all night myself and so was simpatico. I waited as he held up a finger and watched the pump. The wind rustled the palm fronds. I thought how great it would be to live here. The pump dinged.

He finished putting in the gas and came back up to the window and took my money and thought it through for a moment as I watched him do it. It took a while so I was anticipating some lengthy 'this way and that' sort of description to come and was preparing myself. Finally he spoke. "Go down this road," he said pointing with the hand that wasn't holding the bills, "to the Plaza Hotel, and then just keep going straight. There's a little tunnel through the hotel that takes you right out to the ocean."

"Really?" I asked him, like maybe he was pulling another tourist's leg. He smiled then and nodded his head a bit and said, "No shit, man. It's crazy I know but that's the way it is." I would be miles away and he would be snug in bed before I found out if this was his idea of a joke. If it was, it would be a good one, but we were on some wavelength here, what with it being the hour it was and both of us up and about for some reason. Night owls are like that.

He looked in the van and saw the bike, all tied in with its numbered fairing facing forward and its clear plastic bubble making it look like something out of Buck Rogers. "You racin'?" he asked me, with new interest. "I am," I said, "but I got here early and want to have a look at the ocean." "You never seen it?" he asks, incredulous, and I shake my head and start the van and hear him wish me luck as I pull out.

Sure enough after cruising slowly through twenty yellow lights all flashing over their intersections, and crossing the bridge over the inter-coastal waterway, I came to the Plaza Hotel's ominous pink façade facing A1A like a relic from another era. The van's windows were rolled down and I could hear the crashing of the waves but didn't know yet what the sound was connected to. Once I saw the ocean for the first time, I would never hear the sound again without thinking of what waves looked like coming onto the beach. But just now, idling at the intersection and waiting for the only light that wasn't on automatic yellow to turn green, I could hear it and knew abstractly that was what it was and I knew, that in a moment I would see it for myself and that my perception of it would be forever changed.

Surprise was one thing, speculation another, but anticipation was in a category of its own. "I'll give you anything you want for your birthday," she promised. She was sixteen and meant it, I was eighteen and had to say, 'no.' She never got over it. Neither did I.

The sound of the van grew louder as I pulled into the underground parking garage and its rumbling exhaust reverberated off of the low ceiling and concrete walls. This didn't seem right, but there had been a small sign on the outer wall that said 'public access ramp' when I approached so I kept going. I prepared myself for what I was about to see with a certain nonchalance, having seen a great many things, or so I thought, but nothing ever struck me quite like my first personal look at something that was so large it covered the majority of the planet. It was huge; and it moved. I was small and moved only a little by comparison.

There was a rising moon and the water stretched out beneath it to the far horizon. It wasn't just a sight to see, either, it had a smell and there was a constant gusting breeze associated with it in some way I didn't understand, and then of course there was the sound. It was louder than I had expected and it was constant. The whole impression of it was magnified by the fact that less than a block away, on the other side of the hotel's underground garage, none of this was appreciable. I could hear something, but it was not just a quieter version of this, it was the sound of a distant ocean.

Being at the beach, right where the ocean touches the sand and touches you, is not the same as being near the beach. I had stopped on the pad of concrete that spread out from the hotel and wasn't sure how I was going to turn around in such a small space. Then lights appeared behind me and I moved over a bit and a car went on by, right out onto the sand! I waited for it to sink up to its door handles but it didn't. It turned to the right and just kept going so I followed, finding the sand wide and firm and flat and easy to make out in the moonlight. We turned off our headlights.

The other car soon disappeared as it sped down the beach toward a large black structure that jutted out from the lights of town into the blackness. I was too far away to see what it was but figured it was a pier of some kind. Of course I knew that they had driven on the beach at one time, and had seen pictures of it and of races on the beach with cars and with motorcycles, but it had never occurred to me that they would still let you do it unimpeded.

I drove along with the sea at my shoulder and the fragrant salt breeze filling my soul. This was worth the trip. I loved it.

Soon I came to a place where some cars were parked near an all-night diner that was on the boardwalk facing the ocean and pulled into line where others were parked. I figured I could use a cup of coffee. I checked my watch and saw that it was not quite four. The sand was looser and my feet sank into it as I headed up to the stairway that led up to the light. My shoes were soon invaded by beach sand which would eventually find its way into almost everything I owned.

Up in the light was the Volusia Diner with its neon framing over an old low building next to the penny arcade. Inside there were a few stool pelicans perched with cigarettes and cups of coffee waiting for something to happen. They looked to be a century older than I was but did not give the impression of being any wiser for it. I disdained smokers, always had, even though my parents smoked as did nearly every adult I knew. It was part of being around adults then to tolerate their habit so I went in and looked for a seat as far from everyone as I could manage.

The waitress was so much like Lauren Bacall in her manner that I thought she was putting me on. She probably meant to play the dame from that old movie but missed the mark by using the voice of Humphrey Bogart. Her cigarette never left the corner of her mouth and she squinted the eye on that side to keep some of the smoke out of it as she spoke with her head turned just a bit.

"What'll it be?" she asked for the millionth time, each time with noticeably less interest than the one before. "Coffee," I shot back at her, unintentionally playing a Spade, and took a stool that was not next to anyone. She nodded appreciatively and started her 'get the pot and the cup' routine.

She had the heavy white porcelain cup in one hand and the Cory Coffee Pot in the other which she had glided off its burner in one smooth motion with her left hand as she plucked the cup from a stack of identical others with the right. She poured the black as coal coffee in mid-flight on her way over to my spot, landing it a bit roughly before me and sloshing out a pool which we both looked at and shrugged. "Dead men don't wear plaid," I commented.

She just stood there, expectantly, in a posture much like I imagined Napoleon had contemplating his last moves at Waterloo before withdrawing only with more hair spray. I picked up the battered cup with it's predictably 'too small for my finger' hole and took a sip. Horrible; it was simply horrible, and she was waiting for me to say something but beat me to it after a smirk of contempt. I had been set up.

"Cream and Sugar Sweetie?" she cooed, meaning to offend. I was young, and it showed, and might not be man enough for her 50 weight coffee, but I was not a fool. I notice that the other patrons had animated themselves enough to look or listen with cocked heads to hear what I was going to say. The coming exchange was probably what passed for entertainment in a joint like this so I needed to spot the exits and consider my answer carefully.

I noticed there was no juke box and no one was holding up a paper. The first was a little surprising, as it would have fit right in; the second was expected since I doubted any of them could read.

"Is your cooking as bad as your coffee?" I asked her, James Cagney, going along with her tough girl act, and she smiled, tilting the Camel up with her lips as she did so. "Some say it tastes pretty good," she answered, sensing now that the conversation had moved on to things that might mean money, or double entendre.

"Nice ash," I said, referring vaguely to the grey detritious dangling from the end of her non–filtered cigarette. "Can you scramble eggs without getting any in them?"

She looked like I had slapped her, and I supposed I had so I feigned indifference and took another sip of the coffee. Turpentine came to mind. She was offended now, apparently, and took her prop out of her red lips and put it in the ashtray with a pile of others that bore her brand and ran over onto the counter.

"Who the fuck are you," she snapped, out of character, "the Health Department?" "Potentially, I'm a customer who would like to have breakfast and can pay for it," I said in my own voice. I left it unsaid that I didn't want it made by her unless she wasn't smoking but she got the rest on her own and smiled.

There was some rustling noise from the faithful as stools turned and bodies moved around to see if this was going to turn into anything more. "So", she asked in a probing newly friendly voice, "you ain't from the Health Department?" "I am not, "I answered, "and if you can manage it, I would like three eggs scrambled with cheese, please, and dry toast." She nodded and picked up a familiar Guest Check pad that was the mandatory sea foam green and white with blue lines and a red sequential number in the upper right corner. I knew them, and had always thought they looked better than the places where you found them. Art Deco design transcends its global gallery.

She had pulled a pencil out from behind her ear and was writing now and was all business and we were going to be all right with one another. The drama had passed and I was in the fold, at least until I showed myself unworthy, in which case there would be trouble. "Hash browns?" she asked, staccato, and I answered, "No, thank you." "Grits?" she asked raising her eyebrows, suggesting she might have misjudged me and could possibly be a Southern boy and thereby a countryman. "Thanks for asking," I answered, "but no thanks." She put her pad down then, sensing that we might be done for the moment.

"See anything else you like?" "Ketchup" I said and she nodded and slid a bottle in my direction without looking as she passed it on her way to the griddle. The moment for interesting conversation over, the locals went back into their own thoughts and pulled down their shades.

I had finished my coffee by the time she came back with the eggs and she set them down with one hand, holding the coffee pot in the other and tilting her head to one side. I slid the cup over and she re-filled it without a word. This was a dance I knew well enough; I had been on her side of it myself as a waiter in several places. If she was good, she would bring the check and the coffee pot back with her one more time and ask me if I wanted dessert or if everything was all right. She would have figured out already that I wasn't the dessert type and the pedestal pie cover near me had as many flies on the inside with the pies as on the outside and I might have noticed. I had.

She did come back and I gave her the 'hand over the cup' sign and shook my head. She left the check without comment and wheeled out into the audience to make the rounds of her regulars. I paid the check and gave her a tip in the same amount, leaving it all on the counter. No one said anything when I left and it was a new world that I stepped out into.

The dawn was breaking over the ocean and everything was changing. There were soft colors of pink and purple and the sky was going from black to blue in that way that mystifies me still. The breeze had let up and the sound was now somehow different and quieter. The ocean was closer. I took my shoes and socks off and left them in the seat of the van and set off for a closer look. It was compelling.

The water was washing up on the shore in what seemed at first like an irregular pattern but it didn't take much observation to see that it was relentlessly thorough. Someone had told me once that every ninth wave was bigger than the ones before and after and I began keeping track to see if that were true or if I could declare it bunk as I suspected. As I walked along, I let it lap my feet and found it colder than I expected but kept going and didn't draw back from having it touch me again. Here was something primal, something moving and alive that was as old as the world itself and we were meeting for the first time.

I did not think that I would get the impression that it was in any way aware of me, but I did. It was silly, of course, it was so large and I was so immutably insignificant. 'Size matters doesn't it?' I thought to myself, and laughed for jibing with the ocean the way one might poke at a newly made acquaintance and my laughter was carried away on the wind.

I didn't go far, I had other places to be and this was not why I had come to Daytona. I left before I was really ready to go and although it was not a conscious decision, I took it with me. I would always love the seashore and I promised myself that I would come back. Walking back past the diner I heard the waitress greeting a new customer; this time she was Alice from the Honeymooners; the mark would play Ralphy Boy only he didn't know it. She was good.

. . .

I thought of all of this thirty years later as I was near the shore again and could smell it but not hear it. I was meeting Danny Levine for lunch in Savannah and was put at ease by the familiarity of the waterfront. We had spoken on the phone less than an hour before and I was fulfilling a different promise to myself that I would take better care of my friendships.

It was a bit odd that Danny would be in that category but he had shown up in Colorado two years ago at a Vintage motorcycle race in Steamboat Springs, high in the Rocky Mountains about as far from the beach as you can get, and I recognized that he was touching a base from his past of some kind and it was me. He was the Judah Benjamin of our group – more competent than he needed to be for his position and the go to guy when you needed something but didn't know where to go. He was the Poobah of our confederacy.

When he appeared, I had been out to practice on my Yamaha TR 3, a highly strung, temperamental grand prix two stroke twin and had not especially enjoyed it. The course was a combination of public streets and an access road to a housing project that was not yet completed so there were only one or two homes finished. There were curbs and gutters and manhole covers, none of which were good things on racetracks, and to make matters worse it was misting slightly which gave a slimy slick surface to everything. I was a thousand miles from home and two days without sleep on an errand that was about to prove disastrous and I knew it.

I had put the bike up on its stand and was taking off my gloves and helmet when I noticed someone standing nearby. Our pits are not closed off from the public in any way so it is not unusual to have someone come up and say he had one of those and point to a bike or ask if it is like the one he used to ride to school or some such. It's a public relations thing and by this time I had been dealing with the public a good deal so I didn't mind it as much as the weather. Being patient with inane questions was the opposite of what I would have done when I was seriously racing, but then and now are as different from one another as they can be as am I.

I made sure the gas was off and the bike was steady and then turned to face my patient unidentified visitor. "Gregg Bonelli" he said, like he knew me, and in the instant that he said it, the way he said it, I knew who he was. "Danny Levine," I answered, and we shook hands. He was larger and rounder and greyer than the last time I saw him.

"Danny," I said, "I wouldn't have recognized you." He smiled then, and said, "I hardly recognize myself anymore." I found him a seat and set to work on the bike doing the routine things one must do to keep them going. He knew about them and was not offended.

We spoke about how long it had been since we had been together and what we had been doing since. Danny was "Professor Levine" now with a Ph.D. in Art History and was teaching in Savannah. I was a practicing attorney with a doctorate degree in law and had graduated with honors from a Chicago Law School. We were a far cry from what we had been the day we met.

That day had been twenty years earlier and I had just gotten my initial paycheck from Triumph City after two weeks of working with no real money. We had been blown into town by the first blizzard of the season in Colorado while on our way to Oregon where I had been living when she and I met in Southern Illinois. It sounds as unlikely now as it was then and I'll get to it, but for now it's enough to know that I had money in my pocket and was out to convince myself that I was not broke and could buy my new wife a thing or two if I cared to.

I had spotted Danny's shop on the main street of Gainesville, Florida on my first pass through from the interstate to look the town over. The "Subterranean Circus" was hand painted with care and detail on the marquee over the length of the one story building and it made you want to go in and see just what sort of business they conducted. It was a month before I had the opportunity, interest and funding all at the same time and could make that happen.

The bell rang on its spring mount just over our heads when I pushed the door open and showed Stella inside. She was all smiles with her blonde hair and deep tan and was better looking than I deserved which was often mention to me and probably to her as well. She didn't like being called 'Stella' she had informed me recently and had decided to start using her middle name instead, but I had resisted and lapsed back into thinking of her as the girl I loved when I met her rather than the one she wanted to become.

The overwhelming scent of patchouli struck me as we entered and the easy grace of Rita Coolidge's voice was haunting the air as we came in. A striking brunette came over, who was long and tall and very direct and had hair down to her waist parted down the middle of her head which had been the fashion in the sixties, which is what it was in here apparently, while outside things had moved on a bit. Still she was obviously braless and excited to see one of us, which was difficult to ignore.

"Gloria" she said, holding out her hand in response to my introductions of ourselves, and her handshake was more of a permissive caress than I thought it should have been at first meeting. We held hands as she looked into me. It was powerful and her large dark eyes were pools of steady invitation. Then I realized that she must be stoned and let her go and let her know kindly that we were just looking around.

Processing this finally, she gave a sweeping gesture with her long bare arm across the whole scene; several rooms of black light posters, paraphernalia of all sorts, and pottery, inviting us to take our time, and just let her know if we saw anything we liked. She lingered on the word, 'anything' just playing with it herself, suggestively. When we turned away I could hear her saying it again to herself to see if it got a rise out of herself. Surely, I was imagining this; but the steady yank from my new mate told me otherwise as we crossed a threshold into some other world of things in Haight-Ashbury mockery that was in every university town in the country by then.

A parachute hung from the ceiling, sans cords, and the whole place seemed casually very well done and thoughtfully laid out. This had taken some time. A small leprechaun of a man with a beard appeared from the back with round wire rimmed glasses and a quick sure manner who introduced himself as 'Danny; Danny Levine," and commenced to try and sell me something.

He was Jewish, and it was obvious. He enjoyed it and so did I. There had been a shoe salesman back in Robinson that was like Danny who was perpetually cheerful, engaging, and doing business and I had come to enjoy the salesman's shtick as a genre. He pointed out this and that and explained to his satisfaction the value and purpose and savings involved with purchasing everything I showed even a passing interest in.

I was there to buy something, even if I hadn't said so, which please him because he knew then that he was not wasting his time so it was now just a matter of finding the right thing, which was a different task altogether than the one where you just wait to see if someone is a looker or a buyer.

Gloria and Stella had wandered off into another room and were looking at a jewelry display and Danny and I stood together and watched them admiringly for a moment. Then he surprised me and said, "Aren't they gorgeous?" and I wasn't sure I understood him. "The women?" I asked him, and he nodded in appreciation, "Yes," he answered, "we are lucky just to have them." He was right about that, neither he nor I were what anyone would have described as a great catch.

I didn't know him at all but I knew myself well enough to hope I had better things ahead of me. He seemed oddly stuck here, as if it was all too easy to give up and hurdle over some impediment that would be mandatory before he got to a better place in life. It was a strange thing, but he and I seemed to be together in this and I suspected that he felt his days with Gloria were numbered. Couples are hard to figure anyway. Here and there you meet one that is strangely mismatched and you wonder to yourself what had brought them together and whether whatever it was would keep them that way.

The radio playing music when we came in had turned to talk when Rita was done and had rambled incoherently on about furniture sales and weather and such until, finally, it had gone back to music. Then one of those moments in life came along that you never forget.

It was the first time I heard Seals and Croft sing "Summer Breeze" and Danny and I walked into a room of winds chimes and tapestries that seemed made for it. I turned to him and said we would always remember this and he looked oddly at me and raised his eyebrows then and said, "If you say so.." My sense of such things had grown over the years from when I had first begun to notice that some moments stood out more than others, and then extended that hypothesis to others thinking that if I pointed them out when I felt them, they might sense it as well. Calling them out was a social experiment and not everyone took it well, but Danny had seemed accepting enough, especially given our short acquaintance.

Perpetual memories had first become noticeable to me when I was a child and I thought then that it was strange that some things I never forgot and others I could never seem to remember. Over time I had come to recognize their appearance but had not tried to organize them for what they were – significant in a special way that was yet to be revealed. They exist for all of us, but mostly we let them go by without marking them until afterward when we think back and say to our self, 'yeah, I felt that coming."

Reunited and our browsing done, Stella and I selected as a purchase a tie dyed hanging of heavy material with a seam sewn in one end made for a curtain rod. We put it up in our apartment when we got back home. She had shown me a silver ring and tried it on, but I couldn't afford it and was embarrassed to say so. Gloria said she would hold it for me and I thanked her as I told her she didn't have to. She gave me a wink then, which I supposed meant that there was something going on I didn't understand. I knew I would have to come back later to find out what it was.

That turned out to be the next Saturday and I stopped in and ended up giving Gloria $20 as a down payment on the ring that Stella had picked out for herself for her birthday, which was next month, I was reminded. The women had formed a conspiracy in the brief moments since their meeting as Danny and I had 'breezed around the place' as Gloria put it. I knew when the birthday to be was, and I knew that I needed to get her something, but still it was a transaction in which my only part was to provide the money and something about that bothered me. I let it go.

For her nineteenth birthday I cleaned the motorcycle grease out from under my finger nails and scrubbed up and took her out for dinner at the nicest restaurant in town. She ordered a Caesar salad which the waiter prepared on a cart next to our table. She was so grossed out when he put a raw egg in it that she wouldn't eat any. I did not mention that I did not know that was what 'Caesar' salad meant either, and ate it anyway, knowing I was going to have to pay for it. Otherwise the meal was fine, and should have been given what it cost.

We talked about our future and the things we wanted and as I listened to her I thought to myself that it was unlikely that any of this would actually work out. I reformed it into challenge for myself as I listened, thinking it was more likely that I would see it done rather than let it go bad if someone had dared me to; even if it was myself. Some self analysis was in order I realized and began immediately.

My mind was constantly on motorcycles and the next race and the rest of life seemed only incidental to that. It was a bad thing, or at least it had some bad aspects, and I had a good thing here and should do more with it. She wanted to go to college and have a degree because I had one and she was tired of feeling like I was smarter than she was. I was smart enough to understand that and agreed that we should do it. While I didn't think it would make her as smart as I was, given what I knew already and where she was starting from, I failed to see that she thought she was already there and this was a social reform movement for me, not her.

I wanted children, which was why we had gotten married to begin with, and I wanted her to stop taking birth control so we could get started. She agreed, and those two things – her education and intention to start a family, were set in motion. In that one conversation racing went from being everything to me to being tertiary at best. My intention was to bring the sort of luck I had been enjoying on the race track to these tasks as well and I had no reason to believe it would not work out.

I gave her the ring and she feigned surprise. The waiter brought out a little cupcake with a candle in it and everyone in the restaurant sang happy birthday to her as if that was why they were all there. That night was as good as it ever got between us, the rest was all downhill, and as insightful as I thought I was about things, I have to admit that I never saw it coming. Our destiny may not be by chance, but it is not necessarily by choice either.

. . .

The next time I saw Danny Levine he was zipping himself into a set of all black leathers and we were at the Pasco County Fairgrounds in Dade City, Florida. I did not know that he road bikes at all, let alone raced. The Florida Grand Prix Riders had made a road race course out of the access road around the fairgrounds which was a mile and eight feet long and had sixteen turns. It was also the road you drove in on and left on and the whole affair was exceedingly informal. Except for the speed, that is, they really got things moving once the races started and I was startled by how casually people would sit and drink beer in lawn chairs while roasting hot dogs on a grill all just a few unprotected feet from the track.

It was this place that had brought me to Florida to begin with and it was here, among the blossoming orange groves, that I learned a very valuable lesson – Go fast, or stay home. I had not seen Danny there before so I was surprised to see him here now. I went over as he was about to start up his little rotary valve Kawasaki single and was suiting up. He saw me and made the 'two hands pushing' gesture and I nodded my assent and got behind him and waited until he nodded and signaled that he was ready. The little bike fired right up and off he went as I saw the Star of David hand painted on the back of the seat with the moniker "Team Jewish" hand lettered beneath.

I watched him take a lap or two and then went back and got myself ready to ride. When practice was over I found him again and he was in an animated conversation with someone using both hands the way fighter pilots describe a dogfight and talking 90 words a minute. I stood by for a while, watching and listening with pleasure to see someone so enthused about what they were doing.

When he was finished he turned to me and said, "I didn't know you liked to watch motorcycle races." "I don't especially," I answered, "I'm here to race." He looked surprised. "You're too big!" he blurted out and I held my finger up to my lips, "Don't tell my bike," I said, "it's unhappy enough already," and he laughed at that, and I did too, which prompted a series of one liner jokes from both of us each trying to tell them the best and laughing at ourselves and one another. "Did you hear about the elephant that had diarrhea? It's all over town!" Groucho would have been proud.

It was a joy to be in his company and he was fast and won his race. I did not win mine, but I was fast enough to not get in anyone's way and smart enough to know that I needed something faster to ride. Ted Henter won my race and I went over to look at his equipment. He had an easy gracious manner and didn't seem bothered by my presence.

At Dade City there were no private pits or places to hide what you were doing. I looked with open admiration at his domestic version of the Yamaha grand prix 250cc bike, the TD2B and asked him how he liked it. "It's faster than what I was riding before," he said, "and it seems to be fast enough to win so I like it fine." "I ride something that used to be that sort of bike," I told him, and we had a look at my 250 Harley Sprint. This was 1973 and my bike was a factory made special from 1966. It was still relatively fresh in terms of running hours and still pulled hard and sounded good. But, there was only so much you could do to make a pushrod single four stroke go fast and in my own mind at least I was doing it.

Ted asked me how I shifted it, having heard me go past on the straight while he was getting ready to go out, and thinking to himself that it was very quick and seemed too smooth. I told him I used the kill button and explained that it was a detail I had gotten from the guy I got the bike from because the pull on the dry clutch is a bear and it would wear me out to have to pull it in and let it out for every shift. You load up the shift lever in advance with your foot and when you are ready just dab the kill button and it jumps right into the next gear. Then he asked me if it worked for downshifts too, but I told him it didn't, because you had to bring the revs up to get the gears to go down easily. It was a pleasant exchange and we were called away to other things.

We were kids, both of us really, as were most of the racers with few exceptions. Here and there you might find a mature seasoned veteran but they usually didn't bother using up their equipment at club races like Dade City. Parts were precious and hard to come by. If you used one up in practice or when it didn't matter, you would regret it when the time came that you needed it to be at its best.

As was my custom, I shook hands with him when we parted, which told me something. They were strong, but smaller than mine, which was not surprising. He had character, and a kindness that other riders didn't seem to possess, but he was fiercely competitive. Still, I had the impression it wasn't aimed at me, but more at the world that was holding him back generally.

That night there was a short track race over at a sandy oval in front of the grandstands for the fairgrounds. After loading up I was drawn by the sound of one motor very much louder than the others that separated itself from the roar of all the others by its singular constant pitch that did not rise and fall. I went to see what it was.

The closer I got the more it seemed like the scene was other worldly. It was brightly lit within the circle, but walking from where I had parked over to it I could barely see. I was coming from another part of the fairgrounds where we had been racing and so was already within the 'pay to be there' portion of the property. There were no guards or gatekeepers here. It was a warm night and I carried the fatigue of the past few days heavily, suddenly, as the tension that had let me do it began to ebb with the reality that I had survived and would live to race again. There were a few standing at the fence about midway down the backstretch and I joined them at the square link cattle fence that kept the bikes on the track.

It was smooth and flat and orange in appearance but didn't seem dusty. They guy next to me said 'Hey' as I approached, which is Southern for 'Hello" so I said 'Hey' back and asked him what was going on. He said they were about to start the heat races which meant that practice was over. Pretty soon they were lining up some bikes and since there was no announcer or public address system over where we were it was difficult to hear much other than the running motors once they were started. They came around and past us and then stopped on the front straight to take up their starting positions.

I had done this myself many times by then and had more or less put it behind me, but there was still a thrill at seeing it. That was tempered by my lack of information. I did not know the riders or what to expect from them or what size the bikes might be, or whether they were any good at it. All of that would show quickly I knew, so I waited.

The race started. The sound of the bikes increased as the pack of them headed down to turn one and then it lessened as throttles were closed and adjustments of lean and left foot pressure were made and steering done until riders were individually satisfied that they had the turning thing under control and then reopened the throttle, some sooner than others, some gradually, until they strung out and came past us down the back stretch and did it again for turn three and four and then back to the front straight and so on, pretty much the same, until I saw the checkered flag come out and they stopped racing and cruised around and back into the pits. It was so very familiar that it didn't especially interest me. Then another group came out and it was repeated and I was turning to go when I heard the loud booming sound that had attracted me to begin with. "What the hell is that?" I asked my neighbor. "That's a Harley Sprint," he said, baring his teeth in a big grin, "Ain't she sumpin'?!"

She was something indeed, and I knew something of it since I had one and had ridden it all day only mine had never sounded like that. This one made one loud clear note until they turned them loose and then it got louder and ran down to the turn and never let up just kept going. You could see the rider wrestling the handlebars around and getting his foot out and pulling the bike around behind him, next to him, beneath him, and then tucking in tight and putting his left hand out and grabbing the fork leg leaving just his throttle hand up in the breeze as he went by us all alone, way out in front of the others.

There was a wake of sound that followed him that was almost painful as he passed and took the machine into the blackness of the far turn. Suddenly he was upright and then twitched the handlebars first one way, and then the other, searching for that spot where the front wheel would plow just enough of the sandy clay surface up in front of it to allow him to turn the bike and keep the back wheel almost spinning free, just within the powerband, never letting off the throttle not even one little bit.

For a moment I thought the throttle had stuck open and this kid was about to buy it, but he let off on the front straight and they lined up for the start and you could hear him blip it up and let it fall back down, but it sounded very little like the other bikes and nothing like mine. This was the 250 main and he won going away, leading every lap by a greater margin than the one before. It was a beautiful thing to see and hear.

Deep inside the moving vision of flailing arms and legs was a domed piston with valve pockets going up and down inside a combustion chamber at 11,000 rpm while its connecting rod dipped into a well of Oilzum Crystal 50 caster bean oil in its wet sump and its featherweight pushrods were poked up and down in their external tube into machined sockets in the rocker arms without stems or adjusting nuts that rode on eccentric shafts for adjustment instead. Its layout was similar to the street bike version of the same motor, one that was designed forty years before as a 175 to meet the needs of post war Italy. The laydown design had seemed practical and accommodated many of the considerations in a gravity return lubrication system. A small pump sent oil to the far end of the rocker arms through external oil lines that were forever prone to leaks and exposed to all manner of things that might lessen their grip on the pressurized contents within. Despite all that, and its archaic design, this bike flew, and I wanted to know why.

After the race was over I hopped the fence and made my way over to the pit area, walking past the machines and tools and tires and mechanics working on bikes or looking at bikes that were beyond working on. In a far corner I found an old man and a youngster peeling out of his leathers. Up on a wooden stand to accommodate the odd footpegs with the left one higher than the right by half a foot; sat the Harley that had just cleaned everyone's clock. The old man saw me coming. "Hey," he said, "You comin' to protest us?" "Hey, yourself," I said, "Should I be?" I smiled then and he was a little less wary. "We're all legal here and using pump gas," he said, pointing at a can as if I could check for myself." "I believe you," I said, "I came to have a look because I raced one of these all day over on the road race course and mine doesn't run anything like yours."

"Well," he said, more calm now and about to give me the benefit of the doubt, "this here is a CRTT motor, not one of them CRS's and there's a world of difference." "I know there is," I answered with some respect, "I have a CRTT, with the high compression piston and the eccentric rocker arm shafts and the lightweight push rods and all that, but mine does not haul ass like yours does." He grinned large then and looked me over. "Maybe 'cause there's too much ass to haul," he poked me. I laughed at myself and looked at the kid now coming out of the van. "What's he weigh? I asked the old man. "Just shy of a hundred pounds." He answered, his eyebrows going up and I nodded at that. "I'm eighty over," I said, and added, "and I have to starve myself to get there." "Well, eighty pounds on a two fifty is a hell of a handicap," he observed, rightly, and I nodded in agreement. "Still," I continued, "mine has a flat spot in the power band that makes me have to pull the clutch in and wring its neck to get it up over 9500 and if I keep it up there, it sings, but every time I have to slow down, I have to go through it again." He was in agreement before I had finished. "We used to have that problem, too," he said, and I waited to see if he was going to say any more. He didn't. "... and?" I said. He didn't say anything then, just stepped away from the bike so I could have a look at it in the light. Plain as day, there it was; the secret I had been looking for.

Where the Del'Orto carb with its remote float should have been sitting was a strange black rectangular thing about five inches long and three inches wide held together at its corners with Allen head screws. A small mouthpiece stuck up out of the center to which they had attached a giant air cleaner of some kind that looked like it was off a tractor. I pointed at the air cleaner, " John Deere?" I asked. He smiled then and shook his head a bit, recognizing that we were going to be all right with one another. "Allis Chalmers," he said and I nodded as I squatted down for a closer look. "What the hell is that?" I asked him, pointing at the black block sitting on top of the intake manifold. I didn't hear an answer and stood up then to let him look at me while I spoke to him.

"Listen," I said, "I don't dirt track around here and I my CRTT is a factory road racer I bought right out of the back of the Harley team transporter over at Daytona the year Rayborn decided to ride Yamahas instead." "Dick O'Brien?" the guy asked me then, to see if I was telling the truth. "Chews a cigar down to nothing and cusses like a sailor?" I asked and he smiled again, "That would be him," he said.

"I caught him at a bad time and he had moved the bike a couple of times to get it out of the way and he and Rayborn had a back and forth and there was some shouting and pointing at it and I had seen all this from a ways off. Rayborn gets on the big bike and goes out for practice and O'Brien moves the Sprint around the corner and lets it fall up against the garage and turns his back on it like its garbage. I waited for a good time, when nothing was going on and found him trying to relight his cigar and asked him nicely, as nicely as I could, if he might want to part with that red bike over there? And I pointed at the Sprint." "What did he say?" the old man asked me. "Well," I answered, now having his attention and both of us enjoying a good tale, "he looked me up and down and asked me if I rode and I said I did. Then he asked me if I was any good and I said I would be if I had that bike. He seemed to like that answer and said '$300 and it's yours' and I said, 'deal' and went looking for money."

I paused then, letting it soak in. The story was not all true story, but good stories don't have to be true to be good and it was the story of how the bike had come to the guy I got it from so it wasn't very far from the truth as I knew it. "Still got the bike?" he asked me. "I do and it's right over there in that van if you'd care to have a look." He nodded again and then said, "What's the motor number?" which was a test. If you raced AMA you had to put your motor number down on your entry blank and you were not allowed to qualify with one motor and race with a different one. They didn't care about frame numbers because lots of guys had frames that were unnumbered because they had them special made somewhere to some idea of their own about what might be better than a stock frame and in the case of Harley Davidson that meant about anything else. "66CR6030" I said, and she's the fastest 250 Sprint in America." "What about Hollingsworth's?" He asked me and I shook my head 'no.' "Last summer up at Indianapolis I outrun him on the straights and beat him in the final." I said.

This was fact, not brag, and it was a real accomplishment seeing as how Dick Hollingsworth had won the 250 Novice race at Daytona and would be the last four stroke to ever win a 250 race there. His bike had been clocked at 132 miles an hour which was haulin' the mail for a 250 pushrod single. "No shit?" he said, suddenly interested. "No shit." I answered and he pondered this and then asked me what carb I was running and I told him the '38 Del Orto it came with, and then he asked me what I timed it at and I told him 38 degrees BTDC and then he wanted to know if I had the full speed mag and I told him that the 66 had a half speed mag with the big bump on the side of the motor to accommodate it.

The interrogation over, he squatted down next to his bike then and pointed at the black rectangle and I went down to have a look. "It's called a 'Lake Injector' he said and I got it out of a catalogue after my brother saw one run out at Ascot and called me up to say I should try one." "Fuel injection?" I asked, knowing very little about such things other than it was illegal. "Not really," he said, "it's just a flat slide body without a float bowl."

I was puzzled and didn't know what to say. "Jets?" I asked. "Not really, it has different needles that run down the middle through this adjustable thing here," he said, pointing at a brass fitting next to where the throttle cable went in. "How does it work?" I asked, not getting it at all. "Damn good." He said, and laughed, and we stood up then as someone came over and asked him if they were going to run the big bike main and he shook his head and said, "Not tonight," and the guy went away.

He pointed at the intake rubber that connected the air cleaner to the throttle body and it had a big tear in it. "I don't know how much dirt she ate when that happened," he said, " but I'm gonna tear her down and see before we race it again." I nodded in agreement. "When will that be?" I asked. "Next Saturday night in Jacksonville," he answered, and then asked, "are you gonna be there?" I shook my head. "I've dirt tracked enough," I said, "I stick to asphalt now."

I stayed to help them get it all back in their van, lifting milk crates full of the usual stacks of gearing and oil and tools and the like. They had a piece of lumber for a ramp and once we had the bike in and loaded, other than the kid's leathers hanging up over the back window there wasn't any sign that the van carried anything special at all.

I got back to my hotel in town after midnight and watched an old movie, unable to sleep even though I should have been tired. I went back outside and took a lawn chair out of the van and sat under the clump of palm trees in the middle of the spot in the center of the old motel where maybe there had been a pool once. The town was asleep. No traffic came or went for nearly an hour and I soaked up all of the peace available, which the place had in abundance.

Over at the fairgrounds, not far from here, I had been elbow to elbow with other men on motorcycles all day as we had contested each inch of every sandy corner that slipped from beneath us. We had gritted our teeth with the sand that seemed to be in everything and we had laughed about it when it was over. Well, most of us had laughed, some here and there were pissed or disappointed about something or just generally angry at life. I was not one of them. I was living a charmed life and I knew it and knew too that there was probably never going to be anything happen to me that would make me change my mind about that.

I went in to lay down around three and slept still as a stone until the next afternoon when the maid knocked and said, 'housekeeping'. I opened the door after pulling on some swimming trunks and asked her if I could have half and hour to shower and get my things together and she got out a clip board and made a mark and moved her cart on to the next room without comment and there said, 'housekeeping,' to the door and waited.

. . .

The waitress came again to refill my tea and asked me if I was ready to order. I had that feeling I had when 'housekeeping' had awaken me up from a great dream of being contentedly elsewhere. I pushed my glass over and watched her pour in more tea. Professor Levine was running late, but I had time and was here to make up for all the times I had not taken the time to be together with him and our contemporaries. "No thanks, I'm waiting for an old friend who should be here soon." I said and looked around. Just then, coming through the door in a tweed jacket with leather patches on the sleeves came Danny, looking every bit the scholar he now pretended to be. I waved, he saw me, and came over.

He recommended the crab cakes and I had them while he had just a salad. We were both doctors now, but neither of us medical. I was a doctor of law and he was one of Art History or something like that. We were equally unimpressed with one another so far as that went, knowing what it entailed and knowing that it might have been hard to read and remember all those things we had separately had to digest but knowing too that none of that had been as hard as working all day in a bike shop, then driving all night to get to a race just in time for the gates to open, then practicing all morning and racing that afternoon, then driving home catching some sleep somewhere maybe, or maybe not depending on how far it was, and then getting back to work on Monday surrounding yourself with people who did not understand even a scintilla of what you were about.

I had last seen Danny at Steamboat, as I was about to go out for practice, and even though he and I had both said we would get together later we had not. "What happened to you at Steamboat?" Danny asked for starters. Squeezing a lemon into his tea and then pointing at the one I had not used and waiting for me to nod my assent before taking it as well and carefully repeating the process. I feigned suddenly getting squirted in the eye with lemon juice and said, "Fuck!" louder than necessary and offended patrons looked over at us apprehensively and he started to apologize and then caught himself and smiled. "I miss Hyatt," he said, and I agreed, we all did.

"Well," I began, " I was going out to practice having had a front brake problem with the pucks sticking in their caliper, probably from having been sitting too long, and my brother had offered to help since he was there to race as well, although we had driven out separately. So he takes the caliper apart and announces that it's not right and can't be fixed and I have a look and somehow he's lost part of it, don't ask me how, and so I go over to the swap meet down the hill in the parking lot and find a guy who has a complete set up off an RD, the master cylinder, lever, hose, caliper with pucks, the whole shebang, and I buy it for twenty bucks, thinking I am the luckiest man alive, and hike back up the hill not happy since my practice group is being called and brother says he'll put it on while I get suited up so I start putting on my leathers and when I look he's got the brake line off and I have a fit and ask what he's doing and he says he wants to use the stainless steel braided line instead and since he's got it apart already I let him go ahead only when it's all together it doesn't have any brakes."

I take a drink of my tea. "Need to bleed it." Danny comes in to keep the flow going. I nod and pick up the tale, "So I tell him to bleed it and he says he will just fill the master cylinder and use the lever to let the air bubble up and he turns the bars so its level and takes off the lid and then proceeds to stand there and watch the little pool of fluid in the reservoir as he pumps and it perks up little bubbles."

Danny's salad and my crab cakes come. Danny looks puzzled. The waitress asks if everything looks all right and Danny asks for lemons and points at me and I say, "Cocktail sauce?" and she nods and goes away. "Can you bleed a brake that way?" Danny asks. "I never had," I say, and then keep going, "So I wait and we miss a practice session and there is only one more and I am not happy and probably show it, (Danny makes the aside to the audience we both pretend is there that I always did) and then I tell him to just use the air bleeder on the caliper and I get a 10mm wrench and hand it to him and he shakes his head and says he's getting it.

I feel the brake. There is some, but it's spongy and I'm listening to the other groups come and go from their practice sessions and soon it's first call for mine again. I shake the wrench at him and point at the air bleed nipple. 'Just do it, and do it now.' I say and set off to find my earplugs and helmet and gloves which I had laid up in the front seat."

"No sleep for how long?" Danny asks. I shrug; then think about the drive from Chicago out to Steamboat and the week of jury trial before that. "Four days?" I suggest for an answer and Danny has a mouthful of salad now and so gives me the 'go ahead' sign with his other hand and I return to the tale – " so I come back around to the bike and he's gone and you're there and I pull my helmet on and you push and I go out for practice, which means down the hill from the pits onto the front straight then around a little left hook of a turn and down to a ninety to the right and then there's a couple of blocks of straight before another ninety off to the right." I say this and he's nodding, with me on the course, oriented and ready for what's to come.

"So, I sit up and brake hard for that right turn, having gotten up to third gear, which must be about eighty or so and when I pulled the brake lever it hesitates for just a second and then goes to the handlebar and a spout of brake fluid shoots up in front of me like Old Faithful which covers my visor and I can't see shit and have no brakes at all." "What about back brakes?" He asked, now not eating. I shake my head, "You know I never used them, and so I had them backed off so I wouldn't drag them in the corners if my foot touched the lever while making a turn." He nodded and then shook his head and asked, "So what did you do?"

I had a mouth full of crab cakes. "These are great !" I said. "Told you.." he answers, and then I go back to the narrative of the Steamboat Springs incident. "So I have just that moment when things have gone to shit and you realize it and wonder what to do and if you are taking too long to realize that it's the time to do something before it all goes to hell and I stomp the back brake, and there's nothing. I'm already off the gas and have the clutch in; I'm off line and headed for the crowd which is standing behind one of those orange plastic snow fences behind a solid line of hay bales along the curb. Time compresses and I think I see a stagger in the bales to let corner workers come out to flag. There's a worker standing there, frozen, and I head straight for her.

Actually I'm heading for the stagger and hoping I can get through it and onto the cut out in the curb for the handicapped which I know the building codes all require now and since this is new construction even though I can't see it I figure it has to be there somewhere and we are at an intersection after all. I rise up off the seat onto the foot pegs so my knee caps will clear the clipons if the bike hits something solid I can't see and throws me off forward before I'm ready to jump.

I run out of time, crash through the haybales and into the snow fence which now has nothing behind it but an empty field where a street is going to be but hasn't been made yet."

I pause long enough to take a drink of tea to wash down the bit of crab cake still unwilling to let itself go and resume, "I couldn't see it before but there's no curb here at all and the people were just lined up behind the fence and two lines of surveyor's stakes with the bright orange tape tied off on each one snaking off into the distance ending in what will be a cul-de-sac someday. The people have all have scattered just in time for me to arrive and take the snow fence from in front of them and drag it off into the open space with the front of the bike as it slows me down like the tail hook cable on an aircraft carrier.

I manage to stay on the bike and somehow keep it upright into the increasingly soft ground, leaving a deeper and deeper rut behind me, but the deceleration is fierce and I cut the tops of both hands on the fairing ears."

Danny looks up to see that scars and I show him the red marks still visible two years later now and he returns to chase a sunflower seed in his vinaigrette over to a crouton so he can get them both in one bite. "I yanked fifty yards of orange snow fencing away from all the things it had been tied to and pulled over a dozen people in the process who were too stunned or too slow to let go," I continue, "but I was all right and the bike was all right, except for the bleeder nipple in the caliper which was nowhere to be found.

When I had grabbed a handful of brake, the pressure had shot up and over done it for the few threads that held the nipple in just finger tight. Since no one had used it to bleed the brakes, no one had checked to see if it was tight either like it should have been. Turned out to just be finger tight and as I had ridden down to this point on the track, and used the brakes, it had unscrewed itself to the point that it failed spectacularly."

The waitress comes. "How is everything?" she asks. "Interestingly," Danny says, musing out loud, "just like always," and she goes away like it's what she expected to hear. We finish the meal and I pay for it because it was my invitation and he makes no fuss about it. He asks if I'd like to see something of Savannah and I offer that I have already seen the waterfront and he volunteers to give me the nickel tour of the garden district. I follow him to his house and park and we get in his Volkswagen Rabbit Diesel and off we go. The new Danny nee head shop operator wears his Professor suit seriously and is well informed and pleasant, more pleasant than I remember. He has aged well, although I couldn't guess his age. He is timeless.

He has more grey than black hair now, but that doesn't mean anything, and he is no more or less cultured than he ever seemed to be to me and when we get back to his house he invites me in to see his 'pride and joy' as he calls it. He means the house, which is a turn of the century bungalow style cottage that I can draw from memory having rebuilt many such houses and remodeled them as a carpenter, then as a landlord.

It was lovely, with hardwood floors throughout, except for the kitchen and breakfast nook, which still had what might have been the original linoleum. He had kept the built-ins and columns that separate the dining room from the living room too and the fireplace still had its bookcases on either side all under one mantel. It was an English pretense of a manor house in a smaller scale made for the masses and moved to America. It was exceedingly charming and very well done.

It had been his favorite maiden aunt's home and when she got up in years and could no longer take care of herself; Danny had been between life's phases and had come to help. That led to classes at the university and eventually to a place for him there and here, after she passed. I flashed back to the moment at Steamboat when I was about to go out to practice and was holding my helmet by the straps and about to swing it up onto my head cutting off our first conversation in forty years.

He had looked at me then and asked, "Stella?" and I had shaken my head 'no' stopping my routine and making me lower the helmet to start over sort of like making a bowler stop after he has started his walk toward the pins with the ball just beginning to swing down on its arc. I had looked back at him and asked, "Gloria?" and he had shaken his head 'no' aping me and we both shrugged. Then I had gone out to face what was very nearly certain death when my brakes failed. He had intended to wait, but I did not come back, and I had wondered later what he must have thought. Now I would ask him.

"What happened to Gloria? If I may ask," I said. "You may," he said and then explained that after a trip to Europe in which neither of them had behaved especially well toward one another, the charm had worn through their on again, off again, relationship one night in Amsterdam and after that last 'off' it was never really 'on' again and he had heard that she had moved up to Boston and married some guy she had known in high school.

"Typical," I said, in mock exasperation, as if this was what all women did and that all such love affairs had such atypical endings. "Stella?" he asked me. "Her speech impediment got worse, and although I tried to overlook it, her own conscience just wouldn't let her." I said. He looked quizzical, and then nodded, remembering the old joke. "Couldn't say 'no'? He inquired. "Well, she had no trouble saying it to me…", I said, meaning to sound flip, but it was too honest and it hurt and some capped well of emotion overflowed down deep in me as I sat in the presence of an old friend and I had to wait until I could say more. He waited with me.

"Her view of it is different of course," I picked up, going on to fill the void, "I was difficult and distant and more interested in racing than I ever was in her," I said as if quoting her. "Truth?" he asked me and I nodded my admission, "True enough to stop fighting her trying to leave," I said, then added, "later I sort of fell in love with an Austrian girl named Suzanne, spelled with a 'zee' while chaperoning a bus load of high school kids around Europe. She was the tour company liaison.

Remember that I hadn't actually dated anyone since high school; Stella and I didn't actually date, we married, and that had lasted twelve years" I said, annotating. "Happy ones?" he asked, fleshing out the ghost. "Three for me, one for her maybe, but she said when we parted that she'd never had a happy day."

A canyon appeared and our conversation fell into it. He built the bridge; "So Suzanne with a 'z' was, what, exactly?" "I'm not sure," I said, "at first she was just cute and had a pleasant manner and came from the French speaking area of Austria so she had this appealing accent. We spent a lot of time together naturally and I was professional about it all until we got to Switzerland and it was just so beautiful and I noticed that I had finally gotten past being bitter and was just lonely."

Danny was quiet, and looked his hands, but said nothing. He was having some full length major motion emotion drama play in his memory and I wasn't going to bother it. "So," I continued, "I ruined it by making too much of it and the second year I went back and requested her trip so we would have another ten days together and she was distant at first, but the last few days, and nights, we played 'what if' to see if we might really have something."

"Did you?" he asked then, looking up as if I was unloading something here. "Apparently not," I said, "Neither of us would or could see moving to the continent where the other lived and worked and my language skills weren't really good enough to do more than ask directions and get me slapped so we parted rather anti-climatically."

"Then what happened?" He asked, like a therapist. I gave my head the sideways nod and shrug to wrap it up and said, "I moved on, and went back to living the single life like I had most of my life."

We moved on to the next topic of reconnected friends who have not kept in touch; "Kids?" Danny asked me. "Just the one," I said, "and she's very special to me, which is what made me wait so long to let her mother go and what made it so hard in the end." I confessed.

We were quiet a moment, and he got up and went to the kitchen and came back with two Heinekens. I didn't drink ordinarily, but I was not totally abstinent and did not want to be ungracious. We sipped and then I asked him if he had kids and he said, "None that I know of," and was being candid so I didn't laugh. He changed the subject.

So what brings you to Savannah?" he asked me. "I'm really just here to see you, Danny." I said and he seemed totally nonplused by this. "I'm flattered, really, but..." and as he was searching for words I added, "I've realized that there was something special about those days, those people, those things we shared over the years and I was finally able to afford to take the time to track it down." He drank, relieved I think, and glad that I was not about to come out or anything. "I would have gone to see Hyatt first," I said, "but he died," Danny nodded and pursed his lips. "That does put a damper on conversation," he offered. "This one?" I asked and a smirk came then, given such a straight line, in his best Groucho he said, "Last night I shot an elephant in my pajamas;" and I nodded and drank with him as we both understood each other well enough to know how the rest of this would go.

"You and Danny were close, weren't you?" he asked me, Hyatt's first name being Danny as well, "We were," I said, "but I didn't appreciate it much at the time. You know how it is when you're twenty something and life falls into place for you without much effort and you think that things will always work out like that..." I say, but didn't finish the thought for lack of an ending worthy of the beginning. He nods, and said, "Do your remember the time at Stan's…" and I picked up the string, "When he ordered all the pizzas and charged them to Stan telling the pizza guy to deliver them to Stan's house," Danny went on, "…and then called everyone to tell them there was a party at Stan's house?" he said and we laugh together barely able to breath or forget the memory of Stan so red faced and denying that he had ordered any of them.

Hyatt had stood right there with a straight face saying "Oh, and I suppose you didn't invite any of us over for pizza either?" to a room full of people all of whom Stan had welcomed at the door and invited in when they appeared without asking any of them why they had stopped by. In the end, Stan paid for the pizzas then passed the hat to make everyone pitch in, which we did, except for Hyatt who thought he should get an exemption because he had thought of it. If he put any money in he probably took it back out when no one was watching.

Stan lived in a quiet little part of Gainesville known as 'the boulevard' which had a pond that ran down the middle of two one way streets, each going the opposite way from the other, and the houses were old but classy in the tiled roof Florida kind of way and surrounded by big live oak trees hanging with Spanish moss. At Christmas time they would decorate the whole five block length of the neighborhood with candles in paper sacks for their luminary celebration and it was truly beautiful. Whenever any of us drove past Stan's we could tell if Hyatt had been around because there would be plastic pink flamingos in the yard in a variety of compromising positions.

"How did he die?" Danny asked me, and I started to tell him but I teared up instantly and was surprised that I couldn't talk about it. I finished my beer and he got up and went to get us another. It had been ten years now and it was time, I thought, that I come to grips with losing people you can't live without. Not because you see them so much or you have so much in common but because they make your life be what it is, or what you want it to be. "Hey, I know a guy down in Gainesville that can sit on a bike and balance it and play the guitar at the same time…" he could too, but it was the least of what all he could do. Mostly he could be Danny Hyatt, which was something no one else can do.

The beer came and I recounted the story of how I found out that Hyatt had died and how it had just been a short time after I had called him up and he had given me a description of a lap of Savannah without missing a beat and then I had kept calling him every week or so to see how he was getting along and then I got busy and didn't call, which was about the time that he and his wife had started sleeping in separate rooms because of his snoring so badly. Apparently he had sleep apnea but they didn't know it and she went in to see if he was all right one morning and he wasn't – he had died in his sleep.

I cried then, without noise but tears fell, and I felt embarrassed and stood like I should go. Behind me I heard Danny snuffling a bit too. "I went to the funeral," he said, and this surprised me so I turned to look back at him. "How did you find out about it?" I asked him. "Oh, Art called around to people whose numbers he could find, people who had worked with or raced with or just enjoyed the hell out of knowing him," he said. "Nobody called me," I said, adding, "and I was the reason he was in Gainesville at all." "Probably no one knew where you were. You just disappeared one day," he said and I nodded my appreciation of the truth of that and walked into the kitchen and put the bottle on the table.

Danny was standing up now, and the formal parting ceremony was begun by mutual silent agreement. It was time we parted. I shook his hand and he shook mine. We lied and said that we would stay in touch. We told the truth that it had been good to see one another again.

"I have questions about Team Jewish," I said, remembering my real purpose for being there. "Ask Art," he said, "it was his idea," and I said I would. He walked me to the door and I heard the floorboards creak their century old noise as we passed over their joints and commented to him, "I can fix that," and he said, "Why would you want to?" and I remembered again why I liked him so much. He was part of a time and a town that I had loved that had loved me back as much as most others had hated me.

I was hard to love and hell to live with, at least that was what I had been told, but I was unapologetic about it. Leaving Professor Levin's I noted for myself that Daytona was just three months away and I would be there, on the grid, zipping up my leathers again and feeling the sun shine on a free man, who had decided for no special reason that the way to test to see if he was truly free was to do that very thing.

I would work jobs no one else wanted for wages no one else would tolerate and keep my mouth shut about it. I would 'yes sir,' and 'no ma'am' and kiss whatever ass I had to so that when the time came I could get in my van with my bike in the back and enough money in my pocket to get me there and head for the high banks to race again.

Everyone who raced had the winter off, the last race most places being in October. So for three or four months we had waited to be the boys of summer again and we pushed up the time by making it start at the Speedway the first week of March. There were club races here and there, sure, but it wasn't the same and when you went to a national road race, it was exactly that, people from all over the country would be there and if you beat them, even some of them, then you knew that you had really done something.

Ode To A Man And A Motorcycle

A man twists a throttle
An old man
A young man
It does not care

Things are set in motion;
Cables slide through housings;
Slides are raised in their carefully crafted
Tubular homes to reveal their cave like mouths

and their brass jets with their tiny measured holes
feel the breeze passing through its caverns
and meter out a measured mist of
fuel from the float bowl below

The key, if there is one, may be on
and if it is, and the battery has its charge,
electrons race along copper pathways
faster than the speed of light

Signals are sent to an increasing array
of waiting messengers who measure,
translate, interpolate, integrate,
and command parts to move

A piston is sent in measured motion
Orbiting along its elliptical path
Of clearances and notions;
Compressing, pushing

It strokes up and down as
puffs of air and fluid are
Injected or permitted
or persuaded to join

IT RUNS . . .

The old man sits on the running motorcycle and feels the world
    he knows change
back into the world he knew when he was a young man won-
    dering what the world was;and what the mass of moving
    things between his legs; now running faster, now slower; at
    his command, just by twisting the throttle, will mean to him,
    and his world.

A foot finds a gear with a poke or a pull
A hand pulls in a lever then lets it out –
Slowly... moving the bike or making
the world turn beneath him.

An old bike
A young bike
It does not matter.

3.

Baby Steps

Reality and Zen and Racing considered

MATHEMATICIANS EXPRESS PROBLEMS WITH reality in numbers. Philosophers use terminology. Doctors and lawyers use semantics and say that what they do is an art, not a science. All of them, and everyone who is engaged in a discipline of some sort in an effort to be right about something, believe there is a truth out there, whether or not it has yet to be discovered.

Motorcycle racers search for the truths that will bring them speed. It may seem simple at first, but it is complicated. That is because a good deal of their work takes place in the real world while the others do things with symbols and ideas that only loosely represent reality.

Because they deal in abstractions, the numbers boys are more difficult to track for those of us who don't speak their language, and the process is different than what we are used to, but that doesn't mean it isn't real or that they aren't right. They tend to be focused on the conversion of all things into numerical expressions so they can propose relationships which can be worked out by computation and confirmed by experimentation. It is a process that some call the scientific method.

Some of it is truly amazing, like why the sound of a motorcycle changes as it comes toward you and then passes by, fading into the distance, even though the rider neither alters the throttle setting nor hears the pitch change. That would be the Doppler Effect, named for the guy who thought of a way to accurately express that change of pitch in terms that can be dealt with mathematically. Good to know, but it won't make me faster, so my interest in it is of the same sort that I feel toward the Mona Lisa. I appreciate what has been done here; and I see the result; but I don't need it all the time.

Since scientists can do things that give us understandings we would not have otherwise, there is an understandable tendency for them to think that they can express everything in that way and that all relationships to all things are eventually discoverable and scientifically measurable. If you press them on the point that they don't really know what is going to happen next, they push back with statistics and explain that while they may not be able to predict a particular roll of the dice, they can say what the probabilities are that a seven will turn up and how often.

Numbers didn't mean all that much to me until I got the print out of the trap speeds at Daytona and discovered that the bone jarring terror I had just experienced had taken place at over 180 miles an hour. The only thing on that bike that was capable of safely handling that sort of speed was the motor. The wire wheels, the crude suspension, the small diameter mild steel tubular frame, the rider, were all from a different era. Somehow, just then when I read the trap speed, the number gave expression to a thing that was unnamable and I understood how numbers might have uses beyond the obvious.

I also knew they were good for things like calculating gear ratios so that when you put a gearbox together you could keep from having a big jump from first to second and so forth. Why the makers of transmissions couldn't be content with regular intervals was always a mystery to me but apparently they could not resist tampering with it in some way to make it "better", as in giving a lower first gear than was called for so getting away from a stop sign might be easier.

While that might be true, and nice enough if all you needed it for was getting away from a stop sign, in a racing application it was more problematic. There are far fewer starts than there are first gear corners, and since many riders downshift through the gears as they scrub off speed and enter a corner, the idea that one of the lower gears you are about to transition to will be a good deal lower than the rest is untenable. It makes the motor overwind, it upsets the suspension by the sudden yank on the chain, it can break traction at the rear wheel,and make you feel stupid, none of which are good. I used to have to count my downshifts in order to know when first gear was about to be employed to avoid just such things and doing that when I already had enough to think about seemed unnecessary to me since it had been done deliberately by some guy juggling numbers and thinking he was doing me a service.

Philosophers have it a bit tougher than mathematicians, because their work is in ideas, which are more nebulous and therefore more easily imagined as simple. I first gave them a hard look when one of the contestants on an old game show would ask questions obviously intended to tweak his inquiries. "Is it bigger than a bread box?" "Can you paint it green?" were not questions intended to illicit the obvious responses but rather couched in terms that led to inferential information from which understanding might develop.

"How good is God?," would be the same form of question in the realm of philosophy and since I have mentioned it, what would be the answer? Well, since this is an inquiry into Zen and motorcycle racing, I will toss out a possible answer in terms that racers might understand as a starting point:

Today, on this track, he is the best, better than all the rest. His control of all things relevant to the moment is precise and exact and his race strategy has taken all contingencies into account perfectly. He need not be the ultimate all time best, because the race is not infinite but finite and we do not exist through all time, just in this moment. If we are checking our transponder times and all the laps have been run, we can look and see that his times are better than anyone else. Faster than you; Faster than anyone can ever be.

How much does not matter either. We all can have sufficient understanding of the processes involved to find satisfaction in our own accomplishments. We are not in competition with Him.

Philosophers don't think He works that way, but it changes nothing. There is no besting God. I apologize for using a pronoun that makes it seem like God is a boy, because that is not necessarily so, but since I am limited by a language that does not honor all distinctions equally, I follow Western tradition and say 'He' when I might just as well say 'She' or 'It'. It is a limitation of mine that the language I think in has such poor attributes that I have to explain myself.

Arabic has 2000 words for camel they say, but I'm not sure that helps. All languages have their limits and while I'm not sure where that comes from, it bothered me enough to move past it. Where does Zen come in? Well I may offend many by suggesting that the word we use for something doesn't really matter all that much in terms of transcendent truth but I believe that to be the case and take 'Zen' to be something other than what many traditional Buddhists may believe. It will bother some, no doubt, but it bothers some to see tee shirts with tuxedo vest and tie printed on them worn in restaurants that require a coat and tie while I see it as compliance with a rule of a sort. I should define my terms early to avoid setting up an unnecessary tension between groups of believers and do so now.

If I love a Triumph (and I do) but I know that a Kawasaki may be faster (which may also be true) which one I take to the track for a race says nothing about my emotions or my pragmatism. My love of Triumphs is real and sincere and no amount of being passed by other brands will change it. That is because my first love was a Triumph, before I had the mature understanding of what all is involved at the racetrack that comes from hard practical experience. The divorce was not of my making. I would never have sold that bike, but my parents let it go for me as I had moved on as all children do and had others by then. Somehow the thought that it was back there, pushed back in the corner of the garage and sleeping under a tarp for the "someday" that I might come back and get on it again, was a comfort to me.

My pragmatic Molly lime green side might win more races, or my candy apple red and chrome side might get more approving nods, but the reality of what goes on at the track is of a different order. My mind's eye rides its Triumph regardless of what my 'Wanna Win' body sits on. I am part dreamer, and part real boy at the same time.

My notions of what my Triumph could do were a fantasy, of course, and while it may have been imagined to be all things great and wonderful when it was new to me and I was young, the truth was something else. I might have accommodated both had I been more careful about planning it out and had better resources, but since we are talking about ideas and what we believe as well as motorcycles and racing, I need to point out that at least in our hearts, where our minds don't always have the last say, it is all right to love Triumphs as a matter of personal philosophy, even if you don't have room to keep all of them you ever owned out in the garage.

To quiet the fears of Harley riders I put it out there that my first factory road racer was a Harley Davidson and had the motor and frame number of 66CR6030, something I recall about no other race bike I've had since. I loved that bike, and even though it was Italian and my name is Italian in origin, it was as American to me as I was to it. It came to me in gorgeously pristine factory red livery and I painted it orange and black in American factory team colors. If it bled when we crashed, and we did, it would have been as red, white and blue as mine. I didn't let it go because I didn't love it. I let it go because it was too slow and I wanted to go fast. When I sold it, I made the buyer promise me faithfully that he would keep it together as a machine and never piece it out. He lied.

Speed was the goal and the gods of speed do not linger on past progeny. Demigods or not, their race is run. Are there really Gods of Speed, or am I just making that up? Are racers superstitious? They are and they pay homage to unnamed gods whenever they ride and follow some routine that has kept them safe so far. What is a god after all, but something we empower to be capable of actions beyond our control?

Every time I lean into a turn I pray the tires hold their grip. It is not a 'special prayer' said a particular way and it is no longer a conscious act of mine, but deep inside my psyche a little start when I lean away from the vertical comes that is reassured by something telling me it will be all right and the interface of that exchange is my hope or wish or prayer that it will.

Western Philosophers seem to think it would matter if there were other gods and if so what they might be like and what their relationship might be to the real God we think we know and Him to them. Zen does not ask this question because it provides no useful information. We are tangled up with the idea that He looks like us because of the language that says we are made in His image. While I am happy to discuss the literary masterpiece that is the King James Version of the Bible, I may as well say that it has glaring inconsistencies and no amount of saying or praying that it is all exactly and literally true will fix them.

They don't bother me. Its parts had different authors at different times writing for different purposes. Amen. And I have no doubt that they were all divinely inspired. Yet they wrote and spoke in the language of their time and people and as I have already demonstrated, language has its limits.

Sometimes there can be more than one right answer and this is one of those times. More than one countershaft and rear sprocket combination can give you the right gear ratio. Can the Bible be both inconsistent in its language and true in the ideas it expresses? Yes, in my opinion, and I stop there. I stop because this is not that book and to answer fully would be too vast for our uses.

Do we limit the possibilities by making what we call God too small? Or by insisting that if He has good in Him that He be all good? We would not do that with Zen because it is not personified. While it may be personally gratifying that our cultural heritage tells us we look like God, it does makes us wonder why we can't see Him in each other or why we look so different from one another.

We are told that it is possible to see Him in the face after we die if we are worthy, which takes a lifetime of correctness in a great many things and forgiveness of our failures and missteps, which are as inevitable as they are human and therefore expected; But there are a good many things out there in our experience and all around us that don't fit with our understanding of what would be a personification of such a deity and are therefore outside of God, or clearly not part of His nature. How do we explain that?

We contort logic to keep Him pure and tell tales that give Satan a realm and all the rest. We may as well go ahead and believe in dragons and wizards while we are at it, but I think that goes too far. Think how irrational it is for modern man to fall back on ancient myths to understand the world he lives in. We are smarter than that now, aren't we? But are we so smart as to be able to explain everything with science or something like it? I say 'no' to that, and bow to the mysteries that remain.

As for the argument that one only has to consider the great design of all things to believe in God, I say; If creation is divine and therefore perfect and an example of God's perfection, they why does man breath and eat and choke through one passage into his lungs and stomach, which is patently a bad design.

Eyes were made to see; yes I get that, but when I look at a bridge spanning a space, its length looks obvious as well and I do not impute divinity to its designer. Instead I give credit to the natural world for which it was made.

The bridge is not 'miraculous' in its length so much as it is inevitable. All shorter spans would have failed. Once one was made long enough there was no need to make a longer one. End of story. Try not to choke on it.

My grandmother suggested chewing each bite 36 times to facilitate not choking. Tedious work, but effective; I skipped that once I understood that what she intended was that I make sure I chew it enough to be able to swallow it without choking. So too is my approach to all of this wondering about what it all means.

I do not think or believe that any set amount of repetitions of this or that prayer or position or fasting will produce a particular state of enlightenment any more than I believe a set number of laps in advance of a race will assure a victory. I do believe that some are necessary, however, which is why I take the time to rough in the layout of the course ahead of us now.

It has been said by some that God is not reallyeverywhere and capable of doingeverything, but rather that He controls all things in all places somehow remotely through some plan and all sorts of agency relationships with the forces of the universe. Different philosophers have taken a stab at explaining this as well and some of them are interesting and should be addressed.

The French enlightenment writer and mathematician Descartes, for instance, thought that God was the ultimate clock maker and that the universe, and all that was in it, was just something he made and set in motion. God need not continue to be present in order for it to be marvelous or to function as He intended. Likewise it does no good to complain to Him about how one thing or another might seem to have gone wrong as all outcomes are already determined and are therefore inevitable. Respect and even admiration is due, certainly, but it is folly to think that outcomes can be altered at this stage given how vast it all is and what all is going on through time making connections and bringing consequences forward that are completely beyond our comprehension.

Well, there is something attractive and humbling about this view and quite a few people who would like to think there might have been a God once sort of give it a passing embrace and then move on with a clearer conscience since it does not require anything of them now in the way of worship. There is no reward waiting for those who pay homage, if the clockmaker has gone on to other work, and while I am oversimplifying this a great deal and do not mean to offend philosophy majors who are chomping at the bit to correct me, I tell them that it doesn't matter so they should relax and be content that the maker of all things has included someone like me with such an imperfect understanding to say it and tweak them into correcting me.

As one eager to know the truth, I would listen to other riders describe their impressions of the track that they had ridden but I had not. No matter how informative it might be, however, I knew that their understanding would never perfectly match mine and that I would have to decide for myself, as the moments came to me, what they each meant and what was required or was to be abstained from depending on what I was trying to prove to myself about it.

God may have helped me with that; some would say that was a certainty. I am grateful, but it is not unconditional. There are still unanswered mysteries to challenge and I have yet to find the full understanding I think possible. I need to know more. What I know so far is that the best lap I have ever done of the track I know the very best was not perfect and I could have gone faster.

Christianity is not the point either, but I will speak further of it later on. What I came to understand generally through racing motorcycles is that there is something larger out there that should be considered and for lack of a better term I call it Zen. By my definition then, Zen is a discipline of meditation that leads to enlightenment. Where I differ with traditional practice is my belief that meditation has active as well as passive aspects and one of them is found while racing a motorcycle. There is more than one path to enlightenment in my view, and the one that has chosen me is for the few, not the many, and then only for the very few. I see no reasons why Christians cannot believe that Christ was part of creation and that his coming and going was not included in the process that continues to amaze us.

It makes me think, and things that make me think such thoughts as racing does must be inspired by some greater curiosity that is in me so deeply that I cannot satisfy it or be content until I find an approach to the mystery that is all of reality that lets me say, "All right, I get it." Zen takes a step back and asks the seeker of enlightenment to think about their quest.

Traditionally, in Zen, that thinking is regimented into some meditative scheme that has produced results for others. Postures are adopted, phonetic sounds are expressed, and mental states are sought which are intended to empty the mind and extend an invitation to whatever it is that it out there. Science intrudes here with the news that an empty mind belongs to a dead person because to be alive is to have brain activity. Meditators counter with their view that all brain waves are not the same and the alpha and beta labeling of EKG patterns are cited as an example of how someone can effect what they think and possibly invite a mental state to come where new ideas may form. Ooohhhhmmmmmmm, indeed.

4.

The Maine Thing

"*I SHOULDN'T BE HERE,*" That was the thought that kept coming to me as I reflexively drove on through the night of yet another all day all night race to do with racing. It's November 2013 and there's a blizzard chasing me. I raced across the New York Turnpike with the temperature dropping and the radio calling for 10 to 12 inches of snow following the freezing rain that was coming down now. Into Vermont my Garmin generated directions set me off onto Route 9 that may have looked all right to some computer program that was now controlling my time and place coordinates in a way I never would have chosen for myself.

I could have done it the old fashioned way, of course, and used a map, but I had borrowed one of those new GPS things that is supposed to tell you how to get from here to there. Right now I am discovering that 'here' does not exist in its world of maps because the highway department of Vermont has made some changes since whoever did the input into the computer's world had a look at reality so the thing is useless and just displays a little blue car out in the blackness. It would make me feel lost but for the fact that my car is red so it obviously doesn't know what it's talking about.

I fall back on my Boy Scout training and know that where I want to wind up is east of here so I head east. A mileage sign for 'Brattleboro' appears; which is a name I recognize, so I press on through the night on the newly paved black road on which now appear shiny patches of sheer slickness of ball bearing character that make me skitter and twitch as the car does the same. Since they are scattered and unpredictable it is not possible to set the car up for them in advance so my lines through the corners are imperfect. There are speed limit signs and little villages and houses right up against the road, but its past everyone's bedtime, apparently and I have my eyes full enough already looking at the turning twisting ribbon disappear ahead into the north woods that I have little time to pay them much heed.

An old feeling comes on me then, as I climb a little hill, and it tells me to fight my natural desire to accelerate to crest the top and I slow down instead and find a village cop sitting in his car, radar on, just waiting. No telling how long he had been waiting for the chance to justify his salary with some out of state money in fines, or how disappointed he must feel at not getting to read me the riot act about how their little town was not some damn speedway. I wave, but he doesn't wave back and I just go on. I don't know if he didn't see me or if it was all so out of place here and now that the feeling I have that I don't belong here is so true that I am effectively invisible. I know it happens in restaurants all the time where I go in and sit down and waitresses never see me after that or know what to do with the cold food they had the kitchen make an hour ago and see no place to take it now.

I press on and the switchback turns and the ups and downs of the hills and the high bridges over gorges so deep the depths below me are finally unnerving. No lights from other cars, no lights from houses or barns or security lights, only the stars, now unnaturally brilliant when a moment ago the sky was shrouded in low black clouds. I have out-run the weather front and am in another world now, one that doesn't shrink back from the sudden cold but still thinks the warm days of a lingering fall have some time to go. I know something they don't. The death of summer is real and the vacillations of fall are folly as you sit in the sunshine and listen to the brooks babble over the granite boulders in the streambed.

Finally a sign for Concord, someplace I know because that's where we stayed when we raced at Loudon. The old timers still called it Laconia, but that's further up the road and the race there was a mindless slalom between pine trees on a paved road that led up to a ski lodge and back down. Some care was required and I started to think of that but hit another patch of the black ice and it yanked me back to reality as I silently begged for traction but remained outwardly calm. It was a habit, I knew, that I had gotten from racing, and I wondered if it made any difference in the outcome of events ever. I used to think it did - Staying calm even though the facades of your ramparts are crumbling.

I stayed stoic through a divorce I never wanted and was pummeled by a stranger now in the body of someone who was once the kindest most beautiful girl in the world and I had brought her here, to Loudon, to let her see for herself where my sanity and my sanctuary was. My friends were warm and welcoming to her and she never was left to want for anything. "She's so beautiful," one of them told me with her standing next to me, "too bad she's blind." And then we laughed and she got another hug from another stranger who was now a friend as her dependence on me to see the wider world was further eroded.

That spring weekend in June the weather had turned warm but the nights were very cold and it was our first weekend together ever. We had come from a thousand miles away starting out as strangers and loved who we were here, with these strangers, so much that we managed to stay together and pretend that this is who we really were for over a decade. I was not pretending. She was a pretender and the truth of that bit her pretty hard when she hit thirty and instead of a big mortgage and a house to match she had something from the 1930s with a mantel lined with ugly assorted plaques and trophies from groups of strangers who only had motorcycles and bad taste in decorating in common. She was not having the life she had imagined and had to get out.

I could see that, and I didn't hate her for it, even though I had wished she could have stayed. But I raced and she didn't understand what that meant. "You could stop." She would say, and I would agree, I could. "Will you stop?" she would ask, and I would say I would, someday. "When will that be?" she would ask, pressing me now not for the truth but to show me that I had no intentions of ever stopping no matter what the circumstances. "I can't say," I would tell her," I will just know when the time is right." I answered, sincerely, but hearing myself sound disingenuous. "Make it right now," she said, finally, and added, "or else."

When that came, the ultimatum that made me choose between all things with her as they were and racing, it was poor timing on her part. I had already stepped down from pro racing as an expert and now just dabbled here and there with the caveat that all the weekends were hers unless there was a race somewhere and I had a bike to ride that was ready, and I could fit into my leathers. That particular trifecta had only hit once the year before. The threat lacked merit as it merely pointed out how inadequate my effort was to do it and in turn how inadequate I was doing it which translated to 'slow' which is something my nature just wouldn't tolerate.

But, that was sort of the list she had worked against me in good fun for a while. She baked and kept me well fed, thinking that I would not be able to say no or keep my weight down. It was a struggle and she made it that much harder, but I could do it and from Christmas until Daytona, I hardly ate a bite. On my birthday in early February I would get out my gear and see how far I had to go. It was a ritual of sorts; that harkened back to my cave dwelling ancestors who had stayed snug inside through the bad times and now would have to chance to run the hills again and be hunters. Some years were tougher than others, but I could always do it and so would then start going out to the garage and getting a bike ready while she slept.

She didn't go to the races anymore, and there was just one time when I went ahead and took my daughter, then 8, because she wanted to go and had a memory of enjoying the trips. I felt guilty leaving her unattended while I was on the track and even though a fellow racer was there with his kids and they all played together and had a good time of it while his wife supervised, I never took her again which meant that I was where I had started when at the races – alone.

Racing turns out to be a very tough thing to share. If those around you care about your welfare, then they won't want you to take risks that may hurt you which means you must be careful which means you will be slow. They will say that's all right and that they don't care but it will come up that if you are going to put this much time and effort into something and be bad at it, well maybe you would be better off doing something else instead. But if you try hard and do well then it means that you have sacrificed enough time and treasure to be there often enough to acquire sufficient skill to be competitive and then gone out and raced hard enough to win, which means that you took risks that others were not willing to take and managed to get away with it.

When you crash, and you will crash, they will find the courage to mention all the things about it that had been bothering them that they didn't want to bother you with or jinx you by bringing up crashing like just talking about it could make it happen. It is likely that you will be conflicted, I know I was.

But I seemed to have a talent for racing and could make a bike go fast by the things I did with it. I wasn't scientific about it, or especially analytical, I just rode it. I could feel the bike moving under me, whether it was braking or turning or changing directions suddenly and it did not worry or alarm me when it did those things any more that the view I got when I did a triple summersault with a half twist when diving. You do this and then this and then that and splash, you're back in the pool. My coach had been irritated by my ability to translate a description of what was needed into body action in the air without the repetitive walk through my team mates required. What can you say about it? Is it a gift, or a curse?

Racing a motorcycle was like that for me. The body movements required to make it go; Throttle, upshift, upshift, upshift, tuck in, focus on braking point, wait for it, wait, then pop up and brake seriously, feeling the front wheel fight for traction while watching for the turn in point to throw the bike over as I let off the front brake a bit, maybe more depending on the speed I want for the entry, adjusting it all to the apex and then opening up the throttle again as I exit, feeling for the back end to step out, not too much too soon but enough to feel it going and turning into it with the clip on's and opening up the throttle and shifting up and up and tucking back in and then doing it all again and again and dealing with the slower riders and being dealt with by the faster ones until made to stop by a checkered flag or a red one. I was unconscious in a sense when racing, at least in the early days.

Nothing I did with my wife occupied me like that. In considering the parameters of the problem from her perspective I think in hindsight that choosing cooking and overfeeding as a strategy might have been a mistake. Perhaps some other activities might have been employed to greater effect to keep me in doors while she was in bed so that I might want to be there with her, but the opposite happened instead. I am sure the psychologists have some name for it but she claimed that she loved me so much she couldn't stand to think of anything happening to me so she had to stop loving me and learn to hate me instead for the selfish bastard I so obviously was if I was going to go ahead and race.

Such thoughts were never articulated by either of us back then, all those years ago, since we lacked insight and experience enough to know what was in the mix of the emotional pool where we were competing. I hated it that she couldn't be happy with me as a racer since that was who I was and all that I was when we met. Still, seasons come and go and we usually find a reason or a way to be out of racing eventually on our own and I knew that, so I made every accommodation I could to satisfy her demands.

I sold the bikes and gear and tools and cleaned out the garage of every vestige of any reminder that I had once been a big time motorcycle racer. Then an odd thing happened. Having been satisfied that I was willing to give up everything to please her, she was not pleased with me anymore. Instead she had fallen in love with someone else and I had 'changed' somehow and she just didn't feel the same about me, even though she appreciated the effort. I had a decent job by then and kept it and took up new hobbies. I learned to play the guitar, which used up six or seven months and led to the realization that I can play, or sing, but not both at the same time and since my singing voice is so horrible that even I can't stand it, my musical career was short.

I tried racquetball, which I enjoyed a good deal but which my knees found to be too much, likewise tennis. Finally I turned to golf, and recognized that it might cause a drinking problem due to the application of alcohol as an anger management tool. It was supposed to be a social game, and I liked and appreciated that aspect of it, but… all the cussing and screaming was distracting, even though I was the one doing it, so the invitations to join others dwindled to nothing.

I was by then five years out of racing and was post-divorce. I had ridden the roller coaster that divorce brings and been sad, mad, sorry, hopeful, hopeless, holiday lonely, sad, etc… often enough to be at peace with the ride. Then one day, for no reason, I picked up a copy of Cycle News and read through the race reports and looked at the ads and realized that I knew no one anymore that was racing. In the want ads, however, was a Yamaha road race bike for sale with a phone number that had an Oregon area code. I called it and had a chat with a guy who got it from a guy who said it used to belong to some guy that worked in Florence and went off to race and never came back. It was my old TD3.

I bought it sight unseen, and had it shipped, which was probably a mistake. Some parts of it never arrived and instead of the CDI-ignition, Carbs, and expansion chambers I got the $75 it was insured for and someone else got that box elsewhere. It was good to see the old bike again, however, and I felt some inner compass start to gyro me back on course again. Oddly, I felt no sense of urgency and at this point, there was no vintage racing so far as I knew. WERA had some classes for production bikes that stretched back far enough to include RD Yamaha twins, but they didn't call it vintage racing. I would get a rule book, read it, and then build a bike to fit a class. I had once just taken any bike I could get and then gone to the races only to discover that it was cheap for a reason and was 'outclassed' which meant usually that you got to ride around at the back of a group of guys on faster bikes than yours who were not especially happy to have you join them.

Back in the present, Concord came, finally, and it was roughly 3 a.m. My brief exchange with the seller over the internet had been one confusing thing after another. He had a 1965 Yamaha twin road racer for sale. That was not on a for sale page, but just part of a string on a forum for Ducati's but thanks to the thorough nature of word proximity search, Google had brought it to me from a couple of months before because it had the magic words of my search in it.

I wrote to say I was interested, but had to join the forum first so I did. He confirmed that he still had it and that he was asking so much for it. I asked for pictures and an inventory of what I would get if I drove out to Maine to pick it up, which I was ready to do. I got a picture of Gary Nixon's TD3 instead which preceded a series of miscommunications that didn't discourage me but didn't raise my expectations either. I sent a check for a down payment of earnest money and he acknowledged receipt – the deal was on. When I asked for directions he was vague but concluded with the killer red flag in such matters, 'You can't miss it...'

I slept for a few hours in the car at a remote rest stop north of Concord without another vehicle in sight nor any heard passing by. The car was warm when I put the seat back and pulled my coat over myself, but I could see my breath when I turned over to the other side less than two hours later and realized that I was not comfortable and therefore not really resting either. I decided to drive on over to Maine and look for the address I had. It was not much of a road and had the black ice problem only more so. The sun was coming up off to my right and there was an eerie low cloud bank between the clear sky overhead and the distant sunrise that was deep purple and black in a large billowy row that stretched from horizon to horizon but was illuminated underneath in brilliant pink and orange. I had never seen anything quite like it and it was doubly tantalizing because I only caught glimpses of it through the trees when the road I was fighting with turned just right to left me have a glimpse before jogging back to the other direction obscuring my view behind another hilltop

I found the town, which was pretty easy since it was on the main road, but not the address on the houses or the mailboxes. At seven the only diner on the highway opened and I went in to see if they had a phone book, which they did, but which was not helpful because his phone was either unlisted, or a cell phone. I had his number, but so far he wasn't answering and I was beginning to get worried. There were two women working there and the owner was about to take off to go and start his day elsewhere. We fumbled through all the ways you find someone when you don't know where they are and none of them worked so I settled down in my acceptance that I may have just driven across the country again for nothing (It would not be the first time) and ordered breakfast. The younger of the women went away to the kitchen and prepared a truly delicious spinach omelet while the pleasant supervisor girl poured coffee and made conversation. I tried to think of something to talk about.

"Stephen King is from Maine, right?" I said. "You betcha," she came back with the clipped New England accent that is so strangely charming. I smiled. "The accent?" she asked and I nodded. "We rather think you talk a bit odd yerself." She responded. "That I do," I admitted, but it sounded normal enough to me and the food arrived and we moved on to other things. It was very good and I was hungry but passed on the offer of toast even though 'rye' and 'sourdough' were choices. When I was finished I was given the meager check, I asked them if he ever came in. "Yep," the younger one said, "all the time." So I paid for my food, added a tip for them and then held out an extra $5 and said, "Next time he's in, tell him the coffee's on me." And they had sort of an odd look but understood what I wanted and I suppose may actually do it. "What's yer name, then?" asked the one holding the bill. "Montage," I said, "the fireman."

Heading back down the steps to my car in the brilliant early morning sun the phone in my pocket started to vibrate. I answered and got bits and pieces of a guy talking that made no sense until the word 'motorcycle' came through intact and I said that if he could hear me, to give me step by step directions to his door and let me write them down. As I moved over to the car I found a sweet spot the satellite graced with its signal and could hear him clearly. He said he thought I said I was coming in the afternoon. I had said that but the weather was predicted to be terrible with ten to twelve inches of snow today so I came early. I wanted to be south of Boston by then, changing my flight plan from the New York thruway that brought me here to I-80 across Pennsylvania, a difference in latitude sufficient to affect the weather.

He said I had about ten miles to go and he was very close. I followed his directions and found him waiting for me on the steps of his home which had a rustic appearance but was very nicely kept. He probably had been a hippie when we were both in our teens but had managed to make the outlook work for him well enough to manage to put together a substantial little niche in the woods. His wife was pleasant and welcoming and they had two dogs and a cat which required constant reassurance and could detect that I was both a dog and cat person so things were soon well enough among all parties that we could get to business.

They offered coffee and breakfast but I deferred, explaining that I had just had both at the café in town. He went to the garage and then to the basement as she and I talked about the pets. Soon he had a pile of things assembled on the kitchen floor and I looked it over and asked if there wasn't a swing arm for the frame and he went away again and came back with one. That made a motor, expansion chambers, two wheels with axles, forks in their triple clamps, and a strange looking frame. It was enough for me and I counted out the bills on the counter for him and she went to another room and came back with the check they had been holding and the deal was done.

As we began carrying it out to my car we talked about where he had gotten it and who it had belonged to. It was another racer's tale of woe. This guy, who was fast, and was ambitious to be noticed, had gone big time and gotten sponsors who expected commitment and results and he had struggled at the national level and could not deliver either since it was just then that his wife decided to assert her belief that he had a mistress. She left him for a more attentive, more normal kind of guy, which shook his foundations enough to make him look around for support which he found in drinking. Hey, at least he could forget about his troubles for a little while, right? Predictably enough this did not work out and like a lot of racers who dabble in behaviors that are risky, he went too far with it and lost control.

The crash was a slow motion disaster as he toppled from prominence to head shaking sympathy to bankruptcy, both financial and spiritual. At this point, the guy selling me the bike, offered to help. His offer was sincere as he is a good man and he did not look to take advantage of what was a bad situation. The fast once upon a big time guy vacillated between feeling used and recognition that he was holding on to things that were never going to be of any use to him again. Hence the bike that came my way. It was, in 1965, the fastest bike of its kind in the country. I had bought it looking for just a part of its character to complete a project sitting at home on my workbench waiting. Now I had a decision to make, would I undo all of this man's effort and erase all of the special qualities that it possessed for the sake of making something new out of it that quite likely would never be as special or as predominant as this bike had been in its day?

It is a dilemma that all who dabble in vintage motorcycles face. Are they alive on some level as a whole, and do we destroy their karma by taking them apart and scattering the mated parts around here and there with some being used and others never used at all? I had time to think about that and thanked my host for all his kindness and generosity and promised to stay in touch. He had a good handshake, which spoke to me about his character and the time he comes from. It's not a high five or a fist bump but a man to man I'm shaking your hand and looking you in the eye for a moment here to let you know that someone in the world you live in still understands what it means to shake hands.

With that I was away and headed south toward Hartford, Connecticut where I planned to turn right and go west and south until I met up with I-80 and head for home. I wanted to get this done before the blizzard they were forecasting caught up with me and made my long trip even longer. It was by now a forty hour day interrupted by a two hour nap, which had been helpful, but not enough. I could feel my fatigue draining away what energy I had left and knew that coffee alone would not be enough. I would have to sleep soon. But I had miles to go before I sleep… then I caught myself and wondered why it was when my brain ran out of fuel that it turned to poetry.

I remembered coming up to New England that first time and finding it so charming and different from the rest of the country. The secondary roads were narrow and windy and the racers and their bikes had a ratty appearance to them that said 'tough' more than unkempt. Boston Cycles would come, with guys who could ride, but not always the same guys. I liked their graphics and the idea that someone outside of California could make bikes go fast as well. It was before

Kevin Cameron had taken up writing but he was there, and his mind was at work.

Motion Enterprises from New Jersey came to the races up here too and Steve and his crew were approachable and helpful and Henri the brush painted everyone's numbers in a distinctive style that was soon mandatory if you wanted to be known as someone who knew what was going on. John Moyer and I became friends as novices; Jeff, Bart and Schroeder were Juniors. They were waiting to produce an Expert and launch themselves and the shop into prominence. I thought it would happen; so did they.

It was in Concord that I saw my first Dunkin' Donuts, and spent the night with a cute and amorous young blonde who was caught up in the 'run away and join the circus' family atmosphere that we all seemed to share. Now I was back in Concord and heading south on the interstate and except for the Capitol building not much of it looked familiar. The New Hampshire Highway Hotel, which had been a landmark here for no telling how long was long gone and now a strip mall which has already come and failed and is now in its second or third imagining as something else, none of which have been as grand as the hotel used to be.

The radio is on for soundtrack music but I'm not listening until the introduction of 'Radar Love' creeps into my consciousness and then everything is as it was and I am driving south into the sunshine of a new day with a bike in the back and cutting through traffic with an easy motion that seems to magically tell me which lane is about to slow down and where the next move should be. I turn it up.

I only stop for gas and keep my speed up hoping to outrun the complete change of climate that is descending on me. 'This may be the last sunny day' something tells me and I can feel it on my face and hands through the windshield and try hard to store a memory of the feeling that I will be able to bring back when I need it in the long cold grey days that are coming.

Before I leave Connecticut, it's snowing and the sunshine is gone. The roads are covered with ice melt and accumulating moisture that was once just snow or sleet or freezing rain but is now just slop. Everyone is going faster, which seems counter intuitive given the road conditions but drivers know, and racers understand, that there is an urgency built into any journey that makes us go a bit faster all the time as our destination calls us.

At the Pennsylvania state line the increasingly poor conditions become unmanageable on a mountain ridge as we come out from behind a tall cut on I 81S onto a mountain crest that is forty or more feet in the air and curves to the right to line up with the cut in the next range of hills. The only radio station I could find a few miles back was playing non stop Polka music now but I don't have time to make it stop. It's a demonic distraction I'm sure and I struggle to keep the things I am doing with my hands on the steering wheel bear some relation to my hopes for surviving the trip.

I emerge through a cut into a space of unprotected highwaywhere a fifty mile an hour wind gust hits me broadside. The roadway is iced over as it caps a bridge that looks to be a hundred feet above the valley floor below. Sixty yards in front of me the semi I am following into the vortex of snow is exposed to the cross wind and his load comes around past the point where he can straighten it out by correcting with the tractor and he is jack-knifed.

I am full lock and fighting to keep my own vehicle from coming around and pointing backwards. His trailer swings around in a wide arc to clear the road in front of me and then pull his cab into my path. "FREIGHTLINER" it says on the hearse that is coming for me. There is just asmall shrinking space over to the right between the oncoming truck and the guardrail that is closing even as I spot it but I will have to hurry and cannot even think of braking if I am to get there before its gone so I aim for it and accelerate.

It will be my death if I am wrong about this and I know it, but I can imagine nothing else that will save me so I take my chance. Things move slowly. I hear an echo of voices from the future trying to figure out who the remains belong to and why they are here, so far off the route he should have taken if this was a trip to Maine from Illinois. It will be a mystery.

When in doubt, accelerate; someone said once at a race somewhere, I don't remember now which or whether they were being serious.I hit the curb and jump it with the wheels on the passenger's side as the truck swings closer not leaving enough room for me to get through otherwise. I see eighty something on the speedometer. I shoot through the gap just as it disappears behind the grill of the massive rig, wheels locked, tires not turning, headed for the guardrail.

Ahead of me is nothing but blackness and snow and in my mirror I am relieved to see that the trucker manages to stop disaster from taking him over the edge. He does block the road from side to side however, and I can just make out beneath the trailer's belly, the image of cars and trucks suddenly sliding into one another and showing the effects of the laws of motion in unpleasant and unwanted ways.

I know then that behind me all traffic is now stopped and in such low visibility conditions it is only a matter of time until someone plows into the whole mess. I am fortunate not to be on that side of things. I am a lucky man – or something else is at work, but it seems redundant to mention it again and I don't want to do so improperly or show insufficient appreciation so I give a silent prayer of thanks to whatever it is and mean it and move on.

I am ready to call it a day and promise myself to take the first exit that shows rooms for the night. It proves to be three exits further on and by then we are at the junction of 81S and 80 so in the morning I will have an easy time of finding my way. Still in those last thirty miles it was clearly unsafe to be on the road and at any moment the combination of the wind and the ice and the poor visibility could have put me off a hundred times. I pressed on like it would all work out, but I didn't know that at all; In fact I was fairly certain that it would not all work out but the alternatives were simply worse than what was going on already so I stayed with it. That's not so much a choice as an abdication of choosing to do otherwise.

Finally an exit sign appeared with lodging available and I pulled off and found my way to a large and mostly empty hotel that had meant to be a convention center only no one came and there were no conventions any more. It was sparsely staffed and barely heated but it was a respite and I took it. I showered and slept and was awakened by a ringing far off in just a short time and woke up not knowing where I was or how long I had been there.

The phone was across the room and strange to me and I pushed its flashing buttons trying to get someone to talk to me but they didn't and finally it quit ringing. I found my glasses and called the front desk to see if they might know if I had a message. The voice of a cheery hotelier type young lady put out her practiced patter that contained a sentiment that they wanted my stay to be pleasant and inquiring if the room alright and asking if I needed anything. "I need not to be disturbed," I said, barely recognizing my own voice, and knew that it was too late to be pleasant. She hung up without an apology.

I found my cell phone which has become my new age wrist watch where I go to see what time it is and flipped it open. I had been sleeping just over an hour. It was not enough, I knew that, but I also knew that it would be a good bit before I got back to real sleep again.

Back in the soft warm bed with its clean sheets and cozy pillows I wished I had at home I lay comfortably, but awake. My mind was kicked off the ledge of relaxation it had settled on and was not looking for another. Outside, in the freezing cold, sat the disassembled bits of steel and aluminum and fiberglass oblivious to the time or the temperature in any way that I could understand. Still, they had called me somehow to come and get them and now were counting on me to keep them out of a rubbish bin somewhere until the special thing they could do would be rediscovered.

. . .

Once upon a time, on a sunny day up in Canada, they had been combined beneath a young thin rider from Michigan who was both brave and bold. The wind blew there as well and it was cold relative to what it was down in the 'states as they had lined up at Shannonville, a race track made from an old bomber base with its predictably flat topography and difficult to follow lay out. The local boys had it wired, and had shown the way through practice without mercy or concern. While they were chatty enough in the pits, they were condescending in that way that hockey players talk to recreational ice skaters who ask for help of any kind. But when the race had begun and everyone streaked away down the long straight to turn one it wasn't any of them in the lead but this bike, with this bold boy onboard.

It sounded like two run away chain saws running wide open since no silencers were required. This did two things; it ran audibly better than those bikes with mufflers and it revealed to everyone within ear shot just exactly what the rider was doing with the throttle every second. If you let up, everyone knew it. If you lacked the courage to hold it on across the big sweeping bend that jolted and bumped you along across the taxi way from one runway to another all made in a scale so huge you could almost lose your way everyone would know. What they heard instead was the steady scream of a motor held at wide open throttle by the hand of pilot they could now barely see; all tucked in and bent over with his head down and his chin buried on the tank as he streaked away to a victory so large that when the race was over, everyone came over to have a look at the amazing little machine.

'Yes' those are the new chrome bore cylinders from the factory GYT kit'; 'No, I didn't put any additives in the gas, but its AV gas I got at the airport back home;' 'Sure, I enjoyed racing up here in Canada but I really thought there would be more competition.' The last was said with a smile, half serious, half poking the guys who now stood around and looked at something that made their once superior machines just so much slow moving equipment. He got applauded at the trophy presentation and then had driven back home to Michigan.

That was in 1965 when the Warren Commission had just announced its decision that Lee Harvey Oswald had acted alone and no one believed them. How was it that Jack Ruby managed to stand there with a gun in the garage of the Dallas Police Department and wait for him without anyone asking him what the hell he was doing there and how beyond imagination was it that everyone in the entire country with a television set was watching when he killed Oswald right in front of everyone? It was a mystery, but no one thought then that it would remain that way. Then the inevitability of science to reveal everything was believed.

Which was more unlikely? A little bike from nowhere, showing up and beating hard seasoned veterans on a track they could ride in their sleep; or a night club owner in Dallas getting a front row seat with a gun in his pocket right in the police station and taking down the lone gunman? It was a triumph of human will and spirit over logic and the laws of physics. Just logically, if anyone had asked you in advance if something like that could happen you would say not in a million years, but you saw it. When they told you that a disgruntled book depository employee could take three shots with a bolt action rifle from a third story window and kill the president riding by in a moving motorcade you couldn't believe that either, but it happened.

Some things about it could not be explained afterward, sure, but there were always things like that when you tried to figure out the past. "Business or Pleasure?" the guard had asked the bold Michigan boy pulled up to the international border crossing at Windsor before going into the tunnel he hated only slightly less than the bridge that would take him back to his own country. "Pleasure" he had said and the guard stuck his head in and looked in the back and saw the motorcycle. "Got any paperwork for that?" the Canadian asked and the driver handed over the trophy. "Just raced it at Shannonville and I'm taking it back home." "Nicely done," came the response from the customs man, handing back the trophy as he was waved on into the blackness.

I sleep then, the story revealing only so much as I might have known some of it myself, having gone from Michigan to Canada to race at Shannonville and come back again. When you first do such things, they seem exciting and fresh and it takes you out of your routine which had become routine whether it was a pleasant one or not and some people are just not meant to have their lives become routine. It was another life to load up and go racing and it all seemed so impossibly wild and free. The strangest part of all was that it was allowed.

'Yes,' you can go ride a motorcycle as fast as it can go and there are no police to tell you to slow down or traffic lights or dogs or deer or stupid farmers on the road with their big machinery clogging up the highway. You can be shoulder to shoulder with other guys as weirdly crazy as you are and laugh and joke and ride with them around a racetrack knowing that some of you will fall down and some of you will break your bikes but only one of you, just one, will win and they will celebrate with you when you do just as you will congratulate them if its someone else. The racing gods have smiled on someone, was that someone you? Will it ever be you?

I wake up early even though there is no special reason to as I have the whole day to make a half day drive back home. Still there is nothing to be done about it so I shower again and dress for the day and pack up the things strewn about randomly from the night before as I wrestled with fatigue and the strangeness of my surroundings. I go down for the free breakfast buffet and find it as unpalatable as usual and have just toast and coffee and tell myself I will eat later if I feel the need. Back in the car, with the bike's bones protruding here and there from protective piles of moving quilts and sleeping bags, I settle in for the ride home through Pennsylvania, Ohio, Indiana, and back to Illinois. I am near DuBois when the gas gauge tells me it's time for a pit stop so I exit and fill up and see across the street an inviting sort of place that reminds me I have yet to have a proper breakfast.

Déjà vu is the feeling that you are experiencing something that has happened before, but going back to someplace you have been before is more than that and different from that. It's like a portal to the past that you could let yourself fall through or can ignore. Sitting solid and stately in the sunshine of a cold morning was the original Dutch Pantry. I saw a place to park and took it, thinking to myself that it had been a while . . . and waited for the thought to finish itself.

It was all so familiar inside, the smell of cinnamon and bacon in the air, the open beams of the ceiling, the post card displays you have to walk through to get to alcoves on either side where the tables and booths are waiting. The hostess asks me where I'd like to sit and I take the open booth next to the window where I can see the car and the road and sit on the side so that my back is not to the door in honor of Wild Bill Hickok as she hands me a menu. Then the past comes over me like a warm sea and I feel the sand of the present being eaten from beneath me as the wave goes out again and erodes the beach where I sit waste deep in the sun.

I have been here. Right here in this same spot facing this same room in this same restaurant. Then I sat and looked out the window at my new 1972 Chevy van, green with yellow flames painted down the side and my number plate in the cut out next to the driver's door – 74 Q. I could see my leathers in the back window, hanging there to show the other riders who happened to be on the road that it was me; Oregon plates and salt still showing on its sides.

Guys in their leathers and gear were different people than they were in their jeans and tee shirts and the man you raced for a hundred miles and wanted to thank or blame afterward for something could be hard to find once unsuited and back in civilian clothes. They would be even more difficult to recognize once they got back on the highway.

John Long was a white Dodge Maxi Van with Florida tags; R.G.Wakefield was a Plymouth Barracuda with a trailer; the Boston Cycles boys had their off kilter logo on the side of their van with Massachusetts plates; Stan Friddus had the Silver Bullet Chevy van with its old style flat nose and its ancient Norton inside. But the fashion was to hang your leathers up in the back window to show your name and number and to keep the fools with their bright lights from blinding you as you drove. On the roads home from a national race, as we all scattered out back across the country from where we had come, it was nice to run across a fellow racer here and there as you passed by or they passed you by.

Then I remembered thinking that before and looked up reflexively to see if she was coming back from the bathroom. Of course not - She is not here. She could not be here. My waitress comes, a red headed woman of pleasant demeanor bringing me a cup of coffee and a menu and a smile. She looks oddly at me for a little too long and I worry that taking my hat off has made my hair frightening. I order the vegetarian omelet, bran muffin, and a glass of milk. Her face turns pale and I notice that she doesn't write anything down. She looks across the table at the empty chair and then back at me. *'God,'* I wonder to myself,' *is it possible that she remembers her?'*

"I've been here before," I said, to jog her off the loop she's struggling with in her mind. She nods looks again at the empty chair and then back at me. "Honeymoon…" she says finally, and I agree and say, "Sort of, it was our first trip together and we probably behaved like it was a honeymoon, but we didn't marry until a few weeks later."

She smiled then and nodded. "We talked about that, you two were so Ga Ga over each other you hardly noticed anyone else and she made such a fuss about how good the milk was and then wanted another glass!" She was laughing now, sharing a memory of a time when we had stood here, more or less like this, forty one years before. "… and you pulled out her chair and helped her off with her coat and then did it again when you left."

"I'm amazed you remember," I said. "We had just opened and it was my first week on the job," she answered, "and after seeing you two together the way you were with each other I went home and called my boyfriend and told him about it and he said he loved me that much just didn't show it and I told him if he did, then he would marry me." She was pleased with herself and the memory and it showed. I looked at her hand and there was a ring there. "Still got the same guy?" I asked her. "Yep," she said proudly, "and we have five grandchildren now." She beamed.

Then she looked again at the empty chair. "We had some really good years together," I told her, "but sometimes things just don't work out and we parted." "Still friends?" she asked, and I shook my head. She looked at my hand and saw a ring and I answered her unspoken question. "It took a while," I said, "but I found the girl of my dreams finally, and we are very happy together." This sounded well enough but I now felt the need to go ahead and explain the empty chair. "This is a business trip for me and she's at her job and couldn't come but I will bring her next time so you can meet her." This pleased her, and me as well, as we were long acquainted and now unexplainably reacquainted.

She went away and came back with the food then came again with a second cup of coffee and then came back for the final 'how was everything?' inquiry with the check. I gave the expected answers to our call and response worship and then added as I was about to leave, "It was really nice to see you again," and she teared up a bit and struggled to speak. "Today's my last day," she said, "I was given my notice two weeks ago." It came to me that she was probably in her sixties and that no one else was going to hire her to do anything worthwhile and that she was probably about to lose the only job she had ever had along with whatever benefits it might have offered.

I looked at the other waitresses then, all younger by decades and flitting from table to table with smiles and coffee pots, all someone's daughter or grand-daughter and probably not someone's mother or grandmother like mine. I laid an extra twenty on the table and she shook her head and told me it was too much and that wasn't what she had meant by it and now she wished she hadn't said it. "You've no idea what it was worth to me to hear you say you remembered," I said. "Take it with my blessings, and enjoy your life."

She drew her lips in as she nodded and then patted me on the shoulder as I put my coat on. I would not see her again – ever. I knew that and she knew that. She was a good person and a pleasant willing worker who had waited on a young couple more than forty years ago that she had not seen since. It had been on her first day of work. One of them came back and sat in the very same place and ordered the same odd breakfast on her last day of work and the dominoes of her memories all fell into place and it had come back to her like the bittersweet persimmon pudding her mother used to make but she could never seem to get right. For a moment there, it had been like it was yesterday. She had never forgotten it. I hadn't either but to be honest; I hadn't remembered her at all.

It took the rest of the day and into the night to get home. I was glad to be there and glad that I had gone. In a life of racing with memories scattered about the country like natural children from intercourse with strangers there is no telling where or when a reunion might come. Statistically I suppose the odds are against it, but then, racers live a charmed life and don't believe so much in such things.

There had been a moment, up in Maine, as I drove across Route 113 toward the coast in the early morning light, that the mountains were visible through the trees off to the north just now and then. They were illuminated in soft bands of pink and purple and indescribable hues of darker blues as if someone were deliberately making a show of it. The sunrise reflecting off the low bank of clouds to the south was no doubt the cause, but it was four thirty in the morning and not another soul was on the road to see something so spectacular.

I tried but failed to capture it with a photograph and am not surprised to find later that it's just a distant blur. In my mind, however, it's a different story, and in the clear cold morning light I saw a wonder to behold so singular that it told me I was meant to be there, right there, right then and that all was well. Despite the quirky and oddly haphazard sequence of events that took me there and back, this moment is meant to be – it is the Maine thing.

5.

Mindaltering Motorcycles

I WILL NOW GIVE an example of how a motorcycle can make you think differently – I first rode a Honda 50 step through with an automatic transmission. It was marvelous. It was reliable and economical and transported me from here to there with the top down feelings of a convertible extended all around me. People waved and I had the chance to wave back because it didn't go fast or make annoying noises or impute some darkness to my character. I thought about certain things a certain way on that little Honda. I was free to remember to get milk as I went to the store and feel behind me for my homework on the way to school. I was Doby Gillis with a smile and a crewcut and a bright happy future.

Then came the Suzuki X-6. Someone had one and let me ride it. My thinking about nearly everything changed. It make odd noises and seemed like a nest of bumble bees beneath me, some of them sounded angry. I stared at the bright green light in the double handed speedometer face and listened to the distant voice of the owner explaining with a strained voice that it was 'up for first' and 'up for the rest.'

He had not mentioned how many there were in 'the rest' but of course I would have to find that out for myself. I did not want to embarrass myself when I started so I gave it plenty of throttle and managed to get it off the line a bit too quickly and to adjust for what I thought was too much speed already I shifted up but failed to sufficiently reduce throttle to keep it from continuing to accelerate which it did through all the gears I found, as I bent lower and lower over the bars, watching the speed climb up to 100 mph and turning my head to keep the tears from my eyes and the roar of the wind from my ears I finally realized that I had the throttle full on still and slowed down.

Then it happened. I thought that anything less than full throttle was just that, something less. It was addictive. I had to have one and once I had one I had to ride it as fast as it would go all the time, rain or shine, and keep going faster and faster until, well, until it just wouldn't go any faster because it was so very obvious that that was what it was meant for. My Suzuki nearly killed me one night in 1966, or my girlfriend, or both, but that story will have to wait until it makes more sense.

It was a seriously engineered, technologically superior machine to anything else on the road. Walt Fulton III, won the novice race at Daytona on one and that struck a chord in me like nothing else had in my life to that point. A picture of him riding his Suzuki at Daytona was in the cycle magazines and it looked a great deal like the one I had. He surely knew things I didn't but then again, there was a possibility that I could do what he could do, and we rode the same sort of bike.

All of this is starting to sound a bit complicated and far from the race track, which is why we are talking about itearly so I can stop and suit up and spare you from further pre-race tension. If you've raced, and that is in some ways a precondition to understanding what I am saying, then you know there is a comfort born of experience for you there that frees your mind to work on things you do not feel elsewhere. For instance, how do you know what is good or true?

At the racetrack, Speed is 'Good,'and things that make us go faster are 'True' which is the beauty of taking your inquiries into goodness and truth there. That these inquiries may be a part of larger questions having something to do with physics and something to do with an arbitrary set of rules that are man- made may be useful, but our application of them will relate first to racing, and then, if there is something more, to whatever that may be. I will treat the man-made rules first and leave the physics for Adrian to explain later.

"… It's not really a rule so much as a guideline," Captain Jack Sparrow.

6.

Rule And Line And Logic

LET'S TAKE THE RULES that racing organizations impose first because we are all familiar with them, although they may not all be the same ones. They are arbitrary, and exclusionary, and intended to accomplish different things, but all races held under rules are bound by them. In some sense, their necessity is questionable I suppose, but then I have participated in many a midnight drag race where neither of us knew what the other had under the hood.

Thinking you are fast, and having something fast, are not the same thing and while I enjoyed that sport for what it was, what I wanted instead was to test myself against others with as little advantage given to the machinery as possible. That desire came from childhood racing on bicycles and in swimming pools and on cinder tracks. Once I started with motorcycles, the need for some categorical sorting of the machines we rode was obvious.

I give an example: A racer I will call Kenny came to Centralia, Illinois one weekend in the late 60s for a scrambles race where I saw him ride. He was fast; incredibly so. He had the habit of keeping his left foot down and his knee locked rather than flexed and would pivot around on his steel shoe with an easy grace that showed his great mastery of all that was going on. I marveled at his skill. We all did. He won several races, all using the same Bultaco and it was simply unbelievable how much faster he was than everyone else.

I was not in his class, so I had no interest in the outcome, but there was a rumor in the pits that he had been cheating by using an oversized motor and since I was a hot rod oriented kid, and knew the truth that you can't beat cubic inches, I went to see how the dispute would be resolved.It did offer some explanation as to why he was so much faster than the rest of us and human nature being what it is, some tended to think the worst of everyone at every opportunity.

The rules required someone who wanted to claim that another racer had violated a rule to post some money to back it up. That was put up when the formal protest was filed and the protestor had to be rather specific about their complaint. Apparently that was done because by the time I got over to where the crowd had gathered the head was off the bike and calipers were being used to measure the bore and stroke.

I was new to dirt track racing then, and was just starting what I hoped would be a career. I had bought my first race bike because it was reputed to be the most powerful in its class, and therefore the fastest. I chose the smallest class because I knew that I didn't know anything about racing on dirt in competition.

My motorcycle forte at the time was my ability to do 100 miles an hour on gravel roads and thereby leave anyone foolish enough to try and ride with me behind. Every ride was a race for me, and when no one would ride with me anymore, I realized I may as well be racing. The local police mentioned that as well, although they were surprisingly nice about it.

The dyno tag on my 100cc Kawasaki G31m said 20.4 hp, which was incredible.How could it possibly produce that sort of power? I had come to racing motorcycles from drag racing and my 55 Chevy ran C gas and made 1 hp / cubic inch, which seemed awesome enough. This was five times that ratio, which put it into another realm altogether. It had to be magical in some way.

I did not know then that Steve McQueen had one too, but if I had known it, I would have been happy to hear it since his sense of these things seemed close to my own. We both had unit construction Triumph twins too, something I was aware of. Still, he was not a big man, while unlike most of the other riders in the class where I was starting, I was.

If I had learned anything in drag racing it was that weight makes a difference. At the drag races, weight is one of the factors that determined what class a car runs in. It was a recognized performance consideration, the expectation being the more something weighed, the harder it was to make it go fast with a given number of cubic inches. That calculation, together with some other more technical rules about setback and wheelbase, made up the class structure for the Gas class machines like my Chevy. The rules were intended to impart a level of fairness to the competition between racers.

At the motorcycle races it was all about engine displacement, and there were no rules about weight. That was a handicap of its own for me, because I was 6 feet tall and weighed about 180 lbs. ordinarily. I guess I could have been a jockey, where horses are handicapped by weight and the rider's weight is considered, but I didn't like horses and I was way too big to be a jockey. If I took extreme measures to get my weight down, and I did from time to time, I could starve myself down to 165, but that was pushing it and seriously affected my stamina. Most of the dirt trackers I started out with were much smaller than that, probably in the 100 – 120lb. range.

Looking strictly at the physics equation of acceleration, I knew that horsepower and weight were the two main factors in getting up to a given speed. Since scrambles racing was a dirt track race that amounted to a series of acceleration tests interrupted by corners, I thought it would be a good place for me to start so I could see if what I thought I had in the way of talent could overcome the handicap nature had imposed on me in the way of size.

Once I had an AMA license and could race, I read the rules, bought the fastest bike for the smallest class, and went to the first race I could find. That was Centralia where Kenny's bike was under protest so I got close and paid attention to see the rules applied. He stood by, chatting with some of the other riders, and accepted congratulations and handshakes all around when the bike was found legal. Other than the protestor, everyone seemed to take the news just fine that his motor met the requirements of the rules. It was good to know in a way that talent could actually make that much difference even if we didn't have it. That affirmation had cost the protestor some money, but he deserved to be whacked a bit for whining, which is all it really amounted to in the end.

As for my Kaw, (phonetically said 'cow') it proved to be the fastest bike in its class. The little track was laid out on a hillside which had left and right turns, some sharper than others, racing first downhill to the left and through some switchbacks before climbing back up to the finishline in less than a third of a mile's distance all together. Since I had come early, and signed up first,I had the pole position and when the race began, I was first away and pulled ahead down to the first slow corner which was a right where Ray came from out of nowhere and knocked me down with his little Suzuki 100 single and went on to win the race.

I had not seen it coming and although he rode past me a time or two afterward as I stood and glared at him, he did not look my way. I was fuming.

It took a while for me to get up and straighten out the twisted forks where he had run over my front wheel. Since I was in front and already squared off for the turn when it happened, it was hard at first to figure how exactly he had managed to hit me unless he had done it on purpose. I was not happy.

After the race, I went over to speak with him about it. We had our helmets off and he was being congratulated by his pit people and friends so when I came up he might not have known who I was or what I wanted and was still smiling. "You knocked me down." I said to himwith a poke in the chest coming with the 'you' and there was a quiet that came over those gathered around us to see what would happen next. He nodded a bit, and chewed his lip, not looking at me, and then said, "I did." I thought he would go ahead and say something about being sorry but he didn't. Instead, he commented, "That's a really fast bike you've got there." I waited a beat, to see if more was to be said, but if it was, it wasn't coming from him. "It is." I said but didn't go away, waiting for something to come to me, or him, to give the moment some resolution. I was new to such situations and wasn't exactly sure what I wanted from it.

One of the bigger guys stepped up and asked if I wasn't going to congratulate Ray on a nice race since he'd won. I shook my head no and said that if I had to knock people down to win I'd just as soon lose. They laughed, like I was joking, but I wasn't. I went back to my pit and loaded up and went home. I used the trip to ask myself if I had not made some mistake. I was new to all of this and knew it, and where I came from, the idea that someone would deliberately knock you down to win a race was outside the rules. Apparently, at the motorcycle races, it was acceptable behavior and just considered 'good racin' so I had some adjustments to make if I was going to keep doing it.

I hadn't tripped other runners when we ran track, even though it's an easy thing to do from behind. I hadn't run other cars off the highway by pushing their bumpers out of the way to win a race. It had often been the case in racing that the guy coming up from behind has the chance to exercise an unfair advantage and I had never thought it fair play. If it was, then it might not be my game.

It was three weeks before we met again, this time at the county fairgrounds in Marion, where they used a half mile dirt oval as part of the scrambles track. With that much straight there were no machines that had the speed of mine. Once I determined that, I went looking for Ray. When our class was called for practice, instead of going out first, I hung back and waited until I saw him go out. Then I would hunt him down and wait until we got to the slowest corner and turned in, exposing himself completely to whoever was coming up next. That was me, and I ran over his front wheel, knocking him down and went on.

It was a surprisingly easy thing to do. I had not seen it coming when it happened to me, but once I had the concept, it was stupidly simple to accomplish. When practice was over, some guy I didn't know came over and mentioned that I had knocked Ray down and I said that I had. He said they didn't hold with that kind of rough riding and I would be disqualified. I was told to pack up and go home. I went and talked to the referee about it and he said a complaint had been made about my riding and the protest upheld and that would be all for me that weekend. I told him about what had happened at

Centralia and he said it didn't matter to him, he hadn't been there. I could have complained there if I felt like it and I hadn't.

We eyed one another a good bit as this was said and I told him finally that I didn't think much of whiners, or cheaters, or riders who knocked other riders down to get ahead, but if that's what it took, I could do it. He shook his head and seemed understanding. "Son," he said to me sympathetically, "It ain't supposed to be like that." I saw his frustration with what the rules could do and recognized that it's mostly the riders that determine how it is really done and the referee only comes in after it's already gone too far. It's a tough sport, and to survive it, you have to hold your own.

It was arbitrary, and seemed unfair, but I learned from it, and when we raced again at Springfield Ray and I ran into each other at the riders meeting. He held out his hand and I shook it and he said it was good to see me. Nothing was said by either of us about what had gone on between us in a negative way. He never knocked me down again or came near my front wheel and I let him alone as well. These were amateur races, so it didn't really matter how you finished, we were supposed to be learning and this was meant to be the time honored way to do it, at least that was what the AMA thought.

I won some races that first year and so did he and I put the little bike away and bought a 250 so I could move up to the professional points paying novice class at the end of the season. Ray did the same. I bought a Yamaha DT-1 with a GYT kit chrome bore cylinder and expansion chamber. Ray got a Suzuki Savage 250. One night at a fairground somewhere in Southern Illinois he fell in practice and it killed him. I wasn't there and was sorry to hear about it. I liked him, and he had a way of getting around a dirt track that seemed exceptional. It made me realize that some things, not just about racing, are beyond our control. That's really too simple an answer and I do not favor Aachen's razor – the idea that the simplest answer is probably the correct one.

7.

Making A World Of Your Own

SIMPLE ANSWERS TO COMPLEX questions may be easy to remember, and I admit that I favored them when I was a child, but now, looking back, I think there is a great deal more to it than I understood. The explanation that all things are God's will, for instance, and all that's lacking is our acceptance of that and the recognition that we are no one to question the divine plan, seems too simple. It is too simple. If I were accepting of everything then I would have settled for having a pushrod Triumph twin and would still be riding around the back roads on rainy days to enjoy the thrill of wrestling it back into line on gravel roads.

Acceptance of the status quo also gives little comfort to those of us who still live after those we love do not, unless we accept as well that something grander is waiting for us after death and they will somehow be there. That is against the evidence and my image of heaven was disturbed early when Papa told me that dogs and horses were not allowed there. I was seven and Jet, the wonder dog, had just been hit and killed by a truck while I watched so the timing was either perfect for such a lesson, or cruel, depending on whether he was kidding or was telling the truth. While there has been a good deal written about heaven, there remains a complete lack of scientific evidence.

Still, we have control of some things and while we do we may as well do all we can to make our world be the one we want to live in. I will give you an example of how two racers decided to change the world and did so. I traveled alone down to the big track at Talladega for a novice race at the speedway. I had calculated how far it was and used the speed limit to determine when I ought to leave to be there at some reasonably early enough time to sign in and get a good grid position. I drove through the night, knowing that I wouldn't be able to sleep anyway if I waited until morning. As the road ran on and there was no traffic around me, I tended to drive faster and faster as I went, giving up 55 for 80. This put me there very early where I found a sympathetic gate guard just about to call it a night. Down at the far end of the chain link fence, nearly out of sight, another guard was letting in another lone van and we could see one another.

Between us and the gate to the pits was a twisty winding road that I had never seen before. He faced the same thing. I drove along the road with one eye on him and saw that the faster I went, the faster he went until it became plainly obvious that we were racing one another.

It was stupid, or silly, or just plain fun, depending on your point of view and apparently we shared the same one. I won, but it was a close thing and we both turned off the lights of our respective vans and called it a night to wait for things to begin to happen inside. That was some time later, but we were first and second in line when it happened and sure enough once they let us through we raced in, found places to park, unloaded our stuff and pushed our bikes with the leathers draped over their tanks and our helmets on our heads off to find the tech line. It was a foot race in the end and he had a shorter distance to cover but it was still close and everyone was laughing; we were, the AMA tech crew was, and the track man who pointed the way to him as I watched was.

Once there, we were told that it would be a bit before they opened and we had a while to catch our breath. I didn't know the guy, but he had a Yamaha like mine and novice plates so we were simpatico competitors with a weekend ahead of us to get acquainted. I leaned the bike against the nearby shed and went over to introduce myself.

I stuck out my hand, grinning as he was, and said, "Nice race." He shook it and said, "Thanks, You too." I gave him my name and he said he was Danny Hyatt and we were instant friends. In the half hour we had to wait for things to get going we did the abbreviated 'getting to know you'sort of back and forth in which I learned that he was from Missouri and he discovered I was from Illinois. We knew none of the same people although we had both started racing about the same time and there was the possibility that we had both run Granit City the same weekend but I had not recalled seeing him there nor he me.

He had come to the point that he realized that he had to get serious about racing if he was going to do any good which is what had brought him here. Yamaha was coming out with a new bike next year and he knew that his, and mine, would no longer have much of a chance to win. I agreed, but added that I went to all the national road races I could make and had decided that dirt track was not my way to an expert license.

He had done two tours in Viet Nam, dodging nightly mortar attacks at an airbase as he raided other guy's refrigerators while they huddled in bomb shelters. I had managed to avoid such experiences but had problems of my own with the war and its effects so we were on the same side about that. Charlie Watson came over and told us they were ready to welcome the 'eager beavers' and we went through tech and out, pushing back to our pits. I did not see him on the track, but that was not uncommon. It was a huge place and we were strung out so far that it was unlikely you could hook up unless you planned to ahead of time.

I apparently beat him in the heat race and we met again looking at the grid positions for the final. We talked about the usual things; jetting, gearing, fuel mix and so forth. We were both set to go for the final and I wished him luck and he did the same for me. Then I had a thought come to me and I called him back and asked him if he had a moment and he said he did and we sat down on the pit wall as I tried to put into words the thought that was coming to mind.

"Danny, " I said, "I don't know what you'll think of this but I've got an idea and I want to just spit it out and you can tell me what you think." "Shoot," he said, brushing his hair out of his eyes. "I love to race and I am going to have to make some changes to get to a place where I can do enough of it to find out if I have what it takes to make myself happy with it," I began, and he nodded in agreement. "I'm out of college now, and have piddled along at a bike shop barely scraping by so I could be at the races and have something to ride," I continued. "Now I'm going to have to find a spot where I can have a life and race too," I concluded, like it was some major confession.

He said nothing for a while, then told me he was a night floor supervisor at a mental home back in Missouri and hated it and added that the only difference he could tell between the people he cared for and himself was that he had a key and went home in the morning, whereas they stayed there all the time.

I understood that, although I could not imagine having such a job, but I had worked nights many times so we were again alike in what we had done and could manage ourselves well enough to be here. Like me, he was looking to make a change and was ready to try something new if it meant more racing.

"Here is what I am proposing," I finally said, "whether it's you or it's me,makes no difference. Whoever finds a job, doing something we both can do, and gets in a position to hire the other one there, let's work together to help each other go racing." He thought a moment, nodded in agreement and said, "deal", and stuck out his hand. We shook on it.

The following Halloween I married and left Illinois to return to the Oregon coast where I had been managing a Yamaha shop. That job had ended but my things were still out there and I was looking for someplace to be anyway and my young wife simply wanted to be out of Carbondale. We were snowed in when we got to the Rockies and sat in a hotel room looking at our meager finances and a map of the country. "Where to?" I had asked her, and she said she didn't care. I took her at her word and the next day when we got down to the east / west interstate across Texas I paused to consider which way to go.

Stan Friduss had told me at a race in Danville, Virginia that if I was ever in Gainesville, Florida and needed work, he had a bike shop there and would give me some until I got situated. That had been two years earlier and I hadn't seen him since but sitting there at the crossroads and listening to the little Ford eat through the pitiful savings we had left I figured that closer was better than further away and sooner was better than later and turned east. Florida called me; Oregon would have to wait.

It took the rest of that night and part of the next day to get me there and another hour to find Triumph City on the northern edge of town. It was a large modern metal building on the road to Alachua and the owner, George Hack, was the man at the service desk. I thought it was Stan's place.

I walked up with my tool box and announced that I was ready to work and explained that Stan had extended the offer I was now accepting. George was good natured about it, but explained that he was the owner and that Stan no longer worked there and that they did not need any more mechanics. There were three guys watching us talk and I figured they were the mechanics he spoke of. I looked out in the asphalt lot under the shade trees and saw a large number of motorcycles of various kinds and then at the metal holder on the side of his stand up counter that held the work orders. "I'll tell you what," I said, "I don't need a salary, just give me half the labor off the tickets I do and I'll eat all the comebacks for free, it won't cost you a thing to have me work through your worst bikes waiting right there," and I pointed at the herd of mixed heritage.

He thought a good deal before asking me if I had any training and I told him I did and had four years of experience in a Triumph; Norton; CZ; Yamaha shop and had all of my own tools. He pulled out a ticket and pointed at the shade tree. "You'll have to work out there," he said, "and tell me when you're done with this and we'll talk." I went around the other side of the building to where Stella sat in the van and told her I had work and to make herself comfortable as best she could while I did it.

She was 18 and did not argue but took out a book and started reading. She was in the shade and it was not freezing as it had been yesterday so for the moment she was happy enough to tolerate being neglected. I finished five bikes before the shop was to close and George paid me in cash, satisfied that they were properly completed. It was Saturday evening and he asked me what my plans were. I told him my wife needed lunch, which surprised him because he had not known I had one, or that she was with me.

He came with me to be introduced and as we talked he saw his office manager leaving and called her over and asked her if she knew of anyplace we could stay for a while. She said her apartment complex had one unit left to rent and it was the fully furnished model and that the manager had told her she could have a finder's fee for bringing someone to fill it and that was how it began. It was all too simple to be believed and we went, loved it, signed a lease, and slept in comfort that very night. Monday I worked inside with the other guys, who were paid a salary whether they worked or not.

A month later, George decided to make me the Service Manager and moved himself up front, which made us short one man in the back. I asked him if I could hire my own replacement and he said when I found someone that I thought could do the job I could. No sooner than he was finished saying it I pulled out my wallet and fished out the scrap of paper Danny had given me with his phone number on it.

I called him while George watched, unsure of what I was doing. "Danny," I said into the phone, "It's me, I have that job for you we talked about." He asked where and I gave him the shop name and address and the phone went dead. I thought we had been disconnected.

Other things happened to distract me as I got oriented to middle management responsibilities and I thought I would call him back later but I didn't and when I came to work on Monday, Danny's van was parked under the live oak tree behind the service door with him, his race bike, and his tools inside. I woke him up and introduced him to C.N. Lyons, Johnny President, Charlie Pier, and Herbie the Painter and we all pushed bikes out to face the new world - the one that we had made ourselves.

That was the way things went for me for a long time. I was living a charmed life and had done nothing to deserve it. I once thought that as long as I could make it to the grid at Daytona each spring, everything would somehow be all right. I thought it was within my power to make that happen.

Times change; Danny died in his sleep at age 40, Ted was blinded in a rental car accident while in England to race the GP's, Triumph City closed, and Stan Friduss, the man who invented crawling off your motorcycle and sticking you knee out on his 500cc Norton, now sells Moto Guzzi.

Now my motorcycle race at Daytona is in the fall, which couldn't be worse as a time for worshiping the cycle of life. It's the end of summer and warmth, not the beginning, and no amount of good will by all concerned can change that very basic truth. You are not starting another season, you are ending one, and it may be the last. The speedway is different too, not that it matters, or exactly because it matter.

That is the real problem, and not one that I have found a solution for whether I use a calculator or spend time on my knees. It's not that I don't accept it that my racing days are numbered, we all know that to be true, it's just that I have an appetite for something born of experience and I am not yet satisfied that I have gotten all the nourishment from it I was intended. There are ahead of me only so many opportunities to feast at the table. What should I have?

Knowing I can make a world for myself, and knowing that I have changed as I must do, as we all must do, the question now is what part will racing play in the world I make next? I use to just ignore the problem itself and fall back on distractions to think about something else. "I love Lucy" reruns can only do so much to disguise the truth and even she has some 'splain'ing to do. What seems to be going on around me is not as real as I thought reality was supposed to be.

The sequence of events seems wrong, for instance, and I am fairly certain that the speed of time varies, depending on what I am doing or thinking about. Some moments in the past seem more real to me than moments in the present and I have feelings telling me that some moments to come are familiar to me, before I even have them. I am not alone in this, which tells me something else about it, and I have accumulated enough experiences of my own and been told about enough by others, to know for certain that the way things go are not at all the way you and I were told they would go.

So let us begin with baby steps; what do we know for sure and how do we know it? We should start with that and we should agree ahead of time to limit our prejudice toward those that disagree with us to lap times. What is true will work, pragmatic philosophers point out, and no amount of saying you are fast will make it so. As Kenny Roberts was fond of saying, "When the green flag drops, the bullshit stops." He said it at my house, at the dining room table, and made good natured fun with our other guest before he ever thought about sticking his knee out or crawling off his motorcycle to make it go faster. He was just another racer then, and we welcomed everyone. It was a traveling circus and we saw each other and renewed our acquaintances at the races where life was an altogether different sort of thing. It was a small branch of the larger tree of the family of man at large. A nonconforming branch to be sure, but very much alive.

Don Vesco was there too and more or less the whole gang at one time or another and whether some of us were faster than others on the track, and we were, it made no difference when the time came for a good story and a funny way of making things go this way or that to illustrate a point. We were young, we were ambitious, we were having a life, all of us, and racing motorcycles was just part of it.

We moved along and moved on, some of us to other things far from the track, some of us never very far at all. It made us think. It still does. Once at the movies Mike Devlin faked gagging and made noise like he was puking as he poured a large drink on the floor where we sat near the back, letting let it run down the auditorium beneath the feet of unsuspecting patrons in front of us. Was it funny? Oh, man, I laughed until my sides ached. Was it the right thing to do? Well that's a different question all together. Where to begin?

8.

From Whence We Came

NOTHING BEGINS THINGS, NOT really. Sometime before the first moment I can speak of there was a moment that I have nothing to say anything about. It's back there; they are all back there, stretching out across the universe of time in ways we cannot imagine. We cannot imagine them because we are built to process information a certain way, and while all that we can do is marvelous, there is a limit.

If I want to know the truth, and I do, then I must consider everything and begin with what I know and can understand and work out things from there. I was not very old when I first noticed that some moments of time were different from others. Some days seemed brighter, some things registered as more significant in my memory even though I had no idea why. The face of a girl in the window of a passing car; an old postcard written in French and postmarked from Verdun; the way she turned toward the sun as she brushed her hair back from her face; such moments as these have made their way into an album of remembrances for reasons I cannot explain, yet I know they are significant in some ways I have yet to understand.

Other things; phone numbers, names newly heard, directions to the market, the tube stations of London, seemed to make too light of an impression and required writing down. Notes would be found in pockets weeks or months or years later with cryptic clues about what I had been hoping to blossom into useful communication. "Cat food, nail polish remover, Advil, blue masking tape, Pineapple…" Had I been a terrorist in a previous life, or did I just have multiple personalities? Hard to say, but one thing was clear – the secret to understanding the present lies in the past.

...

James Walker Wright was born sometime around 1855 and later married a woman in the Indian territory of Oklahoma. Nine children were born of the union, and the fifth, Roy Earl Wright, was born August 30, 1896 was my grandfather. He was, as the story goes, a hell of a man and a fair hand in the saddle. My memory of him is that he had big ears, big hands, and used few words. His only daughter should have been a son and he called her 'Bill' which is part of my story since she was my mother. It is also a part of the incredibly large series of connected events that make the world around us and all that happens in it a mystery in some ways, and understandable in others, all at the same time.

Roy was awakened one night when he was about ten years old by his father and taken off to Arizona to help him run a newspaper that later failed. He was never told why he was chosen or what had happened to his mother or any of his siblings. When he could, he left his father and went to look for them but they were gone. He returned to complain to his father to find him gone as well. As an adult, a lifetime later, summer vacations were spent searching the headstones of the cemeteries scattered throughout the West in hopes of discovering some evidence of what had happened to the rest of his family. I was on some of those outings and we noted the little things said that were so cryptically noted as to make us wonder. "Died with his boots on;" "Just out of Omaha;" "Complained constantly;" were examples that still bring a smile. Roy died of lung cancer in 1966, without finding a trace of his kin.

He had worked on the hundred and one ranch and played for the Kansas City Athletics as a catcher for a while but mostly his life was spent in the oil business, working on rigs and saving his money to wildcat a well for himself when he could. Some were good, most were not, and his life had the ups and downs of fortune that characterized many in prewar America. When the war came, his self-taught welding skills finally made him a valuable commodity and he spent the duration in the Kaiser shipyards putting seams together for victory and being happy to get paid overtime.

Bill had come along late in the 1920s, although some lying about the precise date was usually done. I did not pin it down until after it fell to me to make her final arrangements. She was a hell of a woman, and claimed to be the first in Oklahoma to have a driver's license although I doubted it. Roy had bought her a 1936 Ford at the State Fair because it was robin's egg blue and was sworn to be the only one in the state. He was flush at the time and the car went home with her at the wheel and took her to Varnum High school in Seminole afterward and on to the State Championship basketball tournament where her team won with her as a point guard, although less than five feet tall. Red hair and a temper to match with the vocabulary of a longshoreman she filled in gaps in a conversation with startling tales that left most bystanders with nothing useful to say.

"Bill, tell us about the time you met Howard Hughes when you drove down to Houston with $500 and a Colt 45 to pick up a drill bit for Roy…" might be said, which would launch the telling of a great tale of traveling across two states driving the '36 with blocks of wood screwed to the pedals so she could reach them from where she sat on a Coca-Cola crate. It sounds unlikely now, but it was still the West back then, and self-reliance was not optional, it was required. She made the trip down and back in two days and some change, which surprised everyone, and did it without stopping to sleep, a trait which I regrettably inherited.

Roy pulled out the string and put the new bit on just in time to complete the well before his lease expired, keeping his promise to his investors. I would like to be able to say that they struck it big but it was a dry hole. The only bright spot that still shows from the whole affair was the ability of a teenage girl to drive across Texas and back at a hundred miles an hour and not kill herself in the process. I made the trip myself years later just to see what it took and even with a modern interstate highway to help could not match her speed. It must have been something to see.

Margaret Parrish White was the daughter of a judge in Carmi, Illinois and was sent west on the train for a visit with her aunt in

Chloride, Arizona. She was charged with looking out for her sister Mary, younger by a year, but only 13. Margaret played the piano and Mary sang. The two of them performed wherever they could muster a crowd to pay for it, which proved to be often enough to keep them afloat. Somehow, through details lost in time, the girls met and married two young cowhands from Kingman, the Bonelli brothers, Frank and Bill, who lived in the only stone house in the Territory. It still stands today as a national historic landmark across from the courthouse. It had a cupola on the top where the boys would watch in the evenings to spy their father coming in from the ranch so the news could be relayed to the kitchen to go ahead with finishing the meal.

The family had come from Tooele,(two ella) Utah, where the primogenitor Johann Bonelli had emigrated from Switzerland in 1859 coming to Ellis Island on the good ship Emerald Isle. He met Johanna Harrison of England either in Utah, or on the ship depending on which source you believe and they began the American branch of the family by picking a new name for it – Bonelli. Some remain right where it all started, others moved on. In the interim many remarkable and mundane things may have happened, mostly unknown to me.

There was a ferry run by Bonellis across the Colorado River and photographs can be found of the boys on horseback, on the seats of freight wagons as teamsters, and together on a motorcycle before WWI sometime. There was a flurry of misadventures with the Parrish girls when they came and no record remains of how it came to happen that Margaret went home to Illinois on the train with a broken heart and two small sons while Mary went on to California with Bill to found a ranch that is now a state park where a race was held and reported in the first issue of the then new "Hot Rod" magazine.

Margaret's younger child was unnamed because it was then the custom to let fathers name their sons and her husband Frank would not. So the boy was called, "Junior" until his older brother, Jack, mangled it frequently enough into 'Judy' for it to stick first as a nickname and later as a name of its own.

Bill and Judy met in Carmi, Illinois during his senior year of high school, shortly before he volunteered for the Army Air Corps despite having a deferment. He recalled signing up on the wing of a P-38 lightening at the White County Fairgrounds flown in for just such a purpose and allowed as how it was the last time he ever saw one. I came along some years later and spent many hours in the offices of the principals of the schools I attended across the country trying to explain that while my parents were Bill and Judy Bonelli, it was my mother's name that was Bill.

We moved a good deal when I was going through the grades and I didn't mind. New towns meant new friends and while l liked some better than others I had something most of them did not – stories to tell, which was usually good enough to keep them at bay while we got to know one another. Those wanderings relocated me from south to north to west and back again, planting me in Illinois about the time I was old enough to care where I was. That is where this story begins in real time, and where I will now demonstrate how all of the things I have said above that you may have thought a self-indulgent waste of time are actually critical to the way things are now.

Stop yourself. Stop doing whatever else it is that you are doing and pay attention just to this long enough to understand what I am saying. Time is what to you? I mean you do have some concept of time, don't you? We all do. We can segment it into categorical slices, sometimes uniformly measured, sometimes more vaguely referenced. For example if I tell you that I 'need a second' before I answer your question, how long will you be willing to wait? If I say I'll be 'back in a minute', is a minute all I get to return? Obviously there is some vagueness built in to our expressing things to one another and it cuts across all disciplines. While 'clarity' is often said to be the legal purpose of having a contract written out between parties, few would say the verbiage that results is all that clear. So we have a large body of things that are fuzzy in their expression and meaning going on in a world around us that seems less so as we consider it.

Outside our windows is a world familiar to everyone with a window. There is a sky and something beneath it and here and there things grow and may have been built upon it, or not, depending on where you are. It has rules and laws of its own that man has discovered over time and applied to do things with it and to it and for himself. Man is frail, after all, and nature can bring fatal forces to bear so it's been a struggle to get to where we are today, which is a position of relative comfort and safety if we choose it. I have a house, Shakespeare had a house, Hemingway had a house, I have seen them all. They had roofs and walls and doors and while there are marked differences they are not all that great given the span of time and the distances between their locations. There was a time when the possibility that one person might see the houses and the ocean between them extremely remote but that time has passed.

Man has learned to move around by artificial means; that is to say without muscle power or the wind being the motivational force. Motorcycles were invented and since they are a necessary element in this discussion we should consider their origin. By my definition that happened in America in Massachusetts and a man named Roper should get the credit, but I'm not an authority that anyone would listen to, just someone who thinks 'two wheels and a motor' makes a motorcycle and anything more is something else.

That discussion will keep, the important thing is what comes next, and that is the event that launched me into the life I live and the way I live it.

I drove out to Tooele, Utah, entirely ignorant of any family connection, to help put on a vintage motorcycle race and I noticed something that made me feel a great deal better about the state of things in general. It had been some time since I had taken the time to follow the pioneer trail to the West, and although all of us have heard about it at one time or another, it is worth repeating to modern man just how difficult a journey it must have been.

I mean, it's a chore in a climate controlled car on an interstate highway at 75 miles an hour, so it is hard to imagine how it must have been on foot or in a covered wagon. If you give that a try, to imagine it, you will probably miss it by a mile; actually by more than a thousand miles.

Oxen or horse drawn wagons were only good for about ten miles a day, if the road was easy and a great deal less if the terrain was difficult plus, they had to be fed and cared for. The journey was so long in fact that they needed to leave as early in the spring as the flood swollen rivers would allow and move quickly enough to clear the mountain passes before the first snows of winter. I do not see how they did it; although I know they did.

There is a marker in Grand Island, Nebraska to note where the Mormons established a stopover and resupply point for their followers who were heading west to eventually settle Salt Lake. Many of them carried their possession in push carts. Most of us try to park as close as possible to Wal-Mart's door so the distance we have to push a cart with our possessions is minimal. We are not pioneers, even if our forefathers were.

I was surprised to find my family name on the pioneer's monument among those of the city founders and spent a little time with the librarian to discover that an unknown predecessor had come from Switzerland to help settle that part of the valley. I was less surprised to read in the city records that a subsequent Bonelli had been asked to leave after invoking self help and a shovel to settle an irrigation dispute with a neighbor. He had used the shovel on the neighbor rather than the irrigation canal which was frowned upon. I enjoyed an impromptu picnic in a lovely city park full of children and their caretakers and mused about my unknown connection to them as the sun shone on us all.

The weather was perfect and everyone I met seemed to go out of their way to be helpful and kind. It was an adjustment for me, but I made it and soon my gloomy depressed attitude that was my Midwestern viewpoint began to soften as my outlook brightened. What could it be? I asked myself as I notice the transformation.

No news – was the answer. In my traveling I had been deprived of my daily diet of gloom and doom as provided by the world news mongers. Things are bad. How bad are they? Why they are (fill in the comparisons yourself here as they vary but are tied to past events in the 'as bad as...' genre) so bad that it has not been this bad since the last time!

I consider myself to be well informed, and when I reached that state I recognized the duty to stay that way. I read a lot, and enter most situations with the hope that it might educate me to be a better person in some way. Consequently when floods ravage Pakistan, as they have for a thousand years, I am interested. I am also mindful that from 1965 to 1967 in this same region 1.5 million people died from the record drought caused when the monsoonal rains failed to take place, no doubt making as many people wish it would rain more than ever, which has come to pass. It is my planet, and they are my people in the same way all human beings are, which make me grieve for them and their troubles, wherever they may be.

Sitting in the sun in Utah, however, they seemed especially far away just then and my spirit felt less burdened not hearing of their daily woes. The blindingly beautiful vista of the blue sky and distant mountains helped as well and it was with a smile that I stopped at Wal-Mart to get some ice on my way out to the track to work. It was there that I met the angel of the day.

She was working her shift at the 'less than 10 items' aisle and greeted every customer with a smile and good cheer. When it was my turn I commented on what a beautiful day it had been, worried that she might have missed it here inside and eager to share my appreciation of it. "I spent it at the park with my grandson," she answered, beaming. Seeing that she had more to say on the subject, I asked her how he was and she stopped what she was doing and said with obvious pride and affection, "He's only four, and do you know what he said to me?", she asked checking to see if I was interested, and continuing when she saw I was; her eyes went up then, to a place just beyond us, as she recalled and relived the moment with obvious relish; "Grandma, I love you wider than the Ocean; Higher than the sky; … and more than chocolate pie!"

Her laughter that followed was infectious and the other patrons who normally grow impatient in such lines, joined me in congratulating her on her great good fortune. My own fortune was increased as well by her reminder that there are good people everywhere and their riches are as great as their appreciation for what's really important.

Taking the time to talk about it is what we lack today, and I fear that may only get worse in the future. The young twenty something woman the track assigned to work as my liaison for race control had a smart phone constantly playing something in one ear as she texted and surfed every spare moment she was not actually talking to someone else. I was sad for her and her generation and could not help but hear her complaining about what a hassle it was to be burdened with a four year old and be a single mother.

When I was younger I would have been surprised by the irony of the answer that came later in the day when her little son was dropped off by his divorced dad. When she finally managed to interrupt her conversations with her social networking peers long enough to rhetorically ask him what he had done today, he said with a good deal of enthusiasm that grandma had taken him to the park. Putting her finger to her lips to shush him, his mother had whispered, 'that's nice' while listening to another conversation in one ear as music leaked out of the other. Looking around, the little boy noticed me and I smiled at him and leaned down to ask,

"Do you love your grandma more than chocolate pie?"

With very big eyes, he slowly nodded 'yes', no doubt wondering how I knew his grandma.

9.

The Phenomenon Of What Matters

You as Racer

I WAS DOZING WITH my eyes half open seeing nothing of the sameness of the highway rolling on ahead as it had been for days now uninterrupted but for the stops for gas my hands no longer feeling the wheel which had grown into me, taken in like a tree takes something to root over. When I did stop rolling, I behaved like it was a pit stop and was antsy to be on the move again getting food or drinks to go when there was no need but once the tank was full I was a fool. Sixty miles an hour is a mile a minute; standing still is zero miles a minute and time and miles are all there is between where I am now and where I want to be.

There had been chili dogs and peanuts and coca cola and sweet tea and hot coffee that turned cold and bitter but I drank it anyway craving the effect and caring no longer how it tasted. The sweet smells of a racing van had been with me so long that I no longer noticed the racing castor and its gasoline partner or the rubber of the tires when the sun hit them or the sweat drenched leather suit hanging like a herald in the back window showing my name across my back shoulders and my number for all to see who were behind me and telling them that's where I thought they should be then they would pass and show me theirs and then the race was on.

Aldana snuck up alongside in the middle of the night and roused me from my cruise control with a cherry bomb under the front of my van and I came full awake with a start and saw him then, next to me, when he turned the dome light on and pointed, laughing like a lunatic at me, then with me, as we reveled together at being young and on the open road with the whole country spread out before us.

There were police, sure, and I suppose some of us got arrested for speeding, but more usually it was some civilian who had come in our midst thinking he could pace along with us without realizing who we really were. There were rules about things. You never lead a pack of speeding cars and truck over a hill, for instance, but rather moved over to let someone else go first and be the first one seen on the radar gun. If some speedy guy came along and followed but wouldn't take the lead we wouldgradually slow down until he had to pass us and then would speed up right behind him until eventually he would decide he didn't want to share the road with us and so would go faster to leave us behind and rabbit away.

We would say we had made a 'rabbit' out of him and then follow his speeding example at a safe distance but still matching his speed so that we got where we needed to go that much faster and then had time for sleep. 1800 miles is a long way between racetracks and the difference between 55 miles an hour and 70 miles an hour is 15 miles, every hour. In 1800 miles it makes 7 hours of difference when you arrive and that's enough time to slow yourself down, get to sleep and rest and then be ready for a day of racing, or enough time to go and drive in the ocean or walk like zombies around in a mall or do anything anyone has a mind to do, or no mind at all to do it with.

There had been a picture in the paper of Aldana and me on the banking at Daytona on TZ750s and it was a great shot. It was a better photograph than it was a race between us as he had a bike that would handle the speed we were doing and I had a jet propelled Conestoga wagon that was trying to kill me. Still, the photographer had captured a moment when Dave had come along faster than I was and slingshot past me, close enough to get us both in the frame at the same time and 'click' just like that he had his moment as we had ours, all of them different from one another in nearly every way you could describe.

To Dave I was just another bike he was passing, although we spoke to one another when we met off of them, but still it was the nodding 'Hey' of strange familiarity said to another racer at a safe distance. It doesn't do to know someone so well that you would think of their situation on the track when thinking of your own is all you can do.

I saw him and Gary Nixon up at Loudon after we had all had our careers behind us and were back for reasons of our own to do some riding on race bikes again. I had a camera and wanted a picture of us together and they were happy to do it, something we never would have done when we were really racing one another. They look smaller than I remembered when I look at the picture now, and I look out of place. Still, we had our moments.

I was in Tooele again just before this book went to press and saw Walt Fulton's name on the grid sheet. I was perplexed. Which one was it? The first of that name was famous, as was the second – who was a Triumph district manager for the Midwest and flew a small plane around his territory with a Tiger Cub in the back and then went on to be the first winner of the Catalina race. His son, Walt Fulton III, was my contemporary hero from my embryonic 'racer wanna be' stage of development that had given me the impetus to go ahead and give it a go at the big time.

I went looking for him and found my friend Dave Roper instead. Dave has an appreciation for history and has made a good bit himself, but I recall when he started racing and have seen him over the years become legend. He enthusiastically answered my inquiry with the news that it was the man I sought and I told him I would very much like an interview if some time could be found.

It was, and so it was that I met Walt for the first time and took him away from his race day routine to spend 40 minutes with me and my I-phone in collective reminiscences of things past. It was wonderful of him to do it and he is a gracious gentleman through and through. He was returning to competition that very day, as it turned out, having ended his active career one day at Laguna Seca when he crashed spectacularly at high speed. Not knowing what had caused it, and being told it was probably just pilot error, he retired rather than endanger anyone else by riding with him again.

Some men might say such things and you wouldn't believe them, no matter how long you knew them, but with Walt, even at this first encounter, there was no doubt that was the truth. He added later that he had found out from someone at the track that pieces of his front wheel had been found on the front straight, which was before the fast sweeping turn where he went down. Apparently, the cast front wheel had disintegrated and when it let the tire deflate, it took him down.

Now he was back and riding a Harley Sprint in a special frame with all the best equipment that his sponsor had gathered to give him a worthy mount. It was odd, in a way, as we were both there to race, and to do a job. His job was to promote his new business, which I had the announcer plug on air; mine was to officiate on the grid, and line the bikes up for their race and then score them. Ultimately that included his, as he occupied a spot on the second row of a grid of very fast riders in the hyper competitive 350 gp class.

I have to admit that there was something about it that seemed wrong to me somehow and it took a bit before it came back to me. Walt wore glasses when he raced in the old days, and they were not insubstantial. He admitted on his own that his nickname had been 'Mr. Peepers' and we all had nicknames back then whether we like them or not. Now he didn't wear any, which is a tribute to modern technology.

There is nothing wrong with his vision, or his riding skills, and he has not lost a bit of his competitive desire. He won his race, finishing first among people who knew who he was, and others who hadn't, but would sure know now. Good for him.

10.

Your Skill Set

YOU HAVE A SKILL set – a brace of things you can do; a quiver of talents that you can use to bring down the prize you've targeted. You may be charming or handsome or strong or brave or thoughtful or whatever descriptive label you prefer but the truth is, you do some things better than others. Doing things, some things, stirs a reaction within you that other things do not. This distinction drawn by our nature relates to one of the fundamental functions of our brain. We are hard wired to compare things.

Oh, this tastes like chicken. Or; this road reminds me of the one to Road Atlanta. Or; that noise sounds like the wheel bearing that went bad in my old Ford van when I didn't know what it was. Big things and small, we compare each sensation our senses register from the time our brain goes to work and it never stops until our life is over. When we sleep, the brain keeps working but doesn't get many external inputs to work with so it makes things up to keep itself busy. We dream.

If you want to test yourself to see if you are hard wired to be a motorcycle racer, ask yourself what you dream about after a day on the track. If it's not the track, then you may be better suited to other things. That is because we have a certain sensitivity to the input of things and if the amplitude of that range is exceeded by our mental limitations then we just can't manage it. It was just "frightening" or maybe "numbing" or worse yet; it made no impression because it was just too much.

I have had fifty years of racing to consider, and depending on where you are in the arc of your career with motorcycles you may have more or less. I have talked to many riders after experiences that did not turn out well and asked them what happened. Their answers fall into two basic categories; the "It all happened so fast..." and "One minute I was doing this, the next minute I was on the ground..." sort of response, and the moment by moment detailed description in abstract terms of the sequence of events that made up the incident.

"I applied the front brake with two fingers and felt a modulation in the lever as the front wheel encountered a depression in the track. The tire began to lose traction and I lightened the braking load which took me off my line so I was now going to miss the apex I had planned for and had to turn in again; this widened my exit point and required an adjustment in my throttle return to full power so my weight shift was changed to accommodate the new setting as I exited the corner." OR

"I don't know what happened. I grabbed me a handful of brake, and BOOM! I'm on the ground slidin' along like a wet dog on the kitchen floor!"

This is as good a time as any to talk about courage. It's a brave man that gets back on and races again who was speaking in the second example. That is because he has little or no idea what caused him to go down. He is not analytical, he is reactive. He may think it's his socks, or what he had at the Waffle House before coming to the track, or because it's Friday the 13th. He may be right, I don't know about him other than I know it takes courage to face danger you can't defend yourself against.

This is not criticism, it is observation. The first of these two examples comes from a cold calculating mind that is up to speed with what is happening and is dealing with the situational data as it arrives and storing it for later analysis if there is a later. It may work out, it may not, but his mind is unemotional about it. It is not screaming "Oh God, Oh God, O God !!!!" to itself as things develop. The man with such a mind is not screaming anything, he is; and here is one of those places where written words show their limitations.

I mean to say, he is not screaming anything, he 'IS'. He is not just in the moment, he is both remote from it and its creator all at once. He is the embodiment of reality as he knows it. This is how blind people go on after they lost their vision. They are still here, the world they move through is still here. The interface has changed, that's all, and some can deal with it more successfully than others. Ted comes to mind.

It's the mind / body philosophy problem extended. "I am not just what I think, I am what I feel" a philosopher would say. True enough as far as it goes. Now put that guy in a leather suit and send him down to turn one at Daytona with 40 other guys who also want to get there first and see what he has to say about it. What motorcycle racers say about it is that it is what they think, and what they feel, AND what they do, that makes their reality.

Motorcycles bring a sharpness and immediacy to experience that nothing else does. We look ahead, or we should, and we pay attention. Unlike in a car, even a convertible, we have a reactive relationship with our movement through space that is both unreal and visceral all at once. It is easy to imagine that there is no motorcycle beneath you and once the ambidextrous and ambipederous functions are automatic, it's you doing it, not you telling some machine to do it while you just sit on top of it. Arcade motorcycle racing games are not like racing no matter how good the graphics are. The horizon is artificial and you are really stationary and can feel it.

The perpetually troubling aspect of all of this is that the elation you feel at doing it is tempered by the presence of someone that can do it better than you can. We are extremely rational on the track, and need to be, but there is an emotional reaction to being passed and left behind by someone who is either riding better than you are, or has a machine that has capabilities yours does not. This little wrinkle cannot be ironed out just by the will, sometimes it also takes a wallet to be a player. Mind over matter? Sure, but speed costs money.

"I can rider faster than you can," is something no racer wants to hear. If what we wanted to have was a test of riding abilities, we would make everyone ride identical motorcycles with exactly the same tires and horsepower, each handicapped to allow for the rider's weight like in horse racing, and then start them all in a single row like in motocross and find out who is fastest. We don't do that.

We did something like it in the seventies when everyone rode 250 Yamaha twins at the AMA races and it was interesting to a point, but even then there were a few who knew things, or had access to special parts, that gave them an edge.

If it was about size, then Pee Wee Gleason would have been national champion and he wasn't. He was brave, and fast, and threw his bike away with true courage any number of times trying to get to the front. At the rider's meetings he didn't come up to my armpit and I kidded him once that I had legs that weighed more than he did. (about a hundred pounds I would guess). Pat Evans was also very small rider, and very fast. When he came to Daytona the first time he made a TD2 Yamaha look big. I made it look tiny so it gives you some idea. Was he really faster than I was, or just smaller? We raced together and as much as I envied his weight advantage, I bet he wished for a little more muscle to keep it pointed where he wanted. Oh, and my feet touched the ground when I sat on it without tiptoeing.

There is a physical aspect to racing and being strong, or at least having a certain level of fitness, makes a difference. When things are going bad and you have to make some sudden adjustment to the course of a three hundred pound projectile the whole mass times force equation has to be dealt with. Even if you are strong enough, you have to have the reflexes to react quickly enough and those are only triggered if you have enough gimble - that function that lets you walk down stairs with a glass of water and not spill it. It's your kinetic balancing ability extended to objects beyond your body. If you can juggle, or ride a unicycle, then you know what I mean. If you can't; well you just can't that's all.

I say all this as introduction because there is more to racing than how our minds and our bodies deal with situations brought on by riding motorcycles at speed in close company. There is something intangible, unpredictable, unexpected, that both intrigues us and keeps us humble. I had the chance to visit with Tim Lile at Millville at the end of summer AHRMA vintage race 2013. He was in bad shape. I met Tim as a new rider some years earlier, struggling to make a BSA B50 competitive. I suggested he try something newer but he stubbornly resisted. Success didn't happen, and it was discouraging. But Tim is a smart guy and he was determined to find out if he had what it took so eventually he bought one of the big Suzuki twins and sure enough, he could make it go. Without the problems of mechanical failures to worry about his riding picked up speed quickly and within a few years, with some luck, he became the class champion. No argument, Tim was a racer.

That did not save him from a road accident at 35 mph that nearly killed him. Some loose material from the shoulder of the highway, kicked up by some carless driver that had run off the shoulder, found itself under his front tire at the wrong moment and his BMW threw him down and stomped on him. It was not funny. All of his ribs on one side were broken and his heart was bruised. He had brain lacerations that brought on memory voids although his helmet didn't look that bad. His shoulder and his arm are a mess and he has a list of injuries that we didn't go into. The good news is that he lives, and he walks and talks and still has a sense of humor. When the doctor asked him who the president was to test his memory, he couldn't remember. When the doctor told him, he laughed and said he had been trying to forget.

So what was it, or what is it, that brings us to our knees and makes us wonder what the (put your own word in here, it varies depending on your viewpoint) is going on? That's the intangible thing about it that makes us wonder isn't it? I have a long, long list of incidents that I can detail for you so we could hash them out together and look for signs of correlation but, what we would find is that other than our looking for correlations, there aren't any. Well, there aren't any in any way that you can name and be right.

Here is where some want to say that God did it, or more accurately that whatever the outcome of whatever the event, it is God's will. Don't go there with me if we're talking about racing. Heathens are as fast as Baptists. If you knock me down on the track by doing something stupid, I am not going to be satisfied with talking to God about why He let that happen, I am going to be talking to you. God and I are OK with each other, but I don't bother Him about such things other than to tell Him I'm grateful, after which I chide myself for thinking he didn't already know. He's already given us the answers and the brains to figure them out, the rest is up to us. Easy answers to life's persistent questions are too simple to be useful in complex situations.

Anyway, if you race, or have, and are any good at it, then you know that you can master a hundred things a second if you need to – if you only knew what they were. "Tell me what knob to turn and what it does and I'll be all right" said the first time pilot to his instructor. Will he?

11.

Why A Picture Is Not Worth A Thousand Words

AFTER A WHILE, WHEN you've stopped saving refrigerator drawings your children and grandchildren drew, you realize that everything is not precious and the great museum and library of your life is not going to be built. You have to downsize and things have to go. It is not as bad as it sounds and there is actually some relief in calling the kids up and telling them those boxes of stuff they left in your care when they went off to college or where ever will be going as well. It's a little disconcerting to hear they don't want them but save yourself the grief of going through them one more time just to make sure there is nothing important in them. There isn't. I know that because I did it just to make sure.

Kodak stopped making cameras. It happened recently and I think my family had started using them when they first came out. I had one for a long time, a little black Bakelite box with a red window in the back that showed the number of the negative about to be exposed. It had been left behind when a WWI veteran had died alone and without family to pass it on to. It had no viewfinder, just some marks across the top to point in the direction of something you wanted a picture of as you moved the little arm that stuck out from behind the lens that operated the shutter and listen for the little "click" that said you had made a picture. Once you did, you had to wind the film to the next spot before doing anything else or you risked a double expose of the picture you just made.

The box was sent in to the factory in the mail and in two or three weeks an envelope of photos and their negatives came back to you. It was an amazing thing to see and people were clearly fascinated with having their picture taken which, in part, explains the multiple images we have of people posing for photos. Looking at them now, as complete strangers, we try to imagine something the picture is telling us. *"A picture is worth a thousand words?"* No, it isn't.

I say that because like a lot of people of my generation I have the accumulated images of unknown relation that passed down from album to shoebox to Wal-Mart bag. Taking any one of them and looking at it for information about the people in them, you begin to see just how little a picture really tells you. Who is that? What is going on that warranted a photo being taken? What ever happened to them? If the picture was taken by a professional studio and if they are still in business and the picture was numbered or catalogued somehow then there is slim chance that a record still remains of something.

After a while, Kodak started printing an abbreviation for the month and the last two digits of the year on the edge of the print. My first photo shows "Nov57" and was the product of an early Kodak camera I had found in the attic. To our surprise, Kodak honored their promise to process the old film and several of the pictures turned out. Rather than return the old box camera loaded with more film, however, they sent me a new one and several mailing envelopes to use to send in the exposed film for printing – in color! Sunsets now became fair game.

Obviously a black and white photo of a sunset does not tell the whole story. All sunsets are interesting but some are also spectacular and makes us wish we could capture it on film. We can't, which makes my point about how many words a picture is worth. Going through the collective photos of the family there were three main types of images; people, events, and sunsets. People are easily understood even if difficult to identify. Groups at a table, at a wedding, at a graduation, at a funeral, all say, "Well, here we are." Christmas morning also seems to be a popular time for these as well and you can get some sense of the passages that come with the children's looks of surprise, joy, or indifference at what "Santa" has left them this year.

Some event photos are also telling. I have a picture of John Kennedy's fresh grave at Arlington taken on our class trip there with my classmates and a picture of the Lincoln Memorial from the same trip. The latter looks remarkably like the photo I took just a few years ago revisiting Washington after too long an absence. Unconsciously I had stood in nearly the exact same spot to capture the angle of the columns and the steps going off in both directions. Holding both photos now, it was obvious that something from that viewpoint compelled me to take yet another picture of it -Then there are the sunsets.

Each photo was an attempt to capture a fleeting moment of rare beauty in nature and each in its own way, was a failure. It's a transubstantiation sort of thing – I wish there was some way to have the real thing again so I could believe in the transcendental power of photography. You cannot do it because the media is inadequate. Nothing is as real as reality. Not 3-D, not digitally remastered, not with home theater sound, not anything. Images can be presented in different and exciting ways, sure, but they are just a trick. Just outside your door, every day, the sun really goes down. How many days do you go out to watch?

Well, a number of people in my family did, apparently, and took their camera with them to try and capture golden red hues with coral and purple accents against a turquoise and azure sky. After Krakatoa erupted, sunsets around the world were unusually and exceptionally beautiful. Photographs of those sunsets are really something to see but they pale in comparison with how beautiful and rare those sunsets actually were. That's a thousand words – get the picture?

NOV 57

12.

Sometimes When I Think Of Nothing

I THINK ALL THE time. They say that once you stop, it's difficult to pick it up again. I wouldn't know and I'm not especially eager to find out if that is true or not. When I was young I fell in love with motorcycles and thought vaguely that they might someday kill me. They never have and I'm still racing them fifty years later.

I knew they were dangerous, but so was doing a double gainer off the high dive and I did that too as well as a lot of other things that could and did hurt me. I had always raced. I played tag with other kids and tried to outrun them so they couldn't catch me. When we got bicycles we played tag on wheels, on roller skates, on skate boards, on go karts, on skis, on anything that moved. When we got cars, we kept doing it.

I didn't think much about any of it when I was young. I just liked the feeling. It was fun to race and good to win, but still a pleasure if I didn't. To compete, just to be a part of things understood by others to be the same thing was enough. I began to think more about it when it began to matter whether I did well enough to gain admission to better racing. I watched professionals race and thought I should and could be out there with them. It never entered my mind that there would be anything about it I could not do. I grew up with kids who were constantly challenging me with "bet you can't do this!" and then they would do whatever it was they had bothered to learn to do. I could do anything anyone else could do, I was pretty sure of that. I could jump up and click my heels in the air twice before coming down, I could hit a home run, I could touch the rim, and I could ride a motorcycle.

Then I met the American Motorcycle Association, who didn't care so much what I thought I could do, they had their little rules about such things and I would have to prove myself before they would let me race. It was not easy, but it was doable. It would have been simpler if I had money to make it less work but then I would not have had to think about it so much. They had restrictions about which bikes could race and which could not. I like their sense of things, their claiming rules, their starting point of showroom models available to everyone with no titanium or unobtainable things inside. It was American, somehow in a Mickey Thompson sort of way, to think that you could go out to your very own garage in the middle of nowhere and work through the winter and build something like no one else had ever thought to build and then bring it out in the spring for the first race of the season and take it down to Daytona and show everyone what you had done.

It was cabin fever expressed in miles an hour. After I got my license and served my apprenticeship and managed to climb up the rankings to get out on the track with all the guys I had seen racing that made me say "I can do that" I learned a great deal about a great many things that never would have mattered otherwise. Mostly I learned to think. Say what you want to, grit your teeth and try as hard as you like, nothing like thinking makes your motorcycle go faster than someone else's motorcycle. Sure you can take risks another rider might not be willing to take, and you can bring yourself to the very limit of adhesion more often than they are willing to but, when you get on the straight at Daytona and tuck in behind the fairing and make yourself as small as you can, it's not going to matter. The bike will only go so fast and at Daytona, that matters.

I liked the whole thing. In a season of AMA racing in those days, after everyone had shown their speed at Daytona, you had other tracks to show them you could still beat them just by riding harder than they did. Past that you could beat them by finding a way to be at races they were not at, or driving further and putting up more than they were willing to put up with. All the time this was going on, you were thinking about racing. "What can I do better to go faster?" was a constant inquiry. We tried different tires, tire pressures, gearing, sticking our knees out, crawling way off the bike, different oils, different fuels, different carburetors, anything that seemed to promise more speed and better finishes.

I left everyone I knew and moved out to Oregon because a guy opening a brand new Yamaha shop promised to sponsor a whole season for me if I would come and set it up and be the manager. It was just after another season of mediocre results and I was at that point when I realized I had to do something, ANYTHING, to either get serious about racing or give it up and just be satisfied having it for a hobby. I worked through the late fall and winter and showed due diligence about business success. It worked and by the end of February we were booming. Late at night, after all the work was done, I worked even later prepping my TD2 for Daytona.

I took off at the very last minute for the diagonal drive across the country and was on the road already tired from making sure everything was done and the bike was ready when something happened that made me see how it all fit together. I had plotted out my own route in the days before Mapquest or Google maps and had gone cross country on a secondary road from the ocean across Oregon into Idaho when I came to a huge gaping canyon that brought me to a halt.

There was full moon that had just risen and it was about three in the morning at that tipping point when you either needed to get a nap or push past it to make it into the next day. I had not seen another set of headlights for hours and the road ran along the rim of the canyon as it headed for the bridge that crossed it. As I looked down over the rim, the moonlight shone on the river far below and I had a sudden urge to stop and make myself take it in.

You know how difficult it is to give up your momentum at such a moment, I am sure. Never stop moving, that's rule number one if you're racing someone and I had this feeling that across the nation from all different starting points, there were other racers like myself with vans loaded with all their efforts from the long winter just ended, now on their way to Florida for what they hoped would be their moment in the sun. I could feel them on the road and even though I couldn't see them, I knew somehow that they were out there racing me.

Still, there was something so striking about this moment, and the lack of anyone else around to see it that made it seem all the more compelling for me to take it in and appreciate it. I pulled over and sat there, looking at it through the windshield. It was not enough, somehow. I turned off the radio. The big Ford V-8 still thrummed along beneath the engine cover pressing up against my leg. The heater motor was suddenly audible and blowing its comforting warmth. Reluctantly I shut off the engine and turned off the lights. I still was insulated from whatever it was that had called me so I got out and closed the door behind me. As is stood there, suddenly chilled and zipping up my coat and plunging my hands into my pockets, I laughed at myself for being a fool. What the hell did I think I was doing?

The van ticked and gave off metallic clicking noises as they do when cooling off. It would be hard to start now, I knew that. The heat would perk the gas out of the carb and I could flood it if I pumped the gas pedal too much or run the battery down if I didn't pump it enough. I worried over this but stopped myself. I had stopped all that I was doing and done what I had done to be apart from such things. Something had compelled me to do it and I needed to pursue whatever that was as purely, and as simply, and free myself from such concerns if I was to fathom what was out there.

I stepped away from the van a bit but it was not enough, its presence reminding me of all that was waiting to be done and all that had been done to bring me there. I climbed up the side of the hill beside the road and around it's crest until the van was out of sight behind me. Now I was alone and untethered. Before me was the river valley in all its moonlit glory. I was still and listened for the slightest sound, anything at all that would tell me I was not alone. There was nothing; just nothing.

Then I saw what I had never thought I would see. Before me, across miles and miles of empty space stretching out to the dark horizon, there was nothing at all but emptiness. Not one light from a single source but nature. No houses, no cars, no trucks, no security lights shining down on anything anywhere for as far as the eye could see and that was a very, very long way. I was utterly and singularly alone - an outpost of humanity at its very frontier.

I took it in, knowing it meant something but not being sure exactly what, and then walked back to the van, trying to gauge for myself what time interval was appropriate for experiencing fully what I had just been drawn to. "Evangeline the Econoline" had been waiting for me long enough that she was still now. I got in and swung back into the seat, my body now unaccustomed to what had just before been a place so comfortable that I had been reluctant to leave it. There was a moment when I wondered if it would start and that broke the spell of not caring if it ever did again.

She did not hesitate and immediately came back to life bringing with her all the accoutrements of the near past; poking me forward. I put her in gear and began to move again. I drove on and although I told myself that I would come back someday and give the spot its due, I never have. It's out there, waiting for me I am sure, but it's in here too, (I point at my chest) in me where it made a whole of something that had never been whole before.

Gene Hamilton was a dandy. He drove a brand new 1963 Chevrolet Impala with fender skirts, dummy spotlights, fuzzy dice from the mirror and a 327 Fuel injected V-8. I had seen him around town on his Triumph Thunderbird and he had even given me a nod once as I gawked at him cruising past. Now he was here in the Principal's office of my school and he looked very much out of place. The Principal looked nervous as Gene's reputation as a bad ass was known far and wide. I had been summoned to the office over the intercom with the usual nasal crackly call from the Buck Rogers looking speaker boxes that hung in every room over the clock.

The box had a curved front of two tone venire that hung out further from the wall at the top than at the bottom which angled the speaker down toward its audience in a way that made you think someone had calculated it and knew it was perfect. It showed some design consideration that I appreciated, but it was never good to hear your own name called and so I gathered up my books with dread and made my way to my locker to deposit them all before climbing up the worn staircase to the mezzanine level where the office was located and went to the counter to make my appearance.

Misses Cat's eye glasses looked up from pounding the typewriter and saw me and jerked her thumb toward Mr. House's door which stood open about half way. I came around the counter and pushed through the swinging door that was just counter height and separated the public from the private portions of the space and marched myself before the firing squad with as much dignity as Humphrey Bogart might have mustered under the circumstances. I expected that I was here having been rounded up with the usual suspects, but was surprised to see a man in cuffed blue Jeans and a black leather jacket seated affably across the desk from Mr. House looking at me as I came in.

I stopped in the doorway, not sure what was up or why I was a part of it. Mr. House spoke first, "Gregg, Mr. Hamilton here has asked for you to be the projectionist at his club's viewing of a movie they have ordered from the A.M.A. and they need you, and the 8518 Bell and Howell projector tonight, can you do it?" I nodded my assent, although I was still digesting the details. Hamilton said, "There's ten bucks in it for you," and gave me a wink. I kept nodding. "I'll have to call Kroger's," I said, "but they won't mind me taking the night off." "You work there?" Mr. House asked and I nodded again. "Two years now," I answered and he looked surprised. "How old are you?" Hamilton asked, looking surprised. "Fourteen in February," I said which was now almost a month ago. Mr. House and Hamilton exchanged looks and then both looked at me again.

Hamilton leaned forward from his slouch and a lock of greasy black hair fell out of the pompadour styling that was a mixture of Brylcream and affectation swept back from the sides of his face into a 'D.A.' at the back, which had only recently been revealed to me to mean, 'Duck's Ass'. "Didn't I see you riding a candy apple red Triumph around the square last Saturday?" I felt the corner of my mouth go up on one side, it was an involuntary reflex whenever the topic of motorcycles came up and the new was still on mine. I nodded with more assurance this time. "You might have," I said, "I ride one."

Hamilton grinned too then, and we were sharing something when the Principal said, "You're not old enough to ride a motorcycle," with some indignation. Hamilton corrected him as he straightened and pulled a comb out of the inside of his jacket, "Actually he is old enough," Hamilton pronounced as if he was giving chapter and verse, "The State of Illinois does not require a driver's license for the operation of a motorcycle." He had his comb up to his hair now and was commencing the few quick and practiced strokes with it that brought the unruly tangle back into submission with one hand while the other hand seemed to mirror its movements as if watching.

"Where do you live, Kid?" Hamilton asked me, now having taken over the conversational lead. I told him and he said he would come by for me at 4:30 on the dot and I consented and was dismissed after being told that he would have the projector with him. It was my first trip to the office without being in trouble of some kind and I got an eye from the rhinestone corners of Misses Cat's eyes glasses as she pulled them down off her face and let them hang on the little chain that dropped them to the sweater she wore that daily matched the scarf in her hair, holding it back and up in the ubiquitous pony tail that seemed to be required of everyone female. My spotlight was brief, however, as Hamilton said some farewell to Mr. House and came along behind me, leaning down on the corner of her desk with both hands bringing his face down close to hers. I was passing through the double hinged door again being careful not to let it slam against its stop when I heard him say, "So, beautiful, who do I have to pay to rent you for the night?" and she giggled and blushed like a Sophomore. He was holding out a ten dollar bill which was apparently for the rental of the projector and I took this in and went on, watching them through the window of the office as I retraced my path back to class.

I used the phone in the hall near the cafeteria to tell Rosemary that I would not be in tonight, and she just said that she would see me tomorrow and made it a question and I said that she would. She was the head cashier and she was middle management of sorts and more or less responsible for me. I had an aisle to take care of but it was her aisle before I came and it was right behind her register so she kept it stocked and neat between customers when I wasn't around. My last class was Gym and I usually didn't go, just walking on past to the parking lot and taking off. Usually no one watched but Coach Roberts was waiting today and called me over. "Get dressed," he said, pointing inside, "and after class come see me in my office." I went through the motions of calisthenics and then a game of dodge ball before we had to run laps up and down the bleachers of the gym and around the basketball floor and then again until the first guy had passed the last guy in line which left us about ten minutes to shower before the bell of dismissal rang.

Coach sometimes watched us shower but today he was not there and as we assembled outside on the oil field pipe fence that made a perimeter of the grass, he appeared in the door and asked me if I hadn't forgotten something. I followed him to his office and he told me to close the door. He sat but when I started to he made a noise that made it clear I had not been invited to sit so I was to stand.

"That your motorcycle out in the parking lot?" He asked. "Yes, Sir," I answered. "You have to be 18 to hold a title to a motor vehicle in this state," he said, holding up a 'Rules of the Road' booklet, "and you are not 18, are you?" Well, I wasn't 18, but the little book he was waving around didn't describe motorcycles as 'motor vehicles' either, which had to have four wheels and turn signals and all the rest. Tractors, scooters, combines, motorized dump machines, and motorcycles were not listed, although you could get them licensed to drive on the highway if you wanted to add all the stuff to them that made them 'motor vehicles' I supposed. He was looking long and hard at me. "I am not, 18, you know that, I just turned 14 last month."

"So are you telling me that is not your motorcycle?" He asked. "Since you put it that way," I answered, "I suppose it couldn't be, could it." This was not the answer he had been going for, but he was not discouraged in that pit bull sort of stupid way that makes it think it must go ahead and bite through this thing in its mouth even if it belongs to his master. "You ride it, don't you?" He said, not so much like a question but an assertion. "I do ride it, yes, Sir." I said. "Well then, whose is it if it isn't yours?" I was in a box here, because I had the bill of sale, but he hadn't asked that. I needed a catch all scapegoat who he could not reach or intimidate. "Butch Wright," I said, coolly. "Who?" he asked. "My uncle, Butch Wright," I said who lives in Lubbock, Texas. He asked me to keep it for him for a bit until his wife Glenda cools down about him buying it." It was liar's poker. "Well, you tell your uncle Butch that I want to talk to him, right now." He said, scooting the phone across the desk at me. I picked up the receiver and dialed zero, which was how you got a long distance connection if you didn't have the number. Before anyone had answered I said, "Operator, give me the Texas Ranger's station in Lubbock, Texas." and coach reached up and took the phone away from me and hung it up. "You didn't say he was a Texas Ranger," he said. "You didn't ask." I said, and we had a stand off sort of.

Coach thought for a moment. "Don't ride that damn bike to school again." He said to me, "Clear?" "Yes, sir, that's clear," I said and I turned and left his office before anything else happened. Lucky for me, my prom date to be just happened to live in a house whose back yard was right up against the parking lot for the high school. I would call her and make some excuse to park the bike at her house, which she thought was exciting and dangerous so she agreed. Tomorrow morning, bright and early, the coach would be able to look out his window and see my bike parked just on the other side of the fence, proving that I had not ridden it to school, but to Judy's house instead. I made a quick dash home, took a Boy Scout bath in the sink and put on a clean tee shirt. Dinner was not on the table so I was excused when the Hamilton pulled up in the driveway and his horn played, "La cucaracha". I smiled at that, who has a horn that plays music? My mother looked out and said he looked like his car had been magnetized and then driven through the Western Auto.

We drove over to the next town to the VFW where the Route 33 Cycle Club was holding its annual meeting. Gene offered me a beer but I declined and he slapped me on the back and introduced me to a grizzled bunch of smoking, drinking, motorcycle riding types who seemed willing to let me live. I sat up the projector with practiced skill and had the movie ready to run in no time. They dimmed the lights and the 16mm clicking of the projector sent images of the Jack Pine Enduro onto the glass bead screen without a hitch. I had to adjust the frame once, and the sound was muddled at first, but it straightened out and I sat mesmerized watching men and women on all sorts of motorcycles crash and slide through the north woods at speeds that must surely cause serious injury if things went wrong and it was apparent that they often did.

In particular there was this one steel bridge that had plates where the tires of cars and trucks would run that were apparently slick as snot and the competitors came to it at a 90 degree angle and then tried to cross it and then go 90 degrees off of it to be on their way. No one made it. Either they fell coming onto the bridge, or trying to get off of it but everyone fell. It was comical, in a way, and everyone got up and went on, but some where clearly hurting from the encounter. The winner of the heavyweight class was a guy named Bob Goodpaster and his teeth showed as the only white on a face caked with mud. I was impressed. When the show was over they had their meeting, and I had to stay because Gene was the President and presided. They followed strict Robert's Rules of Order and referred to a little book about it a couple of times to be sure they had things right. Minutes were read and approved, old business taken up, then new business, and then I was paid my fee by a collection from the membership which netted me $31, not ten and I thanked them one and all.

On the way home Gene told me to watch out for myself on that bike and I told him I would. I dreamed about the Jack Pine that night and when it rained that weekend, I got out my bike and went looking for a dirt road. I had seen it done; after all, which was half the battle, and I was off to have some fun. I did too and the Triumph slithered and snaked up and down the lanes of the county for the next several years as I found it easier and easier to manage.

The coach gave up trying to get me to stop riding it and the principal and I came to an understanding after I had accumulated 67 unserved detentions for my attitude and other things. I was in his office in May of what was expected to be my senior year and he was explaining how every time I skipped after school detention I got two more, which was how the number had gotten so large. Since I knew that already, I probably disappointed him in my registering of alarm. Finally he puffed up and said, "You know, you are not going to graduate unless you serve every single one of your detentions." Well, that was already impossible seeing as how it was May, and I said so. I also added that if I did not graduate it only meant that I would be back next year. That seemed to shut him up completely and we mutually decided to just let things go on the way they were until I was off and away to frustrate someone else.

That was how I came to be a part of the Class of 1966, the best people on earth as far as I knew, and they still are.We had come from all over, most of us the children of WWII's generation and the grand-children of the depression. We stood in the schoolyard together in the fourth grade and looked for Sputnik and later mourned the death of Buddy Holly and the Big Bopper although we were not exactly sure why. Kennedy was shot in Dallas when we were sophomores and his brother and Martin Luther King when we were in college, those of us that got to go. I had a few friends that got motorcycles and rode them, Nolan Wilson was the first of them;Ernie Dees after. He got on a bad list of some of them over differences with his wife after I left town which I knew nothing of, but he saved my life that summer we graduated, and all the summers that came after, I owe to him. He gave me the luxury of time, and I thank him.

Time is not always a luxury, however, sometimes its passage is something else. In racing we need to make correct judgments in real time, quicker than a heartbeat sometimes. While we can hope they are all correct, it is too much to expect that they are. Our very lives depend upon it and even the lives of others, and yet we risk it all to-something we don't have a full understanding of. Some call it 'luck' but that seems too vague.

Examine for yourself what it is you believe makes it all work out. It is a tricky undertaking. If you make too much of it, that is if you build your list of all the things that can go wrong and are so thorough about it that it appears inevitable that something will go wrong and something then does you may begin to believe it inevitable that things always go wrong and that is not the case.

It may be the case that things go wrong once in a while, and most of the time we can look at the particulars of what has happened with hindsight and say to ourselves, 'Oh, I see now, I should have done so and so instead...' which is a common enough reaction to having gotten past an incident. It is far more common, however, that something is about to go wrong and we catch it just in time and can say, 'Man, was I lucky there...' like the time I was going down the back stretch at Daytona and happened to look down through the fairing at my front axel nut and see it turning because I had forgotten to put the cotter pin back in after changing tires.

Its movement caught my eye and in just that moment it came around and off of its last thread and fell away. Now when I put my front brake on instead of just stopping it was going to spread the forks apart as well and I wouldn't have as much brake so I would have to allow for that and go into the pits and fix it. It was in practice, so I was 'lucky' and survived it, but some poor guy might run over it or any one of the million other things that fall off of motorcycles being raced that litter the tracks across the country.

Nothing like that happened so again, we were 'lucky' I suppose, but that just can't be all there is to it. Our collective survival, the continuation of human endeavor that requires so much care and attention cannot boil down to coincidence. I may, but that is unsatisfying even if there is some probability that it could be true. How many times does some guy crash his bike and then in the fullness of his adrenaline pick it back up and get back on the track and rejoin the race. Talk about a bad idea! Still it happens and those riders have it in their minds that they must soldier on, even though most certainly all is not well with their machine once it has been on the ground. Brake levers come apart, fairings come loose from their mounts, dirt and grit and all manner of foreign material is ingested into moving metal parts of close tolerance that are intolerant of it. Now take that machine back up to speed and you have a disaster in the making.

We do it with ourselves as well. We drive all night after a week of work and long nights of after work overtime out in our shop to get ready to go racing. We drink too much and don't watch what we eat and exercise rarely if at all. Once in a while, when we were young and nature forgave such abuse it was understandable I suppose that such things could be done without lasting damage. But season after season it takes its toll and the denial of the obvious truth does nothing to alter its make up even if you can afford to buy increasingly larger leathers. Something is out there, taking care of us, and we have little or no control over it.

This makes the scientifically minded uncomfortable. It cannot be weighed or measured and yet there is a body of evidence to suggest that it is real. Medieval men on the verge of battle made noises at it, made promises to it in exchange for being spared, or devised and then obeyed routines that made them feel a certain comfort about the results, whatever they might be. It goes way back and there are complex and myriad philosophies that deal with a greater power behind the scenes that has and will intervened on our behalf when necessary. The survivors of the Titanic probably prayed for such divine intervention of course, but then so did those lost that night in the same sea. Watch a motorcycle race and what do you see? People in danger of dying at any moment, oblivious to reality.

It is seductively unexciting to behold, and the appearance of control seems real enough when all is well, but let one little thing in the thousands of things needed in combination to make it all work out be altered and a disaster is close at hand. We try not to dwell on it, and to a certain degree must look past it to a positive outcome or we simply couldn't do it. Not to over think it, Hailwood famously said he considered himself already dead before a race so it didn't interfere with his concentration. This comment was seized upon by the press as some sort of bravado of denial but it's not, it's just an expedient way of dealing with the obvious. To take a crazy risk once and survive it is dare-devil. To do it repeatedly over decades is something else altogether.

You cannot count on just yourself to make things work out, there are too many variables involved and you don't have control over enough of them. Some aspect of random chance comes into play and statistics tell us that sooner or later our number may come up. I met Dwayne Williams on the phone one day in December as I was calling the number in the AMA magazine that was listed under 'Road race' for the only event in the United States. I had just finished building my Suzuki X-6 and wanted to ride it somewhere before Daytona and this was the first race listed anywhere. I introduced myself and asked him about the track. What kind of place is Dade City? He was promoting the event and said it was nice. I asked him if it was anything like Daytona and he said yes. I told him three of us would be coming down and was there anything he could tell us that would make it a better event for us? He just said that if we wanted to race, Florida was the place, and so we went.

Dade City was nothing like Daytona. It was a track made out of the access road around the Pasco County Fairgrounds and was a mile and eight feet long with sixteen turns. It was not very wide and the pits were just anywhere you chose to park next to the track. There was no run off or hay bales or anything safe about it and down in the far turn before what was laughingly called the "straight" there was a weeping tree of some kind that shaded the track and kept it slick most of the time with sap. When we drove in and I went looking for Dwayne my first reaction was to express my unhappiness but he was so disarming and straightforward that it was difficult to be angry with him. Frustrated ? yes, angry? Not really.

Practice began as soon as they had everyone in the gate and off the track and it was for everyone. There were no class distinctions here. Some very fast people were there, nationally prominent road racers I had already encountered; Conrad Urbanowski, John Long, Ray Hempstead, Ted Henter and on and on. They were serious about this and I was having difficulty imagining that anyone would actually ride here, let alone race. Still, I came a long way to be here and the Suzuki ran well, even if it was geared waaaaay too tall (I thought it was like Daytona !)

I had a good time getting knocked around by the locals who knew their way around much better than I did. When the final came, I lined up in the back even though we had been gridded by where we signed in which would have put me up front. I had no desire to be in front of people who wanted to be there much more badly than I did.

The race went well, I passed some people, which surprised me as well as them, and I did not finish last. At the end of the day we all packed up and headed home and the smell of the orange blossoms from the many groves in bloom all around us made the scene an indelible memory. I encountered Dwayne a good many times after that over the years and I liked him. He ran the Florida Grand Prix Riders association in a manner that was dictatorial but decisive and if you just put your mind to it, it was all right. If you were a worrier about things like safety, then you might have some concerns.

Years later I was working a race at Talladega with AHRMA and Dwayne was there with his autistic daughter in his pit. I had met her before, but doubted she would remember. Dwayne crashed in practice and so did not return after his session was over and this had upset her because it would upset anyone, and because he was her only link to the rest of the world and he was not there.

People tried to reassure her, but there was no way of being sure she understood that he was all right and would be back soon. I got a call on the radio to go over to their pit and be present on behalf of our club and do whatever I could to make the situation go as well as possible. I spoke to her in a calm voice and smiled and she seemed to understand that I was there as a friend and we waited together until the crash truck brought Dwayne and his motorcycle back to where we were.

In 2007 I walked around the pits at Daytona before the racing started as was my habit, snapping pictures of everyone here and there in case they had no one with them to take pictures. I used to have them printed up at the nearest WalMart and then give them out the second day of a weekend so they would have the images. The ones that were not good enough to print I just stored and left them in their digital format. Recently I was doing some housekeeping and came across those images and took a second look at them.

Every now and then we point a camera at something meaningful and don't realize what we are looking at. There are many such moments in life, I am sure, but still I look for them to reassure myself that life is good and there are things worth noticing. I was sorting through these and deleting those that were not useful and was about to click the mouse and send the blurry shot into oblivion when I thought I recognized Ralph Wessel with two other people, one with their back to me reaching out to a young woman, reaching out to him. I froze.

It was Dwayne and his daughter and I had not recognized them at the time, nor thought much about it. Dwayne was killed at Barber shortly afterward and I had spoken with him just before that race. He said he was fine and the bike was "runnin' good" and then he had smiled that sly grin of his at me as if there was something more to that than he was saying. I wished him good luck and went on about my business.

Now I find this picture of him from out of the past and wish I had taken a better one, or had taken the time to take more of them, or had let him know more often of how fond I was of him as a person who loved to race, loved to be around racers, and loved his daughter. That he died racing was incredible to me, in the same category of Joey Dunlop's passing or any of the other great men who continued to race after there was nothing to prove and really nothing more for them to win. But to having something fail on his motorcycle and distract him, which was apparently part of the cause, I might have thought it possible of lesser men but I never thought it possible of Dwayne. Some shift in the cosmos of things had taken place somewhere far off and a portal opened and he was needed to fill it in some way. It left a hole here. He knew things the rest of us didn't know and he probably didn't write them down. We may never know what alchemy he had dabbled in and made lead into gold with or equivalently made Norton twins as fast as Triumphs, with but it probably wasn't just science.

13.

The Old Gods and the New Zen

SO SHOULD I TURN away from what I was raised with and strike out on my own in some new direction and see if I can make sense of things for myself? Is Dwayne in his grave or riding through the clouds of God's heaven on his Norton which now always starts on the first kick? Tony gave me the answer to that, in his own irreverent way. He was an older kid who sat in the back of the classroom and wisecracked with some degree of impunity when we were in grade school.

He was tough, and would hit you if you crossed him so I kept a respectful distance as most of us did, but he was not especially smart, and did not graduate with us. One day in Health class when I was about 12 and he was already shaving, our prim spinster of a teacher was discussing the seven food groups on a colorful pull down chart and explaining why we each needed to have so many servings from each group each day and so forth, concluding cheerfully with the tag line, "You are what you eat." Tony's reply was quick and sharp, "Well then," he said, loud and clear, "I've already eaten enough shit to last me a lifetime..." He was summoned out into the hallway by the red faced mistress who was struggling mightily to contain herself. We didn't hear what was said, but when she came back in, Tony did not come with her. He was apparently being punished for his honesty.

There was a time when I thought that most people told the truth most of the time. I got over that. Then I went through a phase when I though most people were lying to me about everything they told me. I got over that too. There was no real Santa Claus, was there? Rock Hudson was gay for God's sake! People who told you they would love you forever could change their mind and tell you instead that they never loved you at all. Just when I was about to question my sanity I had begun racing motorcycles where it turns out that you can tell for yourself what is true and what is not.

It's complicated, and it's difficult and expensive in many ways. There is suffering and a degree of endurance required that erodes what other people see as a more normal existence. It can become an obsession, I know that, but what I know mostly about it is that there is a right answer to most of the questions that face us on a given day at a racetrack somewhere and just being there, with that set of known values, is reassuring.

I have either managed my entry and have my license or I don't so I get to race or I don't. I have all of the necessary and properly approved equipment and gear or I don't. The bike is appropriately safety wired and will run. There is a right jetting choice for today's atmospheric conditions and I have made it. There is a correct gearing selection of countershaft and rear sprockets that will provide an optimum overall matching of power band and course characteristics and I will find it. There are points on the track where I should brake and lean in and get back on the throttle and there are degrees of application of each of those elements that will combine to make each turn an experience done as well as it can be done under the circumstances, or perhaps leave a little room for improvement the next time around. These things are not insignificant, they all have meaning. More than half the race is getting there.

I don't want my riding experiences done for me with electronic gizmos even though I know they can be. I don't want my brakes to be 'anti-lock' even if BMW has been doing it on their street bikes for over a decade making me admit that it's not exactly new anymore. I'm old school and not afraid or ashamed to admit it. But then neither do I take available medications for hypertension or have hypertension or sleep deprivation or any of the other things that normally signal some inability to accept the changes that life brings us as we persist in the struggle to understand its meaning. I don't have the answer, not yet, but I am hopeful that it will come to me if I can manage to keep it up to the finish. I've seen the half way flags already, and was a little surprised as I always am by them.

My first 200 miler at Daytona as an expert I rode and rode and rode my guts out and then, just when I thought I had nothing at all left to give, I got the half way flags. 'God,' I thought, 'can I do this? I could as it turned out, making me think that as for the rest of whatever life may have in store for me, I can do that as well.

I may not race as often or go as fast as I once did, but what matters now about racing, is what matters about living, that I continue to do it. I still struggle with building the bikes and getting them to the track and learning the course again for that bike on that day as I try to remember if I have done everything, taken care of everything, and can face the truth of the answers. That truth is that despite all I can do, and every precaution I may have taken or money I have spent or sacrifice I have made, it may still all turn to shit and I will have to eat it just like Tony said so very long ago. We live with our own mistakes, and are responsible for our own choices, no matter who told us something, and none of it is any guarantee that things will turn out the way we want them to.

Why then should I believe things will be any different when I think about what will happen to me when I die? Why should I take someone's word for it that if I do or don't do some things then this or that thing will result in another state of existence that no one has been to and returned from in my lifetime or in the past thousand years or more? Don't be offended, we're all adults here. I am allowed my doubts. Why wouldn't someone doubt?

There is plenty of evidence all around me to suggest that things are less than perfect in the world and that evil as an institution is uncurbed and rather cancerous in the larger sense. Take the weather in England, for instance, is it surprising that I have such doubts? What surprises me more is that I still have any hope, and a degree of faith, in spite of all I have seen. There are things I have not seen for myself but know of, too, which lend some evidence and while I have not actually been to the infamous Dragon Rally - I know it exists. I have seen photos.

Then too, there's Tony. He showed up at Daytona racing a vintage bike and I had not seen him since that day in Health Class. I would not have known he was there but he came over and punched me in the arm like he used to do when I was not looking and reminded me who he was. It was good to see him in a way and he had carried with him through all the years since I had seen him last the idea that his toughness was enough to see him through anything. It was apparently, since both of us were there. We had a good race and neither of us fell down, although he didn't finish ahead of me. He came rushing past a time or two but I knew it wouldn't work out for him given the places he chose to do it and so I would just let him go and then take him back later as he cursed me or his machine, or the fates, or all of them. He faded in the end and while I went looking for him afterward, I didn't find him. Still it had been good to see him and reassuring to know he's out there, tough as ever. There is a limit to that and I bet he knows that as well as I. I don't shake my fist at him anymore, I shake my head.

14.

Thin Ice

WHEN I WAS 9 years old I lived at the edge of small river town in Southern Illinois. One day, in the dead of winter, I was sent out of the house to play late in a gray afternoon. A frozen creek ran alongside our property, separating us from the decent folks in town and I absent mindedly followed it, skating along on my boots and slipping as I went. I went beyond the familiar, bored with its lack of excitement, and ducked under the brush and trees that normally obscured the small stream from view in the spring and summer months to explore new places. Here and there the overburden of vegetation was so low that I could barely manage to get through on my hands and knees, but it was a journey I had only imagined in the warmer months and to be able to do it now, not knowing when I might be able to do it again, was an irresistible enticement. The ice was very thick and did not crack or creak as I went along as it had been very cold for over a month so it did not occur to me as I explored that anything dangerous or frightening might lie ahead.

Gradually, the streambed grew wider and was joined by others which lead to ever larger expanses of ice on which I gleefully played and shuffled about. All of this had taken some time and I looked around suddenly thinking that I had better check my bearings for the trip home which had to be completed by dark. There were few rules at my house, and all of them had to do with the effect something you might or might not do would have on my mother. So rather than trying to remember them all, something I had repeatedly demonstrated I was unable to do anyway, I simply asked myself what she would think about what I was doing at the moment. Well, she was adventurous herself and I perceived in her an urge to follow an opportunity when it arose, and so I thought she might think this little journey of mine to be all right so long as I did not worry her by exceeding my time limit. Looking about, I did not recognize any of the scenery, but in my scan of the horizon I saw before me a huge expanse of ice ahead that surely must be the Wabash River. Unknowingly I had covered a greater distance than I expected and had no idea where I was.

I was not worried, however, as my faithful constant companion "Jet" was with me, the name I had given in irony to the world's slowest Labrador retriever, and she was good at heading for home when told so I would just follow her. There were only a few yards of brush ahead separating me from the wide open space of ice and I could not resist having a look at what was beyond that final barrier of brush. Where their branches came up through the ice, some thawing had taken place earlier when the sun had shown and now little circles of darkness peeked up through them around the brown and grey of their reaching fingers. I bent down to have a look, hoping to get a glimpse of what was below, and when I did the ice beneath me suddenly gave way and I plunged down through crashing layers of frozen sheets of ice some 8 to 10 feet before landing with the shards of shattered ice all around me. I lay in a heap, looking up at the world I had left behind, seeing my breath now expressed before my eyes as it floated up through the jagged holes above.

I took stock of my parts and they all seemed to work and I held my hands up in front of me and could discern wiggling fingers of reassurance so all was seemingly well. If I was bleeding I couldn't see it and if I had broken anything it would wait until later to be worried about. I needed to reconnoiter. I got to my feet and tried to look around, hoping to catch some clue about a way out. It was then I saw it - the most frightening vision of my life that I carry with me to this day; as far as the eye could see, in any direction, were sheets of horizontal ice reaching away into gray darkness interrupted only by the occasional passage of a trunk or branch of some vegetation long dormant from the cold. Down here it was not just cold, it was bitter cold and damp, so much so that it chilled me to the bone all at once.

I had let out a "yipe" when I landed and it was still echoing back to me through the chambers of this heart of darkness. I said "hello" to the void and was rewarded with "hellos" back to me tenfold. This was not reassuring as the voices did not sound like mine helping me quickly conclude that I had had my fill of exploration and investigation for the afternoon and suddenly appreciated the call of the kitchen with its warmth of mother and pie.

Now the question was how? When I tried to reach up to the next level of ice above my head, just within my grasp, it broke off and showered me with snow and debris it had supported before I disturbed it. Far away, in the dim light, I could see Jet, peering down into my predicament. I spoke her name softly, so as not to be echoed again and she whined at me and started to jump. When I saw that, I shouted "No" and was bombarded by a hundred "NO's" from all directions which rose together to make her leap back with a yelp. After that she barked and barked as if to mark the spot where I had been lost to her. A good dog plan I thought, thinking of the time Lassie had saved Timmy from some stupid stunt the same way.

In the fall I had lost my sense of direction so I could not retrace my steps and head back upstream for shallower water and lower ceilings. It was too dark now to see very far and too spooky to look at too often. The day was drawing to a close and all of these things together made me realize the very real possibility that I would be trapped here if I did not think of some way out. Off in the distance, a large dark shape was visible and I could think of no alternative but to move toward it. I raised myself up onto the shelf of ice just above my boot tops, and crouching between it and the shelf above me began to duck waddle in that direction. It was probably not more than 20 yards or so, but leaving the comfort of the skylight left by my descent was unnerving and I could not abate my worries as I usually did by singing or whistling because of the demonic echo, so I just forged along, conscious of my breathing and the little hint of a whimper that came with each breath.

As I grew closer I could see my destination was what I had hoped for, a tree trunk of substantial size that made its way upward through the layers of ice. In reality it had been the fall of the river and not the rising of the tree that had made what I was looking for as the cold had come on and left a frozen mark with each recession that were now the floor and ceiling of my world. When I got to the tree, I started to climb, hugging it like a pole and pushing my stocking capped head up through the opening to the level above repeatedly as I went higher. Some levels were easier than other, depending on how thick the ice, but my progress was regular and so long as I was not stopped I did not have time to reflect on how bad my situation could have been.

A plan was at work and I was working it hard so I did not consider what might be a better plan which is probably the way of most things. We do what we are doing with all our might, or with some recognition that the degree of effort we are giving is what is called for, and having undertaken the plan we don't stop to question how it will work out or if another might be better. Being young and fortunate it did work out for me and I returned to the surface and was surprised to find myself wet and my boots still muddy.

I had apparently fallen through the ice all the way to the river's bed and was spared from drowning only because the river had diminished over time from the winter's effects. Coming free of the last layer I was not as happy as I might have been because it was now fully dark and the neighborhood of my surroundings was entirely wooded and strange and my dog was long gone. I set off toward where I thought home should be at a good pace and within a few minutes began to recognize the stream bed I had followed and saw my own marks on the snow and ice in the dim light. At the first point where the creek was crossed by a bridge I climbed out and looked around for lights. Seeing some on the distant horizon I made a steady march toward it and arrived a short time later without any new difficulty.

It was my house, which was a pleasant surprise, and it was all lit up, which made it that much easier to see. Although it looked familiar, somehow it looked better than I could ever remember it. There were a number of cars in the driveway and I supposed we were having company. I recognized the Sheriff's car as one of them and was excited to see that something calling for "official action" was afoot, my boyhood being full of the Hardy Boys and Nancy Drew. When I opened the kitchen door all conversation stopped. I was only to glimpse the scene for a moment before pandemonium broke loose, but I still remember it - my dog Jet on a kitchen chair, surrounded by adults in various positions of kneeling down or bending over. She was getting the third degree and answering as best she could by contorting her eyebrows this way and that back at each face that was doing it to her while looking for a response. I had learned early that even though she pretended to understand me and what I was saying, actually it was just an eyebrow code, like semi fore flags wagged by signalmen, and try as I might I had never been able to get much in the way of communication from her except that her dish was empty.

She barked and jumped down when she saw me and got to me before the rest of them, who apparently were trying to ascertain what she thought had happened to me. I was relieved at first to see how glad they all seemed to see me, and thought that it might carry me over any concerns I had been working on about violating some house rule about coming in after dark but I was wrong. When everyone was gone after having been satisfied that I was all right, I again repeated my story to my mother as she held a wooden spoon and tapped it into the palm of her unoccupied hand with absent effect. I could tell it was not going well for me, so I elaborated and embellished, avoiding as long as possible the inescapable conclusion of my argument before the court judiciously applied the punishment to the seat of reason.

I was spanked twice that night; once for coming in after dark and missing supper and making her worry; once again for lying, which she said hurt her more than all the worry that I might have suffered a "fate worse than death". That phrase pushed out the usual thoughts about the meaning of words I went through after "now I lay me's "every night, concerning what I was made to repeat. "If I should die before I wake" what was that about and why make a little kid say it before they are supposed to go to sleep? If they were going to die while sleeping they wouldn't know it anyway would they?

That night I lay there in my bed, staring at the familiar shadows cast on my bedroom ceiling that had never frightened me before and knew for the first time where they came from. Just down the creek, only a few miles away, was a dark and empty space about which no one but me knew, and even when I had tried to tell them, no one believed existed. The emptiness that came from those two realizations; that there was emptiness and that it could never be shared, was my new companion that had followed me home from the river that night, and that has painted my ceiling with arcing lines and shadows every night since.

15.

WTF is going on?

TWO WHEELS IN LINE, arcing across a single plane to make a turn, require the machine to which they are attached to be leaned over from its perpendicular position. There are forces in play that physicists try to propagate formulas to describe and scientific papers are out there to express in numbers and symbols that are unintelligible to me. As far as I am concerned, it is an obvious phenomenon: Something magical happens.

Since I believe in magic and don't need a scientific explanation for everything I am satisfied enough that I do not have to be shown the trick to enjoy it. I do realize, however, that there are minds out there who think that everything can be expressed mathematically and explained scientifically. I know also that there are a multitude of descriptions that have tried to express the wonder of it in all manageable and understandable terms. I have seen some of these calculations, and read some of these descriptions and posit a simple refutation - If you can calculate and describe all of these things, why can't you explain why I am faster than you?

Oh, I may have struck a nerve then? Some reflex in the scientific brain was overcome by a Monty Python knee jerk response of 'Are Not!' to which I say without reservation 'Am!' and may ultimately have you out of your league and onto a racetrack enjoying yourself viscerally, unexplainably, unscientifically until neither of us really care who wins or not or who can put numbers to the G-forces we managed to generate. I don't feel them, like a centrifuge passenger anyway, but more as the 'Gee whiz' sort of 'G'.

Anyway, you may as was well try and describe sex as 'just an in and out motion for purposes of procreation' as to think you can describe riding a motorcycle through a fast turn with equations or words alone. It is the same as the difference between sex and love. It is transcendental. It is awe inspiring. It is empowering, and most of all, it is transformational. Remember virginity? I don't know about you, but my first honeymoon was anti-climatic compared to my first lay.

If we were to arbitrarily divide people into two groups in a manner that would draw an experiential distinction between one group and another, I suggest that 'motorcycle racer' is a good one to consider. We do this anyway as we meet one another; get some information from those we interact with in order to know where they are coming from and whether we might be going ahead together in some way. "What's your favorite color?" "Do you like mustard or ketchup better?" "Do you talk during Sex?" "Well, do you think you could if you tried, or have you just never tried?" "Would you like to try and find out?"

You can see how these inquires must be thought through in advance and it is not always appropriate to mention motorcycle racing in mixed company. "What do you do?" she might ask casually when you meet, trying to decide if you are the sort of person she can trust and understand well enough to be with. "I race motorcycles," will end that line of inquiry nine times out of ten because the average person wouldn't ride a motorcycle at all, let alone race one, and the common ground they were seeking to establish conversationally has been yanked away from under them by the image of a maniac in a leather suit rushing around on a motorbike doing impossibly suicidal things for the sake of, well, she really doesn't know why anyone might want to do it and she certainly isn't going to bother to find out.

I was invited to Oxford to a roundtable thanks to a case I took to the Supreme Court about AIDS and a criminal statute Illinois so thoughtfully enacted to stamp it out. Make a condition of ill health illegal, what a great idea! We could have eradicated polio without having to resort to marching dimes if it would work as a concept but of course it won't. It was fate, or coincidence or whatever that put the client with the problem in my care and my sense of justice that wouldn't let him die in a jail cell if I could free him to do it at home with his family whether or not it paid anything. It was a mixed group at Oxford and we did social mingling as a high art with the obligatory get to know you chatter over flutes of bubbly substances until the butler announced that dinner was served. It was grand pretence and I enjoyed it as did many of those I met there as awed about being invited as I was. Still, I was singular in my answer to the question about what I did for sport, or leisure, or for a hobby, whatever the case may have been. It is a topic that leaves the large majority of the public with nothing to say, or even ask, being as dimly understood and largely unreported as it is.

But you are interested in the topic, and here I am safe to say the hated words that every HR manager dreads, "I race motorcycles". I assume this, because you are reading this and there is no reason to do so other than to find out what a motorcycle racer thinks is artful about racing and what, if anything, "Zen" might have to do with it. I make no promises of eternal reward or lower lap times but, I do promise to tell a good tale along the way and I know many. I started racing when very young and am still at it so I've done something right. I also live indoors with the woman of my dreams and can still tie my own shoes, even though I do find slippers outrageously practical.

I have been a National Champion road racer (twice, actually), won Daytona, (only once so far), set a course record at a race track, and have the ability to walk and chew gum at the same time. I speak seven languages; only one of which has been recognized by anyone else, and I am the polar opposite of Winston Churchill because I would rather race than just ride, rather ride than run, etc...

Right. Ready then? Mind your calf on the muffler, it can make a nasty burn if you get it wrong. All set? Then we're off;

The truth of what is in the book came to me slowly, over time, and sometimes it was hidden from me until a good deal later, otherwise I would have just written this down to begin with and would have been famous for it ever since. Like those old dot to dot drawings we used to do as kids, the bigger picture doesn't emerge for some time, and that is not just because we are especially dense or slow on the intake, it is because when we were kids, we had little bitty heads, and inside them were little bitty brains and they were not just a smaller version of the brains we have now.

There were some things they just wouldn't do, like grasping the greater meaning of life for instance, and so we don't listen to four year olds who say they've got it right, we wait until they are fourteen and hear them saying they <u>know</u> they have it right and know as well that we don't know a bloody thing! We have bigger brains now, and know that teenagers know next to nothing about what really matters, but relative to what there is to know we are back to square one.

Separating out the wheat from the chaff in terms of our experiences and how we relate them to the meaning of life, we find four large bins in which we have dumped the events and memories of our past and tagged them for later analysis: 1.Childhood; 2. I'm awake now; 3. Working days and lonely nights; and 4.Finally grown up but not ready to die.I take a peck here at the last category first to spare you some suspense and to accustom you to my idea that things need not necessarily come in order.

No one is ever ready to die, regardless of what they may tell you. That is because there is a great unknown that comes next that we only have some vague ideas about, and have heard some stories about, but from which we are fairly certain there is no coming back as ourselves in the way that we understand things. We all believe this, regardless of what else we believe, otherwise there would be dead people revisiting us constantly and showing up on talk shows to blab about what they had seen or done since dying. I know people who say they don't believe it, but anyone so wrong about their own significance is not really worth listening to.

Ghosts may be real enough, I don't know, but they lack a certain quality to be substantial and so I generally overlook them. I did have goose bumps once walking through a market square in Rouen while escorting a group of American high school kids on an orientation walk about. I didn't know the town well and our tour guide stopped in the same spot where I had stopped the group the day before and shown them the goose bumps on my arm and told them insightfully that, 'Something must have happened here...'

The tour guide didn't have goose bumps, but she did had a guide book, and in frankly horrible English, she described for us '...ow, Jean d'Arc 'ad been flame', fumare', eh, 'ow do you say 'eet? burnted alive' on this very spot in 1431.'

She got a reaction from this. We were all amazed and seemed a bit troubled by the news that something had happened here. We moved away from her and the spot quickly. My initial reaction of the day before lingers still.

This was not the only time that cosmically unexplainable things had happened to me, but it was the first that was so collectively witnesses that I knew it wasn't just me and I began to notice them and look for a pattern the same way I see a big dipper in the stars at night where others only see a bear who is a major.

I could say more about the other categories but you already have your own answers for what goes in them in terms of their importance for yourself. I point them out, but you knew them already. We all were children once, got over it, thought we had arrived at some perfection or other of empowerment and thought, and then had to face our own mortality. It is the bittersweet race we run. There is no winning, at least not in one sense since none of us will go on forever in this world. There is no losing either, so far as that goes, none of us will have to go on in this world past when we should.

Meaning in Life / a Haiku

I wonder if there might be meaning to life,
Or whether the Brits may have it right,
and take in just anyone. Oye!

Ok, maybe it's not a Haiku, and it says nothing and gives us no assurances when we want them but only assonance instead. Sometimes things are like that. They sound good (put 50 lbs of air in your tires and your bike will be lighter!) or make you wonder if they could be right (put less air in your tires and save weight – 10 lbs is less than 30 lbs, right?) when actually they are all wrong. Information is an issue, observation is in play, and the trouble with everything is that it is exactly that – EVERYTHING !

The blessed peace of racing is found in the moments that allow me to kneel and pray upon my bike going full speed that the damn thing won't seize up when I pull the clutch in and I haven't really over-shot the last braking point that will let me make this corner. Racing requires us to stop ourselves from being distracted and just focus on some very real specific things, and then do a certain sequence of tasks in certain ways to produce a performance from our instrument that is the best it can give. I switched metaphors there, did I throw you off? Or did you manage to keep up? "If you can't keep up then you fall behind", which is not a Zen platitude but an obvious truth and I am a fan of the truth and try to speak it plainly.

Examples: Racing is not for everyone, and winning is for the very few. You can get by with being an asshole now and then, but it will catch up with you with a vengeance if you do it around the wrong crowd. Racers are the wrong crowd for assholes. Nice guys may finish last, but guys who don't think about being nice or not and only about what is necessary to win have to do it without being assholes or someone in the crowd they race with will take vengeance on them.

Simplicity is a necessity. Necessity is the mother of invention. Frank Zapa played with the Mothers of Invention and I pretended to like them but couldn't understand a great deal of it because he was Czech and they are difficult to understand even though they do seem to care about making great beer which I understand completely. Nice Driveway!

All right, now that you may be getting the flow of this, let us seriously consider whether chronology is important. That would be the theory that the sequence of events is the key to understanding why things are the way they are and what they might really mean. It is premised on the mistaken belief that we think in a first to last sort of way that we were taught in primary school. So, does that tell me that if I had known when I first went wrong in my past back there somewhere, I wouldn't have had the bike yanked out from under me in the first turn of the first race in thirty years of racing when I finally got to carry the number one plate, breaking my collarbone the week before Daytona in my first ever title defense year?

Not really, and the actual cause was twofold, rain and a bit of oil that decided it would be a good time to float on the surface under my front tire. Since I had just run a warm up lap through there and it had been raining then and all had gone well, I had no reason to think it wouldn't all go well again, did I? That was a rhetorical question so I will just go ahead and give you the answer. Hell no, I had no idea the damn thing was going to plop me head first faster than you can say 'Blue cross, Blue shield' or that some git had forgotten to tighten the drain plug on his Triumph and had slathered the racing surface with a nice sheen of Castrol R for old times sake after I had come by on my sighting lap.

My bike wasn't hurt that bad and I did think for a bit after being released from the Savannah Hospital emergency room that I might go ahead and race the next week at Daytona anyway. Then I sneezed, which brought all of my pain sensors out of their little houses to beat me about the consciousness, and then I laughed at myself for even thinking I could race this way again, which also hurt and yes, I had broken a collarbone before and yes again I had tried to race with it still broken.

That sequence did save me from repeating a pointless exercise when there is no money at stake and there were plenty of races left to make up whatever deficit I was about to have in points before the season ended in October. That actually did work out and I did repeat as class champion so it told me what, about the importance of chronology in the end? Nothing.

Things happen when they happen for reasons of their own and those reasons only seem remote and unconnected when you don't understand how large and how complex the whole is relative to its parts since you are just one of its parts. An explanation may be in order for those who are accustomed to a more linear narrative since this is not that sort of work. The reason is fairly simple; chronology as an ordering of events is not sufficient to connect ideas and their importance in a way that will reveal the truth of all that may be going on. Digressions would be required, flashbacks, and a cue card to keep track of it all.

People on the Titanic did not drown because there were not enough life boats or because the captain was a fool or because the California turned off its wireless and went to bed. They drowned because they were meant to drown, which may be fatalistic and totally unsatisfying in modern terms but does not disqualify it as a relevant point of view just because we have lately come to think we are masters of the universe.

I say 'may' because I have an overdeveloped sense of these things. It came to me from a hundred trips across the country in a transport of some sort crammed with racing motorcycles and tools and fragrances that are immediately recognizable but difficult to identify. I might as well have been a thousand trips if I counted the mental anticipation trips and the instant replays. Just a smell can set one off. Castrol R racing oil, for instance, mixed with gasoline and used to fuel a two stroke motorcycle gives an aroma unlike anything else. Likewise the old Green Label Blendzall had a scent of its own as did Bel-Ray and Yamalube R and so on. Then there is the chain lube and the rubber bits and the silicon seal and scent of your leathers as you take them out and put them on and the inside of your helmet – all of them together evoke a sense of things that is a catalyst for memories and a trigger for future planning. They are at once exciting and reassuring.

The reassuring part was probably hard won because at first you were naturally apprehensive that you didn't know what you were doing. Well, you didn't really, and you hoped to survive the learning process. We all did. Those Novice days could be brutal and even fatal, but if you are reading this you survived them and look back on your abilities now as something you always had. You've forgotten how alien it all felt when you started. Human beings are funny that way. We adapt quickly and tell ourselves we have a knack for something, or we refrain ourselves from doing it ever again. Sally comes to mind.

My grandfather Roy put me on a horse when I was very young, maybe 3 years old or so. He handed me the reigns and was about to explain what to do when the horse bolted and took off for the wide open spaces of West Texas. I hung on to the horn part of the saddle for all I was worth and hollered 'whoa!" at the damn thing until I was hoarse. A horse does not care if you are hoarse or not, but it does care that the end of the day is near and the stable is somewhere back there from whence it came.

That happened on its own, as it turned out, and the unmanageable beast trotted home about dusk and into its stall at no insistence from me. Someone in the house had seen this and had come out to offer assistance. "How'd ya like it?" my aunt asked. "Didn't" I said as she helped me down. It made an impression. I had seen people riding horses and had some primitive idea that it might be fun, but the actuality of it was not at all what I had imagined and I could not reconcile the experience of doing it with my dreams about it from a distance. Just because something looks easy, doesn't mean it is - Like racing motorcycles; or understanding life.

16.

I Race – Therefore I Am

IF YOU ARE A motorcycle racer, it means something. If your name were Bob, then Bob the Racer is not the same guy as Bob the husband, or Bob the father, or Bob the drinking buddy. It's not just a dualism that describes who we are, there is more to us than that. Furthermore, I can be one way in my teens and another way in my twenties and thirties and so on yet even though I may change in those ways, my racer self can remain as it is. I could have enjoyed hunting with my grandfather as a boy and not want a gun now. There is nothing that requires us to believe the same things our whole life long, nor for any particular period of it. Men have logic tight compartments in their minds and while it is good in some respects, like for test pilot thinking and such, it is bad for others.

WE CAN BE A coach or a player in sports and have no trouble switching hats regardless of how different the roles. We can be tough and demanding one minutes and kind and understanding the next. We are not psychotic necessarily; we just have a capacity for thinking in more than one way. Where we get into trouble with it is when the roles require something of us in one setting that is mutually exclusive of our behaviors in another. A simultaneous wife and girlfriend comes to mind. Sure, we can do it, but can they? It is such a part of our nature to so compartmentalize our thinking that we may honestly think we can service both with some integrity at the same time. I'm not sure where that particular mistaken belief comes from, maybe it's how our cavemen ancestors faced danger and were able to forget about it and not dream about saber toothed tigers, but where ever it comes from it is wrong. Fact check that with your wife or girlfriend for confirmation but not both.

STAYING WITH THE RACER in you, however, you must see that any person with a valuable and rewarding existence should not logically risk his life racing a motorcycle. It is illogical. Forget money, they couldn't pay you enough to ride those thing and if Kenny Roberts can say it, then you know it's true for all of us as well. If it's just for the thrill, then go to an amusement park. If you just seek out of body experiences go to Colorado. Stuffing your body in a leather suit and putting it on a racing motorcycle to satisfy some itch in your mind goes too far if that is all it is. Good men, intelligent men, kind men, die racing motorcycles. Others live but do so miserably because they couldn't race well enough to be satisfied with themselves. There is a greater truth here and we might as well face it. Men racing motorcycles are not the men they are otherwise.

GARTH BUCKLES, MY GREAT friend and the best man at my wedding was a kind and thoughtful person. He was insightful, caring, and personified the thinking man for me. But put him on a motorcycle and all of that went right out the window. One sunny day when we were mechanics together at a little shop in the Midwest, we uncrated and set up two brand new Yamaha GT80 minibikes; Two hours later they were seriously used mini-bikes and I had bruises in my ribs on both sides from the ends of his handlebars. We had put on serious race faces for what should have been a little zip around the pine trees out beside the shop and neither of us were willing to say 'uncle.'

TALK ABOUT A HARD riding man; he would not give an inch or be moved, No Sir! No helmets of course, just jeans and tee shirts and it was impromptu, which made it all the better. Any sort of planning for this would have introduced new elements to the experience that would have colored it a different shade. It all started when we raced each other to get the two bikes out of their cartons, serviced, fueled and set up. Then of course we raced to be the first to take a test ride and that was all pretty much a draw, which sent us out the door more or less side by side. The rest just happened by itself. I don't think cavemen had mini-bikes but I do believe that there is something primal about moving along on a motorized vehicle that absorbs us completely.

THAT IS THE NEW dualism I believe takes normal men and makes them into racers. There is something in the genetic make up of some of us that lets us become one with the machine and mentally adapt ourselves so readily to our new environment that the bike disappears entirely and we just go. There is an acclamation period but it is short, and once we figure out what each hand and foot is supposed to do we leap ahead to all the ways we can make it change direction by turning the bars, or leaning or pushing down on a foot peg or throwing out a knee or some combination of them. We are different from one another, so our reaction to having our mind mechanized is different. Some men play the violin, others play the fiddle, but it could be the same instrument. Bob? Oh he was a natural!

Where this leads us is into a battle with science. I like science, don't get me wrong, but philosophically when we talk about our minds and our bodies like they are made of different stuff then we are suggesting that there is a kind of stuff that can't be dealt with scientifically. My mind is what, exactly? How much does it weigh? Is it bigger than a bread box or could I paint it green? Well, tradition has it that is doesn't have a physical existence. Science tells us that things without a physical existence of some sort just don't exist.

Black holes and all the rest of the things we can't see or understand are real and can be measured, they just can't be observed. There are theories out there that try to explain them but the descent into that maelstrom will have to take place elsewhere. There are none in this room and they won't make me any faster so I don't bother them, I just let them be. But science does not return the favor of my mind's indifference to it and persists that all things are knowable.

We have thinking machines now, and if to be alive is to be conscious and thought in progress is the measure of consciousness then I suppose we could say they are alive. Let me compute that for you in racing terms: We have such machines on racing motorcycles, which is troubling, but I was once an innovator myself as we all are who have modified something to make it work in some way we think will be better. But do we want motorcycles to think for us? Do I want a traction control computer monitoring the grip each tire has on the track and doing a better job of it in real time than we can? Do I want my braking input modulated by a system that won't let the wheel skid out from under me but will just turn the kinetic energy of my forward motion into heat and slow me down?

Follow that string and see where it leads. Someday in the distant future laser beams will be built into shut off markers that will slow the bike for us on the approach to each turn and then will only let it accelerate out of the turn at the exit once a set relationship to the perpendicular is again established. There will be a phase there where all future racers do is aim their machines and sit on them. Inevitably, in the name of safety, a camera will be installed in the nose and tail-piece so digital analysis of rider actions can be measured later to see where anything less than optimum input was given by the human component of the 'motorpsyche.' (a new word I may have just made up, but easy enough to see where it came from).

After that its only a matter of time before the human component is relegated to a safer location and the machine is operated remotely, at first from trackside perhaps, but later, once the need for a human face on the whole thing is gone, racers will be able to sit in front of their control panels linked via the internet and 'race' one another on any track in the world and not die in the process or get jet lag or bad food and can hit 'pause' any time they need to use the bathroom.

You think not? Well maybe you do have a mind after all and if you do, you can see how it could be done. Physicalism is the modern philosopher's answer to the old mind-body dualism problem that could not explain the mysteries of causation. What made me think of that? – is an example of a problem of causation. To the physicalists the mind will eventually be explained scientifically and since the subject matter of science is entirely physical the mind must be physical as well. This theory posits that mental states are the product of external stimuli and that by controlling input, we can control the mind.

Of course there are many objections to such an idea but my principal objection is that it leaves no room for a soul. It says that a blob of protoplasm in our skull with electrical current stimulating different parts of it so that they can send little pluses and minuses of charge to one another is all that a human brain, and consequently a human being, has in the way of a mind. At the opposite end of the way we think about our fellow human beings is the Jeffersonian model that pretends all men are created equal. Really? Then why am I faster than other men on the same motorcycle? That would be the question a racer would ask, which I think is a valid point, and which takes us nicely around this lap and back into the pits for a much needed breather.

If racing is real, and I think it is, and if the scientists were correct that the mind does not exist separately from science's ability to know it, then all racers would have the same race and would finish were they started relative to one another all things being equal. That will never happen as any racer can tell you for a fact without the necessity of science being applied at all. I think therefore I am? – That's not it.

I Race therefore I am.

17.

Dead Cheerleaders And Bad Roads

IT WAS JUST A stretch of road in a way; sure it had a name, they all have names, don't they? One is pretty much like another in that way. They are so wide and so long and black or gray and humped up a bit in the middle to make the rain not stand around and puddle and things move over them in one direction or another. You may remember the first time you saw this one, or that one, or heard its name. Dead man's curve; Route 66; A1A; The Goodnight – Loving trail; Comanche Hill; Grapevine Road; Highway 101.

Some names stood out on their own, some because you were there or wanted to be when something had happened. Up at the Laconia ski lodge with the Legends raced their big clumsy bikes between the pine trees hoping they didn't smack one like old Bill had last year, knocking most of his teeth out and breaking his shoulder busting him up so bad he gave up ridin' all together; or the Baja 1000, now there's a race!

The only meal I ever had with Randy Bradesque was at Grattan the week before Baja when he and I had found ourselves awake early and ready to do something so we came to the dining room of the crumby hotel where we found ourselves and had breakfast together as the sun came up, sitting a table apart from one another because we didn't know each other. We talked and I had won my race the day before and he had won his but neither of us had noticed. We talked about that too. It was Sunday now.

I watched him later and he was smooth and fast, leaning his big BMW over until the heads drug and sparked and his knees were out like a canoe outrigger. I didn't know if he watched me or not but I didn't do any of that stuff, or needed to, as I rode a different bike that wanted different things but mostly it wanted to be straightened up and pointed straight so it could just go. We both won our races again and he drove past my pit on his way out and waved at me and I waved back not knowing I would never see him alive again. I didn't have that thought until later when I learned of his death and tried to conjure up the last time I had seen him and then sift through it for any clues.

Some spectator supposedly did something to wreck his bike by stretching something across the course, I heard that anyway, but like a lot of rumors you hear about things you really didn't want to know anyway I didn't bother to find out the truth about it, what would it have mattered?

His picture was in the book I wrote about racing over a decade ago and his widow found me at another race later and thanked me for remembering him even though she and I had never met and she stayed around like being near someone who had been near him brought her closer to his memory some how. I thought that it was like lying on your back in the desert and looking up at the stars on a clear night and thinking it brought you closer to heaven. It is something to see and captivating, but not effective in any way that I can tell other than making me marvel at something so vastly incomprehensible.

I was sorry for the widow a hundred ways. She was grieving and she may get past it on some level and move on, I hoped for her sake she did, but there's not going to ever by anyone else like Randy, and she knew that too. That stretch of road was behind us.

The first time I came up on the big 'S' curve on Illinois State Highway One north of Hutsonville I was riding in the passenger seat of my mother's red and white '56 Cadillac and we had been rocketing down the road like always. She had the radio on and the windows down and was focused on a spot a thousand yards away, beyond the next hill, looking for a sign in that Indian way she had of pretending she knew things before anyone else did.

Maybe she did, I could never tell, but she had sensed something and slowed down and I straightened up to see what was going on. When we came up on top of the curve, and it snaked left and up to a plateau sort of place and then snaked right and back left down the other side before going on south, there were cars and trucks and tire smoke and screaming kids streaming out of a bus and running over to a car turned over beside the road with one side caved in its wheels still spinning. It was bad; I knew that, even though I had never seen anything like it before.

There were no seat belts in cars, or padded dashes, or air bags, or a host of other things. You stayed alive by not having a car wreck and when you had one it was likely that someone died. Right here, right now where I was looking there were dead people only I couldn't see them yet. Then I spotted a leg sticking out from under the side of the car, showing in the grass, with a black and white spectator shoe and bobby sock only the color of the skin was all wrong, sort of blue like and I pointed it out to mom and she let off the brake and eased back on the gas as she pulled off on the shoulder and moved carefully through the whole mess of it driving around the overturned car and the truck that had hit it and the school bus and the other cars and a Studebaker pick up which I found odd because I didn't know that Studebaker made pickups.

When we were far enough down the hill that it was all behind us she pulled over and shut the car off and told me to stay there. I did. She marched back up the hill like she was on a mission and disappeared. A police car went by about ten minutes later, then an ambulance, I just sat in the car and waited. I didn't want to see any of it but I could hear voices from over the hill behind me, and screaming, and crying. She came back looking none the worse for wear, but it was Mom the regular person, not the mother for public consumption that got in and sat down and waited a beat before starting the car again.

'Dead' she said, not looking at me, 'all dead' and put the car in gear. "Who's dead?" I asked her and she was lighting a cigarette so I knew she couldn't talk. I hated it that she smoked, but she was expert at managing the lighter and tapping the end of the cigarette on the dash and then putting it in her mouth and lighting it all in one gesture knowing exactly how long it would be before the thing popped out of glowing orange inside and lighting the tobacco yielding that toasty smell that seemed so deceptively pleasant just at first. It would kill her someday, but she couldn't see it. I could, but she wouldn't believe me. The day it finally came that I was right, I found no pleasure in it.

She took a deep drag, not hiding her need for it and letting me in on her wantonness about it for the first time. "Four cheerleaders and their sponsor." She said, nodding her head back behind us. I didn't ask any more questions; I knew she would fill me in when she felt like it. "Somebody thought it would be a good idea to pass the pep bus and get everyone fired up for the game tonight." she said, as if I might understand any of that. Mom had been a basketball player and a good one, but I was not that sort and I knew it hurt her. Mostly she didn't rub it in.

I had worn her letterman's jacket when I was younger, just fooling around. She had been on a state championship team in Oklahoma where they really played basketball and I had been told about the time she used her elbow to break the ribs of this big old Cherokee girl who had been riding her back all night. She was tough, I knew that and never questioned her inner ability to endure all things, but somehow, this had her shaken.

It was "Dead Cheerleader Curve" to me from then on and even though it was on the highway that was the easy way to the big city from where we lived we never went that way again, instead crossing the river at the old bridge that was a hundred times scarier over the muddy Wabash River fifty feet below just so we could wind our way up the Indiana side and not have to think about it any more. Still we thought about it.

Nothing really changed. The road was still there and would be until they moved it somewhere else and even then the spot would be there where it had happened. Places and their events are forever married.

18.

Sitting Ducks

At Daytona on the pit lane for the first time I was lined up with over a hundred other novices all of us on running motorcycles about to race around this huge place for seventy-six miles together none of us knowing if we would survive even the first lap. One thing was sure, someone would crash on the first lap – someone always did. I looked down at the asphalt under my work boot to see if it held any sign for me, here on the fourteenth row with the start way ahead of me and a pack of running motorcycles as far behind me as I could see when I tried to turn my head around. At least the tach on my Sprint worked. The poor Yamaha riders lost that when they pulled in the clutch so they sat there waiting in neutral trying to hear, or feel what they needed in a minute which was some sense of how much throttle to give the bike in the middle of so many machines running with no mufflers on anything.

We were all about to change our lives and were in it together. For many of us it would be the first time – for the rest of them it was something I had no comprehension of. Next year, when I was back here and doing it again, it would not be the same. There would be changes to the track, to the rules, to the machines, to me and all of that would make it something else. Familiar, yes, but not the same – but this year, my first year to race at Daytona, the question was whether or not I was up to it. I imagined that I was. I had always been a 'do anything you can do' sort of guy, but I couldn't play the piano and some people could so I knew there were limits. I looked at the track surface again, passive and patched with tar and littered with sand up against the knee high concrete wall that separated us from the clumps and groups of guys with concerned faces over there without bikes.

Then there was a change in the pitch of the noise, the deafening noise all around us, and up front, through the smoke, I could see a one armed guy waving a flag and we were off, or they were off, and I started to ease out the clutch and keep the revs up and the bike started to move and then caught and went and then I cut through the rows and rows of bikes ahead of me, not all of them, just those who were getting poor starts and I saw the throng head out onto the banking together and went with them, after them, drug along behind them until I got closer and closer and then suddenly was sucked right in among them, my tach now showing 11,500 rpm and my throttle hand was backing off but the revs were not falling and we were around the banking and on the back stretch and I put my head down and the sound was painful and I had to bring my head back up out of the bubble and held my place as a few shuffled a bit here and there but mostly we just held on.

Onto the banking ahead the pack launched itself at the wall and then went up onto it together like a flock of birds that had changed direction all at once at the same time and now they were bending away to the left as I watched and then went after them and onto the banking where it was a jolt and then a dip and then a wiggle which felt strange.

The finish line went past and I was too far up front and the leaders were taking turn one and I must have passed thirty or forty bikes already to be up here and then the markers came and I sat up and braked and went in with them, not sure from this speed where I needed to start braking but knowing that everyone else was.

A guy off to my right went down like someone had just yanked the bike out from under him then two, now three other bikes went down trying to miss him or his bike and running into each other or locking up their brakes and going down and then they all scattered like quail and I hugged the inside and kept to the left and stopped looking at it and made turn one and then went down toward the horseshoe where the leaders were already turning in, bending to the right, pulling away and I had just made my first racing lap at Daytona and I felt like superman.

It did not matter that I was not winning. Right then I didn't especially care if I ever won again. I was here, there were palm trees, the sky was blue, the sun was bright, winter back home had been long and hard and my bike was running beneath me without missing a beat. I repeated all the moves that made a lap and did the same things the same ways until the checkered flag finally made its appearance after a period of indescribable, undiscernibly altered time went by. Each moment piled upon another and in each the chance to make a fatal error felt like it was ever present and my senses were all on high alert although I was weirdly, almost magically calm about it all. We were all just sitting ducks, waiting for fate to pick us off one at a time.

It is nothing at all what it looks like. The sensations of it, the feelings of doing it, the way it looks from the track from behind a bubble of a racing motorcycle is unlike anything else in this life. No camera or simulator or combinations of words that I might juxtapose to attempt to let a reader know who has never done it can know what it feels like. Think sex talk with a virgin here, say what you want to them about sex, all of which may be accurate, they will still be virgins when you are done talking to them. Your first race at Daytona, if you get past the fears it brings and manage the complexities it offers and find your rhythm and ride it, you know you've done something when that's over.

While you were doing it there was a force at work that you probably were not even aware of. No risk you took was as small as the one the cheerleaders took riding to the ball game with their sponsor who was by all accounts a very good driver. Dead Cheerleaders and live motorcycle racers work with the same set of rules. They will all cease to be living beings someday. Perhaps tragically, perhaps publically, or maybe alone in their sleep, but it will happen. Fate is inexorable. It is too large a thing to comprehend that the universe, which is infinite, is made up of occurrences so disparate from one another that they seem impossibly remote to be related but they are. Man is so vain and egotistical as to think that relationship has something to do with him. I know that it has something to do with me, but that's not vanity, that's harmony. Don Emde tells me that the Daytona Motorcycle race has been cancelled for next year.

19.

Mia Copa

ON JUNE 6, 1966 I returned home from a 'forgive me' visit to my maternal grandmother's home in New Mexico. The mission had been a failure. My grandfather had died of lung cancer as I was finishing high school and the rest of the family went out to be there for the final moments of his life to honor him.

My mother had been by his side for some time leaving the house where I remained occupied only by men. We did not get on well with one another and it was a grudging co-existence that pointed out the need we had for the woman that made the house we shared a home. Still, when the time came to go for the funeral, I begged off and they did not make the effort to persuade me to go.

I had two jobs, one after school and one on the weekends, and we needed every nickel we could scrape together so there was a practical argument to be made. I also had no desire to see my grandfather dead or spend more time with my grandmother who was largely hateful to me. I would miss my grandfather, but I could do that from here and had already begun.

He had given me the tenderfoot treatment and spared me nothing, showing me what the rattling was over in the mesquite bushes and how to flush those snakes out and then hunt them down with a forked stick and catch them right behind the neck before killing them and skinning them and selling the skins to the tourists.

I shot my first gun under his tutelage and was not strong enough to hold the barrel out straight so I had to pull the trigger at the red heart dog food can when the sights were lined up on it as the arc I made with the end of the rifle went past. It was a pump .22 and no, he would not pump it for me but yes, he would push it away if I moved the gun any way that would shoot him or me if it went off. He would do this without comment or explanation as if it was directed at the gun, not at me and say, 'tell that thing not to point at me,' or 'control your firearm.' Nearly everything he passed on to me was like that, full of double meaning with multiple applications.

We were in town one day when a man spotted him and crossed the street and blocked our path on the sidewalk to say something to him. Roy put a gentle hand in my chest and pushed me back, telling me to stay put. It was a big angry man and he said some hateful words and pointed at Roy's chest. Roy said nothing but I saw him make fists with his hands and figured a fight was going to break out. Just then someone else hollered at the other guy and he said something else quiet like and then went away.

Roy came back for me and I asked him what the man had said. 'He said he was going to kick the shit out of me,' Roy said, half smiling, and then added 'But sayin' it don't make it so.' I thought about that and decided I believed it. I still do.

I can say I'm faster than you, or talk about this thing or that, but when we get on the track and the time comes to go, nothing I say is going to change things. Talk all you like, or don't talk at all, it doesn't matter. Racing is reality and it needs no sugar coating or explanation. There are back-stories to be sure, and excuses for this or that, but they don't matter to the track. What matters there is what we love about it. It is an equal opportunity exasperator.

20.

Can You Zen This?

THIS IS NOT FOR everyone. It is just for the few who have the ability and discipline to read what has gone before and what follows with the right frame of mind and then work out what it means. I have the ability to spoon feed but think it condescending to do so and would rather reach those few with the mind to get it rather than lose them in my effort to make pabulum out of tough concepts in an effort to get it to everyone.

Imagine a professor far below you in a lecture hall where you have put yourself at great trouble and expense to be enlightened. He begins at one ends of the black board that runs clear across the front of the room through several panels. His is off to one side, looking at you and all the rest there waiting for the right time. He writes "Nothing matters" and begins to draw a line, more or less straight across the entire thing to the far right edge where he leaves just enough room to write, "Everything matters. Then he says, "If we were to plot on this continuum of possibilities the truth of the relationship between what matters and what doesn't, where would you place the answer?"

Some murmuring breaks out as thought is given to the proposition. Finally, one girl raises her hand and offers, "In the middle." And seems pleased with herself while the rest of the class is just relieved they were not called on. "Wrong," says the professor but goes there and puts an 'x' anyway. He turns and looks at the group and waits. Finally someone sensing that there wasn't another offer makes one and he repeats the process and so it goes on until there are many 'x's and as many observations from him that they are incorrect.

Time is running out in the period so he comes to the lectern, putting down the chalk and says, "If nothing mattered, you would not bother to be here," and pauses as he looks meaningfully at each face looking back before continuing, "if some things matter and some do not, you would think then that those that mattered to you were the ones that mattered while those that happened to your neighbor that you were not aware of did not matter at all, at least not to you, and therefore did not matter," again he looked at everyone before going on, "but your mind is so small that you cannot grasp the possibility that everything matters, and has mattered, and will matter through all of time, whether it matters to you or not."

He waits. They wait. Finally someone opens a notebook and begins to write and he watches them, waiting for them to finish. They do and look up for more. "Time is a human limitation," he says, finally, conclusively, "not a Divine one." In that instant the bell rings and the class is dismissed for the day - Lesson over.

. . .

It is not enough to pretend just to know that there are larger more complex things out there as if we might someday understand what they really are and how they work. I wish it were simple, but it is not. I do not believe that it is as simple as John 3:16. It is a nice sentiment and I agree that for some that might be enough but for others it is still apparent that something more is necessary than just simple faith.

I sat and watched my mother die for twelve weeks from lung cancer and every breath was a little more agonizing than the one before. Dulling the pain took her away but let her live with it a little longer. I had promised to care for her and I did, but it was a promise I would never make again. In the end, no angels sang and no peace came over her. She died hard, leaving marks, and I was too close to avoid them.

That was thirty years ago now, and I wanted to write something about it but had nothing to say. Before writing these words I flew to Germany and looked carefully and methodically for evidence that the answer to the basic questions of man's existence was knowable. Luther had written there and I had taken his teachings to heart for a time, digesting his Small Catechism repeatedly looking for nourishment. It was inadequate for me somehow. I thought perhaps that to be there, under the German sky, looking at what he had seen there might be useful.

It was, but not in the way I had expected. I traveled on to Amsterdam to revisit some significant markers of my past in order to reconsider my interpretations of those events in the light of four more decades of living. I see things now I did not see before and admit that I might have been in error previously. It was not a miscalculation so serious as to have been misdirection worth worry given what I understand about things now. We are travelers and we need to think about where home is and what will get us there.

Neither is it sufficient to admit that we will never comprehend it, whatever 'it' might be. We are temporary, 'it' is apparently eternal, at least so far as we know, so there is very little use in hoping to get comfortable with any of this, let alone all of it. But we do, somehow, come to spots where we can nestled down in the fresh dry leaves beside the path and catch our breath and hold our dog and be grateful in some vague way that we know enough to appreciate any of it.

I live and think and breathe and then I have memories of having done so before on other days and hopes of doing it again on still more days yet to come. It is mystical, it is magical, it is something. For a while, that was enough for me, that and the belief that I was living a charmed life.

We reach a point, however, where we can't be satisfied with that. For some reason unknown we feel like we have some special status in the universe of possibilities to comprehend, to know and even on some level to deal with it. Abraham bargained with God. Sure he did, I think to myself, knowing I am a fool. I think there is a God but not because of Abraham. I think so because God has made himself known to me in a thousand million ways so evident that it is useless to continue to examine the question. It is a definitional belief and I am not especially passionate about it. I am not rapturous about the existence of God, nor the limited good I am able to do while in my present state.

Was there a state before this one? Well sure, I have pictures. I was so young and small that my brain did not comprehend what was going on around it and my body was so weak and tiny that I was for a time entirely incapable of caring for myself. I have memories, but not of that time. My memories may have started younger than some, but they tell me there was time before memory and what does that tell me? I was in another state of existence.

Will that be less true tomorrow or the day after or with the passage of my next birthday? Undoubtedly. Some day in my future a day will come when I can no longer think about such things. It may not be the day my thoughts cease all together, it may be some day before that when I still have thoughts but they take such a form as to be unrecognizable to the person who is writing these words now.

I have seen it happen to others. I have had lucid intervals with them when they could speak about things we had done together and when we could plan for things we might still do but then they faded away and those thoughts were gone as if they had never happened at all. There are scientific explanations but they don't really explain anything. They tell us how the bodies of these mindless husks have managed to perpetuate a sibilance of living after the minds they used to house have stopped being what they once were. The inevitability of it brings some real pressure to our day to day existence, and some of us don't manage it very well and distract ourselves in a different ways thinking it might make a difference somehow.

"Then to the lip of this poor earthen urn I leaned, the secret of my life to learn, and lip to lip it murmured, 'drink'..."

Look around. Who has made a difference that matters in that one singular way that is human life and death? Yes, there are those who have contributed to the health and well being of others and enabled them to live longer and do more before the curtain falls, but it still falls. I suppose if one were to dwell on it, it would be depressing, but that would only be if the life they had lived had lacked some appreciation and understanding of what was going on.

Will I be remembered? Did people really love me? Did I really love them? Was I good, really good? Or did any of it matter at all? These are the persistent questions to life's mysteries.

The good news is not just the one you may have heard. The good news is that God is much, much bigger than you ever imagined and has dimensions beyond human understanding. I substituted some letters there in expressing that news to comfort those who need it. Those who didn't need it, and who would have been alright with 'it' won't mind I know.

That is a thought that you can manage, I think, that things are larger than you realized. That wall at the edge of your conception has a back side and it reveals another universe of possibilities. If you could ever master all the rules and applications of those rules we call science to the extent that you know all that can or will or has happened in this universe, and you are up against that wall, then you know that there is another universe out there, and another after that, where none of those rules may apply.

Take heart, have courage, act as if it all matters. It is not a simple recipe and it shouldn't be. The goodness of all of it is apparent, even in the worst of circumstances. This written work is merely a compass to point the way. It may not be the way forward for you, personally, but it makes no difference in terms of the value of hearing of the journey. Just to know that it can be done is enough if you are one who believes that you can do anything. For those of you who just had the thought that you cannot do anything I apologize for having wasted your time. You should stop reading now and try and get your money back. This book is not for you and you know who you are. For the rest of you, welcome, and settle in for a feast of positively edifying examples of how I know things are going to work out just fine.

21.

The Pegboard Tale

WHAT IS YOUR EARLIEST memory? Whatever it is, stop now and write it down as fully and as completely as you can manage. Don't rush yourself, but don't put it off either. If you cheat yourself in this, the cost will be very high later so don't take this lightly. I can wait, and you want to get all you can from this. OK then, if you are done with that I shall tell you the pegboard tale, which is the true story of my earliest memory.

I was very young, just a toddler, and was sitting in my room on my new green pegboard play thing that had a little seat you straddled at the rear and then a lidded box on the front that slid up to reveal a space for storing the little barrel shaped colored pegs with small little posts underneath that fit tightly in the holes of the lid. There were red and blue and yellow pegs and the board with the holes in it was a medium deep green.

I was sitting with the window to my right side and was making a pattern on the board like the streets of a town and was counting out the number of pegs I would need to make the block I lived on with pegs. I was thinking about what color pegs to use for the houses and the streets and the cars and had some out there already when it happened.

The sun came out from under the eave of the house and shone directly on part of the board. It only took a moment but the line of demarcation between the part that was left in the shade and that which was in the sun was clear and I had seen it travel across the board and change everything.

The colors of the pegs and the board itself seemed to change and now there were shadows where moments before there had been none. I put another peg in just to check and a shadow appeared as a darker green place and was just the same size as the other shadows of the other pegs now standing next to darker places that had not been there a moment ago. I took the peg back out and the shadow disappeared.

I thought about that and that was when it happened. I realized that I was thinking. It was not as important what I was thinking about as that I had a mental awareness that it was going on. Some things I did without thinking, I realized, and other things I did only after I thought about them first. Then, like just now, there were whole categories of things I did while I was actually thinking about what I was doing in a moment to moment sort of way.

In that moment, before I was two, I woke up to the realization that I could manipulate the outcomes of some things by the way I was thinking when I did them. Not just things I did myself, but things external to myself. The shadow of the peg was not there when the peg was not there and I was the one who put the peg down or took it away. I did not make the shadow, something else did that, but it didn't do it without me. It was real. So was I.

I got up and went to kitchen and tried to explain this phenomenon to my mother who was in the midst of making noodles by cutting long thin strips out of dough she had rolled out on the cutting board that pulled out of the front of the cabinets. She didn't listen at first, concentrating instead on her cutting with the knife and pleasantly saying 'uh hmmm.' I persisted and then finally persuaded her to come with me to my room and watch.

She came, because she was a good mother, and partly because she knew I was persistent. With her in attendance I repeated the process and showed her the shadow of the peg, now there on the green board as a darker green shape, then gone after I lifted the peg. I pointed to myself and put my finger in my chest and said, "I do this. I put the peg in and then the shadow comes." She pointed outside and told me sweetly that the sun made the shadow, not me, so I held up the peg and looked at the board and showed her there was no shadow.

It dawned on her then what I was talking about so she articulated it to me better than I was saying it to her. "You are thinking that the shadow is a real thing and it comes and goes because of what you do and what the sun does and even though you don't make the shadow, the sun can't make it without you, right?" I showed her a big smile then and nodded, full of pride. I had a smart mother.

What I didn't see then but only came to understand much later was what the incident meant in terms of the processing of data. My synapses were connecting over an observed phenomenon and my intellect was making the effort to comprehend what was going on. We all began doing that at some age and I believe it usually was about the time of our earliest memory. Some impressions of strange or unusual events may have been stamped in there without being intellectualized, but the one where you thought something through and then remembered it is the one I speak of. We all have it in us, some sooner than others, but that doesn't really matter.

Now read what you wrote about your earliest memory, and see what it tells you about yourself, and how you see your world.

22.

Papa And The Present

I RODE AROUND ON Papa's shoulders, sleepy and barely awake. The big house was full of people, very full. They wore silly hats and smiled and pointed at me and blew horns and kept saying "Happy New Year." When we went from one room to another there would be a whoop and a holler and people would reach for us and pat Papa on the back and shake his free hand. The other hand stayed hold of my ankle to keep me securely up there. He looked up now and then and said, "Remember this! Its 1950 and it's a brand new year" It was the only time I remember that he ever held me. Three years later, while I was living with my brother and parents in Roswell, New Mexico, we got a phone call in the middle of the night telling us he had died and it changed everything.

I wake up and realized that I had been dreaming, or remembering. I am older now than my grandfather had been then and recalled wondering what it would have been like to be him. At 53 my grandfather had been the most important man in town and had the respect of everyone, or their fear. His story was only talked about in his wake, after he had passed by; and then quietly and with some admiration. The little bits and pieces I heard of it growing up had interested me only in so far that they explained something of him to me. But then that was silly since we weren't really related. I have two views of it; what it seems like, and what it was really.

He was a local legend as far as I knew. He had a trunk full of WWI stuff I got to play with rarely, a helmet and trench knife, but mostly there were letters and papers that were none of my concern I was told. They said he has served with volunteers in an ambulance regiment but he would never speak of it to me. He was irrepressibly cheerful and was as likely to pull a prank or tell a joke as be serious regardless of the occasion. He claimed he knew Hemingway and was the Ford dealer in Carmi and a Shiner and had once played piccolo in Sousa's band when he was a kid. He had been orphaned young and lived by his wits and grit and kept folks at some distance who pretended to be better than others. Still, they liked him. How could you not like him? He just wouldn't allow it!

One afternoon he scooped me up out of the front yard of their big house south of town off of Route 1 and announced that he was taking me to the fair. I was thrilled and clutched the shiny half dollar in my pocket he had given me along with my orders and the advisory that he had to go to the Kiwanis tent to make arrangements for the color guard. The fairground was an especially fine piece of ground at the southwestern edge of the town and was situated in a grove of 100 year old oak trees. The grandstands and the racetrack fence wore a new coat of gleaming white paint and the taffy machine was up and running putting the little bits of pulled white taffy into bits of white waxed paper waiting for someone to come along and ask for a bag of them. They were soft and chewy and warm and probably the best thing ever as far as I was concerned.

I stood and looked at the huge pile of them behind the glass counter for a while before moving on to the midway to smell and feel the fresh sawdust between my toes. A huckster was setting up his booth and decided to test out his pitch on a kid with his fist in his pocket obviously holding something. "Three tries for dime" he called out to me, tossing a baseball in the air and pointing at rows of stuffed cats perched on a tier of shelves. I kept walking. "Just knock them off and win a prize!" he continued and so did I. I was nearly out of his territory so he added, "...any prize!" which made me look back and follow the tip of his cane as he circled the heavens of the hanging rewards dangling from the underneath side of the stands' tented roof. I stopped.

Some of the other barkers stopped what they were doing to watch the proceedings out of professional curiosity. "Step right up, young man," the barker continued, and I moved closer to see what there was that might interest me. I was clueless of course about what was really going on. I looked things over carefully and spotted a large stuffed white teddy bear, larger than I was, and pointed at it. "That prize?" I asked, finally finding my voice. He looked around to see who was watching and became uncomfortable. There was a tag on the bear I couldn't read from here so I was just seeking confirmation that he had said 'any' prize before I offered up my precious coin for a try. "You would have to knock off three cats with thee balls to get that prize," he began, eyeing his peers and nodding before adding in a louder voice, "that right, Sonny, ANY prize at all!"

I dug my hand out of my pants and handed over the fifty cent piece. He counted out four dimes and I put them back in my pocket carefully before taking the three baseballs he was offering. "Where do I have to throw from?" I asked, before preparing myself. "You can get as close as you want my lad," he said, magnanimously, "Come right up to the counter if you please." It didn't please me, it was too high and I wasn't that tall and so I stepped back until I could see the bottom row of cats too and then asked him, "From here?" Now he was having fun. He cupped his ear as if I were too far away to hear. "Eh?" he joked, "did you ask me if you can throw from way back there?" and I nodded and he was smiling and gracious and he bowed and said, "When ever you are ready, Cannonball, let 'er rip!"

Now I had some confidence in my throwing ability, mostly from a freakish tendency I seemed to have that made it possible for me to nail my brother right in the ear with whatever I was throwing at him no matter how far away I seemed to be. Corn cob, water balloon, mud ball, snowball, it didn't make any difference if I threw it, it found the mark. But a baseball? Something actually made to be thrown and I something that I had thrown many many times to Grandpa Roy and back as he crouched in his catcher's stance and showed me the one finger down sign in front of his big round glove for a fast ball? Man this was practically stealing! Well, that's what I thought anyway.

I could see it in my mind before I ever started to wind up. I gave it the stretch. Held the man on first; stretched again and fired a strike, hitting a cat square on its small red nose. It toppled over and fell off its perch to the silent stare of the stand's owner and after a brief silence there was a smattering of applause from onlookers. A buzz started to go around in hushed tones as the barker reviewed the rules with me out loud for all to hear, holding up his palm at me to keep me from throwing as he adjusted the cats and put the downed one back in its place. I was twenty feet away but could still see what he was doing. "No cheating!" I called out, like I would to any other playmate. He took offense and started to launch into some pat answer when I threw again at a likely looking cat in the far corner of the herd that he had not bothered to mess with. He ducked as I threw, as if I might hit him, and the second cat went over and I jumped for joy. Two for two! Man I was hitting the marks today.

Twenty or more people had gathered by now and an invisible alley of sorts held them back from where they thought the path of ball would be next. The carney started to put the cat back and I hollered for him to "leave it!" and faked a throw to make him duck again. He disappeared beneath the counter and I waited for him to come back up. There was laughter and it was a shining moment for me to be sure. I threw the last ball and watched it go right where I had aimed it, hitting the center cat on the topmost row at its feet, scooting it back against the hidden rail that kept it from falling off the shelf if it was too far away when it went backward and making it go off anyway. 3 for 3, the big bear was mine.

The cheer was immediate. My heart swelled and I took off my hat and gave the crowd a bow which brought more hoots and applause. Even the carnival guy was good natured about it and seemed to be accepting of his loss as his buddies chided him about how the kid had taken his best prize just like that. I had only begun to explore the midway and already had a huge bear to carry but I didn't mind. It had that new prize smell and I hugged it as I walked along and calculated how many more prizes I could get with the remaining coins now burning a hole in my pocket.

I got some state fair taffy, which was wonderful, and unwrapped and ate pieces as I walked along and looked at the strange and mystical world that was a carnival. I was thirsty and hot and got a snowcone and sat down to have it when Armageddon came and my world was knocked completely off its axis. As I bent over to take a seat, still holding on to the all white bear and clutching my last dime in a closed fist, the ball of ice and food coloring that was guts of the snow cone did a slow motion plop onto the front of the bear and then rolled slowly, disastrously, down its front before disintegrating in the sawdust, completely inedible. I had yet to have even a single bite.

Worse yet, the bear, the perfect bear, the virgin bear, was ruined. It was a word I hated already, and would come to hate more and more but it was true, the bear was ruined forever. I was going to cry, I could feel it, and it made me mad so I sat the bear down, scooped up what snow cone I could salvage, and ate it, sawdust and all. The forlorn bear sat next to me, staring dumbly at the end of all things bright and beautiful. After I had abused myself enough not to cry, I gathered my dignity, and my bear, and set off to find my grandfather to hear his sage advice about the highs and lows of my life coming so close together.

Then came the lesson. A carney saw the moment for what it was and came out from behind his booth to console me, taking out his handkerchief and letting me blow my nose in it. He told me it was too bad that the bear was ruined, and hearing it said only made it worse, but he kindly offered as how he would give me three chances to knock down the milk bottles in his booth for any prize I wanted and take the ruined bear off my hands. I hesitated, but not for long. After all, I was the greatest baseball thrower who ever lived and was on a hot streak. Soon we were into which prizes and where could I stand and all the rest and he had the bear out of sight on his side of the counter and I had three base balls and you know the rest. I missed. My throws were not even close and even though he offered to let me try again for only a dime and I still had one, I shook my head 'no' and was on my way, out the of the midway and the pretend world that I suddenly hated everything about. I was just another sucker and there was one born every minute. As I walked back to the car I could hear their calls, "Step right up, three tries for just one thin dime, one tenth of a dollar, hurry, hurry, hurry …"

I didn't go back later, even though it was suggested, but instead sat in my grandfather's 1952 Ford with the clear plastic roof and waited for him. When he came he asked me if I had enjoyed myself and I told him, "not really." Just then a girl about my size was walking by with her family and thanking her father for winning her the best prize in the whole world. A giant white bear with a necktie rode under his arm and looked blankly at me as it went by. As they passed us, and the tie swung, I could see the stain that had ruined it for me. She hadn't noticed, or didn't care, the prize was perfect in her eyes and that was all that mattered now.

23.

Ready Or Not

I PUSHED MY HARLEY Davidson CRTT 250cc Aermacchi road racer, frame and motor number 66CR6030, out onto the grid for my first AMA National Road Race. It was at Indianapolis Raceway Park, in Clermont, Indiana, just outside Indianapolis. Don Emde was there on the front row, carrying number 5 from Bonita, California, although I didn't know him then or that he would go on to be famous or that our paths would cross again many times. Don Hollingsworth was there, from St. Augustine, Florida riding a bike something like mine. He had won the Novice race at Daytona the previous March and history would later find that to be the last man to ever win a 250cc AMA National road race on a four stroke.

Rusty Bradley was there from Dallas, Texas, and we had pitted near one another and struck up a lasting friendship given that I had lived a while in Amarillo and Lubbock myself and would go down to Austin to run on the streets at the Aqua festival and to Green Valley Raceway between Dallas and Fort Worth. John Long was there from Miami, but wasn't hooked up with Dirty Distributing yet and was still riding a Ducati. He made an odd lanky figure riding up and down the pit lane on his 10 speed bike without hands. Conrad Urbanowski had also made the trip from Miami but was on his fast 'C" model Yamaha twin. Gary Fisher and George Taylor had come from Pennsylvania, Harry Cone from Texas. Bart Myers from New Jersey was there and would go on to become 'Professor' Myers at Rutgers. Wendell Tisdale was in my race from Arkansas with a fast Ducati Diana that had a silly sky blue leatherette covered seat tail. We were all still novices and to a man were eager to get over it. My first race at Indianapolis was truly a national event.

I had been to Indy many times to watch races, but they had been over at the speedway, some miles away, and this was where the national drag race finals of NHRA were held instead. The complex also had a paved half mile oval where the Champion dirt track cars ran but with slicks instead of grooved tires. They were the remnants of the USAC old guard that had yet to get the news that their old fashioned front engine roadster style cars were relics of the past. The grounds had a sweeping road course lay out that connected the parking lots and some grassy areas that the AMA was going to use for their road race but it was a make shift deal at best. For one thing, the drag strip was all rippled up off the start as you might expect and had layers of rubber and debris ground into the asphalt that surfaced at the least bit of persuasion. That meant that the big right hand turn at the end of the front straight was a different road added onto the side of the main straight where it went on down to the shut down area for the drag races. As such, they had different crowns to promote run off and their surfaces were different and the transition from the straight to the right hand exit road was taken at high speed, all of which made it both critical, and dangerous.

At the other end of the straight, back in what would be the staging area for the drag races, the pavement was extremely dodgy and the bikes crossed it at an angle through make shift cones that put them into the next turn at the wrong spot and in the wrong direction, which made for two converging lines by riders that crossed each other requiring the sense of timing of a figure eight demolition derby racer as they would eye each other across the blacktop trying to hit an opening just right.

I had driven over with Ron Muir who was there to ride for Kawasaki, his first factory offer since winning the junior race at Daytona in March. He would be an expert next year for that win, and someone probably should have noticed him sooner. I didn't know that much about such things, but he seemed to be very fast and certainly had the killer instinct that let it be known he would do whatever it took to win. He was quick, very quick, and could catch flies out of the air and did, just to show you.

We had some trouble pleasing Charlie Watson and the tech boys but managed to get through and approved for racing mostly because it said 'Harley Davidson' on the tank. I was relieved to hear it start, and out in practice it ran flawlessly pulling 11,500 down the long straight into turn one where I would let off and turn away to the right and then to the right again, only tighter before a short straight to a left and a short straight to another left with a concrete wall sticking out right were you went back to the right and ran along the outside of the inner oval track that shared the grounds. At the end of this back straight, which was fairly long, was a sharp right and then a nebulous sort of no man's land with some cones set up across a huge parking lot where all the drag racers pitted and staged for their runs.

On the far side of it all, was an exit road that ran off to the right down through a dip that was the road course again but getting from here to there a guy was pretty much on his own. That next right was sharp if you went straight over to it from where the cones let you go and my Harley was not happy with the downshift that required. Upshifts were easy enough because the kill button let you just put pressure on the shift lever and then hit the button at the right time and it would go up a gear. Coming down you had to yank hard on a clutch lever with a level of effort that would make King Kong wince.

On the other side of the parking lot with the cones was a right hand turn with a little dip that led to a big carousel right behind the grand stands which brought you to a weird turn that shared the pit entrance with access back to the two lanes of the drag strip that made up the front straight with the start/finish line.

The racing line from the pit entrance road area took you across both lanes of the main straight as you tried to get it turned left while heading right at an Armco barrier. People were careful there, and it was a good place to be careful. The track surface had been abused annually by the NHRA nationals that took place on this same part of the track and it was slick and bumpy and wrinkled up by thousand horsepower monsters which would have been bad enough but we had to manage these transitions obliquely as we emerged from a tight twisty road course onto something the size of an airport runway.

Back at the parking lot nebulous I had decided to try something different about the third lap of practice and instead of cutting across it all straight to the right hand turn and then braking and downshifting, I went wide left as I exited the back straight over to an imaginary point where I thought I could turn it in and sweep across it all of the in between without downshifting or braking. It was further, that was true, but it was a lot faster provided no one was in your way when you got to the turn.

That was problematic as people you were out there with could see what you were doing and they had to know, at least I figured they did, that you would be coming along at an unstoppable rate of speed across their line and unless they made the turn, and stayed out of the way when they came out of it, things could get ugly.

Well, as it turned out one of those people was Wendell Tisdale. I had seen him ahead of me back on the main straight in practice and he carried good speed through the turns up to the back stretch when I caught him and passed him. He passed me right back, under braking, all out of shape and smoke coming off the back tire and I went wide left as he managed to tuck it in to the right and head across the parking lot. I had not lost momentum and could see him composing himself and heading over to where I was headed by different paths. This was a very odd set up and I have to say that I was never at another track that had two lines into the same corner this far apart and at one point we were separated by a good twenty yards or more.

I was leaned in and on the gas as we looked at one another and I could see by then that he was just sitting up and getting ready to brake. He saw me coming. I saw him looking. I kept my head down. He was squirming back and forth with the nose dipped down and his arms out straight taking the weight. I knew that he would have to cross my path as he exited unless I went wide and if I did that, I would miss the next little switch back and my entry to the carousel. One of us would have to give.

I stayed on the gas and he kept on braking for all he was worth, now recognizing that he had nowhere to go, even if he did get to the corner first and he wasn't going to. It was going to be a tie, and that was not good. How close was it? He had spinach in his teeth from dinner the night before. I knew that because we were both wearing open face helmets and our faces were close enough for me to see him grimacing and a chunk of green showing at the gum line. We missed one another by inches and by the time he got up to the carousel I was exiting it and went on for one more lap of practice.

I stopped after that and came in. Hollingsworth showed up and had a look at my bike and asked me some questions about this and that. I was friendly enough and so was he, we were just talking to one another; that was all. He asked me what I was using for a redline and I told him honestly 11,500, and his face lost some of its color. "No shit?" he asked. "Yeah, really, why?" "Because," he said, "they won't stay together if you wind them up more than 9,500 and that's what I use for a red line. I picked up on that, trying to remember if I had seen another Sprint out there. "You've got one?" "Yeah, but it doesn't wind up like yours does." Then he asked me what I used for oil and I told him I had no idea. He looked worried. When did you change it last? He asked. "Never have," I said, he shook his head and seemed to collect his thoughts. We were the only two Harley Davidson's entered and in some way he decided that it was important for there to be some sharing of information among ourselves.

"I have to tell you that if you don't change the oil, the motor will destroy itself and that would be a real shame because you have something really special there." He was sincere, I could tell that by his expression and I took his warning to heart. After he left, I loosened the dip stick nut that had been wired shut to check the oil level. When I got it off, I found no dipstick on it, which turned out to be fairly common I learned later. So I went underneath the bike and took of the drain plug bolt with its self-contained filter, putting a coffee can underneath to catch the oil. A coffee can shouldn't have been enough, actually, but it was plenty, since it barely had any oil at all. I was mortified. Less than a quart came out and it wasn't pretty. Regardless of how this would turn out, I owed Don big time and would not forget it.

Practice was winding down and then they were going to have lunch and a heat race before mine so I had time to run into Indy and find the Harley dealer and ask him what oil I should be using and whether or not he had any. He made some calls and then came back with the answer – "Oilzum Crystal 50," he announced, " that's the only thing that will work says the factory." I was doubtful but bought some and hurried back to the track. I put in the amount they said was required and rewired everything. I managed to get myself out on the grid in time for the introductions and all the rest and had even had a chat with Wendell who explained apologetically that the sky blue seat was his wife's idea of a birthday present. He had mentioned that a new seat cover might be nice and she had taken the seat off herself and spirited it away to the upholstery shop one weekend while Wendell was out of town. "Blue" she had instructed him, thinking 'navy' might be nice. 'Sky ' was a pretty color of blue too, and he happened to have some of that on hand and hence a rapid black and red Ducati came to Indianapolis to race with a sky blue seat. It was strange, but it didn't seem to slow it down and it was not the strangest thing about his equipment that I noticed.

KR73 Dunlop tires were in vogue then and my bike had come with a pair on narrow rims. My interest was in riding, probably where it should have been, but by the time that race was over with its practice sessions and heat race and the main, I had thirty laps or more on the Sprint and was not a happy man. It ran great, and never missed a beat, and it seemed to go fast when I was by myself, but then when I got back onto the long straight the two stroke twins would simply go on past me like I was just an interesting and noisy obstacle. Harry Cone and I exchanged waves a time or two as he got balked in a gaggle of Ducati in search of the racing line while I cut right through them, scattering them like blue quail from mesquite.

He came back past on the straight and then disappeared on ahead, out of range of what I could make up in the corners. The Dunlop tires had a frightening profile and were pointy and narrow when the bike was upright and didn't have an appreciable amount of rubber on the ground unless you were seriously leaned over. Apparently someone had thought this was a good idea but it went against my Indy car background to have skinny tires. It also became clear in that race that the Sprint was no match for the two stroke twins on top end and this was a 40 mile race with a long straight in every lap. It seemed longer but in the end I loaded up without a scratch and saw later in the results that I had managed to beat Hollingworth which I counted as a victory although I didn't ever see him on the track.

Muir had a tougher day than mine and since the Novice race was first, I was able to be back in jeans and tee shirt by the time his turn to race came and I was standing by in case he had some need to say something. He liked to keep people at a distance until he wanted something and then was insistent that you should have been closer. To say that he was temperamental was to mention that Mount Saint Helen's might be a problem some day. He had a factory set of leathers that I had help measure him up for with a tailor's tape in centimeters that Kawasaki had mailed to him. There was some embarrassed closeness that neither of us were used to. He was a skinny guy and didn't weight much more than a hundred pounds probably. He smoked and his idea of training was to run around the house until he was out of breath and then stop, which took two or three laps. The leathers had come back from Kawasaki some weeks later in a 9 x 12 business envelope and at first we thought it was a contract or some contingency paperwork. Inside was a one piece leather suit that fit him like a glove. It should have, it was made of the same thin leather as gloves and if he fell down in it, there was no real protection.

He wore an open face Buco helmet with the face shield cut way up so that he could bury his chin in the little pad in the dip of the gas tank. He stayed tucked in like that all the time, on the straight or in the turns, and never stuck his knees out into the airstream. The leathers were green and white and he had black Lewis boots with pointy toes. I met the guy in charge of the Kawasaki team, and he helped me weld up a brace for the Sprint fairing the first day so I could get it through tech and was very nice about it. There was a little troop of Japanese guys who took care of the motorcycles and there were A1Rs and H1Rs lined up in rows, all shiny new.

The 500 triples were painted up in the Kawasaki neon green livery while the A1Rs where still in their deep red and pearl paint jobs that were so sophisticated. Too bad they didn't stay together very well because on paper they seemed like a winner. On the track they seized with some regularity and were prone to pitch people off when they did so. I had ridden one but didn't like the way it wobbled around in the turns and while it made a different sort of sound when you gave it gas, my butt told me it wasn't any faster than my Sprint, at least in the sensation of speed it gave you. I may have been wrong about that, but it didn't matter, I could not have afforded one anyway.

When the time came for Ron's race they pushed the bikes out to the starting grid. It was different in those days as they had dead motor grids and the announcer would name the riders and their sponsors one by one as the crowd was supposed to respond we guessed. It took a while and a running motor in the days before silencers prevented this approbation from being heard so the grid guys would stop you and tell you to turn it off with that friendly hand across the throat motion. This was a real problem for a guy like me on a four stroke, high compression single that then had to run and bump it off and since the shifter was on the right side. That meant being on the wrong side from anything you'd ever done that with before. If you got it wrong, the piston just came up on compression and stopped there, sending you off or letting you hold on as it fell over to the left taking you with it, something I did a time or two despite my best intentions. In Ron's case it meant you were given the star treatment and only had to stand there and wave to the crowd and then put on your helmet and gloves and wait as the little Japanese mechanics bustled about and fiddled with the bike then pushed it off when the time came and brought it back to you running and ready to go.

I was over at the guardrail watching all of this go on and he looked a bit silly standing there alone as everyone else got pushed and then did a circle to turn around and come back to their starting spot. Soon enough they came riding back and got off, giving him the bike in an awkward exchange since he was on the left and the mechanic was getting off on the right but they worked it out and when the time came for the green flag all looked well. The sound of those races starting back then was deafening because everyone had open exhausts. I had my fingers in my ears as did a good many others, none of us smart enough to think of ear plugs yet. They all took off for turn one except Ron.

The motor of his brand new H1R had died and he sat looking down at it as a herd of little guys in white coveralls came running out saying things in Japanese no one could understand and began pushing him. They pushed him down toward the first turn and it wouldn't start. They pushed him back and it still wouldn't start. The pack had gone onto the backstretch by now and the AMA officials were getting interested in what they were doing and were trying to signal them off onto the pit lane. Ron wouldn't go, knowing that meant he was out of the race. I walked down and stood a few feet away as they changed plugs and he looked at me, unhappy in the extreme, and I could read his mind.

We had worked together all night through hundreds of nights in all weather inside a corrugated shed filled with hammering noise and whirling machinery. We had to be able to tell what the other one was thinking just from their expression without being able to hear. He had risked everything a thousand times to get a factory ride and now that he had one, the damned thing wouldn't run. I caught his eye and pointed under the gas tank. He looked puzzled and looked down then back up and nodded. The petcock lever was horizontal. The gas was off. He seemed calm but I knew that inside he was seething. He whacked one of the men in coveralls on the head and showed them the petcock and they turned it on, pushed him off toward turn one and it caught and fired in no time just as the pack was coming around the carousel behind the pit grandstands. He was starting nearly a full lap behind the field.

The AMA was not happy and I overheard some conversation about black flagging him but the team manager appeared and explained and since Ron was already gone by then there was no real harm so they just let it go. He had disappeared off around turn two into the trees by then as the pack was going into one together after him. What I knew, that none of them knew, was that this was a man with a temper. He could rage, he could be vengeful, he could be cruel. He used me for a ride to the races when he didn't have a ride in something more comfortable and newer. He had talked me into road racing by taunting me night after night as we ran the big press together and put out another issue of the Daily Egyptian.

He found my weakness and worked it hard. He said he was faster than I was. That was my soft spot, which he may have known but I didn't let it show if I could help it. People could say they were bigger or stronger or braver or smarter than I was and I wouldn't protest and would gladly let them have the claim without a contest. But say you are faster and it was unlikely that I would just let it go. I raced and had raced for most of my life by the time I met Ron, and if the equipment held up, I usually won. I was not going to just concede that he was faster than I was. After this day, however, I would keep my mouth shut about how fast Ron Muir was or wasn't.

He came around at the end of lap one and already had bikes behind him, which meant that he had caught and passed bikes that had nearly a full lap head start. By lap two he was maybe half way through the field, and slower progress was made afterward as the faster bikes were slower to catch. I didn't have a stop watch, but by the white flag lap he was in second place and had the leader in sight. No one could believe it. Part of what made it so hard to believe was the way Ron rode a motorcycle. He was old school and rode jockey style. Feet always up on tiptoes on the pegs unless shifting or braking, hands and arms held in tight against the tank and his head down behind the bubble. Nothing stuck out to disrupt the airstream and it was difficult to see that he was making much of an effort. He actually was, however, and the big H1 was a handful to ride and its reputation for being evil handling was hard to reconcile with what we were witnessing.

In the end he fell short by just a few yards and did not win, but none could fault his effort. He came a close second and in another lap, maybe two, would have certainly caught and passed the bike in front of him. Kawasaki should have been pleased, they had built a bike that was the class of the field and had shown superior speed over all comers. Instead they were embarrassed, having lost face. Ron was a happy enough guy when he came in and I congratulated him as did everyone else. He made light of the start line blunder but it was a sore subject and neither of us knew what the real consequences would be. In the end, the team folded and Kawasaki switched to offering contingency prize money to privateers before coming back out again under different management.

The nice man who had been in charge and who had helped me, a novice nobody, get my Sprint through tech, eventually committed suicide. Ron was offered a bike to ride but had to maintain it himself and could expect no help at the races. He tried to get on with other factories but the teams were made and run out of the West coast mostly and he had no connections out there to speak of and had to settle with being a privateer. It was a bitter pill to swallow and the waste of a great talent.

I kept my distance as he dealt with the team that day and didn't look forward to the ride home. When he came over finally, the expert race was about to begin and he suggested that we walk the pit lane to the far end so we could see them taking turn one. There was something about that turn that he had not been satisfied with himself about and he wanted to take a look at how some of the other riders were taking it. I knew what he meant, it was a real test and because the track was so wide and the run off road so distracting going off straight ahead, it was difficult to find a turn in point and take a good line across the wide expanse of the two lane drag strip off into the narrower right hand sweeper that bent away onto the road course.

We missed the start as we were still walking down to our position behind the Armco, but we were there when the leader came around at the end of lap one. I was transformed by what I saw and should flag this moment as none other if such moments were to be ranked. Before that moment, I was feeling pretty good about myself and the fact that I could race a motorcycle. Integral in that was the conceited self-delusion that I could do what anyone else could do – Then came Cal Rayborn.

Ron and I were standing together, one foot up on the Armco, looking down the long straight when the orange and black bike appeared, all alone at the far end of the straight. It swept across the track, leaned over with Rayborn, sticking out head and shoulders on one side wrestling it away from the edge as he shifted up; once; twice; three times and then no more. He came right at us and we could hear the booming of the big vee twin rumbling along after the shifting stopped. He was coming to turn one and had glided across the track from the far edge to the one right next to where we were standing.

He was only feet away when he suddenly lunged off the bike on the right hand side with his upper body and keeping the throttle held wide opened drug the bike around the turn behind him. Ron and I just looked at each other. Had we really just seen what we thought we had? "He didn't let off!" I said to Ron, who was as surprised as I was. He shook his head, partly about what he had seen, and partly to emphasize what he was saying in agreement, "...not a bit."

The pack came on then, Duhamel, and Pierce, and Nixon and the rest, chasing after the disappearing Harley Davidson. They all let off for the turn, some more than others, but unmistakably, they backed off and then turned. Rayborn did not back off at all. It was a 110 mile race and we watched it all, more impressed as time went by. How he was able to do it we were not able to say. None of the others had his skill or determination or whatever it was that let him defy the moment the way none of the others could. If I had not seen it myself I would not have believed it. Hell, I still don't believe it and I saw it myself.

On the ride home we talked about the day and what would happen at our next race, whenever that might be. Ron was looking forward to another team ride that would never come, after all he had turned in a great performance and would no doubt have won but for the error of his mechanics at the start. He still had team leathers and was in a good position, or so he thought. He had gained enough points this season to be an expert next year and thought he had what it took to get out there and mix it up with the best of them. I thought he did too, and said so. We were apparently alone in that.

He was quiet about my ride on the Harley, which was disappointing, but he had never been one to encourage me other than getting me going at road racing. We had had an early conversation about it when he was trying to tell me what the first race would be like and had said that I would be so scared I would pee my pants. I had just looked at him then, and shaken my head. "I don't pee my pants." I told him. He bet me a case of beer on it, and even though I didn't drink, I took the bet anyway. At that first race I was on my X-6 with chambers and remote float Amal carbs off a TD1. It went well enough and he owed me a case of beer afterward, which he said he would buy me whenever I started drinking. I have yet to collect.

I had been happy with my first National Road race performance but had a list of things to improve on that was longer than my list of things I thought I had done exactly right. In particular it had never occurred to me that there were corners in the world that you could take flat out on a motorcycle without letting off of the gas. I filed that away as new information for the day I thought I might find another, or the next time I came back to Indianapolis Raceway Park.

Likewise I saw it as something other than just a mistake when a team of Japanese mechanics who had been brought from around the world at great expense to come to Indiana and put their pride and joy on the track for all to see were so forgetful as to not turn on the gas when the time came. Someone needed to be certain that all was as it should be or it might not be. On the other hand, it was hard to imagine that someone could do everything themselves and at the time I was stewed in ignorance and just didn't know it. Ironically I would sacrifice more than a year of isolation and hard labor and a move to Oregon for a sponsorship only to travel cross country to Daytona and forget to turn the gas on, having the bike die on the line as the field pulled away and I watched without a clue what the problem could be.

While we had been at Indianapolis at that first national race, another novice had come over and asked me if I had a 10mm wrench that he could borrow between practice sessions. I didn't, but I knew that Ron always carried a nice tool box full of such things and I had it in the back of my car. He was nearby so I gave him the courtesy of letting him know what I intended to do, which was let the guy use a wrench. "Absolutely not," was Ron's response, "I don't loan tools to anyone." "What if I needed it?" I asked him, searching for a way around what I saw as an arbitrary position that served no purpose. "Same answer," he said and we sort of looked at one another then to see if the other were just kidding, or serious, or what. He was serious.

"I suppose it's because you don't think you'll get it back," I continued, and was about to add that I would take it, watch it being used, and return it when he stopped me with, "That's not it." And I waited for him to tell me what was 'it'. "I am here to beat everyone," he said, "plain and simple. Whether I beat them in the pits because they didn't bring something they needed and now want to borrow from me or whether I have to pass them on the track to beat them it's all the same to me and the answer is 'no' I won't let it go because they screwed up."

I had to go back and explain to the kid who had asked to borrow a wrench that the answer was 'no' and he was honestly taken off stride by this. "What a jerk," he said, and I had to agree. "It's just the way, he is," I said, apologetically, more or less defending him. "He's still a jerk and whether he's fast or not, being a jerk has a way of catching up with you," the guy said. I agreed and offered to help the guy find what he needed but he had gotten one from someone else by then and I went back to wait for my race and think about it.

On the way home that exchange came back to me, and while it was impossible to connect the two events directly, I had a little inkling of the larger truth that somehow, what goes around comes around. It's too much to believe it's a one to one sort of thing, that's too simple and the universe is not a simple place. If you don't believe me just look up at night and wait until some of those millions of stars collide with one another. Don't waste your time; it's not happening and there's a reason.

Indianapolis had been a real event for me. I had competed with the best in the country and come away convinced I belonged there. I had made a good friend in Rusty Bradley, a fellow Texan, and even though I was now expatriated, it didn't matter; and I 'have seen the elephant' as they say out West – the thing that everyone knows exists but never really hope to see for themselves. I had seen a talent so great that everyone else looked the lesser man - Cal Rayborn.

24.

WHO'S SORRY NOW?

(a poem about watching a frienddie as he
crashes in turn oneat Daytona).

Musical background: *"I'm so lonesome, I could cry"*
(the original by Hank Sr.)

Pointing from the end of the pit lane over toward turn one I say:

"I was just there, behind the Armco in the infield.
Right there, where they come off the banking
right at you – sitting up, braking hard;
each man jostling for position;
Timing their turns.

I knew Rusty Bradley well and liked him.
We went way back and had begun
together on other tracks years
before. He had moved up –
we'd had fun.

Now I was here to signal for him, show him,
With my hands apart or together or just
Some other sign to help him on his way
So he needn't look behind himself
Or need to look away.

When we joked around, things were the same
for the two of us, but always there
were things that had changed
for him; and for me.
Still, we raced.

Many times I would have passed him if I could;
He knew that. He had passed me plenty
and we had laughed about it and
Poked one another like young
cowboys at roundup.

He had the better horse most days and strive
all I might; no amount of grit or 'getty up'
or digging spurs, no matter how I tried,
would make up for that when what
we did together was ride.

There was that one day, at my place, far back
when we were both out on my little track
with the same sort of ponies. Why, Son!
They'd said it could'a been either one –
Just once; I'd won.

As I said, I always liked him, even though
he was Texan and was covered in glory
like I only hoped to have myself
when my race was run and
they told my story.

We spoke of 'luck' with one another
and I saw him as a distant brother,
a twin from different parents.
It made no sense but still
we were SO alike.

I knew that out there he would do the same
things I would do out there just now –
Coming around the banking
In that first big pack of
"Here's how."

We both knew you can only tuck in so much,
Only hold the throttle open so far,
Only grit your teeth so hard
and wait … just …. a
…. little …. longer –

… Longer than the other guys around you.
Later to brake means first to the turn;
First to lean in, first to gas out,
First to the next turn,
– First.

Let them brake, <u>then</u> you brake; The track funnels in.
Intersecting vectors of physics and stop and go
meeting sunlight and colors of bikes
and leathers of riders you know
you can beat.

There's a limit of course to what braking can do,
But the moment's here; the waiting is through.
NOW you writhe and slither and snake,
Sitting up, gas off – You BRAKE;
(*Passed a few*).

All our heroes were out there, racing with you.
Now you've all come to the turn; now you
think you can outdo, something they do
just as good as you. Only <u>you</u> think
you're better. Pooh.

We sort of knew them all – the immortal Gods of Speed;
Romero, and Roberts and Rayborn and Mann oh, man
What a rush, what a feeling, what a need.
To pass one, then the others
To race with Carruthers.

But you're not that much better as it all turned out.
You thought you were, you had no doubt.
You beat them all in the 250 race.
But it's not happening now,
not at this pace.

Later I wondered as I looked back and plundered
Your last moments on earth as my friend
Whether you were distracted by
moments impacted from the
Laps that brought you a win.

Your front wheel comes unglued – just a bit…
it slides you off course – I'm watching it.
There's not time to correct; just a wiggle,
then; DOWN IN A HEAP!, your bike
in the middle.

It only seemed like it happened in super slow motion,
the images burned in my mind with emotion;
deep in my brain . . .again and again.
You with me;somewhere an ocean,
After that – it's insane.

White arms, hands not letting go, bright green legs straddling
the quickly falling bike that is now losing the battle to
stay beneath you. Your smile, your open faced Buco,
   (buck - oh)
all of the rest. **GONE**. Just like that. Too soon;
Too late - Stucco.

For me there has never been a sound just like it.
The tinkling, crashing, sliding, thumping
grinding, clattering noise of you
dying before my
eyes.

Rusty, if I could have, I would have saved you.
You deserved a long and happy life, but ...
You chose instead to ride that Kaw. (cow)
So, Old buddy, I have to ask,
"Who's sorry now?"

25.

A word about the golden rule:

PHILOSOPHICALLY THE GOLDEN RULE is difficult to apply to the competitive world of racing motorcycles but it is none the less valid. Muhammad is not a popular philosopher these days and his followers have been bad neighbors in the contemporary world, but they do give evidence to what we wish was going on rather by example of what we wish were not. In the year 630 by Western counting he said, "Hurt no one so that no one may hurt you." As is frequently the case, the words have been misinterpreted by some to permit gross hurting of others as a preemptive measure and while I do not speak for the Prophet, I am fairly certain that was not what he meant.

Before him Jesus said, "So in everything, do unto others as you would have them do unto you, for this sums up the law and the prophets."

Like all summations, there may have been particular discords glossed over in that but it is a clear enough notion that seems very hard to reconcile with cutting someone off in a corner or taking an unfair advantage in the rules that others have not seen. As four time Indianapolis 500 winner A.J. Foyt observed, "Winning isn't everything – it's the only thing." But if I want to be a good person, <u>and</u> win races, how do I reconcile the two sets of fairly clear directives at the end of the day? Can I just put my Texas Foyt racer self away in a logic tight compartment and be schizophrenic about it, or is something more required?

I was fortunate to meet him at a USAC sprint race, and get his autograph on my program. He was gracious enough about it, and had a thick beefy hand that was tough to shake. As for doing unto others as they do unto you, he had mentioned elsewhere that he believed in that, and also in doing it first.

In spite of its intuitive appeal, it is less clear how much practical guidance can actually be found in the golden rule. Its sheer simplicity makes it an easy target for critical sniping. People take their pleasures in very different ways ("Hurt me," begged the masochists, "No," said the sadist) including racing motorcycles, an activity which I will describe as an outsider might see it for examination:

> *A group of otherwise intelligent and talented men, who are successful enough to have gathered support and resources sufficient to allow them to travel great distances and be at leisure for long periods of time, migrate back and forth across the planet to meet and race one another on motorcycles new and old on different racetracks.*

> *It is a dangerous and even deadly pastime that involves sleep deprivation, serious injury, strained and broken relationships, and mental stress great enough to discourage all but the most devoted. As a reward they get a small token of their participation and perhaps, if all the conditions allow it, they may win.*

Now if we take this set of circumstances and translate it into any other activity, we would find the average sensible person to be critical of it for good reason. The reward does not justify the risk, leaps to mind. There is no prize money or real fame involved and for many, it's largely personal aggrandizement, which is a selfish act. Put lipstick on a pig and it's still a pig.

As a business model it fails entirely. The motorcycles are far more valuable in other uses than on the racetrack as shown by the disproportionately high prices they fetch when auctioned relative to their cost when new. They consume tires and fuel and internal parts at an alarming rate and all of these have escalated in cost to the point that calmer heads shake at the spectacle that is vintage racing.

So is it a golden rule setting? I think so. I suggest that rather than seeing the golden rule as a moral panacea, it is more fruitful to regard it as an essential ingredient of ethical thinking in a foundational sense. It makes a demand for consistency in our conduct with one another and requires fairness. It requires us to put ourselves in the position of another when considering a situation. It is an antidote for the sort of moral myopia that often afflicts egocentric individuals when their own self interests are at stake.

Do I find joy in winning a race? Yes I do. Do I find joy in seeing someone else win? I am happy for them, and so I must say yes again, but I admit it is a lesser joy. That would be the better man, the expert in a field of novices as it were, if the others are busily worrying only about themselves.

On the grid, when I work as an official and help the riders line up as the grid sheet has dictated, I have a moment or two to observe the behaviors of those about to risk their lives in each other's company. It is likely that none of them see it that way, but equally true that any one of them would admit that the chance of a fatal injury is a real possibility. Still, some are engaged with their comrades and will fist bump one another or give a nod in acknowledgment before the starting sequence begins. Why not? I mean it has nothing to do with how fast their bike will go or whether they will hit their marks and have done all the things that needed to be done for that perfect meeting of machine and moment ahead of them.

Is the tire pressure right for this temperature? Is the jetting optimal for the atmospheric conditions? Morning practice may have been wonderful, but that was hours ago and its hotter and dryer now and there have been other races before this one and things may or may not have been leaked upon the track in places they have not seen. None of these problems or the solutions available now in the form of resource management are affected by the simple act of human kindness that is shown by giving a nod or a bump of the fist to another racer waiting to share facing such issues. The man or woman who has done everything right and continues to do so for the duration of the race ahead will be the winner. There is honor in that.

In golden rule terms we ask ourselves if we want to grid next to the S.O.B. who glares hatred at us and gestures negatively before we begin. It is not in vogue as it once was to be that person and I am glad for the change. Bad Bart may have been able to move over one or two by intimidating them out of his way, but today he would as likely find himself on his ass if he tried it now. It's not just that we are more aware of such things or that we are kinder than we used to be, not really. It is that we are collectively intolerant of bullies, having had enough of them in every other thing we do and now, here on the racetrack, we're simply not going to take it any more.

My business on the track is managing what I have brought to ride to face the forces against me in getting and keeping it up to speed. It's speed after all that wins races. That would be the product in a business analysis of what we do or try to do with our little factories we have put together and now manage from on high. If I can do it better than you can, then I can win with proper management provided I don't misjudge some moment ahead of me. If you can pass me, go ahead, but don't hit me in the process or block my way out of malice or cause another rider to go down. Do as you would be done by, that's my golden rule, and may the best man (or woman) win.

26.

The Shadow Knows

THERE IS SOMETHING SEDUCTIVE about speed. From the time we were
toddlers and headed off across the room toward something we wanted
speed was an issue. So was balance and propulsion and judgment and
strength but not courage. We were too young to know better and did
not think of consequences then. This happens repeatedly with speed.

I was heading back to Berkley in the late sixties and had gone to
a student union bulletin board at a University in the Midwest to find
anyone who might want to go west and help with gas. I found a pair
of New Yorkers who had been casting about aimlessly and had pinned
a simple "Going West?" note up with their phone number. I called it,
an agreement was reached and we were on the road in less time than
it takes to say "Bad Idea". They wanted to light up their recreational
substances in the van and I stopped and put them out and we had a
discussion about things. I was no prude and fairly ambivalent about
what people did to themselves, but I was not going to be a party to
a felony arrest and since we were young and traveling across foreign
jurisdictions, we were subject to stop and search for no special reason.
I explained this to them and recounted the loss of a buddy who was
now living in a Texas prison for something no more offensive than
what they were proposing.

We reached an accommodation – I would drive and plead ignorance if someone stopped us, and they would not partake while in the
van, but would 'rest' themselves at the rest areas if I agreed to stop at

them when they came along. That deal, and two fifty dollar bills, got them a ride to the University of California at Berkley from whence they intended to move on to points unknown.

All went well enough and we reached the outskirts of Denver, Colorado the following afternoon, skirting the city on the interstate. The sun was shining, it was late April, and unseasonably warm. On a hillside ahead, people were skiing and we could clearly see them enjoying themselves. There had been a 'rest stop' a few miles back and my riders were in high spirits and the suggestion was made that we stop and try it ourselves.

I agreed, since I could use the break, and was not about to let them drive. As for trying it, we didn't have any of the necessary equipment so I did not think it I would actually happen. I parked in a snow covered lot that was on a steep slope and deliberately chose a space at the edge right by the exit so that I would be able to back out and be on my way without any drama over the lack of traction that front motor placement causes in rear wheel drive vans.

I went to the ski shop where a 'rentals' sign was hanging out and they tagged along. I was surprised to find a friendly proprietor who looked at the clock and told us there was less than an hour left of daylight skiing and then the slopes were resurfaced overnight so he would give us a discount on what we needed. Boots, poles, skis and one lift ticket for $10. That was within our budget so we agreed and soon the three of us were standing out on the snow with little or no idea of what to do other than the rapid fire instructions and cautions he had told us as we got ready and put our things in the lockers he gave us.

There were two choices; to the left was a rope tow that went up a grade to a fairly flat area where you could turn yourself around and then ski back down the short distance to the lodge as often as you liked until you felt comfortable with it, or, off to the right was the chair lift, that looked like park benches suspended from a wire cable car carousel set up with a short line of people waiting to be collected.

We conferred and considering the time available elected to go for the chair lift, since we only had a ticket for one ride, and the day was about over. There was an operator in the shed watching us, and he seemed cheerful enough as we positioned ourselves like the few ahead of us had and were caught by the moving bench right about the knees and swept up and off our skis into the air. It was awkward and thrilling and the view was spectacular. None of us knew anything about skiing.

The New Yorkers rode together and I was on a bench in front of them with a chatty four year old without poles. To make conversation I pointed that out to her and she said she didn't need them since she knew how to ski already and was closer to the ground than we were so she could get up and down by herself. Then she offered to teach me and I said that if she could do it, I could do it. It was then that I saw the first of the black diamonds.

Ski slopes are rated in terms of difficulty, which translates to speed in my mind, and when I had the boys' attention I told them I was going to take my one and only run on the black diamond trail and pointed at a sign. They nodded and talked to one another and then yelled at me shaking their heads in disagreement. So it was that we parted company the instant we were off the lift because there was no flat ground to stand on and I took the path to the right marked by the black diamonds.

I was immediately in trouble, even though the ski rental guy had given us the shorter easier to manage skis and a bit of instruction about how to snowplow if we found ourselves going too fast. I was going straight down what appeared to be a nearly vertical drop and all thoughts about snow plowing were gone in a flash. There was a turn to the left coming and I made some gestures with my feet but they didn't seem to make any difference about my direction. I was picking up speed all the time and could hear screaming. It took a bit to recognize that voice as my own, but I had commenced to holler as soon as I realized I was going too fast to survive, which was very nearly as soon as I had begun.

Some bumps appeared and I managed to flex my knees enough to soak them up and was flailing around with my poles to keep my balance. I flashed past a little tike fortunate not to strike her and recognized her as my former seat mate on the lift on the way up. She caught up with me in a moment and was saying something but I couldn't make it out so she skied up ahead and bent her knees crouching down and pointed at her legs and then showed me, quickly, how to put more weight on one ski than the other before waving and disappearing on ahead. I tried it, and to my great surprise, managed to obtain a modicum of directional control, although I still had no idea how to moderate my speed.

I began aiming myself across the broad avenue that this steep bit led onto finally and in doing so had to struggle more and more to keep my balance each time as I turned back across the face of it. In no time at all I could see the trail was ending and I was coming to the lodge and the parking lot. It appeared to be the end of all things for me given the speed that only seemed to increase itself with every save from the disaster it offered that I had so far I managed. I wrestled with what to do about that.

Finally I decided the best course was just to sit down and let my butt do the braking, thinking in my addled brain that I would be able to avoid my skis as I did so. I convinced myself in the few instants available that this might work. It's funny what we imagine will happen not having tried something before. I sat down at what I thought was the last possible moment, but instead of missing my skis, I landed right on them and was now picking up even more speed as my bindings held me to the skis and my position decreased my wind resistance and took away any possibility of steering. People were looking and waving their arms like maybe I should know I was doing something incorrectly.

I waved back, I knew that already. What I didn't know was what else to do. I was headed straight for the rental shop and in the moment before I arrived I came upon a large pile of softer snow that gobbled up my ski tips and stopped my skis in a heartbeat, launching me out of them and over the pile onto the sidewalk with an unceremonious thump, which abruptly ended the noises I had been making for some time. Even though I had been telling myself, "Hit and roll," over and over in my mind, when the time came I only got as far as the "HIT" part.

People gathered, I was helped up and someone retrieved my skis for me. I thanked them numbly and then sat on a railing, checking to see if all of my extremities were still working. They did and by some unexplainable kindness of fate I had once again survived a gigantic error in judgment and could walk away.

In time the boys appeared battered and bruised but otherwise all right and we turned in the equipment with our thanks and headed for the parking lot. Well, I did at least; they went off to find a 'rest area' as I headed back to the van.

Here is where the story turns to what I find interesting. My close brush with death was imagined, after all, and falls from skis are survivable and common so all was well. I had already had a talk with myself about the joy of speed for its own sake and had decided that judicious courting might be a better approach than accepting a 'come on in the water's fine' invitation from her next time. More foreplay, less danger of a climatic death, that's the ticket.

She could hurt me. She could kill me. What was I thinking! I got in the van to see if it was going to start this time and to my relief the big Ford V-8 came to life immediately and all seemed well. I waited and thought absently about the moment watching a beautiful glowing sun disappear into the Rocky Mountains. The boys came and piled in, laughing and red eyed, and we were ready to set off again on our journey west.

It was then that I looked in the rear view mirror and spotted the black Porsche with the big wing on the tail that said "drug dealer" or "very expensive" or both. It was parked behind me, on the access road for the parking lot, directly beneath a 'Do Not Park Here' sign. In order to be on my way, I would have to back up in less than ten feet, while turning the wheels sharply away from the car next to me, and then pull forward in the half lane of the road the driver of the Porsche had left to me. It would be close, but I could visualize it and so I believed, as youthful brains do, that I could make it so.

I put the van in drive to see if I could pull forward a bit to make it easier, but my back wheels just spun. We were on a serious slope, after all, and that was why I had parked here in the first place. I knew that if I had parked nose down, facing another person parked, that I could never expect to find the traction needed to back away from them and pull out with the engine up front and the drive wheels in the back. With that in mind I had circled the lot and come back to this spot right before the exit gate where I could pull up hill and park and then just back out without any danger of anyone blocking me in and with the help of gravity and momentum, our great friends in such spots. I thought it had been fairly farsighted. Before WW I, the nations of Europe thought that some entangling alliances might be a good idea too.

The sun was shining brightly and people were streaming out of the ski area at the end of a beautiful day on the slopes. I had to wait a bit until no one was walking behind me before putting it in reverse and then slowly and carefully commencing the maneuver I had so thoughtfullyplanned. You know, you would think that after the reign of terror by speed, snow and gravity over me on the slopes just a few moments before I might have anticipated what was to come, but NO! I went ahead and put it in reverse.

No sooner than the van began moving down hill, on the ice, with its new layer of sunshine born slipperiness, did I realize that I was not going to be able to stop it. I let off the gas and applied brake – still moving backward; I put it in drive and gave it gas – still going backward; I turned the wheels to make it change direction – it did not turn. Nothing made any difference. The drums beat faster at the command of the sweaty overseer from Ben Hur; Charleston Heston pulled at the oars; Ramming Speed!

With a sickening crunch the 2 7/8 inch chrome trailer hitch ball firmly mounted on its all steel, TIG welded hitch attached to the rear of my two ton van caved in the passenger's door of the Porsche and then proceeded to punt it off the access road and into the adjacent ditch as I watched numbly in the rear view mirror. "Some objects may be closer than they appear" it said. Yeah? Not this one, it was closer than it looked and it had looked to be too close.

I looked over at my two help-mates and they looked back at me with worried looks and bloodshot eyes. Police would come. There would be conversations and questions. We were all going to prison. This was not good. Fortunately for me that "Do Not Park Here" sign had caught the rear end of the Porsche and spun it around as it was sent sliding into the ditch where it came to a stop just a few yards off the road showing the driver's door and making it look more or less all right to the casual, up here on the parking lot, observer. My van had stopped on the little berm at the edge of the lot and I got out to have a look.

From here, it didn't look too bad, I went down and had a look at the other side. It looked a locomotive had center punched the door. I was sick. I knew that I could not afford to buy gas for a car like this, let alone pay to have one fixed. I climbed back up out of the ditch with some difficulty to find a growing crowd of spectators and knew from experience that someone in the group would step forward and take charge. My greatest fear was that the owner was either there already, or would soon appear. Nature abhors a vacuum after all, so I decided to fill it.

"All right," I heard someone up the hill say in a big clear voice authoritatively, "Let's get this van out of the way and stop blocking the road." People looked to one another and thought that was a good idea since they all wanted to use the road too. I climbed back up the hill and I got in and steered as they went in a group to the back corner on the drivers side and pushed it sideways until the nose came down the hill and with spinning tires the rear end came around to where it was pointed out of the parking lot. I put it in park, but left it running and got out, not sure what would happen next, but before I could say anything, the taller of the New York boys pulled a pen and a notepad from his pea jacket pocket and said with the same big voice, this time aimed at me, "All right, Buddy, let me see your license!" and held out his hand.

The crowd around us nodded approval, sensing that the right thing was being done and I took out my wallet and handed over my license as he made a show of copying down the license plate number off of the van and then something else as he held the license out before handing it back. He waved the paper around at the crowd saying. "I was unable to locate the owner of this improperly parked vehicle to have it towed, but we will give him this information and take care of this." He pointed at the car resting in the ditch as he said it, and then added, doing a nice job of looking people in the eye, "A wrecker is already on the way to remove it." There were nods of approval and he then scampered down the hill and put the note under the windshield wiper for all to see which seemed to satisfy everyone.

Meantime a huge traffic jam was building up on the road and so we got back in the van and managed to get it moving again and get out of the parking lot and back onto the interstate where I drove along slowly, feeling miserable. What a cruel twist of fate this had been. I could see both sides of it and felt like the gods had been having fun at my expense. Sure the guy shouldn't have parked there, but I had failed to wait for him to move and could have, or I could have been more careful on the ice covered parking lot, or I could have not stopped to ski at all. If only I had done this or that instead. So many unexpected outcomes from so many unseen choices until they were already gone by, like the slopes without the black diamonds.

It was Wyoming before we stopped again and I was still under a black cloud. The boys went off to find a 'rest area' as I fueled. They came back with moon pies and ding dongs from the convenience store, laughing as usual. Making life seem better artificially was attractive at that moment, but I took a pass. We headed off and finally one of them could no longer control himself. "We have to tell him!" He blurted out, jerking his thumb at me, and then laughed harder and harder. The other one seemed to agree but was incapable of composing himself beyond a nod. "Tell me what?" I asked. "Oh, man," the tall one said, "the look on your face when I had you give me your license was priceless!" "Yeah," I said, failing to see the humor in it, "I bet it was."

He beamed at me then and asked, "Would ya like to know what the note said?" "You wrote down my license and registration information," I said but he was shaking his head and grinning. "Not a chance, man, I ain't stupid," he answered and they broke out laughing again and didn't stop for some time. I was beginning to understand that he had written something else instead, for which I supposed I was grateful, although I did feel bad about it. Still, I wanted to know what message awaited the guy with the gleaming new Porsche parked where it shouldn't have been. "What did it say?" I asked him. He composed himself, making a serious face and again assuming his 'give me your license' demeanor. In a deep baritone he said, "This is only a warning! The Shadow." As soon as he said it they lost their composure completely and I had to say, so did I. it was darkly funny.

We were really just kids then, none of us twenty years old, and I had no insurance or visible means of support other than the odd job I could find now and then between races. I worked hard, didn't steal or do drugs and minded my own business. All I wanted to do was race. We did not belong at a posh ski area and no one would ever be able to place us at the scene again given the way events had unfolded. There is another side to the story with insights of its own that I cannot tell. Some guy, driving a car that was too expensive to be put at risk in any way, parks it exactly where he is not supposed to park it which is also directly downhill from a decrepit van full of motorcycles and tools with a trailer hitch aimed right at it on an ice covered parking lot.

He had his chances; that's all I'm saying. I don't know the whole story because I don't know why he was there or what he was doing. I'd bet he had insurance but I didn't know everything then and I don't know it now. It was out of my hands as soon as things were set in motion. I had that same feeling when I got off the chair lift. I felt foolish for feeling that way when the little girl skied right past me trying to give me advice. I had the feeling again for screaming I didn't want to die when I couldn't stop at the end of the run and crashed into a snow bank and flipped over onto the sidewalk out of my skis. I felt foolish afterward for thinking I was about to die in the moments before I crashed when I wound up without injury a few feet away. Then when I sat at the wheel of the van and watched the Porsche getting closer and closer in my rear view mirror and kept trying everything I could think of to keep from hitting it and none of it seeing that none of it was working I felt terrified at what the consequences might be. Seeing the damage, being called to account for it, confessing my liability, had filled me with a sense of dread that was born of that moment of speed beyond control as I slid down the slope to disaster.

But no disaster came because, by some quirky marvel of odd coincidences, I happened to have a companion who can still manage to pull off an authority figure act while stoned well enough to convince a crowd of strangers that he is doing all that needs to be done to make things right. Go figure.

I love life; my life anyway. It is full of things like this, so quirky and uncontrollable, taking their turn at turning my world around this way and that. That night there was no moon and there were no clouds to block my view of the millions of stars shining brightly down on me from the clear dark sky. I didn't know why they were there or what they were telling me. Our only eight track tape had been eaten by the player and there was no radio. I drove along in the forced silence, trying to stay warm and trying to get through this transition into another phase of life that I hoped would be better.

There must be some reason for all of this, that much was obvious, but I was not smart enough to figure it out and there were too many unsolvable unknowns in the equation for a guy like me to sort through. I drove on across the mountains into Utah and then Nevada where the guy at the gas station offered me "double or nothing" on the pump if I just let it click off on its own as he filled it up. I agreed and he stood back with his hands up and said, "Call it" and I said "Even" just before it stopped itself at 16 dollars and sixteen cents. He smiled. "You're a lucky man," and stuck out his hand. "I am indeed," I said, taking it and letting him rub some of it off for himself. Years later I would be assigned number 16 as an expert road racer and I had to smile, remembering that decades before someone had told me I was lucky when that number came up. Coincidence? Maybe, but maybe there was a reason for it.

27.

What if God was one of us?

I ASK MYSELF WHAT God needs from me and the answer is obvious – nothing. I am a grateful person by nature and I speculate that some part of my nature is reflective of its creator although I have nothing to base that upon other than my feeling about it. Does that mean then that horrible awful people without a grateful bone in their body were made by some other God? ; Some lesser God?; Some greater God?

When there is a book out there attributed to God says, "Thou shalt have no other gods before me" is it saying there are other gods out there?

Since I have no way of testing these hypotheses there is little use in pondering them but for my own sake and for my hopeful pleasure at thinking I have some relationship working with some terrifically powerful force in the universe. Still, it is my nature to think about such things and since I am fairly sure at this point in my life that now is the time to sort this out if I am ever going to do it. Actually it is a problem I have been working on as long as I can remember but someone always had a ready answer and I seemed reluctant to trust myself enough to wave them off.

I think to myself what God might say if we were to have a conversation. Right off the bat, I admit that I would be bold enough to ask,

"Why have you given me a mind to wonder and the power to imagine that we might ever have any sort of dialogue at all and exchange views on some level?"

I imagine God might answer, "Why not?"

It is silly speculation of course, to imagine such a conversation, but since I have, I may as well give it some thought regardless of its origins or potentiality. I could only hope that an omniscient, omnipotent being might like knowing that some part of His creation understands some small part of His great work. Knowing that is a foolish personification of a being that exists beyond human limitations and feelings, I still realize that the conversation has already taken place a million times over.

If He is who He claims to be then he knows my heart, my every thought, and knows as surely as I do that I do not doubt Him or his purpose or his abilities. Neither do I question the decision to not reveal it all to me but instead to permit me to thrash around in the dark like this, taking swings at everything I think I can reach, whether I can or not. Some things I don't want to know. I don't want to know when I shall die, or my wife or my children or from what causes. I may recognize abstractly that death is universal and acknowledge my desire to find eternal life in His company but, and this is problematic, I don't see why He needs to hear that from me. It is the human condition after all and surely He knows that.

I have seen my parents die, and I have to admit that there was something deeply troubling about it. I grieved of course, but not as I thought I would, or when I thought I would. Their absence changed my world, and I suspect now that what I grieved most about was that change. When we are young we only think we know what death is. When we are old we hope we know what it brings. Scientists coldly tell us it means nothing other than the end of cell division and the cessation of mental activity followed by the onset of decay. If that is the truth, then I don't know why they bother to get up in the morning or kiss their wives or hug their children or hope for the future. It's pointless, isn't it?

My mother died hard, after a hard life, and I was at her side. My father lost himself in a slow dementia bit by bit two decades later after having had another family. He had not been a loyal person but wandered a good bit from one place or person to another waiting for his luck to come back or for the feeling to come to him that he had found his niche. So far as I know it never happened. I have a picture of him sitting on a model T lined up with other boys his age on theirs before a race at a country fairground somewhere when he was about 12. He told me that he had thought to soak the wooden spoked wheels in the creek ahead of time so they didn't fly apart in the turns but he didn't mention if he had won or not and I suspected that he would have mentioned it if he had.

We were strangers, mostly, and did not spend much time together until I went to work for him in the oilfield where I found him distant and unforgiving, not just to me, but to everyone. My mother was not like that. They seemed fated to be together for a while, what with their odd symbiosis of names. He had a certain charm I supposed and others always said to me how much they like him. I didn't see that side of him since he didn't make any effort to charm me. Mother on the other hand was genuine through and through and had a cocky assurance that made you believe her when she told you something.

She had been overhauling her father's 85 hp Ford V-8 when they met and was covered in grease and oil with just her feet sticking out from under the bumper. He had come to the fender to say something smart to who ever it was that had just asked for the "...damn nine sixteenth" and was surprised to find it was a red headed woman from out west. He gave her the wrench.

Bill and Judy were brought together by an unnamed moment and stayed together over the names they brought to it. "It just seemed that we should be together," she told me once, reminiscing after he had moved on to someone else, "I never thought about what I would do if he wasn't there."

Would a God who has an infinite number of things to consider work out something as small as that?

Well, it's hard to say, but He gets affirmation for the wonder of His creation with every breath I take, with every idea I have, both good and bad and there are and have been millions like me and there will be millions more. That does not mean that I am a subscriber to some particular channel that claims to have a direct connection or high speed access. I see, that's all, I know something of it all, but mostly I know that there is so much more to know.

I like to think I am special but that is my problem, not His, and my wish for His personal attention to my own problems is probably just some delusion of my own. We talk; well at least I have spoken at Him. His answers don't come back to me in the sort of voice I hear in the movies where he is embodied with human qualities but I have no doubt that He's been present a time or two as I struggled mightily with something.

Here and there I have had moments of doubt about whether a kind and loving god would allow this or that to happen; Children dying of painful cancer comes to mind. Despite these lapses, I have to say that I see more good than bad in all that is going on and do not credit mere chance or science or the progress of mankind with making life better on the planet in general. I can see room for improvement, but that can always be seen.

There are things divine at work in the passage of time, I can see that as well. My quantum physicists friends like to see all things as merely some random sequence of events without design or purpose. I find it humorous that someone can be in the presence of such an awesome expanse of created matter and space and think nothing of it other than it is expansive and spatial and so might be measured and weighed and its workings explained somehow by imaginary cats in boxes of poison.

Oh, I don't mock them, I get the paradox and understand some of the math and know how badly they would like for there to be certainty and be the one to point it out so that it can be understood and therefore demystified.

But 'Infinite' is a difficult concept to grasp. Actually it is not amenable to grasping at all, it is too large for that. One must remember that infinite possibilities for the explanation of why things happen are also available, regardless of how one likes to limit their own search for the truth to one book or another handed down from the past. Once you have this universe pinned down precisely are you ready to admit that there might be others? Aachen's razor is as poor an excuse for science as I have heard as the simplest answer is seldom, if ever, the correct one in my experience.

I've lost my car keys in some ridiculous places. If I had limited myself in my search for them to the shelf near the door where logically they belong I never would have found them. Those keys, and the keys to other things, could be in any number of places which brings up issues of probability and the relationship of different possibilities to the truth.

Let's say I've lost my keys again, where might they be? Well they could be on the shelf where they are supposed to be, and since I most frequently put them there out of habit, and statistically that is most likely where they will be, then the law of probability tells me that is where they are. Looking there I don't find them, so where should I look now? If I had made a chart of everywhere I had ever put them, and knew, statistically speaking, how many times out of a thousand I put them here or there or wherever, that may tell me where they are more likely to be found, but it will not tell me where they are. The truth may be something entirely different.

I may pat myself on the back for figuring out a model and making calculations to demonstrate the likelihood of a particular outcome but it may not be the truth of where the keys are. I need the keys, I have places to go. I want the truth, not a theory about what the truth might be, or could be, or even probably is. I have extra sets of keys made and keep them in a particular place for the times this circumstance comes again to test me and inevitably, sometime after I have begun using the 'spare' keys, the lost ones turn up. What does that tell me?

So why bring motorcycle racing into any of this? Because it is a crucible of thought and action and probability. Get it wrong and it can blow up in your face. It has a way of vaporizing all the trivial things that trouble us for a little while and shows us what we can do, or can't do, depending on the circumstances. It is esoteric and enlightening at the same time. Motorcycle racers care about such things even though they don't give them these labels. How fast can I take that corner ahead of me on this track with these conditions? If I assigned the perfect entry speed a number, that is if I could quantify it somehow, would that help me?

The first book I published about motorcycle racing thirty years ago was that sort of book. It described the racetracks of America from the seat of a Yamaha GP bike and suggested that there were numbers you could assign after practice for yourself that would let you remember how many downshifts for this turn or that one and then how many upshifts afterward onto the next straight. It was racing tablature, or that was all it was meant to be. My understanding of things was limited then, but I could play the recorder well and so I got by. The symphony of the universe is far more complex.

That was what racing was for me then. On a finely tuned bike, my thought process mostly involved not making a mistake by downshifting too far and overwinding the motor or coming out of a turn in the wrong gear and losing my drive. I didn't have to worry about where to turn or how far to lean it over, I just let those things take care of themselves. I was sincere about putting out some useful information but sincerity is no measure of truth and I should have been paying more attention to what is true instead of just what worked for me in a given corner on a given day.

Many racers keep some sort of race diary for their motorcycles, and it is a good idea in a number of ways. How many hours on that crankshaft? Those pistons? That chain? Are factors in preventative maintenance that let you know when it's time to replace certain parts. It is only one factor, however, and other means are available and time honored. Holding a chain sideways by the end and seeing how far it droops is another way of telling how much slack has found its way into the clearance between the pins and the side plates of a roller chain. Too much slack lets the distance spread from pin to pin under acceleration and deceleration, resulting in worn sprockets as the chain pulls and pushes against the face of the teeth.

Eventually a chain will fail, which is one of the worst things that can happen since the result can be a locked wheel and a crash so we like to buy new chains when we need to, but not before. It is one of the inherited traits of chain driven cycles that they are subject to chain failure. So why not just put a new chain on for every race? Now we come to the crux of the preventative maintenance problem: if we replace all the parts every time, what is left of the original machine?

They say they have George Washington's hatchet that he used to chop down the cherry tree. The handle has been replaced five times and the head only twice but it's the original hatchet. Keep in mind where we are here in our discussion about all things - The infinite possibilities of what matters in our universe and our quest for the truth of things.

I have a rear brake lever for a 1966 Harley Davidson CRTT 250cc road racer that was built for CalRayborn to ride. I can hold it in my hand and turn it over and admire its design and weight and chrome plating. Is there anything of Cal Rayborn there? Well, no, actually, since the bike was built in Italy for anyone to ride and sent over to America where Harley-Davidson assigned it to him but he decided to ride a Yamaha for Don Vesco, which royally pissed off Dick O'Brien who sold the Sprint which is how it came to me and came to be my first race bike. There were a few spares with it in a cardboard box, two front sprockets, three rear ones, and a rear brake lever. The bike is gone now, along with the sprockets, but I kept the brake lever.

In later years I came to know both Rayborn and Vesco a bit. When they were on their way to and from AMA national road races they stayed at our shop and ate at our house and hung out between Midwest events. So did Kenny Roberts and Kenny Woodworth and a host of other determined fast men on their way to greater things. We had an open shop policy for racers and a large supply of off street parking since our dealership had once been a grocery store.

After Rayborn had finished third at Talladega on Vesco's bike, behind Ginger Malloy who won on a TD2 and Kel Carruthers who was second on a TD3, he crashed it somewhere. Cal needed a new seat as a result of that mishap and Don obliged by putting on a spare he was carrying around with him and threw the old one in the trash at our shop. Sometime after the circus moved on, it was left to me to clean the place up. I found the seat in the trash and saved it.

I didn't save it because Cal Rayborn had ridden on it, I saved it so that I could make a mold off of it and build a seat like it for my own Yamaha, which I did. The original was covered with stickers from Don's effort to get contingency payments and to honor whatever promises of sponsorship deals he had made since the money to go racing is a constant problem for racers. I had the same problem; we all did to some degree. Well, most of us did.

Rich kids didn't seem to have a problem having whatever money would buy but I noticed it didn't by them everything. When they were in a turn with me for instance, waiting for that last second to brake and still make the turn, it didn't buy my moving over for them just because they were rich and I was not alone in that. Racing is cruelly egalitarian. Rich and the poor alike own as much of the track as they can hold on to.

So now I have this seat. It is the very one that Cal Rayborn himself raced on, sat his butt upon, rode as fast as he could make it go and then went too fast somewhere and crashed with. Does it matter in the great scheme of things that Cal Rayborn is the one that did those things with it as I hold it now and look at it and feel what it is telling me?

You bet your ass it does. It may not matter if we weighed it or measured it or ran it through a mass spectrometer to see what it is made of or dissected it somehow finely enough to see what its molecules were doing with one another. But, it matters to me because I knew him, saw what he could do with a motorcycle, and knew that he had something going on there that science has no words for. Of course I also remember how he died and how stupid I thought it was once I learned the details. I don't have words for that either.

Philosophically then, if I were to try to put some meaningful analysis to why things are the way they are and what racing motorcycles might have to do with it, I would point to the Zoopraxiscope. It was a fairly simple device that took a feature of our mind's own workings and created moving pictures from still images. Of course there had to be still pictures first, and that was an amazing development of its own, taking place before our civil war.

Almost immediately someone had the great idea of putting two camera's on a bar a few feet apart to take a photo of the same scene and then putting those images on a card side by side to be put in a viewer which made it look 3 dimensional. Looking at those old images now, we know what creates the illusion. But still it gives us something more than what just a photograph gave us of what it must have been like to be there.

When I was a kid in the early 1950s I had no idea how that stereoscopic magic happened inside the little disc viewers that showed me the world in three dimension from two tiny bits of film. I spent hours on my back looking up at the light so the images would be as real as possible. Finally I had the bright idea of using carbon paper to put over a hole I cut in a cardboard box with a cutout for my neck so I could have it over my head as I lay on the floor. In the paper I had poked pin holes that mimicked the stars as nearly as I had patience for and I could pretend that I was looking up into the night sky. It was an illusion of course, just as the night sky is an illusion of what is up there.

What we see when we look at the stars are light waves sent from millions of years ago that have traveled over unimaginably great distances to be here as we look and so we are seeing the past right before our eyes. Something altogether different may be going on way off out there the moment we look.

In between the time photography was invented and I had made my starlight box, Eadweard Maybridge developed a device in 1879 that took still photographic images of a moving thing, like a horse running past a number of cameras, and put them on a disc to be spun by a crank past a slit where they could be viewed to appear as a moving image. When we look at those discs now, what strikes us isn't that he thought of it, it is how few glimpses are needed to create such a complex illusion. Our mind fills in the gaps from its experience with such things and does it so seamlessly that we are able to suspend our disbelief that there might be a moving horse in there somewhere and see instead the truth of what happened, that someone created a device that gave us enough glimpses of the truth of what had actually been going on to let us perceive it for what it was.

A motorcycle is such a device, or it can be. James Dean raced his CZ on dirt tracks in Indiana as a fifteen year old and later said it was the only time he felt whole. I was also born in Indiana and raced a CZ on dirt tracks but had something of a different reaction. I felt like I was being torn apart rather than being made whole. I enjoyed the speed and the wind it made moving past me, but I was not so big on the grit in my teeth or the bruises on the backs of my calves the solid footpegs made or the blisters on the sides of my thumbs the hard rubber of the handgrips made. James Dean and I were simpatico, or could have been if I had been more like him. Actually we were alike in only a few ways that I can figure, that we are Hoosiers and that motorcycles played an important role in our lives as did racing.

He moved on later to a Triumph twin and when the girl he had fallen in love with married someone else, he was sitting on it, gunning the straight piped motor, as she emerged from the church on her wedding day. He roared away down the street leaving her symbolically behind, or trying to, having turned to his motorcycle and speed to heal his broken heart. I doubt that worked, at least it didn't for me.

He made other mistakes and we've heard about them. The Triumph he rode on the street had nobby tires. He raced cars and had a new Porsche Spider which he had decided to drive down to Salinas for a race, taking his mechanic with him. Apparently Dean wanted to break in the motor of the new car gently, a lesson he had learned the hard way after burning a valve in a newly rebuilt Royal Enfield he had purchased in Indiana and was riding back to New York years before.

That mistake had left him stranded on the Pennsylvania Turnpike in the winter time, where the local radio station was devoted to Polka music. I have been there too. That accordion driven insanity was probably playing on the radio of the Indian shop where he finally had the bike hauled in to be repaired and while he waited for an estimate and tried not to polka, he was smitten by a gold pinstriped 1952 Indian Warrior.

The TT model of that bike had been the AMA national champion the year before and he had to have one. He worked out a trade and had his agent forward the necessary money to make it happen; then kept the Indian in storage in a garage in Greenwich Village when not riding it. A part time motorcycle mechanic there named Steve McQueen made a lasting friendship with him out of their mutual appreciation of motorcycles and racing.

McQueen also moved to California and also raced motorcycles, even though he was both rich and famous by then. But for Dean, the lesson learned about driving a new motor too hard too soon, brings to mind a man who seemed capable of a degree of control, perhaps enough to make him decide to drive his new Porsche to the track rather than have it taken down on a trailer thereby getting in a few precious minutes of break in time.

There was some connection there between those events that we will never know the truth about. Why the Enfield burnt a valve and left the young actor stranded in Polka country in the winter. Why there was a shiny new Indian waiting there to seduce him and why it fell under the wrenches of another actor in the future who also loved motorcycles.

If you have traveled the Pennsylvania turnpike from Indiana to New York you know that it is not an easy journey, even today. Where ever he broke down he was isolated from the two worlds he had inhabited – his hometown in Indiana, where he had been "One Speed Jimmy" on his little CZ, the one speed being wide open, and New York City where a young director named Elia Kazan had taken a liking to him after being given a ride on the back of his motorcycle. "He wasn't much for conversation" Kazan had noted, "but there was something dynamic about him that struck me."

We know now that it might have been his self-image as a man in motion, the faster the better. But it was irony, not speed that killed him, and that is my point. How ironic was it that a man who seemed often to be out of control and who raced motorcycles and cars, was killed in a race car while driving it slowly with deliberate care so he could race it later?

Sew that up however you like and there are common threads enough for anyone who races and knows racers who have died off the track after taking risks that should have killed them racing but didn't. Then of course there is the irony of Pete Conrad, the third man to walk on the moon. After a hundred thousand miles in space he dies riding his Harley-Davidson in a road accident in 1996. David Emde, Don's better looking younger brother, was on a demonstration sales ride along the California coast highway when his bike went off a cliff and he was killed. This after a thousand miles as a professional road racer with the AMA that took him all across the country and back.

Jewish custom says a man dies twice – once when his body dies, and again when his name is no longer spoken. We remember James Dean and speak his name and he still lives, but what of the others who have died that we raced with? We don't even remember them if they died on the track during a race, let alone on the way there or on the way home, or from some related way that others might find obscure but racers would know was as real a connection as a link of 525 chain.

In researching this book I reached out to the American Motorcycle Association and asked for the names of racers who had died at their sanctioned events so that I could append them to this text and keep their memory alive, at least to some extent.

They declined to provide a list, although they did it politely, and instead gave me their assurances that they were dedicated to racer safety and that all that could be done was being done to protect riders at every race. Lawyers made them say that, I knew that, and I thanked them.I am a lifetime founding member and supporter. They have made mistakes, as all organizations do, but my heart is with them.

I loved the motor maids, the Jack Pine endure, the no nonsense style of race promotion that brought crowds to fairgrounds and kept everyone else from having a race the same weekend. That's all gone now, and their racing division is the property of some other group.

I think that was a mistake, but they didn't ask me. Racing at Daytona at night was a mistake too, but again, I wasn't asked.

For me racing with the AMA was good, very good, and when I did it under the old claiming rule I felt like I had a chance to someday have as good a bike as anyone out there. Later on, to woo the factories back, they changed the rules to permit specialty bikes to run with parts that most of us could never hope to have. Now there are faster bikes on the streets than what I used to race on the track. I think that may be a mistake too but it's a free country ain't it? So buy 'em and ride 'em, that's what I say.

As for the dead, I think we should make some effort to remember them. Danny Hyatt, my great friend and a good rider, died in his sleep from apnea. Bruce Bateman, a Harley Sprint connoisseur who only ever raced once but lived it every day, died alone in the bathtub of his remote home in rural Florida when in his thirties. Steve Misus, a perpetual student at the University of Florida whose helmet had Mickey Mouse ears painted on and could make a Honda 350 fly when no one else could. He died with a planeload of contraband coming back from the islands when he flew into a new condo under construction in the glide path of the airport he was headed for after falsely declaring an emergency to avoid customs. He made the trip once a year and used the money to race a season. I know of more, and we should make a list so they will not be forgotten.

It wasn't racing that killed them, even if they died on the track. It was something larger than that and I am not a person who accepts such silly notions as 'random chance' or 'bad luck' as satisfactory explanations for the ending of a life.

That is why, as a successful actor in Hollywood, James Dean's racing was tolerated by the studios who had him under contract. He was not a daredevil about racing, he was a calculating talented man who was taking his mechanic along as a passenger that day out of a sense of caution and as part of what might be necessary to get the best performance possible on the track. He wasn't going especially fast when he died, keeping an eye on the motor for the race to come.

It was the guy in the Ford coming from the opposite direction on the two lane highway that we don't know what his eye was on. Whatever it was, he didn't see the little Porsche and turned right in front of it. Fate had something specific in mind, however, for neither he, nor Dean's mechanic, died in the crash.

For me, James Dean's death was a racing fatality because everything that has to do with racing is part of the race. I can win or lose a race at home in my workshop months before the bike gets on the track. Some modification I may be trying may prove to be as good as I imagined, or some piece of metal I may have looked at suspiciously and should have replaced may fail, putting me on my ass.

Post mortems, like the particulars of what exactly happened to Dean are not all that important. Bodies are not made for sudden stops or contact with sharp objects. Neither is it useful to play 'what if' with the many chances that had come and gone to prevent the occurrence from happening. Each of us have driven toward the same possible death a thousand times and done whatever we did and it worked out for us. Either we slowed down because we thought the car coming at us might turn, or we had sped up to be past them before they turned so they could turn behind us. Either way, it worked for us and it didn't work for him. We are not better drivers than he was nor were we always facing drivers coming at us who were more careful. We lived and he didn't. Does this tell you anything?

Much more was really going on than what I have described above, and it was the Zen of things that it turned out the way it did. Dean has become legend, partly because of this event, and partly because of his persona and his ability to portray on the screen the angst he felt at living. We will all leave the stage someday - the plays the thing .

Ted Henter, whose abilities on a motorcycle impressed me more than any other rider I ever saw, was riding his TZ750 in practice at Daytona after becoming an expert. He was experiencing something only a few of us have had the opportunity to do, which was to be on the track with men whom we had admired growing up that were still racing. In this case it was Dick Mann.

Ted told me of the one moment on the track that frightened him the most in his racing career. He was out in practice and had just passed the finish line at Daytona and was preparing to sit up and brake for turn one. On those bikes it is a real moment that requires both strength and judgment that few have the ability to get exactly right. At those speeds, when you come out from behind the bubble to apply the brakes, the sudden wind resistance on your body tries to yank you right off the bike. It is an all or nothing sort of moment and you need to be right about where you decided to brake and turn in.

Ted was there, had hit his mark and was holding on for dear life and leaning in when, suddenly, Dick Mann went shooting past on the inside of him straight ahead through the cones into the runoff area. Mann was riding a TZ750 too, one of Vesco's bikes and had decided he couldn't make the turn so had just gone straight.

It was a very close thing, Dick just brushing Ted's leg with his fairing as Ted was leaning into the turn. An instant later and they both would have gone down to disaster. As it was Ted had the reflexes to give up on the corner and save it himself, going on straight as well, although a bit rattled when he thought about it later. There was nothing to say about it. Mann had overshot the turn in finding out how deep he could go into one while practicing and Ted just happened to be there.

It might have been that Mann underestimated the speed of the rider in front of him or it might have been that he was just learning to deal with the beast they both were riding. Something spared them. If there was a reason for it; neither of them saw it at the time. They got a glimpse, nothing more, of something larger than all they knew or could do anything about.

Ted was blinded later on the day he arrived in England to begin his GP career. It was a road accident at night and he was leaving Brands Hatch and came upon a car coming at him and as they both moved over to let one another pass they met head on. Americans move to the right, of course, and British drivers go left. For a while they thought they might be able to save his vision but eventually it proved not to be possible. He went on to be the world blind water skiing champion for a bit, the competitive part of his nature not having been injured, and he developed the software that allowed the vision impaired to use computers called JAWS, which yielded a satisfying financial reward.

He was an engineering student when I met him in Gainesville, we were both novice AMA road racers in Florida. Instead of a business card, he gave me a spread sheet of overall gear ratios that were the product of such and such countershaft sprocket and so and so rear sprocket, a handy device I've kept in my tool box ever since. I asked him why he had bothered to work something like this out when you only had so many sprockets to fool with anyway. "Why guess when you can know for sure," he said, and was right about it too. We were in Florida on a warm sunny day when he told me that, and I was there again, nearly fifty years later on a day very much like it when I saw the card again, still tucked in the top of my tool box and still as right as it ever was. What it said was the truth, and time doesn't change that. Neither does it change what happens when racers make mistakes.

I was leaving the track at Daytona in October of 2013 going out to meet a friend at Cracker Barrel and Bruce Hammer's riding school was out in practice. I saw two bikes come together at speed and go down as I was driving along the infield access road headed for the tunnel. Red flags waved, and kept waving. Both men had been killed.

I name them here so that they will not be forgotten – Rick Shaw and Eric Desy, an instructor and his student at the rider's school.

The announcer had just commented that Rick had competed in more laps at the speedway than any other rider in history. The sky was still blue, the sun was still shining and the warm, humid, Florida day was hauntingly familiar.

That is what motorcycle racing does. It gives us a glimpse now and then of something infinitely more complex and knowing than we are. There is a truth to things, racing tells us that. We know there is a limit to how fast we can take a corner or make a bike go in a straight line or make it stop. We push those limits all we can to make speed from stillness, to mesh our animated souls with inanimate objects and embody them with the will we have to race. In the process, we may get just a glimpse now and again of what it all means.

I used to think these images were just about racing itself, but there is more to it. I will have spent the majority of my life as a motorcycle racer when I die, whether I die tomorrow or twenty years from now. I started young and have stayed with it and will stay with it because it is not what will kill me, it is what enlightens me.

Al Knapp raced until his was in his eighties and I spoke with him about that very thing a number of times. He was full of the bravado that a younger man has about denying he would be hurt and how he was as fast as he ever was when those conversations began shortly after I met him. Then he fell at Steamboat Springs one year and broke his pelvis and the recovery from that was slow as he was by then in his seventies.

He was knocked down a time or two after that and while we all respected him, it was still a race and to move over and just let him win would not have been racing. He kept at it, however, until Mid Ohio the year when he fell for the last time and knew as he tried again to heal that it was time to quit.

None of us wanted him to not be there anymore. He was our Methuselah. He held out for us the hope that we all might race forever as he seemed to do. At the rider's meeting at Grattan, Michigan the next month a phone call was placed to him by the referee so that we could all wish him a speedy recovery and return to racing. What followed was an awkward thing.

His wife took the call and told us Al was out in his garden. It had never occurred to us that he might have a garden. It took a while for him to come to the phone but we waited and then we all gave him a big cheer. He declined to promise that he would see us later, and in fact I never saw him again. Sometime after I learned that both he and his wife were later confined to a nursing home. To his great credit, Joe Lachinet, a friend and fellow racer from Michigan, continued to visit them until near the end. Al had lived a long life and had raced for most of it and Joe was there to remind him that we all appreciated what he had done for us by doing so. He faded away slowly until he was finally gone altogether.

I wish I knew what he thinks now. We used to sit on the lip of his trailer and talk about whatever came up in our minds. I would joke with him and he would laugh and joke back. We would talk about the old days, although his were many times older than mine. His tank shift Harley-Davidson was his Stradivarius, and he could play it like a virtuoso, but there were others with newer faster versions of bikes that could do things that his would not and he had trouble with that. "All things being equal," he used to tell me, "I'm as fast as anybody." I agreed that he was when it came to anybody else, but not me and said so, and we laughed at that as well.

He was a good and generous man, he was a fine racer, and he is no longer with us. I'm not sure what that means, but I am sure it means something. I am sure of it because of something I learned a long time ago – when it comes to racing, everything matters. If I burn a valve on a new motor by running it too hard and teach myself the lesson to break 'em in easy next time and take my Porsche down the highway nice and easy a decade later on my way to make myself feel whole again by racing, it won't save me if the universe says my number is up.

28.

Oh, A Knot

EVERYTHING MATTERS, IN WAYS that we cannot see or imagine. That is because all things, past present and future, are part of something so large that we simply cannot comprehend it and have yet to conjure up words or numbers or formulae to describe what it truly is.

The fact that I want to know the truth of it does nothing to change what is true. I can delude myself a thousand different ways by trying to think of everything, or trying to think of nothing, and things are still what they are despite my efforts. Here and there, smarter men that me have put together disciplines that seem to make certain things more predictable but that does not mean they are right about everything and how often do they need to be wrong to miss the truth of it all? Einstein was smart and has been proven wrong about some things. He was right about a number of other things, which were enlightening, but his own discipline has now passed him by quantum leaps and bounds.

There is a place, however, where none of this speculation matters and that is on the racetrack. When I open up the throttle all the way, and tuck myself into the best position my body will manage to cheat the wind, then whatever speed I can manage is a true thing and it is all it will do. That day, the way things are; the fuel, the timing, the compression within the cylinders born of fitment and wear and a thousand things are all working together to make the reality what it is for me that instant. I have an effect but I know that I am not in control. I have my hand upon the throttle and have it to its limit, but there are so many other things, past, present and future, that all come to bear in that instant, that I know I am not alone. I can feel them; I can sense them all around me. It's complicated.

It is even more complicated in the turns, and a good deal less perfect, but I know a perfect corner when I feel one and have left nothing behind. That was it, just there, when I waited as long as possible to brake and had the gearing perfectly matched to the track and the downshift just right for the speed the tires would hold in the turn and leaned in where it scribed a perfect arc from edge to apex to edge again as the power brought the back end around, just a bit, and I rocket away onto the next straight, tucking in again as I went.

Put enough of those together on a perfect day and you can set a lap record, something I managed only once in forty years, but still it can be done and there is a sweet harmony of all things that comes with it. To do everything right, to have made all the correct decisions, and to master a race track, even for one lap, gives you a glimpse. Enough glimpses and you can begin to see that there is something at work here and that you play a part, but only a part.

The next session after I set a lap record I crashed heavily doing what seemed to me to be the exact same things I had been doing before. Something was different. Someone had oiled the track a bit maybe or my tire was more worn, or the racing god sensed that I needed to be humbled a bit. Whatever the cause, I went down and took a chunk off of my hip bone and trashed my left knee again, tearing the soft bits away from a knee cap I had broken at Dade City ten years before and had only recently stopped limping from. That was on a Saturday and I still managed to fix the bike up and race it later that day, winning my class and race it again on Sunday, winning again, after then having a seriously hard time getting my leathers on over a subdural hematoma the size of a football on my hip that was purple and very angry looking.

The next day, and the day after that, and the day after that, I was shoveling cement and gravel and sand into a mixer for twelve hours so I could afford to go racing again and my head was filled with that one perfect lap. Not the crash, or the fixing the bike again, or the races won afterward, but the one perfect lap and the guy coming to find me to tell me that I had set an absolute lap record for the course and wanted to be sure they had my name right for the record book. I remember that lap still, like it was a moment ago, not forty years ago and it is a real thing, as real as anything, and always will be.

Race Day Metamorphosis

A canto of 29 stanzas of five decreasing lines each with
apologies to Dr. Seuss

1.

I sit half in, half out of my van on the back door sill
I am between the two known worlds
I have my gear laid out
my jeans are off
my socks on

2.

I can hear bikes running somewhere in the distance
And the sound of the announcer yakking away
But I can't tell what he's saying anymore
It doesn't matter –
Not to me

3.

They are starting the race before mine and my race is the
    next one.
I have the schedule and have checked it too often already
I would like to be more relaxed and calm but
I have to be sure so I don't miss something.
I simply can't fuck this up!

4.

I like to think that through and through I am mostly a nice
    person
but the truth is there is a part of me in there that rages;

Not in anger so much as against some things
too large to control; too hard to subdue:
Life, for instance.

5.

Quietly I put in my ear plugs wishing I had always done so
There is a constant ringing with us, there it is – tinnitus
but giving it a name and telling me there is no cure
does not make me feel better
or it more bearable.

6.

It is annoying, like a lot of things seem to be now and I push it
    aside
or I try to, by returning to the one thing I know that demands
all of my attention and all of my actions so that
I don't have time to worry about the petty
pieces that make all of the rest of it

7.

"First Call" comes, which means the race on the track is
    half way.
Crossed flags are being shown but I don't have to see them.
'Boots & Saddles' bugles in my mind, John Wayne calls
I step into my leathers and zip up the calves and
Look for my boots and put them on

8.

I stand and stretch and pull my arms back into their sleeves
I mold myself into this new leather clad being by
Sheer will and old memory and new desire.
I want this. I suppose I still need this.
I like to think I can always do this;
But I know I cannot

9.

Someday it will all slip away, that's the beast I fight today
Nothing to prove, nothing to say, just zip it up and go.
Helmet first; not too tight – there just right;
Gloves pulled on, fingers flexed. Squat.
All set? Now where's the bike?

10.

I look in the tank and check the level and move the petcock
   to 'R'
No reserve here, that means 'race' to me, and the fuel flows.
I watch the carbs to be sure they don't pee out their sides;
Nope, the floats are not stuck, so on goes the choke
and the off /run/off thumb thing is set to 'run'

11.

I rock her back and forth and dab at the shift lever looking for
   neutral.
I know it's in there, and I know where it is, so I am not
   worried.
I find it and pull the stand out from beneath the wheel
And look around to make sure that I am clear
and back out onto the pit lane – ready.

12.

I wait for last call now, seeing people around me doing things,
   not hearing.
Some guys go past me, already running and I feel pressure to go
but know it's too soon and the motor will be too hot so I wait.
It seems to always take longer than I think it should.
I know what I should do and I wait since I could.

13.

Now the calls are all made and the track is being cleared and
   I GO.
I paddle along to get her moving then hop off on my left foot

And run along beside holding onto the clip-ons in that
Awkward non Olympic event that is the starting
trot now forgotten by all but a few.

14.

I have it moving now, and give myself a little jump up and
   come down
On the seat just as I let the clutch out and dab it into first gear
Listening for it to fire, wishing I had another hand free
So I could manage the choke lever at the same time
It spurts, it spits, it runs…

15.

I get back on the seat as I rev up the throttle and reach down
Fumbling in gloves for the choke release on the carbs
Then I find it and neutral and take a quick breath
It's going to be all right. I didn't foul a plug.
It runs, thank God, it runs.

16.

It takes a minute to clear its throat and run clean. I am patient
   with it
Two strokes are old school now, which is funny, but so am I
Which is not so funny as I was more the new kid in my
racing past and was comfortable with that being so
when there were more of us than anything

17.

It was special, and not just to me, otherwise why do they still
Flock to see the men I knew when we were all kids?
Still, its nothing like it used to be, we know that -
Nothing ever is

18.

I see riders going out for their warm up lap and decide to go

I pull in the clutch, find first gear, and play quickly with
That moment when the clutch finds the power and
Things start to move along and then I let the
Clutch out completely and just go.

19.

Through the paddock, nodding here and there at old friends,
"Yeah, I'm doin' it again…" and then down to pit out
Where I get the wave of a flag and another nod
And then I'm on the hot pit lane and gas it.
Everything changes now

20.

My aches and pains disappear along with my list of worries.
Speed comes. I feel the turns and tires, watch the tach
and brake markers, looking for that rhythm I had in
Practice that felt just right so I can
get a groove going and race.

21.

The warm up lap goes by and I run hard to be back on the grid
   for the start.
It's a production of its own making what with grid marshals
   pointing andstupidity and impatience and overheating and
   soon enoughit all settles down
to business and the board goes sidewaysand
the green flag waves and – we're off!

22.

I zoom ahead of my body to a spot I need to be and things
   happen
with my feet and hands and ears and eyes and all of it seems
to be working together unconsciously, seamlessly, as I
pick and choose the places I want it all to go
and see it happening. We go.

23.

Down to turn one is a monument of the past and I know what
    to do.
"Ever been first?" someone asked me when I was 19 and
I said I wouldn't know how. He told me that he knew.
"First you have to believe you can do it," he said,
"after that, its just a matter of making it so."

24.

He was right, I found out later the first time I managed it, and
    it was huge.
First to the first turn! A small milestone in a racing career; but a
    real one.
After that it's first to the second turn, then the third and so on
    and on.
Following is one thing; you know what to work on and can see
Where improvements can be made just ahead of you

25.

Leading is something else altogether and not everyone is as able
    to do it.
An empty track ahead of you, with all of it yours to use as you
    please.
You could go over there, or stay here, or take the middle
    and see
just where you feel the best about going into the next turn
and when to get on the brakes, brakes! BRAKES!!!

26.

With the pack behind you, it's a bit too soon, to be all alone out
    front,
in their sights, you loon! No time to look back. Never look
    back!
just do what you do with the track and let the rest of it
take care of itself until you have to do something
else, nothing you can do for it now.

27.

Just to race. How sweet. The feeling it gives makes me
   complete.
The laps roll by, you do what you must, now here, now there
with a cut and a thrust you work through the pack once
Behind you now in front of you, now behind you –
Away!

28.

Crossed flags come, I never know why; then white then
   checkered –
The time seemed to fly. Some may have gone by me I
Can't really say, none came too close though and
I was not in the way. It was good. It was fun.
What a great day!

29.

That's too simply said, it was more than that. I've missed
   something large –
It's not a cat in a hat. I was a different person before it began
someone else again as on things ran
different still, now that it's through.
I ask myself, " just who are you?"

29.

The Moving Finger Writes

I HAVE A VERY used digital clock that sets nicely on my desktop. I know there is a clock on the computer display, but, when that is not on, I like to know what time it is so I can manage, well, so that I can pretend to manage my time. It is a faulty clock. It seems to run well enough when it is going and I am watching, but I suspect that in those moments that I look away, or become preoccupied with other things, that it either races ahead a bit, or maybe stops altogether. Some part of this is an illusion and I am trying to work out which part. This phenomenon is on the order of the song in the small, small world pavilion which is satanic the second time you take a grandchild through, no matter how long or how short the wait. That too is related to time.

I believe that time will eventually unravel for you if you live long enough. There are many theories about time out there, and I have considered most of them, but it is a familiar stranger. We learned early on to deal with it and were taught to be punctual and that others were sensitive to losing any of it even if we weren't. Meeting up with other racers to do things was part of the business a long time ago, and is still today to a certain extent, although FedEx has taken some of the travel out of that aspect of a racing life. Gasoline used to be the cheapest thing I bought associated with racing so it was not a big deal to spend a tank of gas or two getting to some half-way point to meet someone and swap things.

On those trips, there was time to ponder things and that was often the most productive aspect of making them. I always worked a job of some sort during my active racing career and time off was hard to come by so inevitably it was an all night run to here are there and back with an exhausted return to the daily grinding at whatever was making me a living. I could have stopped of course, and opted for some 'real' career at something, but to be the kind of person people are willing to pay to be invaluable you have to be there and I often wanted to be elsewhere.

So it is that now I notice the crochet of time unraveling for those I have known the longest. The 'sharp as a tack, quick as a bunny' friends of mine that always had a quick witticism and novel thought to share about this or that are now staring blankly into a blank future. They are not getting ready for next season or honing a new idea into a shape vision of things to come. They may still maintain their relics, some of which may still run, but they are like forgotten charms on a bracelet that now signify nothing but memories.

My brother has lost himself in thought and won't be coming back. He was always a thinker and seemed constantly distracted by something other than what was going on around him. When he was young, people admired him for being so thoughtful. Now nearly 70, they see it as a sign of early dementia and say it may not be that early. Our father lived to be nearly 90 and was mentally sharp nearly until the end, but he did not race or fall on his head repeatedly and my brother has and apparently it did some damage. He is still here with us in body, but something of his spirit is missing.

I can still talk to him, and about some things may be the only one that still can, which makes it all the harder in terms of guilt at time not spent with him. This has a backhand effect on my time with my own family in which I am now absent physically and often mentally as well as I contemplate what becomes of us and our time with things. He has been tested and diagnosed and the prognosis is basically that things could be a lot worse. He has his old memories and is good with them. He has his motor control and can walk and talk and eat and so forth, but he can't make new memories reliably or be trusted to be alone in the presence of appliances. He no longer seems to have situational awareness in the way that he once did. He can't drive, or ride a motorcycle, because his perception of things is off by a beat or two and his reaction to the changing environment of things on the go is not good enough to manage it. It is for all of us, on some level, a time management problem.

I would stop and think about it more, but there is no real solution, only some accommodation of a situation that seems unalterable. My digital clock stops keeping track of time whenever there is a power failure, which is often enough that I see it flashing 12:00 at me every now and then and notice. This makes me have to manually reset the time by pushing some of the buttons arrayed on its top – "slow, fast, alarm, and time", are the choices. If I push down the "time" button and push "fast" at the same time, the display races ahead through a blur of hours and minutes that are too quickly shown to be comprehended accurately. Now and then I recognize one but it is impossible to get it to stop right on the minute as it were.

If I use the "slow" button instead, and it is not near noon, the tedium of the slow crawl of time seems interminable. For some reason it matters more to me that a digital display of time is exactly accurate that it does on an analog timepiece with hands. There we find some estimation of what time it might displayed. With the digital one, it is either exactly the right time, or it is wrong, which somehow matters more but I can't tell you why.

Women in my life seem to like to crochet and my wife, Vicky, is especially handy at this. There are stitches to count and things to do and she applies herself diligently. Now and then, when she's dropped a stitch, she will unravel a section by just pulling on the end. I watch this in horror. All that time undone; things so intricately arranged and managed and measured just pulled away like that as if the time to do it was all that made it what it was. Such is life. I need more time.

30.

Darkness Comes

I'M LAYING IN THE back of a van and it's moving. Something is wrong. I don't ride in vans, or cars for that matter, I always drive. I have a serious headache, and I don't usually have those either. I start to raise myself up but when I put out a hand to balance with I run into a motorcycle. There are tie downs and I feel them and feel them grow taught and slack as the van swings from side to side moving along. I'm in a race van. Only it doesn't smell like a race van and I know it should. I feel loose parts and rough edges and dirt on the bike. There shouldn't be any dirt. The bike's been crashed. I can't see anything so I say something. "Hey!" the universal Southern greeting, admonition, and all purpose question.

Something is said from the front, but I can't hear them. Feet and hands move all around me and I struggle to get upright and am dizzy and it makes my head throb. "Out!" I say, which is our crew's signal that someone is about to puke and an immediate stop is needed. The van slows quickly and I hear the side door open. Hands find me and I am helped out onto the shoulder where I stand with two hands on the side of the van and heave up nothing but heave never the less. "What time is it?" I ask. "About six-thirty someone says" "Is it dark?" I ask. There is a pause before someone answers, "No, not really." "Then I am blind." I say and turn my face around this way and that to see if any light is detected. None is and the turning kills my head.

"Where are we?" I ask. "On this side of Mont Eagle" comes the answer. "Let me sit up front," I say, "I'm carsick." This is conveyed, people are moved and soon I am in the passenger's seat of my '64 Ford Econoline van heading north out of Georgia into Tennessee and eventually back to Illinois. Someone is driving but I'm not sure who it is. They seem to be doing all right, whoever it is. I stare ahead but see nothing.

"Buns, what's up?" Garth asks from over where the driver would sit so I assume he is driving. "Can't see nothin'" I say, "What happened?" Garth waits a beat. "What's the last thing you remember?" "Looking back as I come onto the straight and seeing your orange helmet catching up with me." I said

"I didn't catch you." He says, and I feel a vague relief, but have no memory of much else. "I've lost a bit of time," I say, "so fill me in." Nothing seems to make much sense but I am not panicked about it. I feel as if they talk about what's going on it will come to me. "Well, we went down to Road Atlanta for the Junior/ Novice combined race and you were riding your all purpose DT1 with a high pipe and an R5 front end while I was riding your Harley Sprint road racer I just bought from you but still owe half the $300 we agreed was the price." He said in a calm voice.

Garth Buckles is one of my all time favorite people, has a great demeanor, no matter what he situation. I never saw him panic and even when he was fucking with someone he was kind about it. "Shorty, come here," he would say, holding the bucket of water he was about to pour on the shop boy after a stray shot from a squirt gun had barely sprinkled Garth. Sure enough, Shorty would come and apologize as Garth doused him with the bucket. Now he was driving my van and I had no idea what was going on. He part about the Harley sounded right though, we had a deal made of some sort.

That made sense. I paid $300 for it and it was uncompetitive, although I still really liked it. "How'd I do?" I asked. "You were the fastest guy out there on a single two stroke and your laps times consistently dropped throughout the event." Garth said. A female voice then came from the middle, which was closer, 'I scored for you and sat next to Norma Vesco and we made quick friends because my name was Norma too," she said. "Norma too?" I asked, not recognizing the name. Garth helped, "It's your brother's wife, Norma." We rode along for a bit. "Is my brother here?" I asked. "No," Garth said, "he couldn't come, but we have Ron Muir and Dave Pfaff and his wife with us." "All in this tiny van?" I asked, incredulous. "Yeah," he answered, "it's a crowd, but we had a good time." "Good" I managed, but couldn't keep talking, my head was splitting.

Something in the future told me that Norma and Norma stayed friends and it mattered but I couldn't work that out, next year, maybe, I thought, but that made no sense. I was conscious that I wasn't conscious. I had no sense of smell. I could feel the van moving and knew I was sitting up and holding on but there was very little else I could manage. I just breathed, and was aware that I breathed, and I waited for it to pass. I may have slept again, I don't know, but nothing happened easily or quickly. I had been hurt before, many times, but never like this, never so badly that my senses failed me and didn't come back. I should have been panicky about it I supposed but that would have required some effort and I wasn't up to it, I just wanted my head to stop hurting. I kept my eyes shut.

Once I had fallen out of an apple tree before I was in school so I must have been five or so. It was tall and they had picked the apples off that they could reach with ladders but up at the top, shining in the sun, were a few that looked delicious. I could just reach the bottom branch and had climbed up and up and up until I was in the limbs with apples and there were only a few above me and I thought I may as well go to the very top and look out over the tree so see the world. I was at the corner of my grandfather's yard, next to the field, and I could see my mother far away hanging out the wash and my dog, Jet, laying near her and the big collie dog of my grandfather's standing guard by the driveway to keep everyone safe. I waved but no one saw me. The view was spectacular. It was a warm day and the sun was shining bright and the corn was up over my head and rustled in the breeze that came through the field and then into the tree where I held on, making a different sound in its leaves even though it was the same wind.

Then I heard someone calling my name, far off, and looked and saw them in the yard, pointing at me and my brother came running as they all watched and soon he was within earshot and I could hear his angry voice telling me to come down right this minute and being bossy and I knew if I did come down they would be mad so I stayed put. He started to climb up but was bigger than I was and the limbs wouldn't hold him so he had to stop, just out of reach and was red faced and angry and threatening and for some reason, once I figured out that he couldn't touch me, I thought it was funny and started throwing apples down on him. He retreated, finally, with a threat to go and tell, and I waited until he was nearly back at the house before I drew my head back in the branches and started down.

Then it happened. A handhold or a branch my foot was on gave way, increasing the load elsewhere and the failures multiplied until in an instant I was hurled to the ground where I landed with a thud, knocking the breath clean out of me. I just lay there, my eyes open, unable to move and unable to breathe. It was an awful feeling. My dog came over and licked me, which he liked to do at the most unhandy times, but I managed to shake him off and in doing so reanimate myself and hear myself take a breath and then another and then slowly got up and shook it off and ran back to the house to defend myself from the trial I was sure that was going on in my absence. One arm moved funny on the way as I ran, and I noticed that, but it didn't seem to hurt. My mother noticed too and made a sling out of a tea towel and told me not to climb in the tree again and not to throw things at my brother and that was it. It was a couple of weeks before I could put that arm over my head again, but I managed, and did it over and over until it moved like it should and went on to whatever I went on to.

When I opened my eyes again in the moving van it was dark still, but I had an impression of light here and there and my head did not hurt as bad. The sun had gone down but the dashboard lights were still on and the headlights coming at us and going past were distinguishable enough that I knew what they were. I was going to be able to see again, I thought absently, and thought that would be a good thing. I had no memory of the race then, that didn't come until later, but it came. It could have just as easily stayed away, I realize that now and the headache and the blindness were caused by bleeding in my brain from a severe concussion. I had had others probably, from football and baseball and boxing, but I was going to be all right;Different in some ways, since some damage must have been done, but all right within acceptable limits.

I was never going to be the same but that is the way of things. You learn to do something, you get good at it, you get hurt, and you can't do it as well ever again. I had been tested every season by some doctor or other for whatever sport was coming up and one of those tests was for peripheral vision. They would have me look straight ahead and then bring something forward from behind me on one side or the other and I was to tell them when I saw it. I could see back behind my shoulders, which they thought was some sort of deformity but I found it useful when I wanted to see what was coming up behind me. After crashing at Road Atlanta, I had no peripheral vision at all. I could only see straight ahead, like I was looking through a tunnel and then at the edges, where there used to be something there was now nothing. It was not blackness, just a void. This was bothersome, but I didn't know what could be done about it. I figured it would either come back, or it wouldn't.

Injury is part of risk and when we do things with our bodies there is always the chance that some damage to the temple will result. We heal up, sort of, or we don't, but we have to live in the temple anyway so all we can do is adjust and pray it heals up. I suppose we could seek medical treatment but I didn't like doctors and didn't especially enjoy plaster of Paris as a solution to why my arm moved funny or why it hurt when I did "that". I had been an accident proned child I suppose, but I didn't see it that way. There was no insurance that covered racing anyway so it was a pointless exercise to consider.

When we moved to Carmi, Illinois I was about eight and had gone to the swimming pool one summer day. I had been to the pool many times before in Roswell and elsewhere so I was no stranger to the chlorine or the diving boards or all the rest and I was a good swimmer. I went off the high dive and went down to the drain and held on for a bit, looking around at the world above me, fascinated with the appearance of things from that perspective. When I finally ran out of air, I shot to the surface and my timing was bad because just as I was coming up, a large boy was coming down and landed right on top of me, breaking my neck.

I woke up in the hospital some time after, with no memory of how I had gotten there and one of those annoying plastic collars on keeping my head stretched up and still, leaving me unable to see myself. I thought I might be paralyzed so I held my hands up to see my fingers wiggle. Someone sitting off to one side said something and soon the room was filled with nurses and doctors and someone shined a light in my eye, holding the lid open and someone else started to gag me with one of those wooden tongue depressor things and I protested and squawked until they all backed off. Eventually order was restored and my mother appeared and told me that I had given everyone quite a fright. I would have to wear the collar until my neck healed, she told me, as I had broken it. "I didn't break it," I protested, "Somebody jumped on me." Then I recounted my recollection of what had happened. Another face came into view, the doctor this time and he told me I was a lucky little boy, an opinion shared by many around us. I didn't see it that way, lucky would have been not to be jumped on.

Doctors and I have a history of disagreement. Once I was racing at Dade City, Florida and crashed in practice coming onto what was laughably called the front straight. While I was away, doing the lap that had brought me there, someone had run off course on the inside trying to cut the corner and had pushed some sand from the shoulder out onto the asphalt. My bike had the pointy Dunlop tires and I wasn't in a good spot with them and the back end came around and I tried to save it but couldn't, not managing to get my left leg out from under it before the large bulbous aluminum cover for the half speed mag came down like a punch press on the side of my knee cap breaking it in half.

In terms of pain, that was probably my worst racing injury, it hurt a lot and there was no waiting. I have been hurt far worse and not felt it for some time, but by the time the bike and I slid to a stop I was at 11 on the pain scale of 10. Someone came over from not far away and picked the bike up, which wasn't damaged since it had used me as a cushion. I probably looked all right, or as all right as I had when the race began, my leathers being fairly worn by then having been down many times before. I was lying on my back, sucking air in between my teeth unable to speak. Dwayne Williams appeared over me and I could hear bikes going by and I could see that he was saying something but I couldn't tell what it was. We got my helmet off and he looked concerned and the bikes were gone by then so it was quieter.

"Are you all right?" he asked me. "No," I answered. "Break anything?" he asked. "My knee," I said. "Anything else?" he asked. "Not that I can tell," I said. The circle of the sky overhead was now ringed with concerned faces, looking down at the two of us talking. I recognized a few of them but no one looked especially worried, which was good. Then Dwayne spoke again, "Well, we need to move you a little further from the track so we can go ahead and start racing, do you think you can walk?"

I was incredulous. Apparently I had failed to convey the seriousness of the situation. "Get the ambulance," I managed to say, sounding more calm than I felt. He made a face, pursing up his lips and turning his head just a bit. "Well, we only have the one here and if we send you off in it, we'll have to stop racing," he said. I spoke more slowly this time, in case he had misunderstood me, with a bit more emphasis on each word "Get. The. Ambulance." I liked Dwayne, but he wasn't a doctor and I needed one to tell me I was all right or not, which meant I needed to be taken to one since I couldn't get there on my own.

He didn't move except for his eyebrows which went one way, then the other and he said, "You can't be hurt bad, you sound all right and you ain't thrashin' around none." My hand shot up and grabbed him by the tee shirt suddenly, twisting it as I pulled him closer. "Get the fucking ambulance over here and take me to the hospital right now God Damn it!" I screamed at him. His eyes went wide and I let him go and soon the ambulance came and they hauled me off to the emergency room of Our Sisters of Torture not far away where they saw a limping motorcycle racer who had been defiling the Sabbath with blasphemous noise who had obviously been absent from Mass. That much they knew because it was still going on and I had not come from there.

That was where my examination began, "Do you need a priest my son?" the Mother Superior asked me. "I don't know, Sister, do I?" The ambulance attendants had found a wheel chair inside the door of this Catholic hospital and wheeled it out and unceremoniously put me in it before announcing that Dwayne had said he wanted them back 'pronto' and taking off. I could hear bikes running in the near distance at the Pasco County Fairground so apparently they had decided it would be all right to go ahead and race without an ambulance present if it was coming back 'pronto'.

She looked me up and down with clear disdain. I was in a one piece leather suit that had once been white and had arm bands of blue with white stars bordered by red stripes. The same sort of striped affair was at the ends of each leg, which had looked good on paper when I drew it up for Bates but turned out to be a bad idea since most boots went over the leathers and tucking them inside was a problem I would sort out next time by just not having them. They were old by now and predated Evil Knevil's Confederate flag get up but people had seen him in and they had not seen me so much so the most frequent comment they brought was about whether or not I was about to jump something.

"I think I broke my knee, "I said, and could feel the leathers tightening around it as we spoke. "We'll take a look," she said and motioned the two attending novices to wheel me into an examination room. I took my boots off with some effort before she came back with a pair of scissors and was about to begin cutting the leathers when I stopped her. "I can get them off," I said, but she looked doubtful. I hopped over to the exam table and stood on my good leg wriggling out of the top and then lowering the pants until I could get it off of the bad one. I could feel my heart pounding in my leg now, and absently wondered if it might actually have moved there.

My knee looked purple and swollen and was oddly oriented. I pulled my ass up on the edge of the table and let the other leg hang but could not manage to bend over to pull off what remained. No one moved to help me. "I can't get that," I said, pointing down at the lump of bunched up leather around my good ankle. None of them moved, the two young ones looking at me and then at their superior and then back at me. I didn't think of it at first, but I was only wearing under-wear which had a dick in it and apparently this possibility had not yet been discussed in the course of whatever training they had so far.

I hadn't thought as far as they had that the necessity of one of them kneeling between my bare legs might be a sin, even if it wasn't going to go that far. "Fine," I said, "I'll get it and jerked and twisted until I got the leg up on the exam table and could reach the sweaty twisted tourniquet around my ankle. I got them off and they lay in a pile, leaving me with just socks and a grimace to keep my tidy whities company. They asked me how I felt and I quipped that I used my hands, holding them up in a mocking gesture that displeased them enough to leave. In a few minutes a middle aged woman with a clip board came in and started writing down my answers to her questions. How old was I?; Did insanity run in my family?, What drugs did I use?; When was my last confession? Did I have insurance? When I said 'no' to that last one, things seemed to take a different course and she stopped showing any pretence of concern.

She wanted to weigh me and told me to stand on the scales. I thought she was kidding and made the mistake of saying so. In a few brusque motions she had me off the exam table and on the scales as she slid the little silver weights back and forth on their tracks expertly until she was satisfied that she would be able to tell the undertaker what I had weighed when living. She handed me a piece of cloth that was roughly shroud shaped but tied in the back and I asked her if it was from Turin and she didn't seem to get it so I didn't bother to explain. Jokes are never funny if you have to go that far anyway.

I don't know why humor comes to mind in such moments but I could have done a stand up routine had I been able to stand. She ignored my commentary and my physical limitations and dragged me down the hall to the X-Ray room which had apparently been a gift from Mme Curie herself, no doubt a good Catholic as well and the equipment no longer suitable for her needs.

It was cold. I was cold by now, despite having finally managed to put the gown on by myself and get it tied. Clipboard lady left and I was left alone in a room too small for its equipment and a disembod-ied voice said, "Lay on the table with your leg flat." I looked around not sure if I was hearing voices, but thinking now that it might be possible. I thought of Feynman and his theory that there was nothing to creation because there was too much stage and not enough drama. Here was plenty of the large menacing mechanism that looked inexplicably complicated and beyond my comprehension, and here was I, defenseless and nearly naked. Still, I had heard a voice and I was trying to work it out if that was a sign of grace when a small face appeared in a grid of glass with chicken wire in it.

"The table," it said distantly, "lay on the table." She might have been pointing, I don't know, the window was too small to see her hands, but there was a clear fright in her eyes and this room was somehow connected to her fear and now to mine. I got up on the freezing black slab and tried to lie down. My left knee would not straighten out of course, still being disjointed and looking for new ways to hurt me. She repeated the command and I finally just told her that I could not do it. It was Dorothy talking to the Wizard but without Toto.

A small door opened somewhere behind a screen and Quasimodo entered silently, grasping my leg with both hands, one at the bottom of my thigh and one just below my knee and pushed down with all the dark hateful force the world possessed and 'voila' my leg was straight on the table. The machine hummed and clicked as I whimpered in pain but the hands did not let go until it was over. I was gasping by then, completely off the scale of what I thought was possible to feel as painful. Bones had touched one another in ways that they were not meant to touch and shoved each other around to satisfy the needs of the machine. It was worse than the time the dentist broke a drill off in a tooth and then had to drill it out with another one, every time he struck it sending sheer pain through my senses so intense that I promised to kill him when he was done, and even though I was only nine, he believed me and left town.

Sister Yanker reappeared and pulled and tugged me back to the exam room where she told me to "Wait here." What choice did I have? The room was only lit by a window of oddly made glass that let light in but didn't let you see through it. I waited while they took the film and sent it off to Timbuktu or wherever it went and tried to be patient knowing that prompt quality medical care like this could make all the difference in terms of outcome. I could occasionally hear the bikes running as another race went off and then stopped, and then another, and then, finally, nothing. Apparently the races were over.

A little man came in that reminded me of Peter Lorry in the Maltese Falcon and I was more frightened than I had been when I first felt the bike slide away past where I could save it. He had round glasses roughly the thickness of coke bottles and very nearly the same color of green glass. When he looked at me, at least I think he was looking at me, his black eyes distorted to large oddly shaped discs that were so disturbing I had to look away. He was holding a piece of film nearly the size of the negatives I had used as a pressman back in college in the darkroom when we shot the flats for the web offset press.

He summoned me over to the window and gave it to me gesturing for me to hold it against the glass over our heads, which I did. We looked at it together, as two colleagues might, and he asked me what I thought. There was my knee, obviously, and running at about thirty degrees across the patella was a bright white line, more or less like a bolt of lightening, from the upper right down to the lower left as I held the film. "Looks broken,Doctor" I said, as professionally as I could manage and I looked over at him, thinking to myself that the Marx brothers had surely done this bit before.

Time stood still. It was one of those moments you never forget, now etched in my memory forever. I could describe this guy to you down to mole on his chin. He was squinting hard, through the glasses, pushed back against his dark bushy eyebrows, and because of his stature he was a good distance away from where I held the X-ray against the milky glass. "It looks all right to me," he said, and that was it, the sum and substance of his medical opinion in six words. He might have said anything else and I may have been able to find some comfort in it or some reassurance that I was not going to be on a poster for crippled motorcycle racers from then on in some public service nightmare.

Our next exchange was a blur, I was still reeling from his choice of words, and he was asking something about whether I would prefer to spend the rest of my life with my leg bent, or straight? And then said that I needed to consider that and let my regular physician know of my choice when I got back home so he could cast it appropriately. Then he left, and took the X-ray with him.

Someone had brought my van over to the hospital and had loaded up the bike and whatever had been lying around and left it in the parking lot. I was wheeled out to it with my boots and leathers piled in my lap. I managed to haul myself up into the driver's seat and was clearly in some distress when the orderly said, "Don't take aspirin, it will only make it worse," and turned and left me there.

I could see my jeans and clothes by the back door where I had taken them off and put on my leathers some hours before, then an agile young man, and now, a cripple. I had to think of some way I might manage to ever get them on again. I got out and hobbled around and sat on the ledge where the doors close. Pulling them up over one leg, then the other, I found a tee shirt that was clean enough that I did not have to hold my breath to put on and did so. I could get a shoe on the right foot, but not the left, it was too swollen.

I noticed the sunset, facing west out the back doors, and felt good about noticing. Despite what all was going on I took a few moments to take it in - My planet was hurtling through space and spinning around just so to entertain me with a glimpse of a rather small star in the universe disappearing four or five miles away below the horizon. I was pulled back to reality by a sudden realization that I was not sitting on my wallet, which I had not thought to look for and which, if lost, would change everything. I didn't want to think that someone might have taken the opportunity to filch it. I chided myself for such thoughts when I found it but thought that it felt wrong and looked inside. A wad of bills looked back at me. I had not had a wad of bills, only a few.

Apparently a collection had been taken at some point; either that or some anonymous benefactor had taken it upon them self to help me out. I was grateful and after getting dressed headed back home to Gainesville, about three hours away, looking for a drive through food stop where I could get a bite and sort this out. I had made this same trip a couple of years ago when I had come to Dade City for the first time and had loved it, everything about it, and willed myself to be there, living there, racing there and had managed to do all of it.

I was on a roll. Life was good and I was lucky. But now, racing had bitten me back and I had proven unexpectedly vulnerable. I would need help with this and wasn't sure where I would get it.

Stan Friduss, a good man and true, had crutches he loaned me from a crash of his own years before but made sure I knew he wanted them back. I had been promoted to service manager at Triumph City by then and it was a chore to get around with crutches but I managed and they tolerated me. A broken racer named Liston Chappel had been working there as a part's man when I had arrived, he was wheel chair bound and paralyzed but cheerful and engaging and I liked him. It all got to be too much for him in some way and he killed himself one weekend later and things changed, like they do when that first cold wind of winter comes in off the sea and takes summer away for the last time.

I was making the most of not being about to do what I had in the past and was determined not to complain. It had been my habit to get down beside a motorcycle to have a closer look by putting my left foot up under myself and sitting on it. My knee used to bend in those ways but not any more. I had not gone to a doctor when I got back, just gone over to Stan's and picked up the crutches. I was living with it straight, so far, and could only hope that it would bend some, someday. Although I had tried hard a time or two to make it be more flexible it just wouldn't do it. Then one day, as I was trying to get down and have a look at a motor number on a Triumph twin to write it on a work order, Danny Hyatt jumped on my back and down I went, the knee giving way and forcing me to the floor. I was speechless. "There," he said, victoriously, "that should do it." I agreed and grudgingly thanked him. It was better after that, although I was never able to sit with my foot up under me ever again. It still hurts now and then and even though I remember it all like it was yesterday it was really forty years ago. Time is a funny thing.

Oh look, my clock stopped.

Sometimes I feel like Frankenstein's monster
Once I get all suited up and have on
my battle scared leather suit with
my helmet's D-rings snugged,
my boots zipped tight.

I listen to the world change around me
through plugged ears and hear
my breathing calm or caught
as all my fears swim inside
the suit so near.

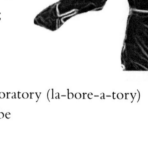

I have new strength and a stupidity
Born of a powerful feeling that I
can do anything and survive;
Things I would never
do otherwise.

I stand in the door of the laboratory (la-bore-a-tory)
that is all my life could ever be
and racing is just the lock
turning as I hold
the key.

Those that love me cannot understand why
I am not satisfied to just let them
do so and have the life that
other men just dream of
while I can only sigh.

Has racing made a monster of me? Or a master of things better
    left alone?
Is this the way I will find my answer? Or only some cold stone
to say 'I lie here,' and was this or that or the other
and now my soul has flown?
That could be –

for someone else; but not for me, never for me.
I am passed that time already and
I have the peace to know.
I will never die Racing.
I am sure it will be so.

31.

Mind Over Matter

SUBATOMIC PARTICLES ARE NO more the building blocks of my universe than grains of sand are a day at the beach for me. They may be there, my physicists friends assure me they are, and they may affect my experiences from moment to moment, but they are not perceived by me in real time and consequently do not matter. They may make matter, but it's not the sort that matters to me. Moments matter to me.

The divine element of human consciousness that subatomic particles do not themselves possess is the ability to notice, and remember, moments in time. While I may ponder what they mean, and may sometimes think I have an answer, the truth is I don't know for sure and may never know. I'm not the Blaise Pascal sort of guy who wants just to 'bet' on eternity, I'd like to know ahead of time if it's possible what waits for me.

There is no easy answer that much I am sure of, and I have some evidence that there may not really be an answer for us living beings at all as well as some to the contrary. The circle is not unbroken, that much I know for sure, and yet I hope. Why that is so is unexplainable to me. It may be chemical, I don't know, but I am a hopeful person and always have been despite a number of falls off of the horse of an easy life into painful circumstances.

My perception of things, of life, has shown me that some moments matter more than others. I don't have precognitive abilities and don't know that I would especially want them, but I do think they are out there. I have been in moments with others who were certain they felt a moment and knew with certainty what it was telling them. "Go ahead and kiss her!" or "Take a later flight, this one is doomed," or any number of other little signals that moments hold for us may have been perceived and believed and obeyed. Later, after the moment passes, it may be logically difficult to give a satisfactory explanation for why we did a certain thing, but that is only because later we have hindsight, which is entirely different from what I am talking about.

Why didn't the Titanic slow down for the icebergs? I don't know, really, although we have a number of accounts that talk about reasons given. I did not spend a freezing night in the garage struggling to finish a motorcycle to race at the first event of the season because I believed the weather report that said it would be cold and bad weather at the track. I went to the race anyway because I volunteer and work for the club that sponsors the event I had said I would be there. I could have as easily said I wouldn't be but it was too late for that. Having said I would, and plans having been made by others dependent upon my representations, I went and made the most of it. The weather was freakishly fabulous. One of those brilliant sunny weekends in early spring that foretell of a blessed summer to come.

I wished I had a bike to ride, but since I had opted not to myself, it was difficult to be too unhappy about it. I thought back to the moment of election, when I choose the path that brought me to Savannah without a bike to ride. It was bitter cold, below zero in fact, and there was snow on the ground and my workshop was unheated. Still, I could have bundled up and made myself do it but I didn't. I have done such things in the past and had mixed results, but back then, for some reason I could not explain, I felt compelled to do it anyway because I felt the pressure of time somehow in a different way. It was as if I was under the impression that time was limited in some form and I had only a tiny allotment of it to be in and work with and try to understand.

Nothing could be further from the truth. Time is endless. I know that because it was going on when I first became aware of it and as far ahead of me in time as I can imagine it is still there. It is the slate upon which thoughts are written and there is no thought without it.

Consciousness ceases without time, although the opposite is not true. Rather than be in a panic about the limited nature of time available and my inability to use it all as well as I might if I knew more, I am at peace that I have any of it at all to even think thoughts like these with. I will always think such things, I am sure of that.

You may ask how I can be so sure, and the answer is simple: I think what I wish for to do otherwise would be to be someone else. What of that? I am an organ donor. What if in the future they figure out how to take a viable brain from a dead body and put it into a living body of another person? What result? Is it me again, only taller now, or shorter, or weaker or slower? Or is it them, with just one new part to deal with and some oddly unrelated memories to who they thought they were. Would a mirror be any help, or would it just confuse the issue?

If you over think reality it can become confusing. Simplify: I know as much as I need to know at any given moment to deal with the moment as it is presented to me. Moments are what matters. I had a moment when I could have chosen a different course and had a different life. When I bought the lottery ticket that didn't win and the guy in line behind me or ahead of me did win, something about those moments, theirs and mine, made life different for us than what ultimately happened. Would it matter if I were a good Democrat and they were Republican or vice versa? What if they were Sunni or Shi'a or Orthodox Jew or left handed? I can't say.

The reason I can't say is that I was not in their moment, I was in mine.

32.

An Even Chance Is An Odd Thing

"I'D RATHER BE LUCKY than good," I heard him say and I had heard it before. He was describing his crash at great speed that had spit him off his bike under the bridge at Road Atlanta and sent him into the banking ass first. Other than a new amount of clearance there, which altered his stride for the rest of the weekend, he claimed to be uninjured. The crash had shut down practice for the WERA Grand National Final and I was there to contest for the championship in my class on my 350 Yamaha twin. Their structure for determining such things wasn't based on annual points accumulated, I would have won already if that was the case, but was a winner take all final ala the SCCA sports car boys which made for a grand finale and a big turn out one supposed at the last event of the year. That was the idea anyway.

It didn't always happen that way. Weather was usually an issue and it also made for travel and work difficulties for those of us with jobs. Years before I had given up working in bike shops and gone into teaching in order to have the summer off so that I could race without the hassle of finding a new job after every event. I had done this after I had moved to Florida with the added incentive that they raced in the winter as well and Daytona was there where the season began each year. It had taken some doing, but I had managed it, and had done so while newly married. Now twelve years later, she no longer came to the races and saw them as a selfish indulgence of mine regardless of what I might do to try to compensate her for the time and effort it took.

I led two lives, effectively, well three if I counted the one at work. Homebody, Teacher, Racer, and never the twain shall meet. It was more than duplicitous, it was maddening. The general rule applied was that weekends with a race in them were mine to use as I pleased but no more than one a month and limited to Friday after work until work began on Monday. This involved long drives and sleep deprivation but so did almost everything else I did so I adjusted. I raced less, as could be expected. The bike failed more often, both from limited resource allocation and time allotted for maintenance. It was not an ideal situation but we all have lives that have nothing to do with racing and I did not want to go without one just to feed my need for speed which I had already proven to myself was not destined to make me famous or rich.

Sometimes I would say I had stopped and would sell everything or almost everything and take up something new. We tried snow skiing until she broke her knee which ended that; and did the summer softball and church choir stints with me playing and singing and her just singing. It was fine. We made friends and had dinners with other couples and generally did all the things that people our age are supposed to do. And then something would happen, usually deep in the darkness of winter and I would get up and go out to the garage and start organizing the mess I had left there when I had last done something with serious intent.

I would find a copy of Cycle News somewhere and look at the want ads. Eventually something old would come up for sale that was in my comfort zone and I would buy it and bring it home and the cycle would start all over again. It was worse than a mistress for her I'm sure since I was distant and dirty and would rather be out in the shop until something was put together and ready to ride and then until I rode it and then until I won with it. After that, being satisfied on some level, I could sell it and be at peace a little and try to make amends again. Nothing she did made any difference. She could be supportive and pretend to be happy about it, or she could pout, or be hateful, or just be gone, it made no difference. It made no difference because I knew if I was going to race then certain things had to be done in certain ways and that included doing them like my life depended on it because it did. She was wounded by my neglect, as one might expect.

Scar tissue builds up over time, however and time does not heal all wounds. She saw continuing our relationship as a choice for her in terms of something she had already done – either she had been mistaken to begin with about who I was and whether she loved me; or I had a mental problem that she was unable to help me with. Once she saw it that way, it was over for her, since either way she had no part in things. So she stayed home and I raced and was not supposed to bring it up when I came back. Whether I won or lost or set myself on fire didn't matter to her, she tried not to think about it and I tried not to mention it.

But finally, at Road Atlanta I had been out in the pouring rain on a good running Yamaha twin and had slithered my way down into gravity gulch and gingerly applied the brakes coming to the bridge as a bike shot past my back tire just off to my left on its side making that 'wups I've been thrown on the ground' clattering noise followed quickly by a rider that missed my front wheel by inches. His trajectory and that of the bike differed by just enough to bracket the arc of my travel with the two moving masses one behind and one in front of me as I negotiated the turn. It was a one in a million chance. Man, was I lucky.

I don't know how fast I was going, but I do know that if either lump had hit me it would have taken me down and someone was going to be hurt and it may have been me. It had nothing to do with me other than I was in the wrong place at the wrong time. It happens. I know it happens because I have seen it happen and even been there when it happened, but it had never happened to me, not yet. One minute I'm tip toeing around at what I think is a limit of some sort, ready to line up to race when practice is over and the next I'm inches from disaster and feel its breath and its spittle on my cheek but it doesn't take me.

I finished the lap and pulled in, the crash truck was already at the pit road when I came back around to it and the rider was sitting up and moving. I looked at him when I rode past and he gave me a thumbs up so I nodded back at him but wasn't sure why. Later he would laughingly say that crashing was a pain in the ass and then limp away. The rain was letting up as I put the bike on its stand next to my van and pulled off my helmet and went to look for a phone. This was before the days of cell phones, which is hard to imagine now, but it added something to the importance of phone calls when you couldn't have them anytime you wanted. I found a phone booth with a working phone and fished out the quarters I had brought with me and dialed home. It rang a long time before she answered. She was not happy to hear from me that was plain. I tried to be upbeat and cheerful and relate something of how I felt. She was silent. Looking for a better ending I told her the race was going to start soon and this might be her last chance to wish me luck. "I hope you die," she said, sounding like she meant it, and hung up.

There are no words to describe the rest of the afternoon, although I tried to think of some then and have tried several times since. It rained off and on; I raced when the time came but made no real effort to win and took no risks bigger than a gold fish. I finished and loaded up and didn't even bother to go and see what my final position was. I really didn't care. I had sacrificed a great deal to be there, maybe too much, but it was hard not to still feel lucky. There would be a bitter divorce and years of unpleasant exchanges all of which turned my daughter into her daughter and field dressed my teaching career and reordered my priorities. It would be some years before I was back on the racetrack again, and I felt like a wounded veteran returning to the scene of a battle where he had been permanently disabled. I vaguely recalled that there had been some fun in it, and having failed to find any elsewhere I had returned to see if it was still there.

That return was at Road America in 1989, the year I graduated from Law School with honors, the year I had absolutely no reason to risk any part of myself on a chattering bitch of a G model Yamaha 250 or anything to prove to myself or anyone else that had to do with speed or motorcycles. Still, when the day was over and the AMA guy came over and shook my hand and said it was good to have me back I had to agree with him. It was very good indeed. I am a lucky man.

But how do we account for luck? What scheme of explanation for the nature of things does it fit into? The baseball player who hits a foul ball into the stands that kills a child is not blamed for it, it was just bad luck. There are protective screens and so forth but things happen, bad things, and despite the occasional platitudes about them and the prayerful relating of the incident to somehow being 'God's will' we are left with the possibility that in any given situation where risk is involved there is an element of luck in play.

I am not lucky at other things. I have no luck gambling, for instance, and will never win the lottery whether I play or not. But still I would not say that I am unlucky. There are different kinds of luck, the one that troubles us most is moral luck. Let's say two friends drink too much reminiscing at a vintage racing function and they both decide that they are still fit enough to make their way home. Bob does so without incident, falling into deep slumber still clothed where he wakes up the next morning with nothing more than a headache. Sally on the other hand, his sidecar passenger in their competition days, does not fare as well.

She holds her own drink for drink and can still put up a good front at closing time, but on her way home a young man on a bicycle fails to yield her the right of way when he should have and ends up dead. Police come. She is arrested and charged with vehicular homicide and faces long years in prison and financial ruin. Bob on the other hand was lucky, and although 'guilty' of the same offense, suffers no such ill effects. Circumstances beyond their control, e.g. the chance failure of a bicyclist to yield when he should have, have passed a moral judgment on one but not the other.

Looking at their intentions, both Bob and Sally were negligent to have driven while under the influence whether or not that caused the incident in question. The fact that it was mere coincidence that she was intoxicated will not save Sally from culpability. Luck saved Bob, but Sally was unlucky. Morally however, shouldn't we judge Bob and Sally the same? Their intentions were identical and neither meant to harm anyone. We form the intentions we form because of the kind of people we are, but there are a number of factors that shape us. Our very character is the product of those factors, both genetic and environmental, and it is infinitely complex. To what extent should we be judged for actions or intentions that just flow naturally from our character?

If someone can't help being selfish or obsessive, if it is just in their nature to be so, is it fare to blame or criticize them for thinking too much of their own interests or whether they left the oven on?Existentialists say we only come to know ourselves by our actions. More than that, circumstances presented by chance give us the opportunity to do so. The American service personnel at Abugrade prison showed themselves depraved and brutal under the circumstances in which they found themselves. We would like to think that we are neither depraved nor brutal but, we have not been in their circumstances. Were they just unlucky to be put in that position? Were they unlucky to be bad?

This idea of luck is grounded in the notion that things happen beyond our control and that when they do something in our character may be revealed to be either morally bad or morally good under the circumstances. I struggle with this hoping to be found good, but knowing that my nature has been formed by forces beyond my control and that some parts of it may be less attractive under scrutiny than others. The first time I saw an ambulance flag at an AMA road race I didn't know what to do. Everyone slowed down and I did the same. I asked the referee about it later, so that I would know what the rule was about passing or being passed and so forth. He said there wasn't any rule. You can't pass under a waving yellow flag but there is no rule about passing just because an ambulance is out there.

This was in the 70s, of course, so it doesn't apply now, but back then they didn't stop racing because someone fell down. Our races were long, hundreds of miles, not sprint races, and there was more likelihood of a crash on a restart than because they were picking someone up off the track so we raced on. This ended when one of Kenny Robert's children hit an ambulance at Daytona causing him serious injury and given the closing speeds in question it was decided to be unsafe. In the early days, however, when my morally bad self appeared, it was nothing to keep racing while the ambulance flag waved and the ambulance circulated. That being true, I would pick up the pace whenever I saw the ambulance flag because I was fairly sure that nearly everyone else would be slowing down.

This brought me some very good finishes when it happened as I would get past large groups of people who were more concerned with the safety of the fallen rider than where they finished while I was the opposite. I was lucky there were ambulance runs at several races and ended the season with the highest standing I had come to yet. Still, I had taken advantage of someone else's bad luck to be there and questioned whether it was wrong or not – simply put, just because the rules allow it doesn't make it the right thing to do.

I had been single minded about winning, or finishing at the front. I had not been malicious, but competitive in a sport that rewarded split second selfish decision making. If it's going to be me or you right here, right now, then It's going to be me and you can go faster or get out of my way. It was allowed, and for a time I thought it was required. I was wrong about that, but I was wrong about many things when I was young.

Does luck favor the good over the evil? I began to wonder, and I felt as though I had done bad things to put myself ahead of others. Selfishness is not a virtue, but it may be a necessity and it brought questions. I decided to manipulate the situation and test my faith about winning at all costs.

I stopped going to AMA National Road Races and raced with other organizations in regional events. There the field was a mixture of new riders, half hearted bike lovers who weren't really racers, and the fast few who favored the particular track where the race was held. To this I brought national level equipment and attitude. I was given deference about nearly everything.

It was suddenly assumed that I knew what I was talking about when questions of procedure or safety came up. I was glad to offer my opinion when asked, but had not suddenly been enlightened to any great extent. True, I had a dozen years of racing behind me by then, and had managed to crack the top 20 here and there, but I was no star, just a competent back marker who could be expected to hold his line when the factory riders came around to lap me.

The culmination of this string about luck comes at Grattan, where I showed up with a TZ750, a wife and a new baby. It was father's day weekend and it was to be my first race since becoming a father. Among my off track friends the talk was that becoming a father would change everything. It changed a lot of things, but I had not been a racing dad and wanted to see if that was changed too. I knew the track well, having been there many times. There were no other bikes like mine in attendance and so I knew I had no competition. I paid my entry fee and let the bike set on its stand and watched my daughter Courtney play in the sunshine.

I could hear the bikes running around the course, a sound which normally would make me frantic to get ready and get out there. I didn't feel that way. Racing didn't start until after lunch and the referee came over and asked me if I was going to practice any. I asked him if I had to and he said there was no rule about it and the bike had passed tech so if I didn't want to practice, I didn't have to. I said I would wait, partly because the bike was not that fresh and partly because I just didn't feel like it.

Lunch came and went and so too the national anthem and the other races up to the final race of the day, which was the open GP class, the one in which I was entered. I suited up and did my usual prerace check of the chain tension, the controls, and the fuel level. All was well. Among my competitors was Torello Tacchi, a guy from Chicago with a water cooled Suzuki 750. It was fast in its own way, I suppose, but nothing like the Yamaha. When they waved us off the hill for a warm up lap, I didn't go, but looped back to the grid instead and found my starting position and waited. In a few minutes the starter came over and said there was a report of something on the track and asked me if I would take a sighting lap and have a look. I didn't think twice, but agreed, and took off to have a once around and back to the start, which I did. I saw nothing that would be a problem and said so.

The board went up, the flag came down, and we were off. I had the lead by the time we got to turn one and was never passed. In seven, which is the bowl behind the pits, I could hear people close to me as I tiptoed along waiting to get it pointed straight again and then zipppppp, quick as that, I would squirt ahead of them and have the track to myself again. Tacchi had gone down on lap one, and blamed me for it I was to learn later, which was bizarre. Someone had spilled something on their warm up lap. It wasn't me because I hadn't taken one and it was seen before I was sent out to find out if it was in the fast line. It wasn't because I never saw it. End of story for me and bad luck for Tacchi. It could just as easily have been the other way.

I realized later that I was sent on a fool's errand when they sent me off alone to see if the track was safe. What if there had been a spill of oil and I had found it and gone down? Whose fault would that have been? As it was I didn't find it even though it really was there, making me what? Well, Lucky I suppose is one label you could apply.

It is unsatisfactory in philosophical terms because it gives you no incentive to be good or not do evil but rather suggests that in some random way people will suffer for things they had no causal connection with. Such randomness does not promote good deeds or thoughtful planning and preparation. Why bother, if in the end it is just a matter of luck anyway?

33.

The Two Headed Coin

LIFE AND DEATH ARE part of things whether we race or not. They are the bookends of our existence and while we like to wring as much out of the former as we can and put off the latter for as long as possible, it's out there and we know it is unavoidable. Al Knapp left us one year and I miss him. I would say we were more acquaintances than friends, but I am OK with myself about that. I never turned him down when he asked me for help, but he never asked me either. Like a lot of us 'younger' guys, we pitched in when we could to make things easier for him.

He rode his hand shift Harley with some aplomb and I will let people who knew more about him and his bike tell the details of his story. I had encountered him first when doing a yearbook for AHRMA and he was engaging and thoughtful and we enjoyed talking. My admiration for him was no secret but it grew exponentially after an event at Hallet, Oklahoma where it rained. I do not like riding in the rain anymore, and while I used to say I liked it, the truth was that I often crashed in the rain and finally admitted that I was not good at making that adjustment. At Hallet, however, Al was not just on the track in the rain, but was pulling away, giving his Harley big slides coming out of the slow left hander and seeming to be in perfect control as he did so. It was his day. The man had skills.

What he didn't have any more was luck. I hate it that people get old and I will hate it when it happens to me. We all will. I remember

of a certain kind who do such things for one another. Later he offered to paint my race van like a Budweiser bottle. I declined.

I helped other people do the same sorts of things when asked because I was young and helpful by nature and didn't mind helping. The needs of racing in those days were small because there were few races and fewer bikes that were competitive and I had one already. Newer bikes might be faster but they would belong to guys who had money and thought them precious and would be less likely to risk destroying them than I would mine. To me, motorcycles were just tools like any other except they made speed instead of pounding nails into wood like a hammer does. I did not worship them.

My riding made me successful at racing, not money and not machinery, and I finally got noticed enough to get a sponsor. Things changed. Now money was spent that was not mine on things which were expected to bring a return. I rode for wages and in that light, the risks involved seemed not to be properly compensated. I could be crippled or killed and what was that worth? I was a young man and might forego a long and happy life for a small bit compensation. I tried to imagine how much money would be enough and it didn't come to me. My joy at having someone provide financial assistance soon soured into bitterness at it not being enough.

A better bike, now had to be the best bike and money was spent to buy things I had never had before, like spare parts. Terms like 'opportunity costs' were heard and learned and applied which meant a box van full of packages of rods and cranks and pistons and all the little bits that go into making them work better than other people's pile of bits. I changed brands of motorcycles as faster better bikes were built by different companies. I rode them well enough, but I felt like a whore. My passion had been perverted for the satisfaction of others. My machines went from having a certain amount of elegance to looking like moving billboards. My results were now recorded. Lap times were abstract compilations of results from parts choices in gearing, jetting, and tire compound. The fun bled out of it, and out of me. It became a grim business.

Finally we got to the time when TZ750 Yamaha's were introduced. At first not everyone could have one and everyone without one had little chance of beating them. Then I got a call from someone who said they could obtain one only if they had a qualified rider, meaning someone with an AMA expert road racing license. I had one and the question came whether I would ride one if they bought it. I said I would.

There is a level of pretending in the things we do that can go unnoticed most of the time. Now and then, when your girlfriend doesn't become your wife and she starts to wonder if you mean the things you say, you get caught. Some things we say hoping them to become true. "I can ride it." For instance, may have passed our lips when we only thought we could and wanted the chance to try.

I had a job, and had to arrange for time off and be careful not to let them know what I was going to do with it. I was not military by nature, but professional racers thought of the rest of the world as 'civilians' in a sense because of the combative nature of competitive racing. They wouldn't understand. I wasn't guessing at that, I knew from experience and had lost several good jobs because of racing. I would be working along just fine, become a valuable member of some ongoing enterprise and then Daytona would come along and I would need to be gone for ten days or two weeks. "You don't have vacation time for that." I would be told and there would be a little tug back and forth about it but in the end, I never missed Daytona.

To miss Daytona was to miss all that had taken place over the winter. It was the annual convention of racing and it was the first event of the year. To come out later and start your season somewhere else just meant that you were not serious about racing this season. I went when I probably should have stayed home and saved my money. I went when I would have been better off keeping that job I left to go there, but I went. It became a pilgrimage. Now the vintage race at Daytona is at the end of the season in October. Who cares? It is not the same in every way you can name. It is for people who don't remember and don't understand what it was before. Now, it's just another race, only it happens to be in a place where things that happened there once mattered more than anywhere else.

It is the Notre Dame of racing in America I suppose. Once upon a time one hundred and thirty novices all lined up here at once and went from the pit land straight out onto the banking and all the way around, without a chicane, and came swooping and crashing together into turn one. It was something to behold. It was terrifying to be a part of but it sorted out the good and the lucky from those that didn't belong there. Running with the bulls? Yeah, it was like that, only you were riding on them. My Sprint once showed 12,000 on the tach when I came across the finish line that first lap. Ordinarily it was good for a thousand less and took some time to get there. This time, as we all headed down the back stretch in a thunderous throng of weaving bikes with riders flapping number vests and hunching over screaming machines, the collective slipstream pulled everyone along to new top speeds. I worried they would all come apart.

They didn't. Here and there one would suddenly slow and then a puff of blue smoke would come off the back tire just a heartbeat before it went down and then took out its neighbors. One guy on the inside ahead of me looked back over his shoulder and when he did the banking came and he was not ready and overcorrected, running off the lip of the wall and spilling himself and his TD1C into the infield. As I rode past, cutting my eyes to the corner for just a second, I had made a mental note not to do that. No one I was riding with had ever done what we were about to do. There was no practice for this.

In practice, we were sent from the pit lane out to turn one where we merged in with bikes coming in from the banking. Here, we came to turn one for the first time after the longest stretch of wide open throttle our bikes and ourselves had ever had. I moved over to the inside after we crossed start finish and let off the throttle just a bit. I was going to brake later and was still in my 'wait and see' mode hoping the clump of people in front of me would sort themselves out into some line I could fall into and follow. It didn't happen. We didn't know what we were supposed to be doing so we all just clumped up together and went to the turn. Someone fell down, I'm not sure why I was too far away, and we scattered like quail to miss him. I went low and now needed the brakes, which the Sprint had in abundance. It still had the pointy Dunlop tires so I had to lean it over to get enough rubber on the ground for the brake to work. Something was churning up the grass off to my right but I kept going and then we were fewer in number and farther apart and headed down to the international horseshoe.

I had an afternoon of less intense racing ahead of me to look forward to. It was such a relief to have that first bit of madness over that nothing that followed seemed like a big deal.'Come on in, the water's fine' the shivering blue boys called up to me on the cliff where the rope hung from the tree. I did of course, knowing they were lying and not minding being lied to. After that novice race, back in pits, if someone had asked me if it was all right I would have said it was terrific. Objectively it was very poorly done in almost any way you could name. They had made inexperienced riders do something they had never practiced in a group so large that there was no escape from the mistakes of others in ways that taxed their machines past their limits. The next year we had heat races instead and started out going into turn one rather than out onto the banking. I had not complained, but apparently someone had and I was glad.

Now many years later I was back there with a TZ750, a bike I had never ridden and had not had even one lap of practice on being asked to do a qualifying lap in the old tradition of what they called a 'flying lap'. You went out alone, down the pit lane into one and around the infield to the banking where there was still no chicane on the back stretch and then did a timed lap beginning when you came to the start finish line and ending when you came back to it. It was the novice experience all over again except this time at 180 mph. Sure it was thrilling, only coming down the backstretch to the banking for the first time I was pretty sure I was going to die and despite preparing myself for what was imminent in every way I could think of I was not ready for what came next.

The compression effect of the G-forces smashed down the inadequate suspension components and pinned me to the tank, my head face down unable to see track ahead. I only had a view of the track through the cutouts in the fairing for the fork legs. I am not exaggerating when I disclose that the force was great enough to part my lips and leave the impression of my front teeth on the inside of my Bell Star helmet. I had been told not to let up on the banking or it might seize so I held the throttle wide open. As soon as I was off the banking, I backed off a bit and there was start finish where I was to being my timed lap.

I coasted into one, not sure that I was going to do this but habit took over and I opened the throttle back up and wiggled around on the big bike a bit to get myself going. From corner to corner it was awesome but it didn't stop all that well and I had no feel at all for what the tires were doing. That was because they weren't doing all that much, being hard as concrete and left over from the year before. I didn't know this, which was just as well, and while they had plenty of rubber and would last the 200 miles to come as well, they were not giving me traction of the grade 'A' sort. By the time I got through the infield I had come to like some qualities the big brute had and thought that I could manage it.

It was an evil thing, a brute, and when you thought you had it under control you were kidding yourself. Think J4 jet engine in a Conestoga wagon - Frightening power delivery, archaic support systems. They would get better, we knew that, but it gave me the end game that I had been seeking. There was a 'fast enough' out there to silence my refrain about having to ride a bike that wasn't.

Before the TZ750s, nothing was fast enough. My 55 Chevy that ran C-Gas and would do the quarter mile in 11.97, wasn't fast enough and it would do 135 on top end and push the whole thing out of shape when it did it because it was so wrongly shaped for such speed. My X-6 Suzuki that would do 100 mph in 1965 when no other 250 on the planet would run 90? Not fast enough so I went racing, made it faster, and still wanted something faster. The CRTT factory roadracer? Faster than an X-6 but not as fast as a C-model Yamaha so not fast enough; the TD2B? quick like lightening and good for 130 plus but not as fast as the TD3 I had next or the TR3 I made it into. Even the TZ350, which was probably my all time favorite match of machine and motor for me, was not fast enough on the long straights and would get passed by the bigger bikes and even though I could haul those guys back in when the turns came, it was a losing battle in the long run and we all knew it.

Nothing beats top end on long tracks and most tracks were long enough for it to matter. I thought I wanted something, finally, that I could say was fast enough, but the leap ahead from the 350 to the 750 TZ was too much for anyone without adequate resources that was honest about what they were doing. I never had control of it like I had all the other things I had ridden. Ours had a motocross rear swing arm and suspension unit and was a made over double shock machine. I didn't get to that comfortable place with it where we were one on the track together, moving from here to there with a thought and a gesture rather than a deliberate effort. It was a pig to ride and it gave little or no feedback of what was going on between it and the track. I rode on it, not with it and the one time I crashed it I hit so hard I don't remember hitting the ground at all and was broken all over when I regained consciousness. I won races with it, was grand prix rider of the year with WERA on it, but it was more than fast enough for me. It was too fast.

35.

The Death Of Big Mike

I DON'T KNOW THE particular circumstances and do not especially care to. "Big Mike"Proffit died on a Sunday at Road America while racing his 650 BSA and I was there. I had only met him the day before when we found ourselves camping next to one another at the track at Elkhart Lake. He knew me somehow, by reputation or some mutual acquaintance I suppose, so he assumed I knew him, which happens to me quite a lot. I had only a short time to set up my pit before my work assignment covering pit out began and he was not around. His pickup truck camper was there, with a neon sign in its window that said "BSA", but he was off to tech or some such and we missed one another that first chance.

There is a flurry of activity when you get to a racetrack and a weekend is beginning and it takes some focus to set things up and get ready. This time is compressed by the track's insistence that you sign in first which is controlled by someone who has stopped for coffee and a chat and is consequently late.

It used to irritate me, but now its expected and even familiar. I just had time to get my radio and give a brief 'hello' to the others on the crew before taking up my station. I had taken the time between races to build a device out of a collapsible sawhorse that was an information sign for the riders. On one side it said "Now On Track" and on the other "Next Up". On top were two 2x2s so that a channel ½ inch wide was made where a painted plywood plaquard sat with a clear plastic pocket attached. In the pocket were laminated signs that said, "Practice Group One" and so on through the groups, and then "Race # 1" and so on through the races.

I had been Pit Out at New Orleans last time and the most common activity was trying to explain to some guy on a running racebike what group was on the track and what was up next. He had on a helmet and ear plugs and the bike was loud; I had on headphones and could not hear him. This does not make for good conversation or an efficient exchange of information. I made the signboard to cure that, hoping as I did so that all the riders could read. In practice it worked even better than I had hoped. We don't let bikes out of the pits for an ongoing practice session when there are two minutes or less remaining because they would delay the next group going out. When I got the message from the starter that there were two minutes remaining, I would turn the whole thing around so that the side that had said "Now on Track" then showed "Next Up " the riders waiting to practice. When someone would try to talk to me, which was inevitably in a group of running motorcycles, I would point to the sign and some understanding of what was going on dawned on them.

I thought of it as a kindness, as a racer myself I know how preoccupied one can be getting a bike ready to go on track and getting yourself ready to mentally handle it. There is a list, whether you have bothered to write it down or not, of things that must be attended to. You have to have been through tech and passed whatever level of scrutiny is applied. That's a funny thing in itself. If you are new, then you are likely to be looked at very closely and there will always be something that is to be done again to make them happy. I dreaded tech in the 60s when racing with the AMA and like a lot of other novices, watched the first practice go off from the tech line at Daytona waiting for approval of whatever it was that they had wanted to see if I couldn't do better. That sort of wore off over time as they got to know me and I raced and did well enough to be noticed. A level of trust came on then and the time in tech was more for paperwork and howdy's than frustration.

I have been a tech inspector for several racing organizations and I don't mind the work. Its not rules enforcement except from the safety standpoint. Drain plugs wired, brakes wired, throttle return, transponder, etc. if they have it all and its done right, then off they go. Still I like something closer to the track if I am to be there all day and am not riding and pit out gives me some interaction with the riders who see me as just some guy between them and where they want to be. The morning practice at Road America went off without incident and when it was over I walked over to the edge of the wood where my race bike waited for attention. I hoped to have time to get it teched and get in a few laps myself.

When I came back from checking in with Cindy at Race Control and picking up my radio, I found my neighbor and a few of his friends busying themselves with whatever needed attention. We spoke a few words, nothing important. He liked the way my bike trailer made up into a cabin and we chatted about it. He was a large man, nearly 300 pounds, with salt and pepper hair and beard and a low gruff voice that he delivered with an odd gait. He seemed cheerful and was clearly enjoying himself. In the afternoon I was assigned as grid marshal and had the chore of lining the bikes up when they arrived on the grid and noting who did not start. As a rule, we do not push bikes that die on the line, but now and then when the circumstances permit it to be done safely and there is help we will.

So it was that we gave Mike's big BSA a shove up the track as far as the exit road where we had him turn off and wait for the crash truck to take him back to his pit. It was a hard push because it was uphill and I remembered thinking that it would have been more productive if he had risen up and come down hard on the seat to turn the motor over rather than just easing the clutch out bringing us to a halt. He was part of the generation of vintage riders spoiled by mechanical rollers that have never had to master the run and bump starting procedure of the Grand Prix circuit from my era. As if Hailwood and Ivy and Agostini were not admirable enough already, they had to push the damn things to start a race.

I made no connection from the pushing incident to my camping neighbor and that night nothing was said about it as we both occupied our respective camps and spoke occasionally back and forth across the darkness. It had been a beautiful day and we had both appreciated the weather and the setting. Tomorrow rain was forecast and we did not look forward to it. I was unwinding and letting the adrenaline of a 'Get to the Race' week of constant worry and late nights flow out of me after an all night drive followed by a long day in the sun with headphones on.

His last words to me, and we always seem to reflect on the last meaningful thing we remember someone saying to us, were something about how he could never get his dog to drink whiskey, but it was still a good dog. I was sitting with our Springer Spaniel, who takes her caretaker duties seriously and was stressed to her limit by all the activity and the proximity of strangers. My response was something about how dogs are good company and he muttered something in agreement I didn't understand as we both turned in.

The next day it rained in the morning and we spoke again about breaking camp before the days activities began rather than waiting to do it after everything got wet. There was nothing memorable in what we said to one another and I admit that I was distracted by what I was doing and we did not look at one another as we exchanged our comments. I was to regret this, but like so many moments in life if we had the chance to do them over I would have done it differently.

In the afternoon the sun came out and surprised us with a fine day for racing. I had been into the village of Elkhart Lake for the first time the preceding evening and was charmed by its devotion to racing and its history. With less than 600 residents it is easily outnumbered annually by the bigger events that come to the track just a mile outside its limits, yet it accommodates them and seems to be happy about it. One prominent sign said that the path by the lake was the roadbed of the old racecourse where sports cars had raced beginning in 1952. I went back in the morning for coffee and had to wait for the only gas station to open since there was nothing that stayed open all night. Still, it was the same girl that had waited on me at closing time the night before and she looked tired.

My day included training a new volunteer to fill in when one of our regular crew is not in attendance and like a lot of clubs we count on volunteer help. He was an ex-racer, enthusiastic and diligent and was absorbing the complexity and importance of his role with admirable efficiency. Something I have noticed over the years about having racers work for me as workers on a race crew, they do not assume anything nor attempt to leap ahead at what you are telling of procedures. This is an admirable trait learned, no doubt, from experience. We were both wearing headphones when the least favorite call from race control came over our headsets – "Red Flag, all stations, Red Flag!" which means that the race has been stopped because a rider was down on the track.

Road America It is a very large racetrack, even longer than Daytona at nearly four miles in length, and the far reaches of its layout are far from the pits. As riders began to straggle in it was determined that the race would not be restarted and they were told. No one complained. Then I noticed one rider visibly upset as she returned to the pit lane where several of us went over to her to see what the problem was. She had come upon the carnage that was the end of Mike Proffit and was emotionally shaken by it. I will not go into detail about what she saw, and hope no one else does either, it doesn't really matter. He had suffered an unsurvivable injury and that much was immediately apparent. Still, like Tom Hanks told one of his girl baseball players, "there's no crying in baseball..." Its unusual, that's true, but it was an upsetting and unsettling moment for everyone. Crying was allowed and we held her bike.

Since I was an official, I was questioned by many during the long delay that followed while the procedural aspects of a racing fatality were dealt with. Because I had a radio and headset, there was some expectation that I might be privy to information that they were not. In our rotation for cross training, those of us that work the races have taken nearly every position at one time or another. On my last trip to Road America I had been race control and had been up in the tower with the track people and their fine video displays of nearly every inch of racetrack. I knew they had seen the incident and by now they had seen it too many times already. There was only silence on the radio, which said more than all the words they could have thought of; when something is so horrible and ghastly that you can't describe it, its time to stay silent.

We counted noses and figured out who was missing. Racers I know well and I tried to place the downed rider from what information we had. It was an important moment. It was as if we were collectively trying to conjure up a memory of someone we had not bothered to get to know who was no longer with us. He was not one of my circle of friends and I admitted that I had no immediate recollection of him by name or number. He had been one of us, however, that much was undeniable, and the loss was ours. It was not until later, when his pit crew had come and asked me what report there was about him that I put it all together.

I knew them from the night before and they knew me the same. When a rider does not come back in from the track, sometimes it is just a mechanical failure, and sometimes it is an injury. If they are to be transported, then his crew needs to know which hospital to go to. If it is worse, and this was the worst of all possibilities, then someone needs to gather up his things and find out who is delegated to drive them home to his family.

I have had that chore and it is probably the worst part of racing. Once you take it on, and things are underway, it puts some distance between you and everyone else there. If you are not a racer yourself, I suppose it is even worse. Everything about the excitement and enjoyment of the sport for you was vicariously driven by your rider's perceptions. When they are gone, his perceptions are gone as well and you are left to deal with the grief that follows. In my case it had been a cross country trip after some arranging that had me in my friend's van with all his stuff headed to his widow's house with the only additions being myself, and a street bike to ride back home. We had spoken twice to arrange the exchange and she was stoic about it, for which I was grateful. Still, there was some resentment there and even though I was from several time zones away, I was not invited into her home when I arrived.

Her brother was there and he was not glad to see me. Somehow he was sure that I was to blame, or at least someone like me. "We" as in the racing fraternity, had taken him from his family by some means they could not understand and they did not have to be nice about it now. Skip the crap about he died doing what he loved and look instead at how young he was and how much he spent of what little he had on his racing. I unloaded my bike, had the guy look over the inventory I had made of the stuff and sign it, giving him a copy and keeping one for myself. I did not know if everything that should have been there was there, but I knew that we had loaded up all that we could find, including the wreck of the bike that had killed him. It's mean business and I had offered to do it out of my respect for him and our friendship. He may have appreciated it, I don't know, but I got no thanks from them about it and have managed to avoid doing it since.

Back at Road America, we went ahead and raced the rest of the schedule after the track was prepared and everyone was ready. I was prepared to call it a day and said so but was overridden. There were people who went home, and I don't know if the incident had any part in that. The grids were not full. There was some good racing and before the day was done I saw smiles on faces again where there had been none. It is a dangerous hobby and while we take great pains to make it as safe as we can, human bodies have their limits and if you exceed them, then you will be parted from it. Since we all will be parted from our bodies eventually, it is a good time to be philosophical about that very thing I suppose, or as good a time as any.

If you are alive, and notice the world around you, and then you race a motorcycle, your perception of things is forever altered. That may be true of a good many things as well, I do not know, but I know it to be true of racing and it leaves a mark. If you have done more than just race, if you have passed any of the markers that racing has within the experience, then there are levels of understanding and appreciation that have come to you about life as well.

When you started, there was the question of whether or not you could do it at all. Then came; Can I go fast? Can I pass another rider? Can I be first to the first turn? Can I win a race? Can I win a race at Daytona (or somewhere in particular) Can I win a championship?

We struggle to achieve these passages and when we do, we change. We might have changed anyway, in other ways, just from the passage of time as things moved along but those changes are not noted in the same way. We are just one of the crowd when we begin and what we desire is to be singularly noted and remembered for what we can do on the track better than anyone else. When we struggle with all of the things that are in our way, we must accommodate the other aspects of life to some degree to fit the time and effort needed to be successful into it all. It makes us think.

Every racer has asked himself, "Is it worth it?" at some point in his career. Well, is it? I don't have such insights. I have seen mistakes made that I thought would apply across the confines of the racetrack to life in general. That was a mistake, they don't apply elsewhere. Men who should have known better have done monumentally stupid things while racing motorcycles that they no doubt immediately regretted. Mike may have been one.

I have made such mistakes but I don't claim to be smart enough to have known better to have seen it coming. I will catalogue some of mine and those I have seen for entertainment's sake, but it would be a mistake to think they should mean something to you. Come to think of it, that might be a mistake as well. They may mean something truly profound.

The really attractive part of racing is the ability it has to point out those making mistakes in real time. Slower riders on slower machines are the product of mistakes in design and preparation and riding. They may be subtle, but there they are for all to see as something faster, ridden with more skill, goes whizzing by. It doesn't matter a whit, either, if the rider is an agnostic or a Buddhist or a Northern Ireland Catholic, such things are not important to the forces in play on the racetrack. And yet we know many a superstition that shows itself as riders prepare to face a possible meeting with death in the race to come.

The difference between life and racing is that in life, death is certain, as are mistakes. In racing, because it never goes on forever, there is a finish line where we compile our lap times and have a look at the reality of who was doing things right and who was making mistakes. Death in racing happens, but it is unexpected. Death at the end of life never misses, and that's no mistake.

36.

You Gotta Have 'Art

IT WAS A BEAUTIFUL thing. The more I looked at it, the more beautiful I thought it was. I had seen some beautiful cars before since my grandfather was a Ford Dealer and it was the 1950s but this, well this had Style! I was sitting in a 1955 Ford Crown Victoria and it was stunning. The parts were all made to flow visually from one into another and the chrome band that ran up and over the outside ran inside too. Slick ! Buddy Holly sang on the radio that looked like it was made to match the rest of the dash, being round and all like the gauges were, and I never wanted anything so bad in my whole life. True, I was young, and had wanted other things before, but not like this. It spoke to me. It smelled great, looked great and when people came in and looked at the other cars and then at this one, they changed.

Across town the boxy little 55 Chevy's with their egg crate grills and salmon pink and grey paint jobs looked pathetic by comparison. We looked, after all they were a competitor, but not for the Crown 'Vic, we had no problems there other than not being able to get enough of them. It was the most striking new car design since 1953 when Studebaker had put out that neat starlight coupe, which only looked good as it turned out, having the same old six cylinder motor as always. Oh there was the little Thunderbird, but that wasn't a car, really, just a toy.

This was all subjective, of course, and I was very young, but I learned a few things about artistic expression in the process. There was a lot of hoopla every year when the new cars came out and design was a large part of it. I drew cars to pass the time while being cared for by my grandfather while the women folk were off doing the sorts of things that womenfolk did. He would put me up on top of the show room sales offices that had a false ceiling by a back stairway with a little school desk and a pad of paper and told me to draw anything I wanted and I did. Usually it was a car.

I kept drawing as I got older and when it came time to go to college I used 'Art' for a major since it was what I did best and what seemed to come the easiest to me. It was there that the problem of the subjective appreciation of things as opposed to reality became clarified. I was attending the University of California at Berkley one summer at a workshop and we had a critique at the end of the term's work in which we were to be judged and for which an overall winner was to be identified. I had done a large canvas of the San Francisco Bay in the spring with which I was pleased and which pleased some-one else enough to buy it afterward. At the show, however, it was not the winner.

The winner was a mounted black and white Polaroid of an un-remarkable living room scene, empty of anything but furniture. The title was, "I took this picture when I heard President Kennedy had been shot." The frame was large and nicely made and the photo was matted in the center with a wide black border of considerable size all around it. We had been in class with one another off and on for weeks by then and I knew the girl that entered the piece and asked her about it. She readily admitted she had not taken the picture, but had found it at an estate auction and just thought of the name and entered it when the painting she had been working on for the class didn't turn out. She had paid to have it mounted, matted and framed so none of it was her work except for thinking of it. I wasn't very sure that any of it had been her idea actually, but I had to admit it was clever, or bold, or both.

The judge was very taken with the piece and went on and on about its creative insight and deeper meaning. I get it, I really do, but its cats and dogs having sheep when you cross categories like that and compare the process of creation in terms of artistic merit to something done by an artist, struggling for mastery of his or her chosen medium while trying to creating something recognizable and artistic at the same time. If I looked at the picture without the title, what would I think? That has always been my test.

Years later I entered a community art show and an abstract piece with yarn and things glued to it was the Best of Show winner. It was titled, "from the sea" in another language, and even after a translation it did not pop into my head that there was anything about it evocative of the ocean; or that may have come in with the tide later for that matter. In fact for me, the only part of it that held lingering fascination was how it won an award at all.

Going back to my artistic training at the graduate level, it was after the photo incident that I decided to look for other work because I was pretty sure that this guy wouldn't like Norman Rockwell either and I did, a decision which has turned out well for me. While I am being critical I may as well say that also in the recent local show were pictures done by elderly ladies from a nursing home, which were drawn first from magazine illustrations for them by someone else, which they then had painted. Charming, and I appreciate the gesture, but its not art, and I know its mean of me to say so but it insults real artists that have labored and created original work of their own that such entries are accepted and shown.

Part of the problem with art is that few people know enough about it to have a real appreciation for it when it comes along. On one level it's a trick; an illusion of some sort where reality is tweaked on purpose by a tweaker who means to do it and say something to you as a viewer when they do. There were some fine original glass pieces submitted, for instance, that were not given an award. They were unique, and nicely done, in fact so well done as to look 'professional'. Isn't that the idea? They were as fragile and as perfect as the dragonflies they portrayed. The difficulty it takes to make such art is not understood by someone who has never done it themselves or seen it done.

An artistic expression in any medium should be judged on its own merits, not by its title, not by its charm, and not by knowing the charming elderly person that did it but by certain concrete criteria laid down long ago. For example: Does it handle the medium well? Is there a composition? Does it evoke something beyond itself in the viewer? It was difficult if not impossible for me to tell if the judge had applied such criteria, and while I am happy for those that were given an award, I question the legitimacy of the process when the rationale stated by the judge that gave them out was that he "liked them". He may like pancakes too, but that doesn't make them art, whether he went to art school or not.

This is the minority view, I might add, as any walk through a museum of modern art will show you. I also prefer old motorcycles to new ones, so much so that if possible I would have one without plastic at all but that is nearly impossible. There was something about polished aluminum and steel being fashioned into a graceful moving object that is artistic and I have felt that way always. For most of my young life it was cars that provided the visual entertainment and the cars of the 50s and less so of the 60s were a grand show. I owned a few in my time that now they call 'classics' but don't enjoy owning them now. My fast '55 Chevy with the Pontiac motor lost favor to a Maroon 1965 Pontiac GTO, that was a beautiful thing and very fast on its own.

From there I might have gone on to other later cars of beauty and power but for a Triumph twin that stopped me in my tracks. It was candy apple red and had the great 'Triumph' harmonica tank badges and looked like it was going a hundred miles an hour standing still. It was easy to start, easy to ride, and while it wasn't as flat out fast as other things I had driven, it was certainly more thrilling. After that, my interest in four wheeled things turned to those that I could haul a bike to the races in and sleep in when I got there.

Aesthetics then, were and are part of racing for me. I want things to look a certain way if I can manage it, and while it may have nothing to do with how fast it goes, a nice looking bike is more satisfying to my soul than a crappy looking jet of a machine. There is a phase that all racers go through when it is just about the speed and the winning. I get that. You will find your own limit.

In Racing, the look of a motorcycle matters otherwise we would not take so much time and put so much effort into getting it to look the way we want. There is a broad range of expression out there and I love it. At the vintage races especially one sees genre expressed that may have come and gone out of style for some but never for others. Jelly bean tanked Ducati's and Black and Chrome Nortons sit side by polished side in garages saying 'look at me' in their own artistic way. Racing is more than riding, it is showing off as well, which is just another form of artistic expression.

While we don't give awards for the best looking machines at a race, those that bring them do enjoy the admiration that comes with having them. Some are so ugly they are cute, while some are so rare as to be admired for that alone. The fact that they run, and that some of them actually put out a good turn of speed is just icing on the cake.

It matters, as all things matter, and that is why racing is part of who I am and what I do. Out there on the track the results are not subjective even though the terms we use to describe the sensations we feel when we do it may be. Bikes are hot or thrilling or exciting, or cool, or whatever adjectives we choose to use to express how we feel about them and yet our transponders translates that all into a digital read out that relates to time and distance in simple truthful terms. Yes, but, we know that is not the end of it. That boiling down of the experience that made the lap a 3:04.26 is exponentially greater than the sum of its parts. How many hours of time and effort went into getting you there, getting the bike bought or built and then prepared just so to let those three minutes happen for you and the machine together? It varies, doesn't it, depending on who you are and what the bike has made you into.

All things being equal, the fastest bike wins the race because of the nature of things that have to do with time and distance. The human factor is the difference and if I go and race and don't have the fastest bike there and know my chances of winning are nil, why would I compete anyway? Simple answer: Because I love to race and it wouldn't really matter to me if no one else was there. My opponents are the forces of the universe, holding me back from taking off at will, other riders are secondary to that and as much as I enjoy a good dice on the track, its not them I beat when I win, or even if I just finish having ridden well, it's the time of my life that I have put behind me for eight laps or however many we just did. That time is filled with moments that string together or run on top of one another and eat away at what time I have on this earth to think and do and try to solve the mystery of why it all matters. It means something.

That is a feeling of mine, of course, but I hold it with as much certainty as I do when I stand before a great work of art and understand that it is great and that it is art. Feelings are not always things that we can translate verbatim into scientific language which seems to bother some people and make them suggest that there can be no certainty about anything without the science to back it up. If science could do creative art without human assistance I might be impressed with it, but it can't. It might be able fool me by pretending it was a person when it made an image but fooling me is no real measure of success and there are many that can tell you that.

I am too easy. I am nice to strangers who may only be out to take advantage of my gullibility. I don't mind that so much since the alternative would be to be unkind to them and that would be against my nature. No, I'm not willing to walk some middle ground while I try and decide for myself if they are well intended. I like to be helpful and I enjoy the company of like minded people. I am reminded of the guy who crashed in the last practice before his heat race at Daytona after having his bike just right for the race. He should have resisted the temptation of one more practice but he couldn't. He crashed hard enough to tear one side up thoroughly, and even though he had not been an especially chatty or friendly sort of guy we all pitched in and got him patched up enough to make his race.

Many of the pieces that were used to do this were loaned to him on an ad hoc basis and there was some expectation that he would return them. Since we were all in the same race, I suppose we thought that after it was over there would be time to sort that out. There wasn't as it turned out, since he didn't finish and came back in and loaded up and left before it was over. He had forty friends waiting to be made and left them all behind for a pittance in borrowed parts. He was the poorer for it.

37.

What's Cookin'?

IF I PUT A generous cut of roast and some vegetables in a crock pot and slice in a bit of onion and then pour a can of Coca-Cola over it all for broth, an amazing thing happens over time after heat is applied – a nourishing meal of juicy tender roast beef with soft carrots and; if you were careful not to add them too early, nicely cooked potatoes as well. The ingredients bear only the slightest resemblance to their uncooked predecessors and the soft drink is lost completely except for making the meat incredibly tender and uniquely flavorful. It is an easy thing to do and while the ingredients are important, their proportions and the manner in which they are combined are non-critical to culinary success.

Racing is like that. If you put what you have to ride and your leathers and helmet and all the rest in a transporter of some kind and drove off to, oh, let's say "New Jersey" one weekend to see what's cookin' what result? Well you would find quality competition here and there but there was also easy riding and enjoyment of a fine facility with some history, the grounds having been a P-47 Thunderbolt training base in WWII. Old friends met, new ones were made, and the larger spirit of racing competition was extended just a little longer for all of us.

I worry that it will all pass someday and while it was interesting to see the electric bike there, and I'm sure it goes like stink, I have to say it does not capture my imagination or my ears like a hunka, hunka burning love thrashing up and down in a cylinder so evocative of what Elvis was getting at when he sang the tune. I also feel a twinge for the folks there who never got to hear a race without mufflers. Every movement of the throttle, each backing off, no matter how small, was audible and identifiable with the guy who had an instrument louder and more responsive than any Stradivarius. We muffled all of this joyous noise some time back and I saw with sadness that the Formula 500 class, my favorite class, had but one entry. (So, just one clove of garlic? Are you sure that will be enough?)

Formula 500 machines were the MotoGP bikes of their day and had been the backbone of American vintage racing for decades but they consume pistons and rings and crankshafts and riders like a campfire in New Hampshire eats firewood. Nothing out there is as vicious as these things were in their day. Short wheel based, highly tuned with narrow powerbands and a propensity to seize at the least convenient moment, they were shod with tires which had the nasty habit of sliding out from under you just far enough to gather up a sudden urge to BITE hard enough to pitch you up into the air where you could only wait for a painful reunion with the earth below. (Should I add the Tabasco now?)

Oh, you've got padded leathers? Good for you. Jump off your garage head first onto the driveway and see if they help. Still, there were lots and lots of two stroke twins in the old days and they were a bitch to ride and a beast to make go fast consistently so they were a universal curse and blessing all at once. They were the great equalizer for all of us novices at one point when the rulebook said we all had to ride 250s to get over ourselves and move up to bigger things.

When I did that, and moved up, it was easier there than the work required getting there and a choice of which bike to ride had more to do with where you finished than your riding did. To have done well in the snarling 250 class where every tiny mistake cost you yards of track on the guy you were chasing you had to be on your game. This was especially true for me since I am six feet tall and my racing weight was easily 50 lbs heavier than the majority of the field. Once I got on bigger bikes with more power, things were different. I enjoyed the difference, but the share of glory for bike or rider shifted to the bike.

John Long lapped the field of novice riders at Loudon on his Yamaha twin and it was impressive, mostly because we were <u>all</u> on Yamaha twins. (Allspice? Is that all the spices together – or something else?). The surprise came when those of us that moved up to bigger bikes and still raced with John found him mortal.

Things happen to people. Actually they happen to all of us, including racers, and it is not unusual to see someone at the top of their game dominating the rest of the field some sunny day somewhere and then find them mid-pack in the standings at the checkers of the first race the next season. (Less onion, please).

Each race is a meal for the soul of a real racer.

There is an after taste of the races before, sure, but it faded on the trip home from that memory and a new recipe was carefully worked out for the next in the mind of a sleepless driver.

"I need more speed;" might have been thought, or "New Tires next time;" or "I will not be bullied in the turns ever again…" The track will be replayed in the theater of the brain as the adrenaline fueled memories that were etched deep in the consciousness render delightfully frightful moments of terror that have come and gone. What's the difference between a good rider and a poor one in a turn at top speed dealing with the moment? The good one is trying things abstractly to make the bike go faster, the poor one is just surviving and waiting for it to be over. (Low? Or Medium? Or high?)

The crock pot crucible of racing has some temperature settings that relate to when and where. If you want to crank it up to max, go to the Isle of Man where our sport began and do thirty eight miles of public roads at insane speeds testing yourself against others doing the same. Is it dangerous? Are you Irish? It's not just dangerous it's deadly and I have to admit it's too much for me now. I had the chance once to go and didn't, and am not ashamed to say that what I want from the sport and what it does for me doesn't require that of me. I can test myself just fine on 'low' now, thank you very much, and the gods of speed don't tease me at night with cat calls of cowardice because I drew a line for myself. Do I admire Dave Roper for what he can do there? He knows I do. Does he also know that I still think I'm faster than he is? Ask him. Are these signs of anything real?

The signs are out there, singularly or in communion with one another, and I know there are skeptics and naysayers who think such thoughts foolish. Ted Henter is a man I admire and have spoken of often. I remind readers that his talent was so great that even those of us competing with him had to admire it. We all have talents, but when we see someone with an ability we don't have it's through admiring eyes more than jealousy. I found I had a talent early on about braking, for instance. It came to me as a matter of necessity born of riding old equipment in a field of faster bikes. I could go in deeper on the brakes than anyone I ever came upon. It's a talent without much use if what you want is a lower lap time, I recognize that, but we work with what we have.

Ted was talented everywhere but the bulge was in his calculation of how far he could lean it over. In a day when no one crawled off the bike or put their knee down it was noticed that he could do something none of the rest of us could do, including John. He could lean it over until you were sure it was going to leave him. Oh, sometimes he crashed, like we all did, but he learned from it and would think to himself that something in the suspension must need adjustment or improvement. I didn't know it then, but he had the advantage of having been a surfer, maybe the first in Panama, certainly the first Anglo. I was riding a crude skate board at the time, dreaming of surfing, but struggling with some of the same challenges – speed, balance, direction and all that.

Finding things in common with someone as keys to their development was a professional curiosity of mine when I was a teacher. Our exposure to this or that has an effect, regardless of how much we want to think of ourselves as a wholly made person at some point and from there make the world what we want it to be instead of the other way around. When I had the chance to interview Ted for this book he told me about how he had seen a dune buggy on the cover of Hot Rod magazine as a kid and wanted one. His father was supportive and paid well enough to make that possible, so Ted's desire to have something was made a material reality. Can you do that? Can you want something and then make it happen? I am certain that you can, although it has its limits. I needn't list them for you, since you probably bump up against them often enough not to need reminding.

The funny thing about hearing Ted's memory of having seen a dune buggy on the cover of Hot Rod magazine was that I had seen it too. It was the August of 1966 issue and when I came back home and started digging through old things for this work I found that I still had it. Some guy in a Yellow Meyer's Manx is jumping over a dirt berm of some sort and has all four wheels off the ground. My ignorance of what they really were kept me from wanting one myself.

In the days when we raced together, if I crashed I thought I had done it myself. When Ted crashed he started looking for what had failed on the machine. His technical approach and reputation for good handling motorcycles landed him a job with Harley-Davidson as the set up man for a young Jay Springsteen when they brought their water-cooled two stroke twins over from Italy to take on the Yamahas. In one of those corporate mysteries a good design was wasted by cost cutting when it came to the bearings and little internal bits and they failed to achieve their potential. Now we're cooking in a larger pot. (How many potatoes are too many?)

I had the pleasure of visiting with Bill Himmelsbach and we were talking about the Harley two strokes because he had one there. Ted's name came up and he smiled. Certainly he had known Ted, and he told me that he had one of the bikes Ted had worked on for Harley back home in his shop under restoration. I asked him how he knew Ted had worked on it and he told me that when he took off a fork cap and looked inside he found a socket there engraved "T.Henter" that had been used to preload the fork for better performance. I got goose bumps. Earlier this season, at Grattan, a 125 two stroke Honda had appeared with an odd looking ignition system that worked like a charm and they had come to show me. It still had its manufacturing label – Henter Engineering.

Ted was blinded over thirty years ago in an accident in England. How 'accidental' that was is probably subject to question in the grand scheme of things, he took it as a sign. He went on to have a successful career as a computer programmer and developed 'JAWS' – a screen reader with audible prompts for the vision impaired. How good was it? Microsoft liked it enough to incorporate its features in their software. How beneficial was it to thousands of blind people who wanted to use computers? Imagine that you can't see this.

The crowd at the New Jersey event wasn't huge but it was substantial. Road racers don't come for the roar of the crowd. Sure, it would be nice if the word had gotten out a little better and the track hadn't decided to be a little greedy about charging extra to let people in the pits to park, but that's not the point. For those of us who wonder what matters and what doesn't, it is large that revelations like Ted's socket still being with us after all this time come to light in such a venue. It is what the French call "*Presque vu*" which is sort of like *déjà vu* only its about the future instead of the past. It's the feeling you get when something is about to happen that you will look back on later and say, "Yeah, I felt that coming."

Racers get it as they zip up their boots and leathers and put on their helmets and wonder what's in store for them out on the track in the near future. If you don't think they are preoccupied, then how do you explain the "don't forget to turn the gas on" notes on gas tanks next to their grid reminder stickers showing them where to go when they get to the start. They don't allow themselves time for such thoughts once the green flag waves because racing is such an all consuming activity and their focus is required elsewhere.

They consciously tamp down these little bumps from their subconscious to work on a smoother surface without distractions. After the race, depending on how it went, they may resurface. If they won, they can ask themselves if that feeling they had before the race was their notice of a win on the way. And if they didn't win, and something else happened, then they may reflect on that as well and consider whether they should have paid more attention to what the signs were telling them before going ahead.

38.

The Zen Of Time

THE TIME IS NOW. Right now, actually, right this minute, right this second – Now!

Wait a moment or two before going any further, that's just a suggestion to get the most out of this but I believe it's pretty well thought out and since I know where its going and you don't it's a warning you might want to heed. Take a break, go to the potty or have a cup of tea or coffee and then come back and we'll pick up the string.

(time passes . . .)

Well, it's later now than it was when you began reading this, assuming you took my advice, and we have built ourselves an interval of time to consider as we go forward which will be needed to show you a truth about it. Time is relative, after all, which is a major theme here. Behind me are experiences which I have been telling you about and which I will continue to tell you about in the hope that they will enlighten you as they have me. I am a fortunate man. Some would say I am lucky, others would insist that I am blessed, but I don't know what to say about it other than I have had a lifetime of unusual occurrences and if I wake up again tomorrow I will be able to say that they persist.

I may be past the midpoint of my allotted time, which would be troubling to those who think about such things, but it doesn't bother me a bit. I left home after high school and I am still gone. I was fully awake and working for a living then, and had been for half a dozen years already. I am still fully awake and working for a living now. I do different things now, and do them differently than I used to but that is to be expected. When I wrote my first book it was with a fountain pen scrawled across three hundred pages of notebook paper. Now I hit yellow plastic squares on this qwerty keyboard attached to a machine I only vaguely understand. I got the keyboard because it was supposed to be easier to see but the letters have worn off from use so that now they are just blank patches of yellow plastic. This changes some things, but not others.

Like all of us, the changes that take place over time make us think about different things. That's interesting in a pedestrian sort of nostalgic way that makes us feel a kinship with people who remember when Cokes were a nickel and the music on the radio was different, but it's not those sorts of things that should concern us. Those things are too easy to figure out, after all, and one has but to look backward with some effort to find a time previously lived to feel some comfort in having been there, been concerned about surviving it, and now feeling bolstered by the present realization that you've survived.

Sprinkle in some opportunities for it to have been otherwise and you start to think that maybe, just maybe, this could go on forever. It's a trick we all do with ourselves – we go to class reunions and watch old movies with new fascination or criticism about what they missed. I have a Ph.D. daughter who teaches about the sixties. I know the sixties, and little of what she believes about them matches my experience. She laughs at this. My methods of knowing are so unscientific and my research from just having been there is obviously biased and limited that she thinks her insights to be more reliable than mine. There are sources to validate and a record of sorts to examine so what do I know?

What I know, and what concerns me, is that I seem to still be who I have always been at the core and was when I went through the sixties. This surprises me. I became self-aware at an early age and was told that changes would come and that I should be ready for them. They couldn't come soon enough to suit me and I jumped into that pool head first, even though I knew it was risky.

Some changes I felt. Growing taller was painful. Puberty was unsettling. Learning to shave made me bleed. Still, it was part of the process of getting out of being obligated to do what you are told to do every damn second and I was certainly ready for that. Ask yourself when you reached that point.

What time is it now? Well, to me its still 'now' because I am still here telling you this same tale that I began a minute or two ago. Could be longer, but if its very much longer you might want to pick up your speed a bit. You might have checked your watch, I don't know, but whatever it says about the position of our planet relative to the location of the sun in this time zone is wrong.

I am not talking about that sort of 'time'. True, you may not have checked your watch but looked at your cell phone instead but it still doesn't matter. No matter how precisely man tries to pin down time with science using atomic clocks and all the rest none of it is precise enough for what I care about. Time is relative to me in the one way that really matters – What you can do with it.

Now is the only time to do anything. We may plan for tomorrow but we are planning 'now' for uses we may put things to at another time that has yet to arrive. Planning is a real thing too. We can't do things in the future, not really, because we have this minor irritating limitation of living in the now. The past used to be 'now' but that didn't last very long. I mean just look back at where this string began and I was talking about 'now' way back then. If this seems to you like a meaningless semantic digression it's because you don't know when I first thought of this and how long I've been trying to work it out.

The idea that time is something real and capable of different qualities and effects came to me after I kissed a girl the first time. She was not just any girl. That would have been October 26, 1962 and I'd have to say it was a real discovery for me. Before then I had never thought much about the time I was traveling through. I thought about the destination, I enjoyed the journey, but I paid no attention to the speed. Ever since that night, I have measured time differently.

We were sitting in the back row of the Lincoln Theater under the Brown Jewelry Store blue neon clock with the word 'Bulova' at the bottom of the ring around its dark face. It was 9:02 pm exactly if the clock was right, and I knew that because her dad was going to pick her up out in front of the show at 9:15 because that's what time the paper said the show was over and I was looking at it to make sure we didn't miss him. I didn't know him, but he had seemed unpleasant when he dropped her off as I waited out front.

To check the time at 9:02, I had taken my dead arm out from around her, where it had been since I had worked the courage up to slip it there after a fake yawn and stretch, and where she had nestled nicely ever since. Before that, I had caught her looking at the side of my head a time or two and given our close proximity it was difficult not to turn and see what it was she wanted but I had managed to keep my attention, and my face, straight ahead. Despite that, I saw nothing and thought of nothing but her and why she kept looking at me.

The pain in my shoulder kept me from focusing on the show and was getting progressively worse. When I couldn't stand it any more, but didn't want to give the impression that I couldn't take it, I leaned forward and turned myself so I could look back at the clock on the wall directly above where we were sitting. It let me get some circulation back without looking like a weenie.

Just then, at exactly that minute as I looked back from the clock, there was a time shift in the universe that was so great it could not go unnoticed. I looked up at the clock and then looked back at her to see if she wanted to know what time it was, and saw that wasn't what she wanted - She wanted me to kiss her. How I knew that, and why I had not known it any sooner I really can't say. What I can say is that there was a moment there when the cloud of doubt I had lived under up to that instant dissipated and I could clearly see my way forward. I did not hesitate, although I suppose I should have, or could have, but leaned down to her and kissed her on the mouth as if I knew what I was doing. I didn't of course, although I had seen it done in the movies plenty of times, both on and off the screen.

I am not sure if she knew either, but we figured out what to do quickly enough and it worked out very well for both of us in the same moment. We continued on for an instant, or an eon, I was not sure, as I completely lost all track of time. There had been no awkward moment or fumbling half hearted hesitation at the beginning. It had seemed as inexorable as gravitational attraction. One minute I was a boy who had never been kissed, the next I was someone's boyfriend kissing his girlfriend the way she seemed to always want to be kissed.

For her sake now, I'll call her Sally, but that wasn't her name. I went absolutely crazy about her in the first minute after our lips touched and before we stopped we were nearly late for her ride. Her grumpy protective father pulled up in his blue company pickup truck from Bradford Supply and did not smile. We had been holding hands and he apparently didn't take it well. He said nothing to me, or to her that I heard, as I opened her door and then closed it after she had gotten in. She just looked at me and smiled and I smiled back.

By the next morning my face literally hurt from smiling and I can still smile about it now. We managed to stay more or less together through high school but that ended brutally while she was dating someone else and I appeared at what was surely a bad time for all concerned. I know now it wasn't malicious but you can't reason with someone who is broken hearted. Later I will tell you what came next, but not now.

Now you need to know that I rode my Triumph twin to school and there were no other motorcycles there and those of us with that unique freedom to transport ourselves where ever we wished stood apart from those who relied on their parents or were seen humiliated through school bus windows as they were taken on a predestined route with the other children. Perhaps to school, perhaps to some prison or gas chamber, who knew? You certainly could not tell from their expressions.

When I showed up on the bike the first day of school no one questioned my right to be there. It was loud and candy apple red and I gave it a nice big slide into the gravel parking lot playing with the throttle to jockey into the space over by the oilfield pipe fence. It was still moving sideways when I got off with a nonchalant lift of one leg and let it slide on out from under me as I held on to the handle bars. I let it come to a stop and then flicked out the kick stand and turned off the petcocks. Guys gawked but they kept their distance. Apparently there was some aura given off by the thing that made people assume you were malevolent, which suited me fine. I was anything but malevolent, but it's not a bad starting point for high school and I had an aversion to bullies.

I was usually late, either from having gotten in late the night before from my night job or from having been out late the night before if it was a rare night off. My day job began as soon as school was out but it was the junior position and I tried to keep them both. Now and then their schedules would conflict if someone else didn't show up and I would be asked to work over or come in early. In anticipation of this problem I had scheduled myself a first hour study hall. These were days in the early sixties and a guy willing to work could find it nearly everywhere regardless of his age. All you had to be to get the job was ask. All you had to do to keep it was be reliable.

Automation was in the future and nearly everything was still done by hand which meant you needed a lot of hands to get very much done and there seemed to be a lot to do. This suited me just fine as when I was working I didn't have to be at home or school where I had to explain myself and be pleasant. I was not especially good at either one. We all have our talents they say, but none of mine fell under the heading of "charming."

I suppose it's the age, as a good many young teenagers still seem to have the problem now. Whether it's an aid or a hindrance to have a motorcycle at that phase of life is hard to say, but it was a means to an end for me and my greatest pleasure so I clung to it. Safety played no part in my concerns and helmets were not required. Tears were a problem though, and they kept me from riding as fast as I wanted so I did buy some goggles, the sort with four little flat panes of glass in them all nestled in a leather holder with padded parts to help them fit my face. They looked goofy and old timey and I was distracted by the lines made across my field of vision by their design. For a replacement, I opted for a pair of the jet age plastic bubble goggles that came in a number of colors. I choose yellow, which really made the world a different place and I liked the difference. Times seeing all things in shades of yellow were special.

It was a perception, of course, I see that now, but when you're young and free and out to see how fast your motorcycle will go you're not thinking of any of that. I wasn't thinking about what was going on between my legs either, where the pistons and pushrods and valves and such were whirring around inside their aluminum and chrome castles. I had no idea how it worked or why. I didn't want to know.

I had enough to think about already and adding design theory and motorcycle maintenance to the burden of things I had to worry about seemed unnecessary. If it broke, I'd fix it, I told myself; but it didn't break - not ever. It just ran and ran and ran. I loved that bike.

The last time Sally and I were together there was a slumber party at Cindy's house and a bunch of the guys had snuck over to be with their respective significant others. Instead of making out she had wanted to 'talk' and had directed me to a bench on the front porch in front of an open window. It was rare for her to take the lead in things so I knew enough to know she was highly motivated about something and went along with it. On the other side of the window her friends listened, I was fairly sure, although I didn't mention it.

I can see now that what she probably was after was reassurance but I blew it and instead expressed my frustration at how difficult women were to please and then made it worse by adding that things would be better if they were like cars and you could just fix them when they broke down or paint them another color if you got tired of the way they looked. Needless to say, this bit of philosophy was coolly received and there was no warmth in our parting. There wasn't any coming from me either, which is regrettable, as I was feeling manipulated and was defensive about it. Give me an ultimatum and I'll take the 'or else.'

I left town to wander for a bit, visiting family in Texas and New Mexico, and neither of us were the same when I came back. We went on to different colleges and I started racing and that more or less was that. Still, I owed her for showing me what time in love can do and how wonderful the world can be if someone shows the way. I still see her now and then but we live in different states and have had our whole lives come and go between who we were back then and who we are now.

St. Augustine struggled with this as well. He had grasped that one of the major things that troubles thoughtful people is the passage of time and their apparent inability to manage it successfully through life. He saw it has a human limitation and I have to agree. Then he made the brilliant suggestion that God doesn't share this limitation since he is divine. I have to admit that I didn't see the significance of this at first and still can trip over the implications of such a truth if that is what it is. He said it in a sentence that has taken me half a century to comprehend. I will set it out for you now so you can get started on that: "Creation was a single act."

It was heretical, of course, but he was a bishop in North Africa and not much notice was taken of Hippo. The orthodox view was that God made the world in seven days and the accepted text on the subject as adopted and considered by the many minds who worked it out since is that different things were created on different days and that on the seventh day He rested.

I knew the story, and had a framed picture of Jesus on my bed-side table that I could see as I said 'Now I lay me…" at night to my listening mother when I was little before the light was switched off. I started wanting the light on once I actually noticed that the words I had been saying every night included a part about dying before I woke, which seemed a bit off putting.

St. Augustine was put off by the logical problem of making God take a week to perform the creation of the universe if He was who we thought he was. After all, omnipotent means all powerful, so it wasn't a problem of being strong enough. (that also adds some mystery to why he might need 'rest' when he was done). He is also claimed to be omniscient, which means he wouldn't have needed more time to think of how to create everything from the void or what the possible outcomes were going to be of everything that he was setting in motion. Descartes would worry over this in Paris during the Enlightenment and finally concluded that God was just a great clockmaker and the universe was what he made and after it was set in motion, since any creation of His would be perfect, there was no need to fiddle with it or watch over it. God need not be present to win.

Descartes said this because he just couldn't believe that a merciful God would allow Evil to happen while he was watching, and since it obviously was happening, He apparently wasn't watching.I got thorough my bedtime prayers without being coddled by my mother's response to my plea that if the light stayed on I might live through the night rather than die. "Let's see what happens if it's out instead," she would say, and then plunge me into darkness and leave me there. I didn't die, but I thought I might once I knew I could and a good bit of time passed in terror of the possibility.

I had not made myself clear, apparently, where as she had. That was something I would have to work on, if I survived long enough, and I have.

St. Augustine had some trouble explaining to people exactly what he meant too and since he had taken it upon himself to greatly indulge in every sinful vice he could find before seeing the truth of things, his teachings were somewhat suspect. He wrote that off to the Devil's work and the weakness of the flesh, which doesn't excuse him. He does make one salient point about time, however, that may be right on the money so I will translate it into an analogy you should understand.

Let's say you're driving from the West coast to race at Daytona, a trip I have made a time or two. And let's say further that you are in Dallas, stopping for gas, right now. Dallas would the present, as in 'now' since that is where you are as you notice it. Arguably time is something different if you don't notice the reality of things where you are 'now' but we'll get to that later. For now we'll say you're in Dallas and it is the present. Buena Vista, where you started from, is behind you, both figuratively and actually since you are pointed east and it is a good deal west of you.

As you stand by the van and look at the tires and smell the gas coming out of the nozzle, and watch the numbers clicking by on the pump robbing you of money, you realize that you are not sure if you turned off the solder pot on the workbench or put the cat outside. This revelation is troubling. Flander's cable kits make great control cables in all lengths with whatever end you need but it takes solder to do it and the best way is with a pot hot enough to melt the solder. You made cables before you left, as you usually take a spare of everything since you are driving 3000 miles to a race where no spares may be available. You also have a shop cat.

You didn't go get one, it just showed up one day to get in out of the rain and it brought you a mouse later and so you let it stay. It goes in and out when it pleases so long as you are going in and out. You put out a little food for it now and then and it curls around your legs sometimes, but it has been kicked out of the way enough to be wary that you could have your hands or your mind full of something you don't want to put down to be bothered with a cat. You are mutually independent of one another. You don't actively care for the cat; it doesn't seem necessary, and it doesn't especially seem to care for you. But now you're going to be gone for a week and a half and if you left her inside there will be no food or water for her and you may find her dead in the shop when you get back which will bring such bad Karma to the place that you will have to move it elsewhere or constantly be reminded of your insensitivity to others for the sake of racing. Danny will draw the outline of the dead cat on the floor in chalk, like a crime scene, thinking it's funny, but knowing that you killed it and he will have one up on you now.

You left yesterday, and have driven through a long night to be here. You worry. When the gas is finally in, you go and pay and then find a phone and make a call. It is still in the early days of my racing memory and that call must be placed from a phone booth and involves getting together a pile of change and listening for directions from an actual human operator who instructs when to deposit the fee. Today you may just whip out your cell phone and be grateful that things are so much better than they used to be but that's too easy.

A conversation follows where in you speak with someone with access and a willingness to check on things for you and you feel better about it and prepare to go on. She's still pouting about not being asked to come along you figure, but then hear another voice in the background saying "Honey, is everything all right?" and you know she's moved on. L.A. may be behind you tonight, but you can still call it, and it will answer.

In terms of your journey, it is your past. Chronologically it is the place you were before the place you are now and so it is the past. Emotionally you may not travel on quite as quickly, depending on who she was to you, but that's not important now; you were calling about the cat.

While you are at it, you decide to place another call to make sure your reservation for the hotel has been delivered and accepted. You call the place you will be tomorrow. It is a different time there so they will be awake you figure. You are checking on the destination of your future person. It is not where you are now, it is where you intend to be tomorrow.

Some one answers from the Pink Flamingo hotel in Daytona Beach. It's tacky, and its fifties, but it's just across A1A from the beach and right next to a liquor store so what the hell. The harsh woman who answers is irascible. "Mable?" you ask, "Is that you, Baby?" and she brightens, vaguely remembering the bike racer that called her "Baby" last spring and the fifth of Jack they shared after he broke into the top 20 for the first time. "Hey, Sugar," she comes back all newly interested and full of anticipation, "Ya'll be here soon?" and you assure her you are hurrying as fast as the law allows and she says she'll leave the light on for you and you are reassured.

Your future is known, in some ways, and should go somewhat as planned. A light goes on in your vision of the place as you picture it, and its out there, just waiting for your arrival. Unlike my mother, Mable will leave the light on.

That's St. Augustine's theory of time and man's limitation and God's power. For him, the past and the future are real, and exist simultaneously and independently from the present. They are connected, to be sure, but not in direct ways as a row of dominoes. God was there, in the past, in Los Angles, and may have been bothered by the cat being locked in the shop and planted a seed in your mind that became the thought that was your recollection of the cat. He was there, in the future, with Mable and everyone else onshore dissipating the ocean currents to keep the sea temperature off the coast of Africa low enough not to give birth to a hurricane just now and He is here, right now, with you at the gas station, keeping the charge of static electricity you bring with you from the seat cover to the hose nozzle from setting you on fire.

He is all these places because He can be and it is not an effort for Him because of who He is.

That's complicated, and it's difficult to imagine, but that doesn't mean it's not true. It makes perfect sense in at least one way – if God can do anything, and we say that He can, then He can be there in the past right now, even though we cannot. Likewise He can be there in the future, which we have a little less trouble conceiving because we know we are not there but will be if all goes well so it's a smaller leap to think of Him being both places at once. It's a mystery, that's for sure, but knowable.

Now let's see where this leaves us. if God can operate in the past, and do so from the present, or the future for that matter, what is it we can know to be true that has already happened? All we can know is what we remember or can find a record of someone remembering and it could be argued that our memories are suspect too, since He could 'make' them as well. If God can make the leap somehow into our past to change something, anything, then he doesn't have to change all the rest of it because it will be changed already. If for instance your great-grandfather fought in the civil war and he and a Yankee faced off across the battlefield and fired their muskets at the same moment and one was killed and the other survived imagine if God changed that result and reversed the order.

All who came after as descendents of that one soldier would leave a void rippling down through time to the present and on into the future. Oh, you think you would know if something like that happened? You never sleep I suppose and have total recall of all events that have taken place in all of time? You know you don't and you could wake up to a new reality every day and not know the difference.

It's a ridiculous argument of course and we assume that nothing like that happens but it's a topic we need to consider that seldom comes up in motorcycle racing. How do we know what the truth is about anything at all?

It is the classic epistemological question and is something that philosophers have been working on for centuries, maybe longer, since a good many of them thought about such things before they invented ways of preserving their thoughts. This is where I think motorcycle racing has something to offer. Absolute truth can be found there.

How do I know what is the right gearing for the coming race at a given track?

It is a problem with some real meat in it so let's tackle it together. Racing motorcycles have a rather narrow band of usable power and a limited number of gear ratios so it is necessary to calculate a final drive ratio that is most desirable and then obtain it by the right combination of countershaft and rear wheel sprocket teeth. I first saw this on the back of a business card that Ted Henter gave me and it was a spreadsheet with countershaft teeth in the vertical axis and rear sprocket teeth horizontally displayed. In the box where the two values met he had calculated the resulting ratio. At first it looked useless to me because numbers are not ordinarily my friends, but I understood what he was showing me and what jumped out was the number of times the same over all ratio resulted from two sets of values. I had always thought, as I had been told, that changing one tooth on the countershaft was equivalent to changing three on the rear sprocket. So for instance, if I had a 19T countershaft on my TD2 Yamaha and a 34T rear, then changing up to a 20T countershaft (yes they did make them) would be the same as leaving the countershaft alone and changing the rear to a 31T.

It was a rule of thumb, after all, and it had served me well enough I thought so why bother to calculate something like that out exactly? The answer was because the TD2 did not have a perfectly spaced set of gear ratios in its gearbox and the jumps from one gear to the next might fall outside the powerband of the peaky little bugger if you had your gearing wrong and depending on where you were on the track, it very well might add seconds to your lap time, which over a large number of laps, would move you down the finishing order to the 'may as well have stayed home' range.

This was exactly the sort of thing I didn't want to know when I started racing, but I was four years in now and the insight suddenly made sense. All those time when I had been screwing up the courage to dive in deeper so that I might come out harder were in vain if I was up against someone like Ted who saw the problem entirely differently. The motor made so many horsepower at 9800 rpm and so many more at 10400 and if he had the gearing correct and rode the machine accordingly then he would be back on the gas at the exit right in the power band where he needed to be and pull away from inept hard chargers such as myself who lacked his vision.

This did not come up in the dirt track ranks where I had begun racing. Sure we changed gearing, but that had more to do with track conditions and there were just two corners usually. On a road race course, however, where the speed requirements might vary widely, the need to select the proper gearing could be critical. What parameters would we apply to the problem? I suppose it could be done abstractly, as in calculating the maximum length of the longest straight and the apex of the slowest corner and then generating some sort of formula that figures in the overall gearing ratio and the rpm range you'd like the motor to be working in.

Thankfully we don't race abstractly, or this would turn racing into nothing but a math problem and would keep guys such as myself off the track all together. Racing is real. It is so real in fact that it will bitch slap you hard if you monkey around and don't pay attention to what's going on. All the senses need to be engaged in the task at hand and must be asked to blend together after sufficient practice to lap a track on their own leaving the conscious effort free to address little problems like how to get around this guy in front of me who is just as fast as I am and so forth. To solve the problem of what's the right gearing? I needed some shortcut. Here it is:

Gear for top speed down the longest straight if more than half of the track is wide open throttle. Bikes with telemetry can give you a quick answer to that precondition but generally you are talking about tracks like Daytona, Ontario, and Road Atlanta. If it's that sort of track, where you spend a lot of time tucked in and just going faster and faster until you top out, then it's not hard to find the right gear. You stack on the highest gearing it will pull (biggest countershaft, smallest rear sprocket) and then add just a bit more.

The first part of that you find out in practice. Yeah, it pulls 10,500 on the banking and that's the redline so it's good and I'm happy with the gearing. Happy in practice is not the same as happy in a long race and the races I was dealing with were very long, Daytona being 200 miles. So I would hunt for optimum top end gearing and then give it a tooth or two less on the back for the race, usually finding as the race went along that I would pick up speed and end up running at the red line in the end. There were exceptions, such as when the wind changed directions and my top end fell because I wasn't in the optimum part of the power band any more but such things are not predictable. That makes them rare enough not to nix the notion that something about racing was real and I could know it. I could know, in a race, when I had chosen the right gearing.

That sort of knowledge is as real, if not more real, than wondering if an imaginary cat in the box might be alive, or dead, or something else and then making up an equation to explain it. I am not making light of theoretical physics, here, I'm just saying that the cat won't make you any faster one way or the other because the answer to the question it asks doesn't relate to speed like having the right gearing does. Belief in the truth of something is called justification in philosophy and much has been written about it. It was put forth long ago but boils down to a three move quick step sort of dance that goes like this:

1. A proposition is true;
2. Someone believes the proposition;
3. Someone is justified in believing the proposition.

American philosopher Edmund Gettier put a hitch in the stride of this theory by suggesting that the relationship of the truth of a proposition to the belief that someone has in it is not sufficiently related. Let me give you an example.

I was racing at Road Atlanta and Scott Autry was there, both of us riding TD2's. We were pitted close to one another and I had been out in practice and seen him flicking his knee out before going into a corner and I had asked him why he did it. Those bikes had very little room between the shifter and the footpeg and he was wearing clod hopper construction boots that did not have room to do the typical rock your foot on the peg up and down teeter totter sort of action to downshift. Instead he just wedged his boot in the gap and when he moved his knee out it rotated his boot in the other axis and the downshift was accomplished. I tried it and it was easier for me than what I had been doing and his information was useful so I trusted him.

He later asked me if I knew that I could take the turn at the bottom of the hill in fifth gear, which was high gear, stating that he had been able to lower his lap times significantly that way. I asked for particulars and he said he upshifted coming out of from under the bridge at the top of the hill and let the momentum of the drop down to the right before finish line at the bottom just bring the revs up as he came on through the turn. Well, it sounded good and it was an awkward transition anyway as you came to that bridge by climbing up out of a drop on the other side known as gravity gulch where all of your suspension travel was used up and a good deal of your nerve, bringing you sweeping up the hill to the bridge faster than you really wanted to go and leaving you to decide whether to downshift once, or twice, to take the turn that apexed under the bridge.

If you did it twice, as most people seemed to do, and took that turn in third under power, then the back end would lose traction as you crested the hill and tried to drive out down the hill on the other side. It was a brilliant layout by whoever had built the track and it had occupied my mind a good deal trying to sort it out. It was a blind turn and there were a lot of crashes there, which told me it was on other people's minds as well. But Scott told me he short shifted up to fifth saving himself the danger of losing traction in a bad spot and skipping the unsettling aspects of an unneeded shift and the extra downshift to get there. I told him I would try it.

I went out in the next practice session and he had the mag cover off setting the timing and didn't go. I meant to do it right away but forgot, the habit I had already learned being hard to alter. It was the second lap before I had it in mind to change my pattern. I was in fifth down the long straight and into the gulch, muscling it over from right to left down through the bend at the bottom and downshifting only once as I braked going uphill to the bridge. It seemed way too fast, and unnatural to take a turn that far out of the power band on purpose, but I forced myself to do it and then dropped it up into fifth when I crested the hill, skittering over to the left and coming close to the bumps that set the pit return road apart from the track. I rolled the power back on as I headed down to the next right, cutting back across the track from my new entry point far left of where I had been before and carrying more speed into the turn.

Before, when I had been doing my usual rotation of up and down shifts, I had been in fourth here, under power, and was charging down the hill, but that brought me there so quickly that I had to let off and brake to make the turn and then power out in fourth again down the front straight where I would not get back into fifth until nearly half way and then only for short time. Testing the proposition that Scott had put forth, I was in fifth the whole time, and although the motor was revving less than what would have been normally acceptable, as it gathered momentum it picked up the revs and shot me through the turn and onto the straight in a higher gear the whole time down to turn one.

It was quicker but less dramatic as you didn't get the fun of shifting up and down as often and I was disappointed in myself for not having seen it sooner. It had not sounded like a good idea, and yet I had someone I trusted telling me it would work and that it worked for them and that I should try it. I tried it and it was true. After the session ended I went back to the pits and found him there, cleaning his bike. He saw me come in and came over and asked me if I had tried taking the last turn in fifth. I told him I had and thanked him for the suggestion and then described the adjustments I had made to get myself to do it and how I had the time to make sure I got the line just right so I didn't cram myself under the flag stand on the exit. He had a funny look on his face but waited until I was finished before commenting, "So, it really is possible…"

I came up short then. "You mean you haven't done it?" I asked him. "Nope," he said, "but I heard some guy in the bathroom telling some other guy that it ought to work so I thought I'd try it." "Yeah, but you didn't try it," I said, "You got me to try it for you!" He grinned and shrugged his shoulders. "Hey, don't get so uptight," he said like someone from California would, "It worked didn't it?" I wasn't really mad at him, I was just incredulous at being fooled like that. I made a mental note to not trust other racers when they tell you things, but it was one that I failed to remember a number of times which I won't go into now.

Right there was the three step proposition of epistemology stood on its head. A proposition that was true was believed by Scott to be possible. He thought he was justified in believing it true but he didn't try it himself but instead had me try it first. Did I know what Scott knew about it? No, we each saw it differently. He thought it might be true but did not know for sure. I thought it was true only because he said he had done it, and he lied. Regardless of his lying about having done it, the truth was that it could be done and that it worked. What does this tell us about knowledge and the relationship of what we think we know to be true and what is really true?

Necessary and sufficient conditions existed for my belief in the knowledge proposed. Philosophers had given a good deal of attention to what sorts of factors matter and do not matter, focusing on things that lie outside the psychological states of the putative knower. Why? Because sincerity is no measure of truth. I knew kids who believed in Santa Clause with all their hearts. Do I have to go on? Wanting something to be true does not make it true, no matter how badly you want it. James Jones was wrong but he managed to convince a large group of sincere gullible people to transplant themselves to the jungles of South America and then drink poison Cool Aid after killing their own children. Did they all go to heaven together then? Well, I don't have an answer for that but I have to say that it is doubtful under most of the schemes laid out as a precursor for such a journey.

The promotion of true belief to actual knowledge is dependent on relevant external factors. My belief that a certain turn at a certain track could be taken a certain way was real but misguided. I blundered into a fortunate occurrence that revealed a truth to me. Its truth was not based on the reliance I placed in another racer telling me he had done it. I had only met him the day before and while he was likeable and had imparted useful information about a downshifting technique that I had already applied and found true, it did not mean that everything he put forth was also true.

He had a sense of humor, a bit dark perhaps, but real none the less. When I told him I had done it, he went out and did it himself and we laughed about it afterward. Not quite in the same way, but we laughed none the less. As time went along and I returned to the same track, I tried to apply the proposition again and found it no longer true. I had told the story to R.G. Wakefield, a good friend of long standing who I would not mislead about anything. He and I were riding TZ Yamahas by then, a 250 for me a 350 for him. I cautioned him that I wasn't sure it would work on the faster bike, although it had held true when I moved up from the TD2 to a TD3. The speed differential there wasn't all that great so it was just a bit riskier and the exit took you close to the edge of the track right at a bad spot where the base of the starter's stand was supported.

I couched the proposition with as much caution as possible and issued the disclaimer that it was on him should it go bad. He tried it and it went bad. He went down and the bike immediately wedged itself and him up under the starter's stand where he went unnoticed for some time before help came. He had a broken nose and other injuries, but survived to race again. I felt bad about it and apologized for suggesting that something false might be true but he shrugged it off. He had a brilliant mind full of trivial things and here and there a real gem of useful knowledge. The problem was he could not sort them out all of the time which left some gaps. That lack of a proper filter led to some poor decisions later, one of which killed him.

I will finish this discussion of the nature of true knowledge with Jett Tharp and a trip I made to Green Valley Raceway near Dallas, Texas. It was a drag strip track and the return road connection was a simple 180 degree loop of slicker than snot asphalt that had the charming aspect of having been made with sea shells in its aggregate. This was of course a mistake, since few things are slicker than sea shells and motorcycles trying to make a sharp turn back on themselves don't need much encouragement to go down. I shared the problem and could not find a solution other than putting my foot down as a good many of the other riders did. Its one thing to take the turn on your high barred street bike with your foot down, but it's another to do it on a peaky two stroke grand prix bike. Jett seemed to be able to do it effortlessly.

Other things in the immediate environment should have tipped me off that all was not well. Women still wore bee hive hair do's for instance, which just looked wrong and all of the places we ate offered to add chili to anything. We were into the sixties far enough by then that the natural girl, long hair parted in the middle wearing a tie died shift or bell bottom jeans and a tank top braless was the model of attraction. Barbie doll outfits over pointy cones of breasts and high heels were just funny to look at, even if the girls wearing them did have a charming drawl that was intriguing. We had come for the Pearl Beer festival of speed which supposedly was a money race and I had gathered up everyone from my part of the country who wanted to come to race or just have a look at Texas.

I had struck up an acquaintance with the local go fast guy, Mr. Tharp and explained that I had found the track surface difficult to come to grips with. "Tire Pressure," he said back to me like a mantra until I figured out what he meant. "Fifty pounds," he added, "that'll do 'er." Well I believed him and put fifty pounds of air in my tires with predictable results. He laughed when I came back to complain about the prank and suggested I live and learn. I mentioned that he might now never want to ever be in front of me when I was close enough to accidentally knock him down. It has yet to happen.

39.

Ghost Riders In The Sky

IN 1970 I MOVED to Florence, Oregon, as part of an offer of a racing sponsorship. A man there owned a chainsaw shop and dabbled in dune buggies. He wanted to add a Yamaha franchise and through an attenuated set of circumstances heard that I might be interested in working for him. I was interested in racing and he thought we could work a deal.

He offered me $500 a month and all expenses paid to the races for a season in return for coming out and helping set up the business and then working as service manager between events for one year. The AMA schedule was fairly busy and taking into account travel to and from all of the events to his shop, after expenses, I thought it a fair offer so I accepted. If he had been a man of his word it might have worked out all right, but he wasn't, and it didn't. As it was I had another life in Oregon that I might not have had so it wasn't all bad. Most of it in fact was fairly terrific. I went to just one race as a sponsored rider and he fired me while I was gone but forgot to tell me so I had to drive all the way back from Daytona to get the news.

When I moved there, Oregon was in the midst of a marijuana drug reform movement aimed at ending prohibition in favor of something less restrictive. Couched in terms of "decriminalization", it was a change of penalty classification from a crime to a citation much akin to a parking ticket. You could have it, in reasonable amounts for personal use, and not be a criminal as a result. I was not a user and did not have any, but many I knew did and I was able to observe firsthand the effect of policy changes on real people. I may be a libertarian in a lot of ways, but too many people are too weak to say no once they start such behaviors and I was not a supporter of making it legal.

Once it was OK to have it, the question on the street became how much could you have? People who had once panicked at the sight of a police officer because of a hidden joint in their jeans, now contemplated buying ten times as much as they had ever had before because it was now "legal" and they might get snowed in somewhere and not be able to find their connection. With increased availability came increased use and as much as I heard people say that they would adjust their intake over time back to their comfort level as before that never proved true with the stoners I knew. That they seemed happy made it difficult to get a sense of whether it was a good thing or not, until you talked with someone who cared about them and had to feed and clothe them.

I had a pack of room mates come and go while the renter of a trailer in college and much of the 'going' had to do with drug use. I was a vocal opponent and the land lord. I came home from an over-night shift one morning to find three of them sitting at a picnic table out front with a double album cover that would fold in the middle using it to sort the seeds out of a pound of pot they had just bought. They were so proud of themselves for having thought of it.

We had an exchange of views about the wisdom of doing it out in the open for all to see and since I had the say, they decided to move indoors and very soon after moved on. One of them, who was a kind and intelligent young man, went to prison later for his enterprising ways and his grasp of the laws of supply and demand, which was better than his understanding of the laws that forbid such activity.

It was a universal mistake of my generation to want to get higher and higher, fostered by a good many things including our age. For those who set their minds to it, the thrill of being stoned on Marijuana turned so routine as to no longer be thrilling and the drug itself became suspect as impotent. A period would follow where other substances containing THC, such as hash and hash oil were located, tried, learned, and then passed over as they moved on to other things.

I doubt the knowledge of self proclaimed experts in the field I hear now saying that marijuana is not a gateway drug to the abuse of other things. It was the addiction of choice for many of my young friends who were lost to me almost immediately. They might be funny or ridiculous when high, but the low that came after made them too cranky to be around and the sink hole in their wallet it created usually took them away from any of the things I enjoyed doing, most of which cost money.

They were quick to argue that it was harmless fun but then they were in the goldfish bowl mentality where things all looked good from inside and everything else they look at is distorted by their altered state. I fear some of this mentality may be coming back as I write this and have made a note to avoid places where such is the case if possible. Colorado already has the distinction of having more mass shootings than any other state, which was reason enough to not be there, but now the possibility that the driver next to me going through the mountains may have a nice buzz going and a Colt 45 on the seat next to him will certainly keep me away.

The Oregon venture did not work out. As soon as I had set up all the bikes, sold a good number of them while the boss was on vacation in Hawaii and his son had trained to be a mechanic down in L.A., I was fired. I had spent my last dime getting back up there, keeping a careful account for reimbursement of my expenses as we had agreed. I had bought a small trailer to live in back in September when I had come out and it sat down the slope in a grove of trees from his nice new A-frame log home. I thought it had been kind of him.

Actually it had been his intention to keep it and when the day came that I was let go I noticed that he had already taken the license plates off of it so I couldn't take it with me. I had been screwed, plain and simple. The Sheriff himself was at the shop waiting for me when I pulled in from the other corner of the country. At that point I knew nothing of course so I thought it odd that he was there.

The old man who ran the saw repair shop in the same building came over to my side of things as I unloaded my tool box and gave me the news. I reacted poorly of course, being young and stupid and stabbed in the back as I was, but I dug out the expense voucher

I had made up and gave it to him and demanded payment from the till while the law looked on from behind Cool Hand Luke mirrored sunglasses.

The Sheriff was standing there and I explained the terms of our agreement to him and why I had come to town, which had always been a mystery to him I supposed. There had been a small piece in the local newspaper about it and a photo of the bike I was to ride at Daytona with me standing behind it so it wasn't like he had never had a look at me.

A very awkward stretch of time passed then as the old man went into the back, supposedly to get the reimbursement for my expenses. The holster of the Sheriff's gun kept creaking as he put his hand on it and moved one way or another, his eyes remaining steadily fixed on me. I wore my hair long then, and my jacket had a prominent peace sign sewn on the sleeve showing my objection to the war that had torn our country apart.

I thought he was going to shoot me if I gave him any excuse, at least that was my impression and he did nothing to dissuade me. In a bit the old man came back and shook his head. "He ain't gonna pay ya," he said and before I could react added, "and I told him I wouldn't work for him no more."

I tried to talk him out of quitting but he wouldn't hear of it. We had spent many hours together working in that building just the two of us, helping each other when something needed extra hands, and a long winter had passed as each of us tended to our respective business. He had seldom asked for my help but when he did, I gave it and we got along well enough.

He had watched me work 18 hour days for weeks on end to get the initial order uncrated, serviced, displayed and sold and I had let him handle all of the money so there would be no question that I had not done things properly. In all of that time he had been mostly quiet. Now he had quit his job because he thought I wasn't being treated right.

He left us and went back into the saw department repair shop and started putting his tools in his tool box. The boss wasn't physically there, as it turned out, apparently unwilling to face me. When the exchange about my expenses had come it had apparently been on the phone as had the old man's resignation. Soon a rusted out International Harvester Scout was pulling out of the drive, loaded with tools and saws and so forth and off the old guy went, down the highway toward the beach.

"I'll get my tools and be on my way," I said to the Sheriff, who countered by saying that his instructions were that I was to take nothing with me. "You watched me carry them in," I said, "and you can watch me carry them out." He held up his trigger finger. "I'll have to make a call," he said, intending I guessed to call the boss and get 'permission' for me to take my own tools with me when I left. When he went to do it I moved quickly and took my things out to the van parked just outside the outer service door and had it all loadedup when he came back.

"He said to make an inventory of what you wanted and he would look it over and let you know what you could have. He also said not to come back to the trailer because it's on his property and he'll have you arrested for trespassing."

My mind was racing. I had driven for two days and nights to be there and had last slept on the side of the road near Wendover, Utah too long ago to remember clearly exactly when that had been. I looked rough, no doubt, and I had no money and only one friend in town. I wanted to say something but knew I had to be careful. My brain was writing checks for my mouth to say that I knew I couldn't cash.

Sunshine broke through the window just then and the rows of neatly arranged and carefully polished new Yamahas caught my eye. I had done good work here; there was no argument. I held my temper.

"Notice that my tone with you is friendly," I began, "and notice also that no one has disputed the truth I told you about what my agreement was with the owner and why I am out here from Illinois." He nodded slightly and I went on. "I know this must be a difficult situation for you and you know that I am going to be gone soon and you are going to be left with a guy like that to deal with every day." He nodded again, the slightest hint of a grin coming to his face but he said nothing. "I'm not going to cause anyone any trouble," I assured him. "I'm going over to a friends place and sleep for a while and then I am going to my trailer and get my things and go back home to Illinois."He shook his head 'no' but I continued, "I know that you are supposed to enforce the law and you know that I haven't broken any so we're done here."

"When I get a call that you are trespassing I will come and arrest you for it," he said. I looked around at the shop and it was a nice looking business. I had spent too many hours of my life alone here making it what it was while the guy who was screwing me over had been far away just waiting for me to be done. "You can't be two places at once," I said, and turned to go. "What's that supposed to mean?" he asked as I walked away but I didn't stop or answer, in a just few strides I was out the door and in my van and driving away. I had not closed the door and had not looked back.

I went down to the breakwater drive which was a huge pile of rocks that stretched far out into the ocean to keep the waves from eroding the beach. There was a two lane road on it with a shelter out at the end and I parked behind it so my van was out of sight and crawled into the back and slept the sleep of the just. It was dark when I woke up and I had no idea what time it was. At first I had no idea where I was either, which is always disconcerting, and I struggled to put it together.

I found my cooler and had a warm Coke and sat up for a while, watching the moon over the Pacific on a very cool night. I probably smelled bad and I knew I needed clean clothes and had none with me. I went back to the floor between the bike and the tools and slept some more and hoped something would come to me about what to do next knowing that just now nothing came to mind. Not every decision has to be made in an instant, sometimes things need to be decided after the dust has settled.

When I woke again it was full daylight and I wandered over to Bill's place and saw his beat up Datsun pick up in the driveway so I knew he was home. He had been my first customer and had bought the only DT2MX that came with our first order of bikes. I was going to tell him the story but he said he already knew what had happened and that he would go with me to get my things. We went up to the trailer, which had deliberately been parked so that it wasn't visible from the big house. There was a new hasp and padlock on the door but it magically came off when I needed it to. We had gotten some empty boxes from the grocery store and had been filling them up with my stuff from inside when the Sheriff drove up.

Most of the filled boxes were sitting in the back of Bill's little pick up by then, there really wasn't that much, and I was cleaning out the cabinets and regretting the past year more with each passing minute. I heard Bill and the Sheriff talking, but there wasn't any of the laughter I usually heard when Bill talked to people. When I came out, the Sheriff had backed up and pulled off to one side to give us room to go when we were done and I didn't say anything to him. "He wants you to leave town," Bill said as we pulled off down the gravel road to the coast highway. "I want to leave town," I said, "but I don't have the money to buy lunch, let alone travel." He nodded and thought for a while as we drove. "We'll fix that." he said and we drove on to his house. We did fix it, but that story is for another time.

40.

Losing As A Way Of Life

ONE OF MY FAVORITE questions when talking to other racers is to ask them how they got started. Those who were encouraged to do it when they were very young apparently have an edge of some sort, at least if the Rossi / Edwards model is to be believed. I did not have a son so they were spared any spill over from my own enthusiasm for the sport, but I would feel badly if I had brought them into something that they could not opt out of on their own without risking some fear of my disapproval or a loss of their own self-respect.

This is probably true of fathers who encourage their sons to do anything I suppose, but taking up the guitar doesn't seem as bad somehow and it won't kill you. Racing will kill you, and fathers have lost their sons that way, not the least of which of my own acquaintance would be John Surtees who lost his son in a racing accident in a car. His case is special, having been the only man to be a Formula One champion and a Grand Prix motorcycle champion as well. The lesson there for me would be if it can happen to him, it can happen to anyone.

I met him at Barber one year when he was our guest starter and I was acting as the starter's assistant. He was a pleasant man, not very large in stature, and seemed easy going. When I knew he was going to be there I took the time to read up on his career and was impressed. Now that I shook his hand and we spoke it was difficult for me to relate to him in terms that I could manage. He was the son of a motorcycle shop owner and had a mechanical mind. No doubt he had put bikes together, taken them apart, tried to get them to perform better, all of that. I had done those things. He had also raced them and so had I, but there was no real comparison in what we had done there.

To say that we both had done the same thing in that we had raced motorcycles would have been silly. I have looked at the stars, he has been there. He had opportunities in times that no longer exist and for whatever reason was successful when his moments came. Some things he had done had not worked out, but some had. Some of each had to do with him, no doubt, and so I was happy to shake his hand. Any more than that, any pretense at fathoming the depths of his understanding of things past and now remembered would have been presumptuous of me. Still, he was gracious and kind and seemed to enjoy being spoken to about his past accomplishments. I decided to take a chance and ask him a pointed question. I asked him whether he thought himself more lucky or talented.

He thought briefly before answering. In a self-depreciating way he said that there was a good deal of luck in his accomplishments and then added that given the length of his career and the number of opportunities he had for things to go wrong that he liked to think he had a measure of talent as well. Some decisions would probably always be on his mind. He did not stay with Colin Chapman when Lotus was young and be second driver to Jim Clark. He did not stay with BRM when it was being developed and left one season too soon. But he had driven with Ferrari when it mattered and had been the world champion, which is something few men could say. Likewise his motorcycle career was across brands and some of his choices worked out better than others. The best machinery usually wins because speed is a product of planning, not courage and is mostly mechanical in origin.

I thanked him for speaking with me and he left after waving the green flag for our first race and I didn't see him again. Certainly he had more than a small measure of talent, but he didn't seem averse to talking about 'luck' as if it were a real thing. Dirty Harry came to mind then, "Do you feel lucky, Punk? Well, do ya?" things are what they are in the real world and on the race track, and the bad patch of pavement that waits for you or me is already there before we come to it regardless of what else we may have done before we get there, or manage to do about it after. I can feel lucky and say I am lucky and pretend that life is all going my way because fate has dealt me a winning hand. Then someday, someplace, something may happen that will later make people shake their heads and say, "Man, that guy was just unlucky."

Since all this has to do with time, I may as well take that topic up again now and see if we have had some similar observations about it. I will begin with some notions we may share when it comes to racing and move on from there: There never seems to be enough time to do all you would like to do to the bike before a race. Well, time is a commodity that man has some control over, albeit in odd ways, and it is one of the three pillars that holds up our life, the other two being money and relationships. Our lives can be parsed down a number of ways for consideration and I suppose my physicists' friends could give me an equation. Just for giggles I wrote one for them: Life = Money + Relationships / Time or to be algebraic about it; $L = M+R/T$. Some will fuss with the proportional relationships, but I don't mind that so long as we keep it simple and not cube anything or sign something unless we are hearing impaired.

My life, your life, anybody's life has its limits. History tells us that as does science and religion making it one of the very few things about which there seems to be much agreement among human beings. It is such a constant in the equating of life that it has been called the 'human condition'. What happens when time runs out is debatable, of course, but I can't do anything about that argument and neither can anyone else since the result of the action of dying is beyond this realm of consciousness and so far as we know it is an irreversible process.

That may change in the future, which is a frightening prospect, but as I write this dying and living are mutually exclusive states of existence. I think that as it should be as it adds a degree of importance to the things we do and makes us pay attention to many of the details of our lives which might otherwise go unnoticed. My life in law school was 90% what I was reading, 9.9% what I was engaged with in the lecture hall, with the rest smashed in between by a huge accelerator of social dimension. If it were a real mathematical problem we were working out then it would be obvious that I had other moments in which I ate, slept, loved and tried to get from place to place all the while trying not to forget that someone's barrel of beer had rolled out of the top of their tavern onto the top of a passerby and established the principle of 'res ipsa loquitor' in the process.

The volume of things I was expected to have at ready recall expanded exponentially as my legal education unfolded and there was a good feeling that came with graduating with honors and passing the bar exam on my first try that had to do with managing a difficult task. Still, I went back to the track that same summer with my AMA license I had maintained by simply paying the annual fee. I had done that because it had been so hard to become an expert and so easy to retain by just paying the small honorarium that I wouldn't give it up.

Many I knew who had sacrificed a good deal of my attention and company to have me relocate to Chicago and live alone through the tough law school times were not keen to see me risk it all for nothing by going back to my leather suit and putting on a pretense of safety by wearing a helmet. I reassured them that the risk was not that great but it turned out to be a bit more dangerous than I had imagined once I got there. Still, it was worth it a thousand times over because it was the last time I ever saw Danny Hyatt.

My brother had purchased a new TZ Yamaha 250 for another rider he was sponsoring since we had parted harshly and I had hung it up. I don't know the specific denomination, whether it was a "J" or "H" or whatever, but it was still a parallel twin but with power valve exhaust and separate cylinders. It was before the aluminum spar frames and was a nice enough looking bike with mag wheels and all the rest. I noticed that it had new tires, which was a luxury we never afforded my ride. This left him with an 'old' bike, without a rider which was a 'G' model and he offered it to me if I cared to ride again; with the old tires from three years before of course.

I had never ridden one, my last GP ride being a TZ750, after which I had seen some handwriting on a wall about money, tires, spare parts and mortality. The 250 was a step back, but it was still racing and it was still a production GP bike from Yamaha so I thought it should be properly designed at least as opposed to riding some home made thing put together by someone who thought 'pretty' meant more than properly prepared to go racing.

It looked like a proper GP bike as well. It was a water cooled twin with both bores in a single casting like I was used to and it had the same sort of bottom end and dry clutch arrangement my TZ350 had enjoyed so I was not worried there. I expected that it's powerband was probably very much like what I was used to, although it did have Lectron carbs where I had stayed with Mikuni's myself. The frame had a dropped tube at the top which reminded me of Hugh Humbles Harris lowboy that he used to terrorize the bigger 750s with at nationals that happened on real road course layouts. That allowed for a gas tank that nestled down lower in the frame rails and probably lowered the center of gravity a bit. Hugh called it a 'lowboy' after the Triumph triple frames of that name but they were made by different people.

The front forks were no larger than what I had seen before and the monoshock rear suspension was nothing special. Actually, it was a nice looking bike and it ran well. The frame tubes were mild steel and were no larger in diameter than Yamahas of twenty years before. The head stock support was no better and neither were the motor mounts which were still solid welded in the frame even though Phil Read's winning GP 250 Yamaha of 1972 had rubber motor mounts and this was 1989.

I had my old leathers and had tried them on before agreeing to come. They were loose, which said something about my enjoyment of life in law school. I had more room than I could ever remember in them. I took the bike out for practice to get acquainted with it, and to have a look at the track again, since all I could remember about it from having run there before was that it was long and I liked it. After the first practice session I decided that these particular Yamahas were called "G" models because that was what came to mind at how easily the front end could be made to chattered horribly if you pushed it into a corner and it phonetically began the words most commonly uttered – "Gee sus Christ!.." after which a good deal of prayer and thrashing about might be rewarded with staying upright if you had been a good person.

When I came in I mentioned this to the new rider, who had ridden it before apparently, and she said she hadn't noticed it. The new bike had the same sized frame tubes so I didn't expect it to be much better although she said that it too was fine. "Fine"? was that her favorite word? Was front end chatter like an air hammer 'fine'? I was merely making an observation anyway, as it was an old problem, one I had met before, and there were a number of things you could do about it, most of which had to do with keeping as much of yourself up on the front of the bike as possible.

I sought and got permission to make some changes and cut back the ears on the fairing and shortened up the bubble enough to let me manage the handling problem by crawling up on the tank and putting my chest down there as I pushed down on the bars. Here and there I got a bit of a 'whoop' sort of sensation after the frame had gathered up a lot of side load and then given it all back at once in a long corner like the carousel, but the majority of Road America is straight and wide sweeping turns but it was good weather and was shaping up to be a nice weekend and I was looking forward to the main event on Sunday.

We stayed in the pits and had a campfire going, several of us who had pitted near one another had struck up the race track kind of proximate acquaintance that can last a lifetime. It was late and we had cooked several packages of bratwurst and eaten them on rye bread with coarse German mustard washed down with Heineken and it was an all together satisfying cultural slice of outdoor life even if the potato salad was suspiciously bland and free of bacon grease. After it was dark and the fire was low, it was difficult to recognize the faces of those that came and sat on the logs around us from time to time and listened to our chatter.

Finally a familiar voice asked me how it had gone today and I was honestly surprised to be hearing Danny again picking up a conversation as if we had left it off a moment before. "Well, Danny," I said, "It went well in some ways but the front end chattered like a bitch and I did all the usual things to sort that out." I gave him the run down and he listened and poked the fire as I detailed the day's adjustments. "I tried all of that with one of those and it didn't fix it," he announced and then added that he had moved on to GXSR Suzuki's himself which he liked better. We spoke about them, since they were foreign to me, and what he and I had been doing since we had last seen one another. He was there as the team manager and mechanic for Nobu Nakamura, a Japanese junior rider who had come over to get some seasoning and Danny had been tagged as the man to help with that. It was a cruel choice for poor Nobu, who had no idea what sort of comedian Danny really was but a bond grew between them and I had no doubt that he was getting his money's worth in terms of racing experiences .

I had hired Danny myself once, to work as a mechanic for Triumph City the day I was moved up to Service Manager, a job I loved but didn't get to keep. From there I moved to another shop and he stayed on. Later I had moved to Illinois to be closer to my wife's mother who had been diagnosed with cerebral palsy and he had left Gainesville for Palm Bay but was still in Florida. The evening stretched on around the fire as we caught up with one another through a series or racing parables we had been involved with. Then he told a classic story that made me love being at the races and hungry for butterscotch pie.

He had been endurance racing down at Palm Beach International Raceway, sometimes called 'Moroso' and had been on his GXSR. It was going well and he had a team put together and their lap times had put them ahead of their class. We both had raced there enough that we could talk about the track without having to go into too much in the way of description and he asked if I remembered the twisty bits down by the canal after the end of the front straight and I said I did. "Well," he said, "I had the most frightening thing happen there on a motorcycle that has ever happened to me…" and we all perked up a bit, because Danny had never spoken of being frightened at all, not in any of his Viet Nam stories, or as an attendant in an insane asylum back in Missouri, or in all of the crazy antics he and I had done to-gether at Triumph City, many of which I thought were frightening.

He continue, "Just past where they had put a skinned alligator carcass the year before, right out of the canal, I was leading the pack into the left and back to the right turn when out of the bank of fog ahead of me a ghost rider appeared in the sky coming right at me." His voice trailed off, and he was visibly shaken, and I wondered if he was going to go on. He had gone back to the memory like it was happening all over again and it had pegged him just as hard. "I sat up," he said, back with us and now milking the moment because he had us on the edge of our seats, "The ghost rider sat up," he went on then paused, " I slowed down," he said then, "and the ghost rider came closer, and then, just to make sure I wasn't imagining it, … I waved."

Now if anyone else had been telling me about a racing experience and added that they had thought to wave at what they believed to be a ghost racing them as they thought they saw their own death coming for them, I wouldn't have believed them, but Danny had a funny sense of things, and it was difficult to ever know what he might do in any situation. He went on after a beat or two, "…and he waved back at me."

It was a night session of an endurance race he was talking about and the upshot of it was that his shadow from the headlight of the bike behind him was being caste upon the wall of dense fog before him. Although it took a moment for him to grasp what it really was, he didn't shake the spooky feeling he got from seeing it. "Even after I had figured it out and knew it was just my shadow," he went on, "the winding bits of road had it moving all round me, in front of me, beside me on one side then the other, all depending on where the guy behind me was shining his headlight. On one level you can tell yourself you understand what it is, but on another more visceral level, there's more to it. Racing your own shadow through the fog all night leaves an impression, "he admitted, as if it were just the two of us talking, leaving off the part about it being a bad one.

It was very well told tale. Normally his style of humor was of the sort that included a can of beans left on an open fire without a vent hole while Nobu was instructed to watch to see that it didn't explode, but this had been something more insightful. There was a ghost rider in the sky and it was Danny, and he had seen it for himself.

I led the applause, and he seemed surprised. "Great story, Danny," I said, with genuine admiration, and then added, "I've missed you." "Well," he responded, "I'm still out here." We talked on into the wee hours and then when the kettle ran dry and the beer was all gone decided to call it a night. I got his phone number before he left and gave him mine. I told him we should do breakfast and wished his rider luck tomorrow in the race. He promised to call and so did I but it would be another year before we spoke again, and by then things were different for him and me as well. This was our bond, being at a race far from home and being together.

I miss Danny Hyatt like I miss the homemade butterscotch pie our housekeeper Rosy made for me when I was a toddler.I looked for him the next morning but he was gone, having packed up and headed back to Florida sometime in the night. I intended to buy him breakfast, but missed my chance. Back out on the track for practice, and then the race, the G model ran like a watch and behaved itself well enough to finish. I didn't ever get comfortable enough to push it around much, but the old reflexive feelings came back readily enough and I would tuck in for the straights and pop up and downshift at the entry points and all the rest without having to think about it too hard. It was a small field and I didn't know the other riders but it didn't matter. A few people came over to shake hands and talk about this section or that one that we had spent some time together in during the race. It was typical post-race adrenaline talk and I enjoyed it. I was offered the bike for a very reasonable price but passed, it was not competitive enough to run up front and if I was just going to race for fun it was too expensive for me, whether or not I had been to law school.

The new bike was not for sale as they had the idea that they were going to set the world on fire with their new rider. She was young, and very small, and I suppose was brave enough to do it, but she was not fast. Watching someone else ride when you know how to ride yourself you can tell when someone is at home on a bike and is having their way with it. She was not that sort of rider. She sat ready to react to something disastrous about to happen and seemed relieved when it didn't. This wasn't the way to the front of a pack of riders who loved every second of what they were doing and who had no thought in their heads about things not working out.

I had known only a few women riders during my career and had no understanding of any of them or what they might be thinking. That is probably my fault and my over identification with other men doing the things I was doing and my assumption that were thinking about the same sorts of things. We may be on different pages altogether when it comes to racing, I don't know. It is difficult to tell in real time what is in your own mind, let alone someone else's. Beforehand their impressions are clouded with apprehension and may be tinged with bravado and so less than honest. Afterward they tend to be full of survivor's elation and are speaking in the past tense so they aren't really giving it to you as it happens but rather as it happened. They were tense and now they have changed and in retelling the race it's the verbs that have changed tense.

Still, I would rather hear an insightful retelling than see a movie of it. Now that we have modern technology we can make digital movies of people as they are doing something and could record what they are saying I suppose, but that was foreign to me and I for one have to say I liked things better that way. Motorcycle racing is an experience that cannot truly be captured in any media for vicarious enjoyment afterward. I've seen laps of the Isle of Man and all sorts of helmet cam images and no where is there the least bit of G force felt or sliding off of the seat or centrifugal force in play that makes racing what it is for me. It is a visceral thing, after all, and I don't want to see a movie of someone eating barbeque and wiping the sauce off of their face, I want brisket! I want to taste it and be filled up by it and savor it and enjoy it and then order up seconds if I have the stomach for more. Hot? You damn right it's hot, it's supposed to be, and that's not in the movie either.

41.

You Bet Your Life

How WELL DO YOU know someone, anyone that you have not risked your life with? I have people I know and have known for years and done many things with that I would not trust as much as a stranger in a leather suit after ten laps elbow to elbow through a closely fought race. Sometimes I would seek them out afterward, and shake their hand and acknowledge my pleasure in their company on the track and then off of it. Here's a photo of John Ellis and I at the off camber turn at Grattan in June. Sometimes I don't see them again until the next race, but there is still some solace in just knowing that they are out there. To be modern I suppose I would say women too, but I am not modern, I am vintage, and women did not race with men when I raced seriously. They do now, and I honor them for that as I would any racer, but I have no idea what they are thinking or why they do it so I will let them write about it themselves. As for the men, I know what they seek.

Men want to understand other men and want to be understood. Men want to trust other men and be trusted. Men want to win and race with men that want to win so that their victory is not a sham, which brings me to an AHRMA race at Millville this summer and the recent NASCAR scandal. In both cases, it was not a race, it was a sham. I will take the latter first, as it is easier and more widely known.

Someone in a team at NASCAR calculated what someone else needed to be in the "chase" and spun out on purpose to bring a yellow flag out when they needed it. The chase is the final ten races artificially separated from the rest of the season to heighten fan interest and keep people coming out to the races after a championship might already be sewn up. It is a problem with all racing series – how do you crown a champion? If it is simply cumulative on points of some sort, then the last races of the season are probably going to be meaningless because the chances are that the fastest riders have already won the most races and so the most points which means they do not need to race any more to be champion. Racing is dangerous and expensive and if you can win a championship with less risk and less expense then the smart thing is to do so.

Some time ago WERA decided it would make the club more money to have an all or nothing final race of the year and make all the races that led up to it be just qualifiers. Something about a one race championship appeals to people who weren't winning already, but it leaves too much to chance and one bad incident to be a real championship. I went a number a years, but the years that I dominated the local races and then went to the Grand National final only to find it raining again at Road Atlanta I have to say I was not all that happy with the concept.

AHRMA separates out the last two races of their season now as a "world championship" and uses the earlier events as qualifiers to be allowed to compete at Barber and Daytona a week apart, but it is dubious if they amount to a world championship. Regardless of who might appear when there were a dozen races before on tougher tracks across the country that had winners and losers and champions crowned of their own it is tough to say it is equal to a whole season. Still, it's a strategy to make racing successful in the vintage area and we need all we can get so more power to them.

What we don't need is what NASCAR has, which was phony manipulation of finishes to give a result to someone they did not deserve. At Millville I was working the grid for the Honda 160 start, which is unique in that it is a Lemans type affair with bike holders and all of that. It was a small field, very small, but someone took it upon themselves to run up and down the line and get a quick word in with the other riders before the start. When the green flag came, and most of the field took off, there was one rider that had difficulty getting their machine going but found that all of the others had waited for them to come and then let them pass them all before going on to their 'win'.

The Honda 160 group is just a club race that is run with AHRMA's blessing as part of their weekend, I get that. I also get that they probably had the best of motives in deciding that this particular rider deserved, in whatever way they had selected them, to be the "winner". BUT… it wasn't a race and I was bothered by the spectacle. If what they wanted was just a parade, then have a parade, but don't pretend you're racing. Fixing the results of a race, any result, makes all other results suspect.

I have an older brother and when I was little I was eager to play checkers or whatever game I could with him. He won, of course, because he was older and smarter and knew what he was doing. I dreamed of the time when I would finally be able to win myself and when it came, what did he say to me? "I let you win." I told him that he hadn't let me win, that I had won fair and square but he was adamant that he had not tried his hardest and had deliberately made me a winner by choosing to lose. I didn't play him after that, never knowing if he was sincerely competing or not. Since this was just a two party affair, I suppose it sounds petty, but expand the notion to people who have raced their motorcycles the entire season and are in a points chase for position. When manipulation of finishes is done deliberately by racers who sandbag to let others finish ahead of them and thereby gain points what can we do?

The answer really is nothing. There is no rule that says you must try your hardest or go your fastest when you race and you can behave any way you like about it so long as you are safe I suppose - Yeah, but it's not racing, and it irks me because it violates the tenant that there is something to be said for the integrity of the sport. Maybe you don't see it, I don't know. Maybe you think Pete Rose didn't bet on baseball and should be in the hall of fame. Guys who try hard and can be trusted have my respect and admiration on and off the track. Guys who disrespect what racing is about don't get it and won't have it. That goes just as much for the riders who let them win as it does for the 'winner' of such a display.

I am proud of the races I have won and admire the men who have beaten me and there are plenty of them. I want them to know that I didn't let up for a single second in any one of those races and if they won, then they accomplished it competing with someone trying their hardest to keep them from doing it. Yeah, it's old fashioned I know, but I think I already mentioned that I was old fashioned.

42.

A Failure To Communicate

ANOTHER RIDER PULLS UP to my post at Pit Out with his motor running and calls me over. I have on radio headphones and my official shirt and am holding a flag. Other guys in leather suits are lined up here and there with their motors running to. It is nearly time for practice for Group 3 again and his bike clearly has a Group 4 tech sticker on it. He wants to tell me something, or ask me something, but it hardly matters which, I will not be able to hear him.

There was a time when I might have heard him, but I have spent too much time in a crowd just like this one and when I pull my headphones off to listen my ears are again unprotected and the roar of the running engines is quite literally deafening. He is saying something inside his helmet. His head is shaking back and forth with emphasis now but his hands are still on the bars. He has the clutch in and is keeping the motor running as if it won't idle. Few racing motorcycles will since that function plays no purpose in racing. I get closer and lean down to him and point at my ears and shake my head. He jabs his foot at the shift lever for a while and rocks the bike back and forth hunting for neutral. After he finds it with some effort, his left hand is free to reach up and open the visor on his helmet and then gesture me closer. I lean down again, cupping my hand over my ear. He is screaming. "adllangla; Whaioat! Kwhioco!!"

I have no idea what he is saying but would like to be helpful. I point at the sign I made for that purpose that displays the practice groups and it says, "Now on Track" and has a placard that adds, "Group 2" on the other side of the saw horse is a sign that says, "Next Up" and when race control tells me there are two minutes left, which is the time I have been instructed not to let any more bikes out of the pit lane and onto the track, I will turn it around and show the placard "Group 3".

He doesn't seem placated by the placard. I remove the headset completely and get closer and finally can distinguish what he is saying, "I need to practice !!!!" his rasping desperate voice yells. I nod agreement and hear 'checkered flag' in my headset as I slip it back on. That means that bikes will be coming in and I have missed the 'two minutes' marker while I was trying to communicate with an excited gladiator. No harm done, I'm not sending anyone out. I have sympathy for the guy, after all I am a racer. I know he is full of worry and adrenaline and is probably pitted somewhere that the public address system is inaudible or, worse yet, that the announcer has not given the calls for practice as he should.

I key my radio and say, "Pit out to Control," and hear "Go ahead" in that reassuring Southern drawl that is the cigarette raspy voice of Phoenicia. "Have all calls been made?" I ask. There is no answer so she is either on another channel solving someone else's problem or checking on mine. Like most of us, I have served in the different positions and know that announcers can be called to multi-task and miss calls they should be making or maybe are not told when to make them as something else was going on.

"Copy" she says to me finally, meaning that she has heard my transmission and it is understood. Over the P.A. in the distance I hear the announcer's voice saying, "Second, Third, and final call for practice Group 3" and know that the matter has been taken care of. I don't need her to come back to me and say anything, I'm just a cog in the machinery here and doing my job as she is hers. Something happened in the tree that kept the calls from going out, now that's been corrected. It will irritate some, we know that, but we are doing the best we can.

I go over to Frankenstein, which is what the red faced guy on the running bike has become. He is 900 miles and a sleepless night past unhappy. He has spent too much to be here, has missed the first practice round and is now worried he will miss his only chance to practice at all. There are critical adjustments to be made to old motorcycles about to race and if he misses his chance to make them then he may have wasted his trip.

I motion him off to the side and give the others a five minute gesture with my hand and look them in the eyes one at a time and make them nod that they understand. Some stay in line, others decide to circulate. They are the smart ones, these old bikes are air cooled and if no air is moving over the fins then they will overheat unless they have an oil cooler which also needs airflow so it's best to be on the move.

We have starting rollers out on the pit lane. I go over to Frank, I think of him in the familiar now since we have spent so much time together and his inner monster no longer frightens me. I point to his tech sticker and hold up four fingers and then point at him. He nods. I point at the board for "Up Next" and then hold up three fingers and he nods again. Then I point at his bike and shake my head no. His head falls then and I think he may weep. He stays like that for a bit and when his head comes up I point at my wrist like it's a watch and then point at everyone else and then back at him and give him two fingers followed by an open palm. Then I gesture out the pit lane. He thinks a bit, then nods. Yes, he would still like to go out with this group and will wait two minutes for them to go first.

Meantime I hear over the headset that we have a green track, which means that all bikes are in from the last session and the course is clear for the next group. I give Frank the palm again, holding him there and wave the green flag at everyone else. They go. It takes a bit for them to all straggle out after one another but soon enough it's just me and Frank. I key my headset and say, " Pit out to Control, I have a late arrival here who would like to go out with this group and promises to be careful." "Send him." Phoenicia says and I point at Frank and wave him out with the flag.

That evening a guy in blue jeans and a motorcycle tee shirt finds me at the worker's barbeque. His eyes are bloodshot and he moves like a man who has been pulled through a knot hole backwards. "You pit out?" he asks and I say I am. "Just wanted to thank you for being patient with me this morning, I couldn't hear the calls and was frantic to make a practice before my race." I nodded and he continued. "We had a flat on the 'Jersey Turnpike and the hassle of unloading everything to get to the spare and the jack and then get it all back inside and then talk to the police about doing it on the shoulder instead of going on to an emergency lot took all of our travel time and we got here late." "Done that," I said and he blinked and a beat went by before he said, "Really?," a bit doubtful.

"Yep," I answered, "In '69 on my way up to Loudon, only it was in Hartford, Connecticut at rush hour on a Friday night, pouring down rain and then I found out that none of the choices on the ends of the four way I had brought fit the eight lug nuts on wheels of the big Dodge I had borrowed and that my girlfriend at the time got her period about an hour before but hadn't said anything and really, really didn't want to spend another minute in the van without a bathroom in sight." This stopped him dead. His tale of woe had been trumped, which wasn't my intention. I was shooting for simpatico but missed the mark and got the heart instead. He wanted to say more I could tell so I waited. He sorted through possible things he might say next. "Is she all right?" he asked then and I turned my head like those dogs do when they are pretending to understand what you are saying but you know they don't.

"Say again?" I asked him, although I thought I had heard him right. "The girlfriend, is she all right?" he asked. I smiled. "Who knows?" I said, "that was forty years ago and she's someone's grandma now I'd bet, but she survived the trip and we had a little fun together for a while." He nodded like he understood but I knew he didn't. I changed the subject.

"How'd it go out there today?" I asked him, and he brightened at that and launched into a soliloquy of turns taken and people diced with that ended with a number indicating where he had finished. I had heard that sort of thing before and had listened for pauses as if some opportunity for input my offer itself but none did so I just listened. When he was done I told him we were glad he came and I wished him better luck tomorrow and he thanked me and then reassured me he would be with the right group for practice in the morning. I hoped he would but whether he was or not we would accommodate him if I had anything to do with it.

Racers have enough problems without assholes with headphones adding to them. Arbitrary power is too often abused and it only takes an extra second or two to be nice about what it is that needs to be done to make things go better. Motorcycle racers could die racing anytime they leave the pits, the least a lowly gate keeper can do who sends them to their fate is be kind about it.

43.

Dueling Dualism

I CAREFULLY AND QUIETLY closed the front door behind me, holding the awkward box camera against my stomach with the other hand. My dog was in the back yard and I was sneaking out the front door to try and take her picture. I had only two interests at the moment, my dog, who was my constant companion when out of doors, and my discovery of an old box camera in the trash at the apartment building my grandmother owned across town.

I had been taken there with my mother who had the chore of cleaning out the place after the tenant had been so thoughtless as to die and leave it full of his things. Letters had been sent out to known relatives but none had come to claim anything and whatever period of time to wait on such things had gone by and it was time to let the stuff go. Cartons and boxes of things had been carried out onto the stoop to be picked through by anyone who might want some of it and eventually a trash collector of some kind would come and take the rest. I sat there with it in the sunshine of a pleasant spring day as inside she pulled on rubber gloves and set to work with bleach and a pail and a mop to erase the traces of humanity left behind.

I looked in the boxes. I had nothing else with me but my curiosity and I wasn't allowed to bring Jet since she didn't know this part of town and might get herself into trouble. She was a small Labrador looking sort of black dog with a distinctive white streak under her throat. I found her one day while out playing in the woods and she followed me home and I fed her and she stayed. She would follow me where ever I went, listen to my questions, and give good advice. She counseled patience in most circumstances, with the offer of a hug sometimes. Rarely did she get her hackles up, even when threatened, but instead relied on speed.

That was what I liked about her. She wasn't fast, but she thought she was. When she would run, she would put her head down and lay her ears back and move her legs back and forth as fast as they would go. I was just nine but I could outrun her, which told me something – she wasn't very fast. When I had mentioned this to my grandfather he had commented sarcastically, "Yeah, she's a real 'jet' all right," and the name stuck. She was one of several dogs I had by that name, all small and black and all with the same distinctive streak under their neck. I would have mistaken them for the same dog but the sex varied, which was too obvious to ignore. Still, they came when I called them by name so the spirit was there.

But Jet hadn't made the trip this morning and so I had to entertain myself within the confines of the concrete landing at the top of the few steps that led to the apartment building and its four one bedroom worlds for people without a family to take care of them. The two upstairs had tenants still, but now both of the downstairs units were unoccupied and I had heard concerned talk about this and the need to get them ready and rented as quickly as possible. I sat patiently for a while, probably not very long but it seemed interminable. I started looking through the box next to me. There were old magazines, mostly Reader's Digest and Ford Times. I had seen them at home and thought I might actually recognize some of them. There were letters with writing on them I couldn't make out, except for one which was framed like a picture. It had a seal on it and some big words but I had seen one like it on my Grandfather's library wall and knew it was his discharge from the service. Apparently the guy who died alone here had been in the war as well.

There was a photo album and I looked at the photographs tucked into their little corner ear pieces glued on the black paper pages with some writing under them. "Basic Training" one said, and another was a group of young men crowded onto a bunk somewhere all smiling and making faces at the camera, most of them holding cigarettes which just said, "The Boys in Company B". I turned the pages and saw the sorts of photos I had seen in the one of these that was kept on a shelf in the den; People standing in groups in front of cars or in front of a house or seated at a table, somewhere their significance unknown to me. Some had writing with them. "Aunt Clara" looked back at me severely from a photo with scalloped edges. A group of men in uniform marched in crooked lines past a band playing behind them in another. Someone should care more about this, I told myself and decided to save it from the trash. I looked for others and found some in little envelopes mailed back from whoever had developed the film and at the bottom of the box, in the corner, I found the camera.

It was just a black box with a little red window at the back made out of plastic of some sort. There were knobs on the sides and a strap that went around your neck. I went inside and bothered my mother, which she had told me not to do unless it was important and I thought this might be. She needed a break apparently as she didn't seem too upset at being interrupted and told me to wait until she finished mopping the floor and so I did. The old linoleum squares of yellow and gray ran down the length of the little room. She had pulled the table and its chairs out and now it was just the rounded refrigerator still there. She went to the far end with the mop and methodically swept the floor back and forth as she came back to the sink and then wrung it out with her hands. The mop went back in the bucket then and she repeated the process down the next few rows and the ones after that until she was done and she had time for me.

"All right," she said, "Let's see what you've found." I showed her the album and the pictures and the camera. She looked at them with me, explaining what some might be, and made sure that she gave each one the respect it called for. She wasn't dismissive about them, which surprised me as she was dismissive often. Something about them struck her and she paged through the album as if she was remembering something. Finally she said to me, "Mr. Albert didn't have any relatives that we could find so none of the people in these pictures are still with us." By then I knew what people meant when they talked that way, my grandfather was 'no longer with us' either.

"They're all dead?" I asked her, which seemed to be a bit blunt judging by the expression on her face. It took her a moment to gather herself to tell me, "As far as we know, yes, they're all dead."

"Then can I take the pictures to the newspaper?" I asked. This seemed a surprise to her and I was preparing a response to her asking why but instead she just agreed and gave me the usual cautions about crossing the street and not talking to strangers. The Carmi Times was only three blocks away, but I would have to cross Main Street so that would require me to be on my guard. I gathered up the album, and the loose photos and their envelopes and made as tidy a bundle of it all as I could. I carried in against my chest with both arms around it and set off for an adventure. I had been to the newspaper office before and liked it. People were busy there and there was a smell about the place that was unique but not obnoxious. My arms got tired but I didn't stop to rest or put it down because I was afraid some might get blown away.

Main Street was made of brick, and the tires of the cars and trucks going by made a whirring sound when they rolled over them which was good because it helped with the chore of looking both ways at once so you didn't get run over. I only had a vague sense of what being 'run over' meant but the way it was said to me it sounded like something to avoid. Someone else was going into the building when I got there and they looked at me and saw I had my hands full so they opened the door for me. I thanked them and they told me I was welcome and I went in, carrying my little burden over to the desk where the lady sat and directed you where you really needed to be. She was talking on the phone and held up one finger and I nodded and waited.

She had looked at what I had, then taken me back to a man at a desk in a room full of people at desks and sat me down in a chair with the pictures and such put in a pile in front of him. He looked at them and then at me. He asked me questions about them. I told him I wasn't supposed to talk to strangers and so he pointed at the sign on his desk with a name on it and then stood up and reached down to me with his hand to shake. "How do you do?" he said, then, "My name is Bill." I shook his hand and told him my name and now that we were properly introduced I supposed that he wasn't a stranger any more and so I told him what I knew about the pictures. I had the urge to tell him that he had the same name as my mother and planned to work that in when the chance came but it never did.

He called Henry over and they talked between themselves but I could hear them. Then someone else came and they looked at the pictures and seemed rather excited and then Bill asked me what I wanted them to do with them. "You can have them," I said,"I just didn't want them to be thrown away without someone knowing about it." "You've come to the right place," Bill said and thanked me.I took my leave and felt good about it. There was a lot of talk going on behind me and glances came in my direction as I found my way back outside to the sidewalk and then went back to the apartment. In my preoccupation with the pictures I had forgotten to give them the camera, which still hung around my neck, and I thought about going back, but decided I would ask my mom first. She was ready to go when I got there, the pile of trash now a bit higher than it had been before. She said I could keep the camera and I was hurried into the car and we went home.

Some time later a copy of the paper appeared with some of the photographs in it. Names were under faces now and addresses and dates here and there. The story came to me from bits and pieces but apparently the guy had been a veteran who served in WWI with my grandfather in the ambulance corps with the Ford volunteers as the paper called them. The ambulances were model T's and my grand-father had gone over as a driver and mechanic at the expense of Mr. Ford himself.

Later on he came to own the Ford Dealership in Carmi and had bought an apartment building which he rented out to anyone so long as there wasn't a veteran that had no place to stay. He allowed them to stay for free until they got back on their feet and found a place of their own. A good number had done exactly that, apparently, all except for one. Mr. Albert had never gotten over the things he had seen in the war and had just kept to himself and lived out the rest of his life in that apartment. Another war had come and gone since then, the one my father and his brother had been in as well as my aunt's husband.

Dad flew over Europe, Uncle Jack flew in the Pacific, and Harry was a Marine at Guadalcanal.

There was something wrong with them all that I never understood. They didn't seem to like each other very much and they didn't talk about the war at all. They sat off to themselves whenever they could and I was kept away mostly and told not to make any sudden noises. I wore the camera around and pretended to be a reporter now and then and one day Uncle Harry called me over and asked me what I had there and I told him the story about it. He put me in the car and we went to the drug store downtown and handed the camera over to the man behind the counter who came back with it 'loaded' and gave us a brown manila envelope to send the film off with when we were done.

Uncle Harry showed me how to look in the back of the camera through the little red window and turn the knob slowly in the direction of the arrow next to it until a number appeared right in the window. Then I was to put my hand over the lens and pull the little lever up and listen for the 'click' which meant that the shutter was ready. Then I was to open up the little hidden door on top of the camera and reveal the distorted upside down image of what I was going to take a picture of and move the camera around until I had it framed like I wanted.

He showed me how to do this and was very patient. It was all so strange to me but I was grateful and appreciated that he didn't have a tantrum and yell and scream like he sometimes did. We took a picture of a tree outside and once he was satisfied I knew the drill, he went back to doing whatever it was he had been doing. I wanted a picture of my dog, because I knew she didn't have any family and that no one would remember her when she was dead. I don't know why that bothered me, but it did. I called her over to me and told her to sit so I could take her picture. I fumbled around with the process and had to step back to get her centered in the viewfinder and of course she got closer the further away I went thinking we were playing some sort of game.

I tried to explain it to her, but either she didn't understand or she didn't care about having her picture taken but either way, I didn't get it. In frustration I finally did take a picture of her tummy which she was showing me and wagging her tail so I would pet her. I stopped trying to take her picture then and went back inside to think about it. Lunch came and we had grilled cheese and tomato soup, a real favorite, and I sat in the kitchen looking out the window and saw Jet setting in the sun in the back yard. It came to me then that if I went quietly out the front, and came around the side of the house all ready to take the picture, I could get her before she saw me and came running.

Once I had been excused, I got my camera and went out the front door quietly as a mouse and got myself all ready, rolling up the film to the next number and then loading the shutter lever and opening up the little window. I was more used to it now and decided that I would frame Jet in the view finder and just walk toward her until she saw me and in the instant, when her head came up and she started to run over and see me, I would take her picture. I thought it was a good plan. I had not counted on how quickly she would see me, or how distant the viewfinder made everything look, or what things looked like to the camera in black and white compared to what they looked like to me.

It's about perception, after all. I still have the picture. It was weeks before I got it back from the mail in developer place and by then I had almost forgotten taking it. When it came, I went out and stood there again, in the same spot, and looked at the scene down the side of the house. There was little similarity. In the photo there was a distant black speck that was my dog Jet when she had seen me. At the time I had managed to see her head come up and watched her begin the process of running over to me. Now as I compared it to what I saw before me I hardly recognized what was in the photo. I showed Jet the picture but she didn't seem interested. I worried that I would not remember this, or that her family would never know what had happened to her. She was a stray, after all, who just started living with me one day for no reason I could think of. It didn't occur to me then that one day she would no longer live with me, but that happened too.

I was disappointed with the camera but I treasure the photograph. It is an icon of another time. The image it shows in inaccurate and I am not the same person I was then and Jet is long gone, but, still there was a time when all those things were as real as they were then as I am now thinking back on it or as someone may be a hundred years from now reading this as archaic crap about a time they know nothing about at all. Technology may bridge the void someday, I don't know, and may whittle down the human limitation of being stuck in the 'now' a bit some way. It's hardly imaginable to me but so many of the things we have now were unimaginable when I took this picture that it creates a possibility that it may really happen someday.

I took the picture in the fall of 1957 and started the fourth grade in the fall. That October I stood out in the schoolyard with all my classmates and teachers at recess and stared up at the sky. Sputnik was up there, orbiting the Earth, and it was put up there by men in Russia. Suddenly people looked up differently at the sky that had always been benignly there their whole lives. Now they were suspicious, now they were frightful, now God was not alone in the heavens. Man had pushed back the boundary of the mysterious just a bit and we thought it was horrible.

What did we know, anyway? Our perception of all things was so very limited by our circumstances that it seems foolish now. We tend to think that people back then really weren't all that bright but that's not true. They had brains as good as ours, or even better, and they plowed through monstrously complex problems by hand, without the aid of a machine to do it for them. This mind-body problem we have with the world we live in is classic. Nearly everyone notices it at some time in their lives. We have thoughts and feelings that are private to us that are not always directly associated with our contemporary surroundings. We dream, we scheme; we imagine things that have never existed. We are more than the sum of our experiences, much more. How much more depends on us, I suppose, but I'm still working on that.

44.

Miracles And All That Jazz

I KNOW MOTORCYCLE RACERS are keenly aware of the differences of the two worlds. Their body is doing many things while their mind is focused on winning, or perhaps more particularly on passing the guy right in front of them. They hug a machine that miraculously changes chemicals and electrical impulses into kinetic energy and provides a forum for its translation of it all into speed across the planet. They fly. They watch themselves doing it. They engage themselves on every level their mind can conjure. It's a real thing, and there are not words for me to describe it to you if you have never raced a motorcycle.

It's like telling a Presbyterian about transubstantiation. They may hear the words spoken to them on one level, and intellectually have some minute comprehension of what is being said, but the magnitude of the experience is beyond them and so is its importance. I dated a Catholic girl when I was in college and hoping to be a serial monogamist. During our time together I was serious about our relationship and our future and so, unknown to her, I took instruction in the way of a Catechism course on campus at the University. They had materials for me to read and there would be little meetings with groups and then singularly as I worked my way through what they believed and why they believed it. Actually, the why part came easiest, as I was on board with the basic story having been raised with it myself. Then we came to the part about the Holy Eucharist and how the little wafer and the wine were supposed to actually and physically turn into the body and blood of Jesus Christ himself. Not symbolically, or in some remembrance sort of way, but actually.

Well, two things leapt to mind right off the bat; I'd like to see some analysis done of that in a scientific way, and, even if it were true, who wanted to eat anyone or drink their blood? Yeah, I got what it was about, and I could see how it was supposed to do something spiritually for the true believers but, hey, I had to say 'no thanks' about the catalyst of 'true faith' as the ingredient that changed the stuff chemically from one thing to the other. Then there was the whole aspect of people being able to summon God to do a miracle by saying magic words; that seemed too unlikely to me at nineteen. I wanted it to be true, though, and I stayed with the girl for a bit longer and didn't tell her of my doubts.

Whether that was out of respect or some hold out position that it might be true and by being with her I might be saved by proxy sort of thing I'm ashamed to say I'm not sure. There was the whole thing with her body telling my mind what to do that was a problem of its own as well but sure enough, they had a rule about that too.

Of course there was purgatory thrown in on top of the rest of it and someone would be needed to bail me out after I died and I had the very great premonition that I was going to die young. Since that scheme required the living person praying my way out of purgatory to be a Catholic, it made some sense that I stay with her for that if for no other reason. My early demise proved not to be true, either, to my great relief. Our love was found equally false as events proved later. She married a nice Jewish boy and moved to Miami after he had convinced her what she was feeling for him while she was stoned was the real thing. Maybe it was, who can say?

She had given me an all saints medal to wear when I was racing after Saint Christopher got taken down from the roster of saints and there by lost his power to protect travelers. The triangular shaped piece of metal had tiny figures stamped on both sides and hung on a chain. I wore it because she had asked me to and I liked her. I didn't fall down when I wore it so I figured it was lucky that way but knew that was not what it was meant for. Still, I wore it. I had been sent off to boy scout camp one summer years before and managed to fall and break my collarbone running down to the lake as soon as I got there. They wrapped me in a plaster body cast which I got wet of course and when they took it off they found the resulting fungus infection had eaten the pigment out of my skin leaving a mark where the cast had been. I had forgotten about it more or less by the time I started racing and sweating in a leather suit but the fungus hadn't and somehow got itself onto the medal and its chain.

When we parted, I gave her the medal back and wished her well. It was years before I saw her again and it was in the summertime, which had always been her favorite, and she was tanned and wearing something that showed it off as she had done when I was with her. As I got closer I saw something else. Around her neck, and down to her chest, was an untanned streak as if she wore a necklace of some kind that had eaten the pigment right out of her skin. She had. Loving someone leaves a mark after all.

If my mind is telling me the oyster cracker I am washing down into my body with Welch's grape juice is human flesh, at what point will the two reconcile with each other? I'm not sure to be honest, that sort of dualism never melded for me. On a race bike, however, I had a different experience. I fell off a lot when I started, which is fairly normal, but I survived it without losing the fun of going fast, which may be rare, I can't say. I can say that very few of the guys I started racing with are still racing now, at least not with me. But even if we had been at all the same races with each other over all the years and out on the track side by side, we wouldn't have experienced the same things. Since I am suggesting there is some universal truth that is revealed by racing, then that's a problem.

The nature of that particular problem lies within the mind-body problem as philosophers see it. Gilbert Ryle said that the traditional view of this dualism we get from Descartes was wrong, but mostly was just a matter of categorical confusion. He asked us to imagine a tour of Oxford University and I have to say right there, that if you have not been there you may as well wait just a bit and I'll come back to racing. But Ryle says a tourist having seen the library and the debate hall and all the individual colleges in Oxford would still complain at the end of their tour that he had not seen the university. My college there was Lincoln College, which has the unique distinction of being where John Wesley gave thought to these same problems. His teaching there led to the set of beliefs that now are the foundation of the Methodist faith, still Christian, but not Catholic, which is just a word that means 'universal'. When I learned that I wondered how they felt about it on Pluto – which used to be a planet but now is something less, sort of like the universe relative to the Catholic faith.

Back to our tourist and his problem with not getting to see Oxford University; he had seen what there is of it, but he wrongly ascribed the buildings he had seen and the University to the same category of existence, and by doing so misrepresented the relationship of the two. One is not the other, nor are they mutually inclusive terms. In a similar way, Descartes was wrong to think of the mind and the body as two separate entities that might possibly exist separate and apart from one another. If you're lost now, I will go back to my first Harley Davidson race bike and see if that helps. I speak of it at length elsewhere so this is a brief use of its nature by way of an example.

My 1966 CRTT road racer was the sweetest little pushrod four stroke ever made. I thought so at the time, and nothing has changed my mind about that in all the years since. It had a dual nature power band, due in part to poor carburetion probably, but I did not fiddle with such things then being fully occupied in learning to ride at speed. It would start and run up to 9300 or so and then stutter badly and act like it could go no further. That did seem like a lot of rpm compared to my experience with American V-8 motors in cars. Fortunately the guy selling it to me explained that it had another existence of which I was not aware and to get there, I would have to pull the clutch in when it stuttered like that and rev it on up to 10,500 or more and go, using 11,500 for a redline. I thought him insane, but at the time we were in the formation process of making a deal and it was still his bike so, hey, 'if you say so, mister, I'll do it.'

To my great surprise the motor was entirely different and pure joy running in that rpm range and just sang its little heart out right up to the redline which, when put together with kill button shifting, made it a wonder to ride. Of course it was also the loudest thing I ever road and a good deal of my deafness now is attributable to sticking my head in the bubble of that bike at Daytona for a novice race of 76 miles having forgotten my ear plugs. Ouch. My point there is that everything about the bike, its nature, the way it handled, what I thought of it, how it behaved, was entirely different once I wound the motor up to the new plateau. I could have bought that bike, raced it below 9300, and never thought much of it. Even Don Hollingsworth who had won Daytona on his sprint and was the last guy to win an AMA National for 250cc bikes there didn't wind his up that much which I learned when we raced them together later.

If you think I've lost you, you're wrong, here's the fusion of all that precedes this.

45.

After the Fall

DON EMDE SHARED THE news after I left the October race at Barber that there will be no Daytona 200 next year. Apparently, it's over - the dream of every American motorcycle racer wannabe of my generation to race the premier of all American races at Daytona is now just a nostalgic fantasy. We had all read of and seen photos of and heard tales of races on the beach and down A1A and back and tried to imagine what they had been like. Then they built the speedway. I went there for the first time fairly early on as things go, shortly after the first U.S. GP that was an F.I.M. sanctioned event. I had seen pictures; the grandstands were empty. I won a Formula 500 race there many years later, and the grandstands were still empty. As exciting and challenging as it is to ride, it is not an especially good venue for spectating. That is not just true of motorcycles, I have been bored by stock cars there as well. But for me, or for any racer, the questions of their careers and the arc they make through time are not just about place, or time and they are not even just about results.

More importantly, on a personal level for each of us; the question that matters is - what were you in the end? There is an end to all things finite and you are a finite being. It's not an easy thing to admit, that you will not go on forever, but you don't; nothing does – not even Daytona. So what is it that you think this marvelous and wonderful thing called life has been for if the final outcome of all things is going to take place after you've left? This is where many fall back on some popular institutional notions that they have been told since childhood. I know them. I suppose on some level I believed them. But I can no longer deny that I am uncertain whether or not they are actually literally true as some like to say.

It is comforting to believe that they might be, and I love that, but the examples that they are not are filling the scale at the other end of the balance with examples of just why they are not. God does not tell men, any men, to behead other men on video, or to crash airplanes into buildings, period. Neither does He let children die of cancer; or beach goers be swept away by tsunamis; nor generations of young people be decimated by war. God's will as a sweeping concept is undeniable, but to step around or gloss over the bad parts and say somehow that they are good parts we just don't understand defies more than logic, it ignores the truth.

Smarter men than I have written better books than this one to explain that away. My favorite of those would be "The Screwtape Letters" by C.S. Lewis, which is an artful piece of fiction that makes an entertaining narrative out of how bad acts and evil events are all the devil's fault. I read it in grade school and found so many of the examples cited to be present in my own life that I concluded that what he was suggesting must be true, or truly based at the very least. Sadly, I have to say I know better now. It was just a story. A good story, to be sure, but not one based on real events.

At my last race, (and here I get to use those words accurately with sufficient vagueness to make readers wonder if I mean I am done racing or am just talking about the last race I rode before I wrote this), was not at Daytona where I had always imagined it would be, but at Barber Motorsports Park in Alabama. When this project began I had decided to return to the fast and fierce world that is Formula 500 racing and resurrected an old machine with new tires and fresh fittings and made myself more fit as well so that I could handle what it required of me. These are the bikes I rode in the best of my racing days. Not as fast as the awesome TZ's that came later, but fast for a while in a short race and the races now are that short.

The classics of the class would have been TR3 Yamaha twins, such as Don famously rode to win a race at Daytona, which are real factory GP machines, but which are too precious now to risk for such small rewards and which have mostly gone to museums and collectors. Their successors in interest on the street were the reed valve RD400s that Yamaha produced, which turn out to actually be quicker in terms of lap times and easier to ride thanks to a broader power band. No one seems to mind that they were not out there in the old days, and I have some, but I don't race them. I race the 350s still, because I race for a different reason.

The class also allows 500cc Honda four cylinders and the new generation of Honda 350 twins that make horsepower like the old ones never did and of course Dave Crussel, when he is fit enough and feels like it, will bring his H1R out to thrash us all and show us what real racing looks like. They all make more horsepower now than they used to, and to put that power to the ground, bigger tires are put on fatter rims than most bikes had when they were new and were raced in the 60s and 70s. Bigger tires means more traction, which is another way of saying more force applied to the twisty bits of a motorcycle frame and there are inevitably twisty bits. This class was born of a street bike homologation formula from the A.M.A. which meant many machines have the mild steel, small diameter tubing of their progenitors' designs and it was immediately put wrong by the addition of longer swing arms and fatter tires that the riders liked because it made them faster, but were put off by when the physics of it all literally put them off.

When all of this was starting, I was already racing. We went from narrow pointy Dunlops to wider cross section tires and I have to admit that I was one of the initiators of such practices, believing in my Indianapolis 500 way that fatter tires meant higher corner speeds without understanding what else it meant. It was the time of Parnelli Jones and the first 150 mph lap at the brickyard which was done on lower wider tires mounted on 15 inch rims while the older roadsters used taller skinnier tires that tradition had said were required.

In terms of vintage formula 500 bikes, big rubber means a propensity to high side if you get it wrong and the bikes loses traction in the rear first and you don't give it up quickly enough and just let it go. There is a moment there, early on in the sequence of events that can become a crash, that a rider has a choice of whether to try and save it, or just go to the track and save himself. Usually it is like this; the rider is in the turn and throttle is being reapplied after it was reduced under braking and turning. The rider has chosen his exit line and plans to sweep out to the next straight while accelerating. The maximum lean part of the turn has passed and the bike is being returned to vertical to maximize the available traction for the application of power. If all is well, it's a smooth transition. For those that have never done it, but do ice skate, or roller blade, I would describe it as that time when you step one foot over the other, moving sideways and forward at the same time because the forces trying to pull you away from where you want to go are too much otherwise. Before you learned to do that you just had to wait to go forward again as your feet were already doing all they could do to keep you upright.

Well, on the motorcycle you can't give the tires a break and have them step one ahead of another, they have to just eat it in terms of what to do with all that force you are making them take. It's not a matter of courage, or technique, really; it's more a matter of science, which will prompt Adrian to give us some formula to ponder later in his book about racing and the immutable laws of physics.

In real time, however, you set your line, sweep through the turn feeling the signals the bike is giving you about traction and power and so forth, and then you begin to accelerate out of the turn. The back end comes out a bit – which is expected and which is not a bad thing if you can control it. There may be other ways to negotiate corners quickly I suppose, but I don't know them and this is what came to me from sliding my Triumph around on green lanes so long ago that I doubt I could learn them.

So here we are at this moment in the curve of all things related and for some reason; either the tire is not up to the task, or the track is more slippery from some recent addition since the last time you calculated this, or the motor is giving more power, or the chilidog you had for lunch has dissipated after being converted from a solid to a gas, whatever the reason, the level of available traction falls below the standard necessary to maintain contact with the track. The back tire begins to break loose and the rider feels it.

There are multiple paths forward from there, and depending on which you choose, an outcome can be as good or as bad as it gets. You can maintain the throttle setting as it is, adjust the angle of attack with the steering and climb forward on the machine putting as much weight on the front end as possible. It's risky, and it was R.G. Wakefield that first told me about it and explained that it was how he turned his Kawasaki 500 H1R when the back end started to come around. It happens quickly and appears as a little lurching twitch to the trackside spectator who may not realize that it was a heart stopping moment for the pilot who managed to pull it off.

When he told me about it, I was riding a Yamaha 350 twin, which had less weight, less power, and narrower tires than his H1 so it was an entirely different moment for me and I had less to work with in terms of available thrust to make it all work out. But when it did happen coming over the hill at Road Atlanta in turn two, I was able to apply it and although it seemed counter-intuitive to me since I had a tendency to stay as far back on the bike as possible so I could keep my head in the bubble, it worked out. It also worked well as a technique to make a speed wobble stop, which was even more beneficial to me when I moved up to superbikes and rode one of the evil handling Kawasaki GPZ750s of the first generation. To review then, choice one is move forward quickly, adjusting the steering angle to prevent jack knifing which leads to high siding, and going on.

Pathway choice number two from the 'rear wheel going away' moment is the 'get off' choice. You are laid over anyway, and the track is as close to you as it is going to get before this ends so just go there now and release your grip on the bike, making sure you get your leg out from under it before it goes down and breaks something. This is why we see riders with their foot off the peg as they brake for a turn. It is then that this traction mambo can begin and they are just anticipating the dance. If it doesn't happen, then they can put their foot back where it should be and go on. But when you can't save it; regardless of the reason, and the bike is going down, you may as well get yourself down with the least possible amount of harm so release the hounds, get down, and slide.

If you build your own bikes, it's harder to do. All the hours of effort and piles of money you put into it are about to be destroyed and you have abandoned ship. I won't go into that other than to say if you're a builder, and think you might hesitate here, then you should probably have hesitated sooner – back there when you were about to put your helmet on and go out on the track. No motorcycle is worth an inch of your skin, no matter what it is once you've decided to race it. Give up on the bike, save yourself, and let it go.

But sometimes, you don't have the choice. Rarely, you are in that moment, accelerating out of a turn, and someone clobbers you in the back end having misjudged a pass. It may not have been malicious, or it may have, it does not matter a bit to you because it feels the same. If you are at Barber, in turn 15, as I was when it happened, then your first instinctive reaction may have been to save it from being knocked out from under you by straightening up and giving up on the corner all together. That is the third path and we try to avoid it entirely whenever we can. That is because once you are off the track, your choices that allow a good outcome are as limited as the resources you have to work with. We race our vintage bikes on the same tracks where vintage cars race, and they are made to keep car drivers safe and only incidentally designed to spare motorcycle racers injury. We have air fences now, which are a good thing, but the tracks have Armco barriers everywhere else, and they are deadly.

Armco is a highway department of transportation guardrail put at a given distance from the edge of a racetrack where it is intended to prevent harm that would happen if it were not there. No one designs a racetrack with evil intent; well except maybe for those figure 8 races out in New Jersey and we don't race motorcycles there. Armco keeps cars that have gone off course from going further off into something worse and protects spectators in some cases. An unintended consequence of their design and placement is that sometimes motorcycle racers are forced into them in unexpected ways and they are killed. It has happened at least three times that I know of, possibly more, because we do not speak of the dead in racing often among ourselves and officially not at all. As I mentioned elsewhere, the sanctioning bodies of our sport will not disclose how many of us lost our lives racing or who we were.

When I was hit, I saved it from going down, so the two paths described first from the moment were already lost to me. The third one; the one in which we just attempt to ride it out, is alien to our training, experience, and is mostly out of our control. When I hit the gravel trap I was moving and upright. If I just held on, and kept it going straight, I could see that I was going to end up in the Armco or flip it if I used the front brake and the wheel dug in. I did not know how deep the gravel was or how large, both of which matter in moments like these. I had no feel for what was going on other than the feeling that I was moving in a direction I did not want to go. I steered deliberately away from the Armco, down the hill and across the face of the gravel trap. I nearly got to the edge of it and was looking at the skinny patch of grass waiting there for me before the barrier supports and trying to imagine making a turn in that little space when the bike lost enough momentum that the front wheel augured in and the bike was yanked out from under me. It wasn't a hard fall, but it was awkward enough that I didn't manage to keep the bottom edge of my helmet out of my shoulder and collarbone by getting my hands out quickly enough and the familiar (way too familiar) contact was felt vaguely as all things filled with marble sized gravel.

It was a successful end to a trip down path number 3 in nearly every way you could imagine given what was available to work with and the alternatives. Other riders in similar situations at Barber making different choices have been killed. Is that the track's fault? I think not, being killed is a possible outcome of any race, albeit an unpleasant one. It is one that racers seek to avoid whenever possible and so I asked myself right away, in fact as soon as I knew I had survived it, what I could do to prevent something like it from happening again.

I got up and waved my arms in the direction where I was sure my wife was watching from, some distance away on a terrace in the control tower. I was pretty sure she couldn't see me, but was equally sure that someone could and should tell her I had done it, letting her know I was signaling them I was all right – or at least able to get up and wave my arms. The corner worker came running down and wanted to pick the bike up and get it over to the Armco. The seat had been knocked off in the fracas and his attempt to use it as a handle failed. I told him I was done. He told him the guy had just hit me and gone on. I asked him who it was and he said he didn't know. I left the track later without finding out.

Earlier that day it had rained, and I don't like to ride in the rain, but it had stopped before my race and so I had decided to go out and be safe and just finish. In fact I had written those very words on my bike's fairing stay, right where I could see them, just before I went out. I was alone, which is usual for me before a raced, and I sat in the back of my van after getting my gear on and having finished my preflight checklist and just took in the moment. I was trying to pick up any signals that the universe might be offering about the moments to come. They are there, of course, but mostly we ignore them. I have had feelings of dread so great that I just took my helmet off and said, 'not today,' but this day I didn't get that.

Instead, when I stood, I saw a hole in the clouds moving over us that gave me a glimpse of a sunny blue sky above and allowed a visible beam of sunshine to angle down like a postcard onto the far hillside. I have seen this before, and when I was a child my grandmother told me when I had first asked what it was that it was the path God made for angels to go to heaven and back when need be. As children do, I believed her. Now I think that there is probably some name for it, since it has happened often enough since I first saw it to wonder if there isn't some name for such things somewhere. With that thought, I put my helmet on and made a reminder to myself to find out what it was after the race.

I will miss Daytona. I literally did miss the race because of my injuries after this crash, but more importantly, I will miss the running of the event generally as it said something about our sport and our place in the world of sporting events. It will not miss me. Racing is not sentimental, even if we are sentimental about it. Riders have less to do with outcomes than they used to and even Rossi, who I think a hoot to watch, cannot control everything or overcome deficiencies he did not create, or avoid the fate that awaits him eventually. Something may be written about him someday that properly describes his place in the pantheon of all things, I hope it is. More important to me would be the place that men like Ted Henter deserve and won't get unless someone takes the time to tell the world their story. That is what's next for me should anyone wonder – or even if they don't.

46.

Do You Mind?

I'M NOT SURE WHEN it first showed up on my radar but rather early on I realized there was a difference between the world my mind saw and the one my body experienced. I was holding a dartboard for my brother and his friends to throw their darts at down in the basement because there was no place to fasten it to the wall. I was four going on five years old and did what I was told pretty much. He and his three friends were the regulation distance away for dart throwing they said and I was holding the board up against my chest and watching the wooden torpedo shaped metal tipped missiles thump home. I never thought about it being hazardous and neither did anyone else apparently. Certainly our parents had not mentioned it. I would remember something like, "If you go down to the basement to throw darts don't make your brother hold the board for you while you do."

Predictably it went wrong and I was watching as a dart that had been launched with admirable force found its way onto and then into my knee cap where it stuck. A moment passed. I did not drop the board because I had been properly threatened with what would happen if I did. I did not yell because not three minutes before this my mother had opened the kitchen door and commanded us to "Keep Quiet!" in no uncertain terms.

Instead I just look at the four of them, ashen faced and cringing, and said, "We're done," letting the board go to fall to the floor and marching upstairs for supervised dart removal. There was a good bit of adult angst displayed but I was calm about it. It really didn't hurt, it just looked like it should, and so I sat on a chair while they gathered 'round and discussed the best way to remove it and finally one of them asked me if I could pull it out myself. I nodded, grabbed it, and worked it out with a few wiggles this way and that to get it out of the bone. My mother was downstairs leaving no doubts about who was going to have their asses beat and who was going to do the beating. She was a real suffragette in the field of corporal punishment - No need to have someone else do what you can do yourself.

I heard the shrieks and sounds of a belt on a butt and then more murmured consternation and then the drama repeated until everyone was satisfied with their punishment and their penance. I sat in the chair until she reappeared and she asked me if I wanted Iodine or Mercurochrome as an antiseptic. I asked her what the difference was and she said one of them burned but she couldn't remember which one. I said I guess it didn't matter then and she got a bottle with a glass rod in its cap and dabbed some of the brightly tinted liquid on the hole where the dart had gone in.

It was out now, laying on the table, but I had seen it in my knee and now saw it there in my mind still. There was no permanent damage to my knee from it that I could tell, but my mind had been morphed into a different creature all together. Now I could 'see' things that were Dali-esque in a way, like the clocks he painted drooping over the landscape only for me they had more to do with darts and such, protruding from people unnoticed as they smoked a cigarette or read the paper and ignored me. The longer I looked at them the more that appeared, in their nose, from their forehead, anywhere their skin could be seen. I'm sure there was something wrong with me and thought so then as well, but it proved to be an effective attention getter.

When I wanted someone's attention I would just imagine them with a dart sticking in them somewhere, and then another and another until they finally got the point and wanted to know what I was looking at. I wouldn't tell them, even though I knew that having a dart poke you didn't really hurt, but would take the opportunity to go ahead and say what I had been waiting to say anyway. It wasn't real, I knew that, but it really worked, which was significant.

I was using my mind in imaginary ways to make real things in another realm. The Sorcerer's Apprentice? Yeah, I had seen that and recalled that Mickey got in a lot of trouble conjuring up the brooms to carry the water from the well so I stopped.

Years later, I sat in the school library and looked at a picture of Mike Hailwood on a grand prix bike Honda leaned over with a grim determined face. He was on cobblestones and there appeared to be rain on his windscreen. The caption read, "Mike the Bike averages 100 miles an hour at the Isle of Man." I tried very hard to imagine what that must be like and had great difficulty. Part of that difficulty was caused by never having ridden a motorcycle. Another part had to do with being very familiar with 100 mph and the nature of averages. There must have been parts of the circuit where he went much faster than what showed in the photograph and the bike must have some terrific top speed.

I had been to the Indianapolis 500 by then, and had seen men wrestle Offenhouser powered roadster machines around a course made of bricks at an average of 140 plus. My family had made attendance a sport of its own and from 1958 through the 1970's we never missed the Memorial Day circus that was the Indianapolis 500. Somebody we knew had a gasoline alley pass and we all got in to mill around with the drivers and the machines being worked on in their tiny little wooden garages. They weren't just photos in a program to me, they were living breathing machines that smelled and felt slick and had leather seats and lots of decals for sponsors and all the rest. Since I had seen them with their skins off and had gotten autographs from Parnelli Jones, and A.J. Foyt and Jim Clark, I had no problem believing that what they did, I could do. Sure it was tough, but all kids imagine they will be able to do tough things and nothing about it looked magical or impossible.

But when I saw Hailwood at the Isle of Man in the photo it stopped my imagination in its tracks. I knew that at Indianapolis if you had the most powerful car with the right tires you hardly needed to let off the gas all the way around. With its big turns and wide open spaces the speedway was a place that let you average 140 something. I knew those guys and had watched them do it. Yet here was a guy tip toeing around a bridge abutment in the rain on paving stones at something like pedestrian speed in a photograph that said he averaged 100 miles an hour over 38 miles of public roads that ran through towns and up and down a mountain. What must the rest of the circuit be like? What sort of a man could do such things? What sort of a machine would allow it? It was a milestone of my thinking about speed.

As time went by and I got a motorcycle and began riding and then racing that marker grew in significance for me. I imagined things, then I did them as I imagined. That was the pattern. I was on the community swim team and raced the free style. I had no training and not much style, but I hated to lose and could make myself go faster than the guy in the lane next to me. The team did well and then we were invited up to the university to compete in a state wide meet. There they combined the scores of the swimmers and the divers for a team total. We didn't have any divers.

The coach apologized for wasting our trip and was beating himself up about it. Two of us volunteered to dive for the team. We had to tell them in advance what we were going to do and most of the diving I had done at the pool was to splash the girls sunbathing in the lawn chairs off to the sides. Now I was supposed to not make a splash when I got to the water and they wanted me to do some things in the air before I got there which they said were 'compulsory'. I got thorough those things well enough by watching the other divers go first and then imagining how they had done it. Knowing a thing can be done is a great incentive.

Someone had done the math after the swimming events and it came down to one last dive. If I could do a double gainer, that is two backward summersault in succession, off of the high board and get a 6 or better, we could win. I had no idea how to do that, and had never even seen one. One of the divers from another team heard me say that and came over and explained how it went. "You spring on the board as usual going forward but when you go up to do your summersault you do it backward, toward the board, and then do another, and then go into the water feet first." I asked him why he hadn't done it here if he knew how. He reached in his mouth and pulled out his front teeth on a plate. "That's why." he told me and I got it. Once you jump up off of the board and start doing summersaults back at it, the end of the board is flexing up and down as you turn in the air above it and then go past it. If your timing is wrong, and you are too close to the board, it is coming up as your head is coming around and 'whack' it gets you right in the mouth.

Knowing this made it was worse for me because instead of having a mental picture I could make a reality, I only had a picture of what I didn't want to happen. I was about to change my mind about trying it at all when they called my name and I climbed up the steps to the three meter board and waited for the signal from the judges table. The word had gotten around that I was trying the dive for the first time and it got pretty quiet, or it seemed like it to me. I had done dives off the high board, but all of them had involved going forward, or rotating away from the board, never backward. This was not going to be pretty. I stood still until the judges were ready, then I took my three step and hop approach sprung up into the air and hoped as I was coming down that I had it right in my head what I needed to do.

. . .

Tony Foale is a man I admire although I haven't ever met him. He is an engineering genius apparently, judging from the things he's made. When he posted photos of a rotary valve two stroke motor that he had made himself, I wrote to him and asked him what made him think he could do that? I meant no offense, but wasn't careful enough to say so and he took it a bit wrong and was put off by my lack of deference to his talents.

I was ignorant and admit it, I should have done a better job with my inquiry but things like tact and tone, do not appear in social media so there are bound to be misunderstandings. I was just thinking that when I began trying to make a motorcycle go faster, it never occurred to me to pour aluminum into a mould and change it into something else altogether. It was a double gainer for me. I'd never seen it done or even described. What I knew about cars, drawn from the American hot rodding tradition, had to do with changing parts, not design. We could increase performance by putting different cams in them with more lift and greater duration and high compression pistons and carburetion with greater flow and exhaust headers and all the other things people did to make them run faster. It was complex in a way, but there were places to buy the stuff and you just had to pick and choose and put it together. To make something entirely new, and to change the design in the process, well I wouldn't have known where to begin. Apparently Tony did so I had asked him about that leap, from knowing you have no idea how to do something, to thinking you can.

. . .

Back on the diving board, I leapt into the air, pulled my arms in and bent my knees up and threw my head back to start the first rotation, keeping my eyes open so I would know when to come out of my tuck. I brought my hands down and pulled my heels up against myself in the back. I came around once and saw myself heading for the end of the board, and had the urge to pull out and call it good. I had my eyes open and could see that the board was still flexing and that I was coming down even with it as I came around the second time. Now I needed to straighten out and go feet first toward the water with my arms at my sides and to do that I would have to pass the board that way, eyes front, and let the end of it whip up and down right in front of my face before going on around and down into the water. The closer I came to the board, the higher the score.

There were seven rivets on the end of the board and an empty hole where an eighth should have been. I could see them all clearly when they went past. Having seen that, I straightened out and held my body locked in position, toes pointed down, and waited for the entry which came with just a ripple in the pool and then I was in the water. 7.4 overall average from the judges, not bad for a first try. I had done it, but I had no idea how it had happened, not really.

The next weekend I went to Terre Haute, Indiana to their red clay half mile dirt track and watched the AMA national race half mile race. Dave Aldana was there on his BSA twin and carried the number 38. I hung on the rail at the end of the back stretch in the infield right where he went into turn three. He would come at me all tucked in, left hand on the fork, right hand on the throttle holding it wide open. He would peer just over the number plate at the track ahead waiting for the spot where he would suddenly set up and pitch it sideways, pointing its nose to the inside and getting his weight where he wanted it, partly on his steel shoed left foot and partly on the right peg as he throttled around the turn, giving it more or less gas depending on what he wanted the back end to do.

It was a beautifully simple thing to watch and I saw him do it lap after lap the same way. The same parameters in play, the adjustments made in real time to direction and power relative to available traction. It was impressive, but it became amazing when there was a late challenge for the lead toward the end of the race.

Jim Rice showed his front wheel up the inside of Aldana near the end and things got serious. Dave held him off, but it changed things. Now just before he gave up his tuck, he would go from head down on the tank, to looking back under his arm, upside down, to gauge the gap between the two of them before popping up to take the turn.

Let me walk you through that. Imagine what it's like to be Dave Aldana, tucked in looking out over the number plate and waiting to go from your high speed tuck posture, to your cowboy steer wrestling posture in an instant as you pick your spot in the inside of the turn and pivot yourself around that imaginary point like an airplane at the Reno Air Races. I'm not saying I can describe it well enough for you to imagine it, I'm asking you to actually be him, doing it. Can you do that?

Two distinct body positions; two completely different sets of concerns, both requiring total commitment, one with all attention focused straight ahead, the other the polar opposite, looking backward and upside down. Now add that view of your rival upside down in a disappearing landscape as the bike continues away from what you are looking at. Now translate all of that into when, exactly, you need to yank your head back out from under your armpit and launch the bike into turning mode with just two laps to go so you don't blow the lead or give up the line he's trying to pass you on.

What is it like to be Dave Aldana? That was my question. When he came around with the checkered flag on his victory lap we all waved and gave him a thumb's up and he nodded at us across the void that separated everyone watching from him and his BSA.

In 1974 American philosopher Thomas Nagel wrote an article about a person speculating what it would be like to be a bat. His point was that there is a subjective character of experience – something that it is to be a particular organism for that organism that can never be captured by reductive science. Reduction is the process of turning reality into some measurement of scientific perception. Nagel was saying that the essential truths of what it means to be a bat are so subjective as to be incomprehensible to science. Bats navigate and locate insects in complete darkness by a system of sonar and echolocation using their high frequency squeaks and the reflection of those sounds. They form perceptions completely unlike anything in human experience and so fundamentally different in every way that any reduction to scientific numeration would be meaningless to us.

It is a mystery how the true character of experience could be revealed in the physical operation of an organism that is not like us. What's it like to be Dave Aldana, however, would arguably be a different matter. We are human, he is human, so if we measure, quantify and sufficiently duplicate the experience he is having we should be able to comprehend and replicate it for ourselves, correct? Science would say 'yes' but I say 'absolutely not.' Dave is a great guy and I know him. At the time he was a stranger to me and to himself as he is now. Then he was a young clown on the loose having fun. He was a nineteen year old prankster who would do silly things for a laugh despite the risks. He was not, and may not now be, a cold calculating racing machine. Whether he thought in terms of risk and reward, I can't say, I never asked him. But would he throw a cherry bomb at you in the middle of the night on the highway? You betcha.

47.

The Zen Of Flow

A photographer for the Daytona Beach Morning Journal took a photo of Dave and I on the banking at Daytona one year side by side. Both of us are riding TZ750s and the caption notes that he seized his motor but went on to finish 10th. It does not mention that I finished 33rd or that I was riding on the same set of tires we had used the entire season the year before.

We both took chances and probably had some moments of doubt along the way. He had a new TZ750 and I had a converted double shock 700 with a dirt bike swing arm. I had too much power for the chassis the motor was in, he didn't have enough. Such is racing.

Could I tell you from that photograph what was in my mind when it was taken? Do I have a running recollection of what the experience was like for me so that I could tell you about it now? No one does that. They may have recollections about it later, and there may be little things they can recall here and there, but the experience of motorcycle racing is transcendent of the common place and runs the mind out onto another plane that is all together different.

We do not remember days, we remember moments. Those moments may be date stamped so that I can recall when my anniversary is or when my children were born, and from those dates I may recall specific events but I do not have a specific recollection of all that happened that day, or any other. I know there are people who claim to have such a memory and I suppose it might be possible, but I am not one of them.

Psychologist Mihaly Csikszentmihalyi wrote a famous investigation of "optimal experience" claiming to have revealed that what makes an experience genuinely satisfying is a state of consciousness he called *flow*. During flow, people are supposed to experience deep enjoyment, creativity, and a total involvement with life. He claimed to have thought of a way to replicate the mental response to optimum experience in our daily lives by ordering the information that enters our consciousness, allowing us to discover true happiness and greatly improve our quality of life. Maybe so, but it seems artificial to me.

Can I replicate mentally the inputs of sensations and concerns that surround me when racing? I think not. I think there is too much about it that is ethereal, like the dream that seemed so real yet dissipates so completely when I wake. I have a survivor's feeling of elation when the race is over, and may be aware of a sudden weariness that I had put off by an effort of will while it was going on, but I cannot simulate those things just by thinking about them anytime I choose.

I knew a man who loved to be at the ocean. He loved the beach, the sand, the salt air, and everything about it all no matter what the weather or the time of year. When he got older, I would visit him and he would talk about how much he missed the sea. I asked him why he didn't go anymore, since we both lived in Florida at the time and it was less than an hour away. "Oh, I don't need to now," he said, "I have my memories..." in my experience, the further away from an event our recollection is called to remind us of it, the less accurate and detailed it becomes. There is some need to be back there, even if it is just to remind ourselves that we are not the same. Science has no measure for this. It is not a physical phenomenon.

Physicalism – the notion that science can know everything – has its limits and one place where there is a glaring deficit is at that edge of reason that is racing on a motorcycle. It is so occupying of the senses to do it at all, that what is left is a purer form of consciousness than man may have anywhere else. "Flow" gives some credit to this notion, the idea that optimal experiences are psychologically distinct from routine life. I think that so obvious as to not need explanation. I also think that such experiences leave an impact on the mind of those who do such things whether it is mountain climbing or skydiving or whatever. The body is gone and the mind is occupied but consciously dealing with things so important to the continued existence of the mind's vessel that normal thinking is impossible. The mystery is what is it occupied with? Why men in such a dire situation are not filled with a fear so great that they are paralyzed to inaction is a question worth asking, but they are not, or the ones that survive to recall it are not anyway.

They are not really afraid, well not of very much. I was always afraid that the bike wouldn't start. Once it did, I was fine. There was an experiment done by a cardiologist that hooked motorcycle racers up to heart monitors to record their pulse rates while racing. What he found was that the increase was comparable to what you would expect to see with a good physical workout in a gym. Effort was applied and the muscles demanded more oxygen and so the heart increased its rhythm to supply it. What he did not find was that fear played a part. Little dumps of adrenaline may come and go during a race, giving a little clarity to the mind's processing of what is going on, but by and large the human reactions to great danger while racing a motorcycle is minimal. Something happens on a bike that overrides the human fear of the consequences of crashing.

Long after I had been up and down the career escalator of racing motorcycles and had convinced myself that I could do it but didn't need to keep doing it to prove anything anymore, I learned of the story of Rollie Free. We all want to be free, but I didn't know until later that I wanted to know what it was like to be Rollie Free.

When I first saw the photograph I thought it was a stunt. I mean here's a guy on a Vincent going 150 miles an hour at Bonneville wearing a bathing suit. Who does that? Well it was a stunt, in a way, since Rollie was the type of guy who was paid to take chances and had done stunts for the movies. The Vincent was not up to speed as it were, in terms of where they wanted to be, and his leather jacked and pants ballooned up in the slipstream and flapped around and he thought it was slowing him down. Was it dangerous? You bet your ass it was dangerous, but he knew that. It was a risk and he had a degree of confidence in the machine having already ridden it at speed that told him he could be just fine and that he would go faster if he only had on a bathing suit.

That part of it, the idea that you just wear a bathing suit, sort of escaped me when I first saw it. I mean I raced in the early days in blue jeans and a tee shirt, but I never road in shorts, not even on the street. Things happen, bikes go down, and bare skin on asphalt is bound to cause grief. On salt it probably does too, as those who have fallen can attest. So where did he get the idea that it was even remotely acceptable to don a bathing suit and swim cap for such a thing?

Well, the answer is that he had seen it done and the man he credited with giving him the idea was none other than Eddie Kretz, the first man to win a motorcycle race at Daytona. Ed had done it at El Mirage dry lakes where the Southern California Timing Association held meets to measure top speed and establish records of same. Ed had peeled off his leathers and ridden in just a bathing suit to reduce drag and it had paid benefits. Since there was no rule against it, Rollie had done it too when there was nothing more he could do to the bike to make it go faster.

My connection to these two came around much later, in 1991. I was riding with the American Historic Racing Motorcycle Association at the Daytona Speedway in a vintage race on the same TR3 Yamaha I had ridden there twenty years before. I was on my way out of the track to take lunch at Sonny's Fatboy Barbeque. I saw a guy there by the side of the road in the infield next to an old Indian motorcycle selling tee shirts. I stopped to see what he had. It was Eddie Kretz and I was flabbergasted. Why didn't he come inside the pits where he belonged and we could all honor him for what he had done? I asked him. He said he had tried to but some guy said he had never heard of him and the track wanted money for him to be an official vendor so he just set up out here.

I was embarrassed for him and for us. Of course I bought a tee shirt and I paid too much on purpose. I wouldn't take change and I asked him for his autograph on the shirt, which I have never worn and never will. I skipped lunch and got out my lawn chair and sat with him through the lunch hour and into the afternoon. He was not especially impressed with himself, but instead claimed that he was lucky and had good machinery. He told me about racing on the beach and his stories were peppered with names I had never heard of. My stories are too, I realize now, but those men were someone, really someone, and not just to him. I wished I knew more, and said so. He wished the same. He's gone now and the loss is real, not imagined.

All people are someone, I know that, but few of them do what motorcycle racers do, which is reach out and touch something vastly larger and transcendent. For the most part they can't express what it is; they only know how it makes them feel. We were just getting to this when I heard my race called over the public address system and excused myself, promising to come back, but by the time I had gotten back into the pits and out onto the grid it was time to race and then we had a red flag and a delay and then my race was pushed back in the schedule until later so that by the time I was finished and loaded up and came back down the same road he was gone.

There was nothing there to mark his passing. It was the same, sandy scrubby sort of place the infield had always been. Still, I had the shirt, and a photo of us together, and that was something. It was twenty years later that I read Rollie's account of how he had seen Eddie ride bareback and taken his inspiration from it to do it himself. They are both gone now. Off to where ever men like that go. When they were here, their time to race and do things was before my time. I thought their machinery quaint and there accomplishments small relative to what technology now afforded me in the way of enablement.

Before I was done I also won my race at Daytona and exceeded Rollie's top speed on the Vincent. I didn't have to go to Bonneville to do it either, right there at the speedway I had managed just a hair over 180 mph. But still, I wondered what it was like to be them, to know the subjective character of their experience while racing. Some of that mystery has been revealed to me by racing myself. Now, they have gone on to another experience and they are no longer physically present to talk to me about it. Now, I really want to know what its like to be 'Free.'

Flow get's it right that there is something special going on during an optimal experience, but I don't necessarily agree that I can just imagine it going on and fool myself into a state of grace as a consequence. To me it's like swimming in a warm sea next to a giant whale. You know its there, you feel it's presence, and you project into it the possibility that it knows consciously, on some level, that you are there as well.

That is what racing is for me. Thinking about it later, or writing this about it now, does not do for me what racing does because those things, this thing I do this moment with these computer keyboard keys, cannot kill me if I screw it up. Racing can. I don't want to be protected from that until it becomes so remote or unlikely that I no longer feel it's danger. That brings the truth of existence to me like nothing else and I don't want to give that up.

48.

Oh Baby

I WAS A LONG time racer when I met my wife. I had been looking for her all my life. She was not looking for me. She is a librarian at a small community college where things are mostly quiet and carpeted and air conditioned so when I took her to her first race to work as a volunteer it was an adjustment. It was also Daytona and the rowdy group of fellow workers and racers that are my racing family were there to set up the annual awards banquet. It was an auspicious moment. Racing was important to me, she knew that. These were my best friends, she knew that as well. She was nervous about making a good first impression.

We entered the banquet room to a mixed greeting of friendly hellos from the busy troop as they were carrying out their assigned tasks. I stopped them with my announcement that I had brought someone with me, which was new to their experience, and that I wanted to introduce them, which was something I had never done.

I waited until they were all there and had put down their tables and chairs and so forth and assembled more or less attentively to see what would happen next. She stood by me expectantly, smiling, looking her cheerful best. Sensing the right moment had come, I said in my best public announcer voice, "Hey, everybody, I'd like you to meet Vicky, she's an exotic dancer from Valdosta, Georgia." To which they all said their 'Hey's and 'Hellos' and went back to work.

She was mortified of course, and had no idea I was going to say it. She might have suspected had she known me better but where's the fun in that? To their credit no one made the slightest comment about what I had said, either because they didn't mind having an exotic dancer on the crew and she looked good enough to be one, or because they didn't believe me, which was equally likely.

As the evening wore on and the dinner progressed through the tedious process of handing out plaques and awards to the various classes and individual awards she would engage in conversation with some of them when the opportunity came and try to explain that she was actually a librarian, not an exotic dancer. Her body and their acquaintance with me made it seem all the more unlikely, even if it were true.

I was also conversationally prodded to explain why I had suddenly ended years of well known racing celibacy. "Yoga" was my only answer and then I raised my eyebrows meaningfully.

Women have problems with racing, and although I promised I wouldn't talk about women racing, I'm not, I'm talking about women who love men who race. To begin with it must be noted that they have in them a cosmic power that men do not – they can bring forth life. That they can die doing it, and have frequently done so, adds something to the experience for them that sets them apart from men, and while men may whine that they do their part in the process too and are therefore equally valuable, I know better than to bother to make that argument.

They have a different view of things, as a group, and those that can see that men brush up against death while embracing life appreciate the similarity to what women do who are willing to risk themselves for the sake of bringing forth children into the world. It is compelling, I must admit, and it gives them a unique status in the world, or it should.

As for the love of my life, I was able to convince her truthfully that I have only every loved one woman and she is the one. The rest, and I am somewhat chagrin at having to admit that there were any, were simply cases of mistaken identity. Had I known where she was, and had I been able to wait until she were of legal age, we could have begun this perfection that is our sharing of life sooner.

We have had our misadventures, but not with one another, which was a blessing for both of us. She is tender and kind and patient and I am as undeserving of any bit of it as ever. Still, she brings out something in me of the person I wanted to be all along and I am grateful for that. No doubt a good many others who knew me then and know me now are as well. Whether we should have met sooner or had a dozen redheaded trouble making kids together or not is speculation for another time.

The gods are kind. I had lived alone the majority of my life and had come to the point that I expected that would be how it ended before I met her. I am a lucky man. That was some years ago now and as with all things many of the group I raced with have come and gone. Some moved on to find better uses for their time and leisure, some disappeared without a trace, but there are some who hang on, for reasons of their own, having found some meaning in what we do.

I suspect it is the same sort of performance junky atmosphere that pervades the back stage of every Opera Company or theatrical troupe. Public performances of any sort call for a certain immediacy that elevates the ordinary to the exceptional in some. Hope is in the air. Finding out if someone might be one of the exceptional is a central theme in why people race motorcycles at all as it is in every competitive arena.

Somehow, in ways difficult to explain, the performance aspects of racing extend beyond the track and become pervasive. Take R.G. Wakefield and the famous tablecloth trick for instance, or how a racer convinced their radar detector and cruise control to talk to one another, or the time an Idaho State Trooper turned out to be more sympathetic than anyone could have imagined – and a woman. Those are stories for another time.

49.

Mind The Gap

WHAT HAVE YOU DONE lately? Another year has come and gone and I'm adjusting to writing different numbers to designate the year in which I now find myself. It is unbelievable, isn't it; that time can go so quickly in the larger sense while creeping along through the parts that seem endlessly untenable? We gather ourselves up from our desk or cubicle or work station and take a look around now and infrequently ask ourselves how our life is going.

A New Year is good for that. Punctuate the process for yourself with the news that a man has been set free after spending the last thirty years in prison for a crime he did not commit and you find yourself counting a blessing you did not even know you had.

The evidence of his innocence was in the hands of the great State of Texas the whole time. His conviction had been appealed three times in the past and each time he had lost. There is a limit to appeals and he had had his. Since I have worked in this system a good part of my life I was not as surprised as some that this could happen. It has happened here. People are fallible and resources are not always available to those charged with a crime to prove their innocence. In Dallas it was the election of a black State's Attorney that agreed to cooperate with the Innocence Project and permit DNA testing of their stored evidence that produced the startling confirmation of the claims of innocence made all along from the depths of his prison cell by the wrongfully convicted non-rapist.

Couple that with the fortunate coincidence that Dallas keeps its forensic evidence refrigerated, and justice has finally prevailed. The preservation of evidence is partly the result of the assassination of President Kennedy in Dallas and the debate about what really happened in the decades that followed.

Race mattered in this case, but not in the way you think. It was eyewitness testimony that nailed down the conviction and everyone from the original prosecutor to the forensic expert to the jury was absolutely certain of the guilt of the accused. White victims and equally white witnesses are simply incapable of making positive identifications of black suspects because they have not had the practice of looking them in the face often enough to sort out one from another accurately.

That's not a racial condemnation; Blacks and Asians and Hispanics are no better at identifications across racial lines. In the Texas case, the accused had no alibi, was positively identified by the victim and witnesses, and his blood type was the same as that found in the victim. His claims of innocence simply sounded like the ranting of someone in denial of his own guilt and not on the way to redemption and forgiveness. Texas leads the nation in executions too, so in a way the guy was lucky. Thirty years lucky? The majority of his life was forfeit. He said he was grateful to be exonerated but sad that his parents had both died without seeing him freed. He has some surviving family and his freedom now but little else. Oh, and there was an apology from the judge on behalf of the State.

He had been found guilty beyond a reasonable doubt by a system that is anything but reasonable. Here in Illinois where I practiced law, when arguing for my clients in criminal cases we were not permitted to define the term "reasonable doubt" even though it was the standard used to determine guilt or innocence. I thought it silly to suppose that the average man or woman off the street summoned to jury duty had a sufficient understanding of that legal term and was likely to apply the evidence in any particular case to the standard in a way that would produce an unbiased predictable result. Scientific evidence did not result in much more certainty and was as often misused by legal advocates in an effort to "win" a case regardless of the truth.

That's a harsh judgment, but in my years of practice it was not unknown to me to be familiar with cases that had been wrongly decided. Any honest attorney with similar experience would tell you as much, although they may be reluctant to tell you the details. It happens; it shouldn't but it does; and the things that need to be done to reform the system go against tradition and the canons of ethics that bind and blind lady justice in her work. I still love the law – but more in the aggregate than in the particulars. If I had a thousand cases and only three were wrongly decided would I say it was a good system? I would, but I wouldn't call it justice.

For instance, why wouldn't it be required that all evidence containing DNA gathered in connection with a crime be tested and the results of those tests be part of the compulsory disclosure of the prosecution to the defense? The answer is it costs money and the system is set up to require that discovery be conducted according to certain rules. In Florida the defense can take the sworn depositions of witnesses, including police officers and prosecution experts, before trial. In Illinois they are not allowed to do so. As a result, only some general idea of what will be said is available to the defense and it is very difficult to prepare for generalities when guilt or innocence turns on particulars.

Our system is supposed to be based on the principle that it is better to let a hundred guilty men go free than convict one innocent citizen. I never believed that was the way things were really done but I sure didn't want to believe the opposite true either. Our collective intolerance of injustice must be shared and our outrage at its results must be felt. We can fix this. We should. If we let someone waste their life in prison for a crime we know they did not commit what does that say about us? I use "we" there in the larger sense as in "We the people" which is what happened here. What New Year's resolution should we make about injustice? If you had thirty years to think about it, I bet you would have no trouble getting it right.

Time is not always a luxury as it turns out, sometimes its passage is the punishment. In racing we need to make correct judgments in real time, quicker than a heartbeat sometimes. While we can hope they are all correct, it is too much to expect that they are. Our very lives depend upon it and even the lives of others, and yet we risk it all to something we don't really understand. Some would say 'luck' but that seems too vague. Examine for yourself what it is that you believe makes it all work out. it's a tricky undertaking. If you make too much of it, that is if you build your list of all the things that can go wrong and are so thorough that it appears inevitable that something will go wrong and something does then you begin to believe it inevitable that things always go wrong and that is not the case.

It may be the case that things go wrong once in a while, and most of the time we can look at the particulars of what has happened with hindsight and say to ourselves, 'Oh, I see now, I should have done so and so instead...' which is a common enough reaction to having got-ten past an incident. It is far more common, however, that something is about to go wrong and we catch it just in time and can say, 'Man, was I lucky there...' like the time I was going down the back stretch at Daytona and happened to look down through the fairing at my front axel nut and see it turning because I had forgotten to put the cotter pin back in after changing tires. Its movement caught my eye and in just that moment it came around and off of its last thread and fell away. It was in practice, so I was 'lucky' and survived it, but some poor guy might run over it or any one of the million other things that fall off of motorcycles being raced that litter the tracks across the country.

Nothing like that happened so again, we were 'lucky' I suppose, but that just can't be it. Our collective survival, the continuation of human endeavor that requires so much care and attention cannot boil down to coincidence. It may, I suppose, but that is unsatisfying even if there is some probability that it could be true. How many times does some guy crash his bike and then in the fullness of his adren-aline pick it back up and get back on the track and rejoin the race. Talk about a bad idea. Still it happens and those riders have it in their minds that they must soldier on, even though most certainly all is not well with their machine once it has been on the ground. Brake levers come apart, fairings are loose from their mounts, dirt and grit and all manner of foreign material is ingested into moving metal parts of close tolerance that are intolerant of it. Now take that machine back up to speed and you have a disaster in the making.

We do it with ourselves as well. We drive all night after a week of work and long nights of after work overtime out in our shop to get ready to go racing. Some of us drink too much and don't watch what we eat and exercise rarely if at all. Once in a while, when we were young and nature forgave such abuse it was understandable I suppose that such things could be done without lasting damage. But season after season it takes its toll and the denial of the obvious truth does nothing to alter its make up. Something is out there, taking care of us, and we have no control over it.

This makes the scientifically minded uncomfortable. It cannot be weighed or measured and yet there is a body of evidence to suggest that it is real. Medieval men on the verge of battle made noises at it, made promises to it in exchange for being spared, or devised and then obeyed routines that made them feel a certain comfort about the results, whatever they might be. Sacrifices were made, entrails were read, prayers repeated. It goes way back and there are complex and myriad philosophies that deal with a greater power being behind the scenes that has and will intervene on our behalf when necessary or justified. The survivors of the Titanic probably prayed for such divine intervention of course, but then so did those lost that night in the same sea. Watch a motorcycle race and what do you see? People in danger of dying at any moment, oblivious to such a reality.

It is seductively unexciting to behold, and the appearance of control seems real enough when all is well, but let one little thing in the thousands of things needed in combination to make it all work out be altered and a disaster is close at hand. We try not to dwell on it, and to a certain degree must look past it to a positive outcome or we simply couldn't do it. Not to over think it, Hailwood famously said he considered himself already dead before a race so it didn't interfere with his concentration. This comment was seized upon by the press as some sort of bravado of denial but it's not, it's just an expedient way of dealing with the obvious. To take a crazy risk once and survive it is dare-devil. To do it repeatedly over decades is something else altogether and that is what we do.

You cannot count on just yourself to make things work out, there are too many variables involved and you don't have control over enough of them. Some aspect of random chance comes into play and statistics tell us that sooner or later our number may come up.

That takes us back to wishing we knew the truth. The poor guy in prison in Texas may have been freed by some state official just owning up to having the evidence he had claimed he didn't have or if it really was just an oversight by taking a second look when it was needed. If it was intentionally done in the name of some false sense of justice then I hope real justice is done to whoever is responsible for having done so in the end, out there where we have no say in things anymore and poor excuses won't hide evil intentions.

50.

Get Your Time And Tide Right Here — No Waiting

THERE IS A TIDE of emotion that comes and goes with racing. Like any visit to the seashore, it is ever new and always sad in its own way. You can't live at the beach. There are some that have found a way, sure, but I won't be one of them, and it's hurtful. You can come and see it and appreciate what it has to offer and experience its sunshine and noise and inexorable qualities, all of which are meaningful to me, yet it is bothersome on some level that I have to leave it eventually and know it. Every day cannot be a day at the beach. Life is like that.

If it's been a while since I've been to the races the old excitement of preparation takes over as I look for, find, and combine the metal and fiberglass bits and pieces that turn a pile a parts into a race ready machine. No matter how I left it last time at the end of last season or whatever season it last ran, it has to be freshened up to ride again.

Oil gets sticky and tarnishes metal things with residue which needs to be looked at, cleaned, and freshly lubricated. Some bearings may have corroded their surfaces, just a little, while exposed to the elements, and will have to be replaced. If I don't hunt them down and cast them out now, they will fail on the track somewhere a thousand miles from here and I don't want that.

They seem like a simple enough tasks but there are as many things to do as there are possibilities for failure. The hours build up and no matter how early I begin it seems as though there is never enough time to do all that I would or could do if I had all the time in the world.

Some parts are just worn out and can't be found again. It's the nature of antique things that have morphed through the phases of becoming 'recently outdated' to 'obsolete' to 'discarded' and then revalued for their rarity and age.

Racers go through some of this themselves, and I have parts that don't work anymore either but there are no replacements that interest me. I used to jump up and click my heels together twice before coming down – now I can't jump up. I dislocated my shoulder when I was in high school, now I can't sleep on that side without it coming out again. I broke my knee at Dade City in '72 when my Harley spit me off as I was pointlessly chasing Ted Henter and John Long and Conrad who sadly may have died in prison this year.

I got knocked off my TZ750 at Loudon one year and cart-wheeled down the track breaking everything that hit the track first with each rotation; elbow, collar bone, wrist, knee (same one from Dade City), ankle (other leg) and then lay in a heap unconscious and totally un-aware that I had fallen. The last thing I had seen had been the sky flashing across the window of my Bell Star at an odd angle and I had barely had the time to think that something was not right about that when the lights went out.

When they came back on I was face down on the track and could hear bikes around me but no longer had one of my own. I jumped up to wave my arms to show the corner workers that I was all right but I wasn't. For one thing only half of me jumped up and only one arm waved and it's hand was on at an odd angle. Nothing hurt yet, but I was pretty sure it would soon enough.

Gary Scott was coming right at me out of the turn that brings you on to the short straight before the pit wall and I stood there, crumpling back to the pavement, with one arm waving. He waved back, which I thought was nice, and then I went down again and stayed there.

I had gone from 35th on the grid to 18th position in five laps but overestimated the willingness of those I was passing to give way. In the end I went underneath two guys, passing them on the inside, and the last one clipped my rear wheel as we exited. It was not a lot, but it was enough and I had the power on and that was it for me. He could have let me go and given way, but he didn't. I guess he showed me. I never found out who that was, no one would say later, probably because it was apparent I wanted to have a conversation with him about it I suppose, which would have been pointless.

In the ambulance my wife had asked me "how do you feel?" and I reached up at her and said, "With my hands" making two 'got your boobs' gestures, an old joke, too old apparently. She got out, angry again and wondering why she had come. Eventually she stopped coming, but not before the ultimatum – "It's me or the racing!"

There was no choice to be made there, not really. After the Loudon crash, some of my friends helped load up my stuff and brought it to the hospital while the medical folks were assessing my injuries and plumbing the depth of my insurance coverage. They determined I was broken in places but could not afford their care so they discharged me in a wheelchair out to my van where a kindly orderly was good enough to help me into the driver's seat before handing me a bottle of pain pills and telling me to make sure I didn't take any until I was out of the state.

Recalling this, my knee hurts again sharply and brings me back to the present. I am standing here in a daze of recollection. I used to worry about such moments, now I think they are beneficial. "It's not a seizure"; I tell those that may have seen me," its meditation."

Once I finally call a halt to fabrication and have finished the assembly process, its time to load up. I used to 'load and go' out of necessity because the mechanical work would extend into the driving time required to get there. My preference is to load up a day early and sleep on it, giving me time to remember something I might have forgotten otherwise. I once drove all night to get to a race and had left my helmet, boots and leathers in their duffle on the porch back home. No one at the track was my size so I couldn't ride. I suppose I could have been angry about it, but instead I just saw it as fate sparing me from another crash that was waiting out on the track for me.

Luke Connor just had a moment like that at Daytona last year when he forgot to put gas in his wife Barbara's tank after remembering to fill his own and everyone else's. Just to make it worse, she was winning and beating him when he passed her once her tank ran dry as they were headed for the checkered flag. I'm not sure how philosophical she will be about it, but she should be grateful. He certainly did not do it on purpose which means that some greater power in charge of the events that result from omissions saw to it that she did not crash and burn instead. I'm sure she was compensated somehow and equally sure that Luke won't let it happen again. Still, such things happen.

After I forgot my gear, I made a checklist to look over after loading, but I don't stick to it very well. Mentally, that list starts with "Helmet, boots, leathers…?" now, which is my mantra for packing up and getting on the road to the races. After I think I have everything loaded, I take one last walk through the shop. It is an odd moment and is what I want to write about here.

I am alone, of course, all of the 'tag alongs' being somewhere else impatiently waiting to get going. The shop is quiet now, and a little less crowded as the months or weeks or just days of hard labor have been expelled from its bowels into the van and trailer. There is money here, I can see that. The tools accumulated over half a century; the space that seems to shrink and grow as projects come and go; the old leathers hanging up on the walls like trophy skins from big game safaris; the helmets once the source of recognition like a knight's standard, now just lumps of plastic in a row with their linings rotting out.

I am sentimental about my friends, but I am not sentimental about motorcycles; they are just tools for making speed. I have liked some more than others but what I liked about them was how they ran and how they propelled me through space magically and disappeared beneath me as they did so. I do honor the craftsmen that made them, but in the same way that a bridge looks inevitable in its design when finished, I know there are better ways to build them now.

A modern bike would be much easier to ride and less work to maintain but they don't interest me. Electrons are not warm and fuzzy and computer chips are not human kind extended but alien to my being's circuitry. I have a troubleshooting list in my head that says "Compression?" "Fuel?" "Spark?" and doesn't extend on to a diagnostic plug for a laptop readout of all things relative. Racing is not a science experiment for me, it is an art.

I should have stopped by now, no one need tell me that. I do not ride as fast as I used to, but I know I still could if I wanted to. I could climb off further than I do and risk more than I do and make it go faster by leaning the mixture out and pouring in fuel additives as other racers do. So if I could do these things, and I know how, it may make you wonder why I don't. It's because I have won enough races to prove to myself and anyone else that I can win races. Now I race for a different reason that is harder to explain and even harder to understand. I wish I had a word for it, but I don't, not yet.

As I've said, I use 'Zen' because it's a word that talks about discipline and meditation and achieving a mental state that is available but seldom obtained as we are distracted by the requirements of our daily lives. For traditionalists, it means clearing the mind of all thought and using a number of repetitive exercises to help do that. For me it means zipping myself into my leathers and working my fingers into gloves that seem stiff and unfriendly at first and then become my second skin and starting up a racing bike and getting out onto the track and assuming the position. You know the one – the one where your head is down but your face is up, pushing the back of your helmet into your shoulders as you peer out through the bubble and watch the tach climb up into the redline as you go through the gears until it just stays there and the speed builds.

It's the position you put yourself in with your elbows in and your feet done shifting and the throttle held wide open as you go for top speed in high gear. The one you get only here and there for just a bit unless you go to places like Daytona or Road America or Savannah. Yeah, they call it "Roebling Road" now, and I've raced too long to explain why it used to be called Savannah. If you've never been over to the old waterfront there, then you've missed the Masonic Temple that bears the lodge number we all seek on our motorcycles so for me, it's still, "Savannah."

I see in the corner of the shop the gathering of sponsor gear from different eras. Valvoline, Spectro, Blendzall, Koni, Champion, all having played their roles in making whatever we were riding then go faster or just go at all. They faded away, as did most of the motorcycles. They are not why I am here. I am here looking around for something I will need in another time zone, far away, thinking I will get a feeling about what it is I will need there when I see it here. It has happened before and I honor the tradition of that event with a moment of homage to its effect. Once it was a tire pump, and although I had one in the truck already, I saw one just setting there that sort of spoke to me so I picked it up and took it along. Sure enough, the one I already had loaded failed the first time I tried to use it so the silent prophecy had been fulfilled.

There was a time when I took everything. All of the tools, all of the spares, all of the parts and tires and tubes and everything went for a ride to Florida, or Texas, or California, or New Hampshire and then back again to Illinois where they lived. Money spent and time wasted for the most part, not to mention the effort of picking it all up, sorting it all out, keeping it organized, and on and on and on in a never ending mental trap that detracted from the I freedom sought to not be burdened by such things.

It's about the riding, isn't it? - At least when I started that's what I told myself. I didn't know a thing about what was going on inside a motorcycle when I started riding them and I was deliberately ignorant. I became educated over time on a 'need to know' basis. I couldn't afford someone to manage it all for me and if I wanted to ride, and it broke, I had to fix it. That led me to a job as a mechanic fixing other people's motorcycles for money, which led me to being a partner in a dealership eventually which expanded to add another brand and pretty soon we were so busy that there was never any time to ride. Instead of a motorcycle racer I became a businessman and it was only coincidental that the business was about motorcycles because business was business.

The all consuming passion of motorcycles had consumed me too and turned me into something I never meant to be. I stepped back, I walked away, just a bit, and told myself things like I would put it behind me. I tried that. I failed. There is something about it. I can't put my finger on it exactly or pigeon hole it precisely, but its there. I can feel it.

I stand in my shop alone with the hum of the florescent lights. I look around for whatever the thing is that I will need desperately miles from here that is here now for the taking. It's like that friendship from my youth I neglected and never said thanks for, or the chance to show some kindness that I let go by. I don't want that moment behind me to cloud my sunny day ahead with a shadow of needless regret.

I pick up a small set of deep well sockets. There is no easy substitute for them and I hadn't packed them so it fills a need to do something, even if it's the wrong thing. Somehow it is better than doing nothing. Vaguely I bow my head at the service and pray that I am praying the right words to get me where I need to be with what I need to have with me when I get there. I will have time on the road to distract myself from this, but I am beginning to understand that this may be the real issue.

I know what is out there in a general way; another track, another bike to ride; an infinite variety of experiences compressed into one another at great speed with some danger peppered in to make it spicy but not necessarily deadly. I have been to the table many times. Still I am here and it is ahead of me, unknowable, like what is ahead of me when the racing is all done and I have nothing to look forward to but my past. I look back to my shop and close the door behind me, locking it, and recite, *"Never look back; Never look back."* and move on.

51.

Delusions Of Grandeur

AM I DELUDED? I mean have I been fooled by things that people have told all my life and that they believe are true but that increasingly look like a well developed fantasy to me? Am I so afraid of just the notion that there is something more, or less to all of this than I imagine that I am paralyzed by the idea? It's a tough topic for sure, and not for the feint hearted. I think myself brave enough to entertain the idea despite the threats from the proponents of other ideas to the contrary.

"Thall shalt have no other Gods before me." I get that, at least I understand what the words say, which may be part of the trouble. I can still hear Charleston Heston in my head being Moses on the mountain bringing down the Ten Commandments. I'm not sure at all that it happened just that way, but then neither am I convinced that the angel Gabriel showed up in western New York one hot day while Joseph Smith was taking a break and delivered the book of Mormon. Don't get me wrong, I am not a cynic, but it is the twenty first century and we are talking about a story from several thousand years ago that was written in a language no one speaks now relating to life as no one lives it anymore.

Basically it's a Santa Clause tale dressed up, which may be part of the problem. If you're good (well behaved and do this and that in the right ways, and don't do the forbidden things or things or the allowed things in the wrong ways); then you get rewarded and your name is on the list. In the children's tale 'rewarded' means a b.b. gun or a new doll house or a bicycle or some such childish notion indicative of the age. At some point someone spoils the fantasy for you by telling you its just make believe but as Walt Disney can tell you we don't easily give up our childhood beliefs. Heaven is a tough idea to let go. I mean it's so attractive in so many ways.

I like being good better than I like being bad anyway and at my age I know that the things being good or bad bring are temporary in the long run so what the hell does it matter what I do? The answer to that is easier for someone who has done a great many things than it is for someone who only hopes to do them. I enjoy being a good person, that is someone who actively does good, because it suits my nature. It's as easy as that for me. Like a 12 sting guitar happily tuned to 'E' so that any strum brings a melodic chord regardless of what its fretting about, I give off a vibration when doing good. Other's can't always see it, or hear it, but its there.

I've also done bad in my life, most of us have. I'm not proud of the times I lost my temper or said unkind hurtful things to those that didn't always deserve it, but in the heat of a moment here and there I confess my intemperance. It's tough to be tolerant of everything and I admit that I am not. I hate bullies and have often stepped in and taken a punch and given a few when I saw them dealing out their brand of vitriol. Still I have enough vision to see that if I am intolerant of those who are intolerant then I am not better than they are. That tells me there must be some external set of rules or tuning devices somewhere out there that lets us know when we are doing the right thing. My mind is incapable, however, of grasping the sort of crap that tells Jihadists to fly jets into tall buildings killing everyone on board and many inside. No god wants that: that was some perverted human notion of what some god wanted and it was wrong. I may make some list of theirs by saying it here but they are already on one of mine.

I have no trouble with that judgment and it does not require examination of any tome or book or litany of perceived grievances from the past to persuade me. It was classically the wrong thing to do and it will and has made life worse for millions. What sort of belief would want that to be their goal? The easy answer would be: 'None that I can tolerate' and there we find ourselves again, questioning whether to turn the other cheek.

It is not the dilemma we think if Scarlett O'Hara was correct, and the more time passes, the more I believe she was. "Tomorrow is another day," was her answer to all things behind her in Gone with the Wind, but Rhett would neither forgive nor forget and the temporal clouded the eternal aspects of their existence perfectly –a good story. That may be our story too. We may try to be high minded and look beyond the failing bodies we all inhabit and imagine what comes next.

Here in America we have an especially hard time of it thanks in large part to our Civil War. A large portion of our male population was thrust into deadly encounters over forces that predated their lives by centuries and seemed institutionally inalterable. Once the idea caught hold that we could do without slavery and that words like 'equality' and 'all men' might really be used in a sentence together to express the truth of things, many of them died more or less willingly so that the generations that came after them could have such a world. They succeeded to some degree and their sacrifice is noted. It could hardly be overlooked. Since so many of them died far from home in a time when death customarily was witnessed by friends and family it left no closure.

Enterprising business types thought of embalming the bodies and sending them home by the boxcar load so they could assist the living with a ceremony of the passing. This caught on to the extent that it's a national institution now and part of the religious tradition that dead bodies rise up and are given life again. I am not as insensitive to this as I sound, death is a real thing and it has meaning, but I don't think it should take your life's savings to get it done properly.

When I taught history there were always three places I wanted my students to see: Gettysburg, Arlington, and Normandy. There were other things, too, and depending on the course and the time period I made the effort to take them there in some way. But when you unload a bus of Midwestern teenagers onto the grass of a cemetery filled with the dead of nearly their own age who gave their lives so that these kids could have the lives they do, it makes an impression. Typically I gave them the task of finding a grave with their family name or from their state, neither of which was very hard to do.

We all went to school and we all had things happen to us there that made a lasting impression. We sort those out for ourselves, even though some adult had a hand in fashioning a good many of them. We have cultural traditions, we have national traits, and we have religious diversity. I have no objections to those so long as they don't engender bigotry and hatred.

Like most of us, I have a diverse family background. I know about it far enough back to know that Irish and English and German and Swiss and American Indians all crossed some taboo line or other in their own time to make me who I am today. They were no doubt disapproved of in their time and yet, here I am. If they knew what I knew they probably would have felt differently about some of the things they believed in their lifetime. They passed those beliefs down to their children who were then faced with a different reality than what their parents had lived with as I am and you are faced with now.

Should I persist in believing all the things they believed? Or should I turn away from what I was raised with and strike out on my own in some new direction and see if I can make sense of things for myself. Tony gave me the answer to that, in his own irreverent way. He was an older kid who sat in the back and wisecracked with some degree of impunity. He didn't graduate with my class so he either dropped out or was thrown out so I'm not sure whatever happened to him. He was tough, and would hit you if you crossed him so I kept a respectful distance as most of us did.

One day in Health class our prim spinster of a teacher was discussing the seven food groups and explaining why we each needed to have so many servings from each group each day and so forth and she concluded with the tag line, "You are what you eat." Tony's reply was quick and sharp, "Well then," he said, "I've already eaten enough shit to last me a lifetime..." He was summoned out into the hallway by the red faced mistress who was struggling mightily to contain herself. We didn't hear what was said, but when she came back in, Tony did not come with her.

There was a time when I thought that most people told the truth most of the time. I got over that. I went through a phase when I though most people were lying to me about everything they told me. I got over that too. That was because I had begun racing motorcycles where it turns out that you can tell for yourself what is true and what is not. It's complicated, and it's difficult and expensive in many ways. There is suffering and a degree of endurance required that eats into what other people see as a more normal existence. It can become an obsession, I know that, but what I know mostly about it is that there is a right answer to most of the questions that face us on a given day at a racetrack somewhere and just being there, with that set of known values, is reassuring.

There is a right jetting choice for today's atmospheric conditions. There is a correct gearing selection of countershaft and rear sprockets that will provide an optimum overall matching of powerband and course characteristics. There are points on the track where I should brake and lean in and get back on the throttle and there are degrees of application of each element that will combine to make each turn an experience done as well as it can be done, or perhaps leave a little room for improvement the next time around. These things are not insignificant, they have meaning.

I don't want those experiences done for me with electronic giz-mo's even though I know they can be. I don't want my brakes to be 'anti-lock' even if BMW has been doing it on their street bikes for over a decade so it's not exactly new anymore. I'm old school and not afraid or ashamed to admit it. But then neither do I take available medications for hypertension or have hypertension or sleep depri-vation or any of the other things that normally signal an inability to accept the changes that life brings us as we persist in the struggle to understand its meaning. I don't have the answer, not yet, but I am hopeful that it will come to me if I can manage to keep it up to the finish. I've seen the half way flags already, and was a little surprised as I always am by them. My first 200 miler at Daytona as an expert I rode and rode and rode my guts out and then, just when I thought I had nothing at all left to give, I got the half way flags. 'God,' I thought, 'can I do this? I could as it turned out, and as for the rest of it, I believe I will be able to do that as well.

I may not race as often or go as fast as I once did, but what matters now about racing is that I do it. I still struggle with building the bikes and getting them to the track and learning the course again for that bike on that day as I try to remember if I have done everything, taken care of everything, and can face the truth of the answer. That truth is that despite all I can do, and every precaution I may have taken or money I have spent or sacrifice I have made. We must live with our own actions, and are responsible for our own choices, no matter who told us something, and none of it is any guarantee that things will turn out the way we want them to.

Why then should I believe things will be any different when I think about what will happen to me when I die? Why should I take someone's word for it that if I do or don't do some things then this or that thing will result in another state of existence that no one has been to and returned from in my lifetime or in the past thousand years or more? Don't be offended, we're all adults here. I am allowed my doubts.

Why wouldn't someone doubt? There is plenty of evidence all around me to suggest that things are less than perfect in the world and that evil as an institution is uncurbed and rather cancerous in the larger sense. Take the weather in England, for instance, is it surprising that I have such doubts? What surprises me more is that I still have any hope, and a degree of faith, in spite of all I have seen. There are things I have not seen for myself but know of, too, which lend some evidence and while I have not actually been to the infamous Dragon Rally - I know it exists. I have seen photos.

52.

Zen As The Answer To Questions Racing Asks

I HAD A CHANCE to pass on the next to last lap. He took the final turn a bit wide, I thought, and where we exited there was room for me to go a little wider than I had been so I waited. I was sure he knew I was there; I had been right on his tail for a while. There was a turn over on the far side of the course that he was much better at than I was and he had passed me there some time back like I was standing still and I had been following him ever since to see how he was doing it. I knew if I passed him too soon, and showed him what I had, he would use it himself and my chance would slip away. Now we had seen the white flag and there was no traffic to play with on the lap to come and so I had to decide if I would take the risk and go for beating him across the line or be happy to finish where I was.

We were racing for position. This wasn't one of those 'who knows what class that guy is in' moments, but an AMA national road race and I needed points if I ever wanted to get over being a novice. There were two ways to move up as far as I knew; you could win a national road race, in which case you would automatically be a Junior the next season, or you could get enough points from your finish positions to move up, but points only came for top 20 finishes and with 40 or more on some grids it wasn't easy, that and the same guys were up there at the front all the time and even though they had their points, they kept coming.

I had no idea exactly where we were running, but every position mattered as far as I was concerned and so I had a lap to decide whether or not to risk pissing away a great finish for a shot at one position better. Did the ends, justify the means? That was the question. It's a question we ask ourselves all the time, whether or not we are aware of it. We want something, we have to do something to get it, is it worth it? I had worked nights at the student paper running the press and worked afternoons at a motorcycle shop to pay my way through college and get a degree. I had traveled around and lived poor, sleeping in my van, just to get from race to race rather than miss one and gather resources by not going. There were trade offs; most of them having to do with personal relationships, but I couldn't seem to find another way and wasn't willing to go without racing.

There were not all that many to go to back in the sixties, and so it wasn't a frequent dilemma. The National circuit had both dirt track and road races since the championship was consolidated in those days. It made sense to me – one champion for all disciplines. Well, not all – trials were not considered racing even though they were competitive in their own way; neither was cross country for that matter, although I thought it hard when I did one. The combined calendar meant that Mile, Half-mile, Short Track, TT, and even Motocross dates had to be fitted into just so many weekends with road races as they could be arranged with tracks and so forth. Apparently the least consideration was paid to whether riders wanted to drive coast to coast to coast in consecutive weeks but, hey, no one made us do it.

Daytona had always been the first race of the year until they had the Houston Astrodome to use as a venue, which was a hoot. But for most of us, including me, Daytona was where we all started, which was odd in at least one way and that was because it was the most important race of the year. Everyone went who was seriously going to contest the series for finishing position. The new factory bikes were there to be considered. New modifications to old models were on display and up for evaluation as well as the aftermarket products that you could not judge just from how they looked in a magazine.

My first Daytona was more instructional than successful. I used the spare time after to have a look around and see what was what. There were a group of riders from California who acted like the rest of us were only there to get in their way, which was irritating; there were some east coast riders from the Virginia area and a gang from New England. A few called Texas home and even fewer were from Florida. One of them won, and as we were in Florida, and I was enjoying myself immensely at just being there, I told myself if I ever got the chance to move there I would. It was a means to an end for me to live in Florida. I wanted to race, they had races all the time, and back where I was living they never had races at all. It was another of those intersections of things that affect our lives in ways we can't imagine when the seeds are planted, but it took root, and when the chance came to be there, I took it.

As for the things I saw when I first went to Daytona, it occurred to me that the factories had a basic ability to make anything they wanted, only they weren't all that good at getting everything right. They put out machines that handled horribly or weren't reliable and left it to the consuming public, sparse as it was for these machines, to find and fix whatever it was about them that was poorly made. On my Sprint, there wasn't much that wasn't right about it. I had the model with the half-speed magneto, with its extra lump on the outside of the case for the gear reduction mechanism. They used a Bendix unit which I thought looked familiar. It was exactly like those used on stationary motors in the oil field and was rated far below what the motorcycle engine would rev. It was a weakness, but it was so much better to have it turning slower that everyone thought of it as a wonderful improvement.

Walking through the displays in the armory it occurred to me that I was out of my depth so far as the handling aspects of the design of the machines were concerned. I had long exposure to complex machines made for flat out speed from years of going to the Indianapolis 500 and spending time in Gasoline Alley ogling the cars and listening to the mechanics. There was even a guy in my home town who owned an Offenhouser midget and we used to go down to his little concrete block building and watch him take it apart and put it back together.

Not so many parts, really, and he was a friendly enough sort who would explain things when he felt like it if you asked the right way. It was there that I had learned about cams and valves and heads and seats and all of that four stroke magic that made things work. My lawnmower and his Offenhouser had things in common. I could see that.

Two strokes, on the other hand, were a complete mystery to me until I was at Ron Muir's shop one evening as he was tearing down his X-6 from yet another seizure. He handed me the head to look at after he got it off and we saw a hole in the top of it's Wiseco piston. I turned the head over a couple of times and asked, "Flathead?" expecting to see the valves in the block somewhere that let the gas in and out. He shook his head and asked mockingly, "Dumb ass?" and I had to admit that I probably was but didn't enjoy having it pointed out. While there never was a formal 'this is how it works' talk, he did explain to me the finer points of two stroke tuning afterward in the time I knew him. There it was – my ignorance displayed to dissipate my self-assurance. I had no idea how the thing worked even though I had ridden an Suzuki X-6 like the one we were taking apart and had even broken one down into little pieces myself, albeit without the benefit of tools.

Did I see in that moment some need to educate myself to further my racing ambitions (was I a consequentialist?) or did I recognize a duty to be on board with the joint effort that I was a part of and get up to speed with the theory and practice as applied to increase my usefulness (was I a deontological being?). The moment did not illuminate the choices before me in quite that way but I did feel the need to retort to Ron's labeling. "Fuck you," I said, "I'm still faster than you." It's that racing jargon of competitors, half joking, half serious, that pushes back and our ages and my lack of experience relative to his had nothing to do with it.

That was how it had started between us. I was a poor slob of a sophomore tired of cleaning 200 toilets a night to bridge the gap between income and expenses. The janitor job was the university's response to my honest reply on the questionnaire about student work when they asked me if there was anything I objected to doing. I had written simply, "clean toilets," without expecting to find my supervisor was a returned Viet Nam vet and I was a draft age kid who had not done his duty so, "Toilet Cleaner," it was. My only out was to get hired somewhere that this jerk off didn't control which turned out to be the newspaper. I had to work nights because there were not enough night classes offered to keep me above the minimum limit for enrollment hours and be considered a full time student and therefore '2-S' for draft purposes.

As the newspaper was my only hope, and there was a guy I played softball with who worked there, I went to him to see if he could let me know when an opening is coming. "Are you kidding me?" he asked, "there's about to be an opening tonight because I've had it with those guys. Come along and I'll show you the ropes and you can see if it's something you want to do." Starting time was 8:00 pm and we got there just a few minutes before. I drove my 55 Chevy, which looked intentionally horrible, painted flat black all over, chrome and all to be non-reflective. He came in something else and was waiting in the parking lot when we got there. Some leisure suit Larry pulled up in a Volkswagen beetle just as I was shutting down the Chevy and got out and made some crack about the car. I didn't hear it because the Chevy was too loud but responded generally, "Faster than you," which was my generic come back to whatever anyone might have said. The guy flipped me off and went on in the building.

"Who's that?" I asked my friend. He smiled, "That's your boss if you take the job, and this is the last night of my life that he's mine."

Now brace yourself for what I saw next. Across a short span of worn gravel drive, hidden in a large grove of trees, was a faded Quonset hut of WW II vintage. It's difficult to tell how big those things are because they hunker close to the ground but I would say it was about twenty four feet across the base and whatever that makes it at the top of its arch inside wasn't much. It had a set of swing out double doors at the back and a pile of paper and cardboard tubes next to a trash dumpster that we had to pass to get inside. We opened the doors and stepped into a very small space, no more than six feet deep, that had a row of hooks off to the side of the door where we hung our coats. Immediately before us were huge rolls of paper stacked on a carriage of immense proportions with a dangling overhead carriage that had a double hooked chain hoist and an electric control box that hung down to let someone move it around its track and take off empty spindles the rolls turned on and pick up new ones with it from where they were stored just around the corner, wedged under the low curve of the buildings outer wall.

Beyond that, stretching into the near distance, was a triple web, full color, manually operated Fairchild News King press. It filled the space from side to side and to within a few feet of the peak of the roof. A narrow catwalk ran down one side with an even narrower one down the other. A small door opened off to the left of where we stood with a bare red bulb glowing next to it and the word, "Darkroom" over it in large letters. Welcome to the pressroom.

As overpowering as the visual image was it was secondary to the smell. I had never smelled anything quite like it, pungent yet provocative in its own way. It was the dual perfume of printer's ink and newsprint that I would come to love and hate over the next months and it never failed to get my notice. I was led down the catwalk pass the huge machine to a relatively open space where a chair set low to the floor with its legs cut off up against the wall that we had to step over. It faced a conveyor belt about two feet wide and about six feet long that came out of a stack of rollers and hidden things known as the folder. This was where newspapers came out, jumbled this way and that from the violence done to them in the thirty odd feet before they got here and where I would sit in the early morning hours and jog the papers into line, county one hundred at a time and bundle with a quick crossed length of twine and tie and stack as the continuous steam piled up in my lap to be caught up with, counted, and done again and again until the run was over.

The speed of the jogger was what controlled the speed of the press run, which was an odd thing since there was a manual control on how fast the press could go and it was just a matter of human ability that throttled it. There was no mechanism for sorting out the mess it made if no one was there to keep order at the output end and so a set of fast hands and a cool head was what was needed. I was introduced, my introducer announced he was quitting at the end of the shift, I was hired as his replacement and he was appointed to train me.

There were three full time civil servant employees, two of whom I met that night. Tom did the paste up and layouts of the pages and sometimes handled the dark room chores and burned the plates but preferred to have helpers do that if they knew how. I came to know how, but it wasn't what they kept me around to do. Some guy I never met worked days as the news room editor supervisor and he was gone home by the time I came. Tom was the swing man who left once the flats were shot and opaque and ready to burn. The third guy was the guy in the swingin' seventies outfit – Ron Muir. He was small and quick and seemed too bright in a cobra looking you in the eyes sort of way. Naturally suspicious of everyone, he liked to have a handle on what you were there for and why you were in his circle to be dealt with. We shook hands and I noticed that his hands were small, as he was, and that there was not much meat there.

"That piece of shit Chevy yours?" was the first thing he said to me. I nodded as we shook hands. "You think it's pretty fast do you?" he continued and we were done shaking hands and said, "It is." "Yeah, well how fast do you think it is?" he went on, pushing a bit. "It's faster than anything you've got," I bragged, having no idea what this guy might have and not caring. He made a face and looked around at the others nearby who were watching. "You think it's faster than my motorcycle?" he asked. "I do," I said, "at anything more than a quarter mile, but bikes are pretty quick off the line so I'd allow as how you might have a Hog or something that's a fast starter."

He was called away and I went off to learn my new job and we let it go at that. It was past midnight and I was standing next to a guy sitting in the chair giving me my next job's description when Ron came up again and picked up the string. He had to shout to be heard since the huge machine was running now and its noise and pounding made your heart match its pulse despite your desire to be your own being. "I've got a Suzuki Hustler that will clean your car's clock on top end," he said, and by then we were more or less co-workers so I backed off a little on my sword grabbing and nodded passively. "We'll see," I answered him, and his eyebrows went up. "You want to race me?" he responded, somewhat incredulously. "Sure," I said, anytime." "We'll have to set something up," he shot back. "What's wrong with when we get done here?" I answered.

Letting someone 'set something up' in racing meant bad things to me. My race machine was built and ready and parked outside. Sure it was crude but it had two things – power and light weight. I would bring the rest. We got the paper finished a little after four and to celebrate my first night we went over to the only all night restaurant in town and had Italian beef sandwiches. It was a treat. When we left there it had been many hours since the challenge had gone out and been called but neither Ron nor I had forgotten. I followed him up to Dowell, a small burg on Route 51 and famously the home of Minnesota Fats and Mel Kenyon, the latter a race car driver. He went in to change and say things to his wife and have some coffee leaving me in his shop to wait. It was tidy and consumed a two car concrete block garage. There were miscellaneous motorcycles here and there but one sat on the workbench prominently.

It was the first real road racer I ever saw up close; a T-20 Suzuki 250 twin with all the full blown racing modifications. When you're not a racer and not sure what you're looking at it is difficult to appreciate what all has been done or how rare the things are you are seeing. The cylinders and heads and expansion chambers were all factory race parts or some hard found equivalent. The fairing was hanging on the wall and the logo on the side had taken the "S" in Suzuki and turned it graphically into a stylized crouching rider. The seat was small and sat way at the back with a very large gas tank stretched out bulbously in front of it. It looked wrong to me, unbalanced, and ungraceful. Ron came in saw that I was looking at the bike and asked me what I thought. He asked with obvious pride and an expectation of the creator of an object d'art. I didn't want to hurt his feelings, since he was a mechanically creative guy and I had to give him points for that. "Cool," I said, which was honestly what I thought about it.

He peeled out of his jeans and had swim trunks on underneath. He grabbed a big gym bag and began pulling out a set of black leathers which he struggled a bit to get into while sitting on a milking stool. Boots were next and he had his gloves and helmet sitting out when he came over to the bike and stepped on a pedal beside the bench and it hydraulically lowered to the floor. He twisted the gas cap and peered in. "Down to the next town and back?" he asked, as if we were back in the midst of our race me conversation. "Sure" I said, "How far is it?" "About four miles," he answered and I nodded my agreement. "How do you want to start?" I asked him. "Once we get it running, you go ahead and I'll chase you." He grinned and I shook my head. "All right," I conceded, "It's your call."

I helped him move some things out of the way and it was early daylight before we were ready. He had to mix up some fresh fuel and it had a pungent odor pouring in as I held the funnel for him. Once that was done and he had on his helmet there was no more talking. I pushed him down the driveway after he had turned on the petcock and was honestly startled by the raw, ripping, dual chain saw scream of the exhaust. He sat on it blipping the throttle and watching the tach as he warmed it up. I waited. Finally he nodded to me which I took to mean he was ready and so I went over to the Chevy and crawled underneath and undid the header bypass caps in a few quick motions. I crawled out, got it and fired it up. The sound it made obliterated the little motorcycle's shrieking.

It had taken me the better part of a year and more than a pound of knuckle skin to get the 421 Pontiac V-8 into the engine bay of the little sedan. I had also cut out all unnecessary metal and replaced it with aluminum panels or just left it out. It weighed 2980 lbs and would turn the quarter mile in 11.97 on its best day, which had netted me a first place trophy in C/gas which was a drag racing classification that meant nothing here. I put the Borg Warner T-10 four speed into first and pulled out of the gravel drive onto highway 51 and headed south, giving it full throttle in each gear. In my rear view mirror I saw Ron in the distance making his way up onto the pavement and starting to come toward me.

I wasn't worried and returned my attention to the road ahead and the coming of a new day. He went past me. I didn't think it possible but it was and it had happened very quickly. We were still on our way down to the next town and even though I was in fourth, I had left myself some margin and not overdone it so I still had some pedal to use. I pushed it up to 6000 rpm and the Stewart Warner speedometer was showing just a touch over 130. It was extremely unstable at that speed and I had my hands full as we came into the little town.

He was pulled over in an empty lot, looking down at the bike and I pulled over next to him. "Beat ya!" he said, and I shook my head, "We were racing down and back," I answered, "we're only half way through." He frowned as I did a circle around him and headed back north to his house. He had shut the motor off, thinking he had proven his point, and he might have had I not been keeping some in reserve. I pulled back onto the highway and did not spare the horses, or the neighbors as I roared up the highway. I saw him fiddling under the tank and getting off to push and then saw him back on the road half a mile behind me. I kept it floored in every gear and made it to his driveway long before he did.

He pulled in sitting up with a sick sounding motor and a sour expression as he rode past me and into the garage. He came back out and motioned for me to pull around behind the garage and I did. He was taking off his helmet when we heard the sirens and closed the garage door, standing back a bit to watch through its windows and the trooper went past chasing the phantom drag racers. It had been fun for both of us. Finally he said, "That's a fast car," meaning my Chevy. "That's a fast bike," I conceded, and added, "faster than I thought possible." He nodded and then said, "Well, it was before I stuck it trying to catch you on the way back." I wasn't sure what he meant by 'stuck it' but was fairly certain it wasn't good.

He took it apart as I watched, and once the head was off and could see the top of the piston, the neat little hole in its crown was visible. He put the head back on and said he would fix it later. The birds were singing when we came outside again and he had me come in and sit while he made coffee and we waited for the police to satisfy themselves that the roads were safe again. Whatever it was we had wanted to prove to one another we had done and so were content. His coffee was horrible and I said so, which made him smile and suggest that I not drink it. Afterward I capped up the headers and drove back to my trailer for a few hours sleep before I had to get up and go to class and start another day.

That was how I got started road racing motorcycles. That was eons before where I was now, sort of, and yet it was right there, with me as we bumped our way across the parking lot section of the track for the umpteenth time and I set him up for the last turn pass. As before, he went wide and stayed right on his line. I went inside him with good momentum and our paths didn't cross before we got to the apex where one of us would have to give. He saw what I was doing, but couldn't do anything more than watch since he had committed to the turn and was using all the available traction and road his line could give him. I had been looking at the wider exit and was ready for some marbles out there so when the back end twitched a bit I didn't let off and told myself just to ride it out.

It probably wasn't perceptible to a spectator, but to a rider in those times each of those little lurches were a heart stopper. Sometimes, they were all the warning you got before you were on the ground. This time it worked out and I kept my head down and beat the guy across the line. He came up along side after the checkered flag and we had a look at one another. Then he gave me a thumbs up and I nodded and gave him one back. It had been a good race and a clean pass. Later I found out it netted me a 12th place finish, which was my highest yet at the time. You don't get a trophy for a 12th place finish and there is not much to say about it other than it's better than 13th.

I had taken serious risks to get it and may have gone over some line in terms of what was reasonable so far as risk was concerned. There was no money in it. I didn't know the guy I was racing. The grandstands were empty and there would be no mention of it in the sports pages here or back home. In a way, it was like it never happened. Sort of like that pre-dawn blast down Highway 51 when I had raced my car against a guy on a very fast bike for nothing more than getting to say, "Beat ya!" and I hadn't even bothered. I questioned why I was doing it if the means were going to cost me more than what I got in the end.

That was forty years ago now, and I know a great deal more than I did then. I know for certain that it is not worth the risk if it is just for some tangible reward you get afterward. I have a closet full of wooden plaques and cheap pot metal trophies that have accumulated over the years. They are not worth much in themselves. It must be something else.

Zen is my answer, which is the word I used to mean 'Everything'. It's everything, all the time that matters, and it's racing motorcycles that taught me that and keeps me conscious of it in a way that nothing else can. For a long time I couldn't put my finger on it but that's because you can't put your finger on 'everything.'

53.

Zen At The End Of
A Racing Career

THE RUBRIC OF THE PROBLEM NEVER CHANGES:

Given: *A rider and motorcycle in competition with another;*
Variables: *All things that effect performance and outcome;*
Operation: *Solve for what it means.*

DAVE CRUSSEL HURT HIMSELF at the weekend's vintage race – well that's one view anyway. Another would be that TZ–750s have claimed another victim; still another would be that cold tires on the first lap of a practice session are unpredictably dangerous; and yet another would be that racers are men and women participating in a risky business who should agree to eliminate every possible dangerous condition they can before putting themselves in harms way.

It was a fairly simple high sided get off with a brutal landing on the point of the pelvis. Bone density, lack of protective padding and angle of impact all combined to send a shattering force across the artfully curved and divinely designed structure to its detriment. The result was a fracture, or a series of fractures that were not revealed fully until a CAT scan some painful time afterward.

I spoke to him briefly as he was deciding what to do next, sitting in his garage space, looking at his nicely organized and well prepared stable of vintage racing motorcycles. He has an exceptional mind and mine was not the only voice suggesting that he needed more information that only professional medical attention could provide. His insistence that he would be all right and the bravado that brought it out were worn through as he posed in what was probably the most comfortable position he could find. He did not look comfortable. We have all heard the stories of our predecessors who sawed off their casts or pulled the pins out of mending bones and then went out and won their races. No doubt he was measuring himself against such tales on some level.

I offered my assistance if needed but his mechanic and his wife are fully functioning even in crisis mode and things were sorted out and he was off to the hospital and did not return. Later his motorcycles and their transporter were gone as well and as I was on the grid for the day I missed any exchange of information with whoever might have had some. No matter, they know none of us wished this to happen and they know as well that most of us would do anything we are asked to assist in the best outcome. That is a clannish behavior among racers and its one of our best qualities.

Vintage racers are more interested in other things than their own ego fed self-aggrandizement. Well, most of us anyway. Here and there you will find the diehards who think it is still being etched in stone somehow on some monument yet to be built about them and their lofty place in the annals of speed. Yeah, I see that happening...

So, let's learn something useful from this if we can. Spare me the obvious observation that bad things happen to good people, it's not helpful and it makes us feel like gamblers in the lottery of life. What could have been done to prevent this?

Well, Dave could have been more careful on the first lap comes to mind, not just mine, but his as well I wager. An easy truth, but it speaks to a set of circumstances somewhat beyond our control. Tire temperatures can be warmed before we put our tires on the track at speed and it begs the question if we could do it, why wouldn't we? Some just don't do a lot of things they could and that's a choice which does not bother me. They have a sense of these things that lets them function in their own way with the problems to be solved. But if there is science available, it does make modern men wonder why someone who could afford it wouldn't take advantage of it.

One answer is there could be a rule about it that kept him from using tire warmers on that sort of bike. If there is such a rule then we need to change it, but more than that, if there is such a rule and it's practice we are talking about then we need to ignore it which brings up another issue. The whole mechanism of getting together and participating in vintage motorcycle races together is a cooperative effort. We have suggested rules, voted on them, refined them, and over time have done ourselves well and ill with them. Most of my working life was dealing with rules of another sort, called laws, and as any lawyer can tell you, the interpretation of rules is an endless process. Some situations call for their being passed over, some don't, it's a matter of discretion and the moment and it is rarely simple.

We have officials for such things and they can be mistaken. They are human too, well all but that one and I won't mention names. They probably drove all night to get here like you did and are tired and off their best game and by the second 16 hour day of standing in the sun in the vice like grip of a pair of headphones mashing their ears to crepe suzette dimensions their attention may have wandered. It happens.

It happened to me when I was racing and it happens to me now as an official. I wish it did not, but I do not wish to be less human so I just accept it. We do our best but being unhappy with an official, or the rules, or anything about what goes on with our club is just being unhappy with ourselves in the end since "we are them" as Charlie Brown would say. Live with it. Volunteer to help, which will not only be helpful but will also give you some insight you may not have.

The tension between historic authenticity and safety is real and has been dealt with before. Will Harding decided at one point in his racing career to mount a tank shift Indian and to tackle riding it with the same determination he had brought to many other more modern things. It wobbled. It wobbled so bad that he put a hydraulic steering dampener on it to keep its head from shaking so violently. It worked, but it violated the rules.

A protest was brought by well respected class scion Doc Batsleer, a Daytona Beach native and rider of the same sort of Indian. Ordinarily, the deciding of that protest would have been a simple matter, but Will was not just any rider, he was a prime move in the beginning of our club, and a respected competitor and a vocal advocate of fair play.

With all that in mind, the powers that be listened to him telling us that we need not kill ourselves to keep vintage bikes authentic if what we mean to do is race them rather than just parade them. Doc was not pleased with the outcome, but the decision came down on the side of safety first and Will's bike was not disqualified.

So too should it be with tire warmers. I know we didn't have them back in the old days, but then we didn't have back protectors either and we not only allow them now, we require them. Safety is a different concern than being true to the past or we would still race around in puddin' bowl helmets wearing skin tight suits without padding and no gloves and I don't think anyone wants to go back to that.

Another possibility suggested for Dave's dilemma was for him to have been "extra" careful. Geeze, I tire of being cautioned, don't you? We are called on to be careful about everything we do our whole lives on some level and if you can't let it go when you take the meanest nastiest race bikes ever made out for a spin, just exactly when did you think you were going to allow yourself the liberty? My morning had begun early with my long time friend and the fastest realtor in Florida blasting Steppenwolf's "Born to be Wild" from his stereo just to set the mood in his pit adjacent to mine. I was all set to be irritated but the lyric got to me first and I had to say, Well…. YEAH!!!!

Finally, I was grieved to see David Roper in a neck brace. We love him, but we also know that he is fragile and has broken things before, sometimes while racing elsewhere. I was so bold as to ask how it had happened and his look was apologetic. It was not a 'fog on the mountain' sort of story to etch on the monument mentioned above but rather a mundane 'run to the grocery store' tale from a street bike argument with a car; him being on the bike and the car having done a u-turn from its parking place directly into his path.

That sort of summed up the whole thing for me. Fate is the hunter, after all, and we are just pigeons. On my 14 hour drive home to Illinois to make my 6 a.m. bus run the next morning to safely deliver children to school I came across another racer on the Pennsylvania turnpike and I recognized his bike from scoring its number many times over the weekend. He is fast. He is fast on the track and on the turnpike and I fell in behind him and played back door in our little convoy until the next fuel stop when he needed to pit and I didn't.

It reminded me so much of the days when the AMA nationals were sometimes scheduled on opposite coasts back to back and an entire herd of crazed speed junkies in vans packed with race bikes would set off more or less together and pass each other and repass each other across the deserts and over the mountains and prairies of the whole continent running nearly free on gas that only cost fifty cents a gallon and listening to Steppenwolf blast full volume from their eight track tape players.

"Born to be Wild…."? You betcha!

54.

The Zen Of Racing

ZEN DOES NOT SEEM a likely philosophy or discipline for a motorcycle racer at first blush, but after some serious intercourse, the truth of it is indisputable. Let us dispose of the 'God' thing first. There is one, there must be, otherwise there would be no need at all for me, or anyone else to be worrying about whether there was one or if life had any meaning and if it might, what part we might play in some plan that a God might have.

'He' or 'it' or 'she' are not sufficient monikers for something so large that it encompasses everything from the moment of creation to the instant that all things everywhere cease to be. I know that some are fond of quoting scripture to explain their own satisfaction with an image that can be suitably molded into plastic to sit on the dashboard of their car and give them comfort and let them feel safer or whatever feeling it gives them. I am not offended in the least by this and to some degree they are at least as right as I may be. But any particular image that man makes is an inaccurate substitute for the grandeur of all things. Since I cannot see everything at once, and if I could, would be unable to comprehend what it all means, I have a problem if I want to understand at all what my life is for or what it means.

That I want to solve that problem sufficiently to know that there is an answer does not demonstrate that there is one, however, and no level of semantic argument or amount of computation or clever experimentation may be able to answer it for me. That is because I am finite. My intellect has its limits and the time I have to consider the problem and work on the answer is infinitely smaller and shorter than whatever name you give to all of it. Undeniably it is 'all' something and I call it Zen, respectfully, because it seems mysteriously sufficient to me to do so. That the word has been used before does not bother me any more than the fact that there are other people out there who are called by the same name I am and we are no more alike than day and night so to use that name, or any name, fails as a complete description. Those others with my name, however, are people too and we are more alike than not relative to all things and since our name is the same may actually be relatives.

So when I look to the heavens and see great things done by a great power, why do I not see just the vastness of space and cold emptiness instead? Because to me, my presence in creation is evidence of the greatness of its creator if I can do great things and I can. This larger truth is more easily digested when we make a comparative examination of it relative to ourselves. Consider that creation is all of everything for all time and that we are just a speck of matter for a moment. Then how great is creation compared to us?

We are bloody marvelous, after all, and there is no dispute about that. We can laugh and love and think and belch and fart and race motorcycles when too tired to drive another mile and too weak or hobbled by pain to take another step. We know of men, we may even know some first hand, that are inexplicably gifted and capable once their hands take the grips of a moving racing motorcycle but who are not to be trusted pushing a shopping cart on their own and cannot find the keys to their car. They can recite the motor number and valve clearances of their bike but have forgotten their children's birthdays and their wedding anniversary (was I married once?) so often that it is now expected. Still, they can drive back roads and detours from their shop door to the race track gate in record time through the dark of night without a break or a map and talk the whole way or say absolutely nothing and it will have no effect on how fast they ride. Casts have been cast aside, pins pulled from broken bones, fingers taped together so a mangled one can manage all just so they can race and usually they do so for nothing if we think in terms of profit. What sort of men do such things?

As a group, racers are widely scattered individuals across the ability board of life and love and all things to be considered. They are characters, they are parents and single men and mechanics and boxers and painters and dancers and all sorts of people. R.G. Wakefield, for example, was a master machinist, but was also a world class comedian. He joked with a straight face and a fu Manchu moustache mixing moments of brilliant insight with pure foolishness. He was animated and rambling across all subjects and just to be in his company was electrifying.

After a hot day's racing at Indianapolis Raceway Park he invited a group of us over to the Checkered Flag Tavern on Washington street where he knew the owner, apparently, and a special table had been prepared for the party of us that sat around and ate and drank and talked long into the evening. R.G. was in his glory and seemed to draw energy from our presence and stood, finally, to thank us all for coming and to perform for us what he described as his "famous tablecloth trick."

He made us all move our chairs back away from the table and take our elbows off and pick up our napkins and drinks. Once that was done, a good deal of the show was devoted to several circuits of the table where he would reposition plates and bowls and take wrinkles out of the fabric with what appeared to be deliberate intent, all the while paying homage to the "Great Bodine" who had been the first to perform this very same astonishing act while with Buffalo Bill Cody's Wild West Show on a stop in Kansas City at Jake's Barbeque Emporium just off Center street less than a block from the cattle yards.

The staff had come in to watch R.G. from the kitchen, apparently having been tipped off that this was going to happen and the owner himself stood in the doorway of the alcove where we were all seated. R.G. gestured behind himself to make room as he took several passes with just his hands and arms at what we all began to believe would be his yanking of the long white linen tablecloth off of the table from beneath the dishes and cutlery in a single instant. Drum rolls were heard, although none were present. A hush fell over the crowd. History pressed in upon us to take notice of the moment to come.

Finally, it seemed that all was ready and he rolled up the end of the cloth with a good deal of care and took several tugs on it to get the tension of the individual threads raised to just the right level to have his grip just so, one hand palm up, he other palm down, the knuckles white. This took some minutes as he was now clearly transported beyond us and into the event to come, that moment of unexplainable action when things that seemed as though they could never happen might be possible and would indeed actually happened. He seemed capable and determined and it made us feel it to as if, once he had done it, we would be able to believe it possible where now we only believed it might be possible because he said it was so and he seemed so certain.

He tugged at the cloth and spoke of the coefficient of friction of linen as opposed to certain other types of tablecloths and wished aloud for silk as he had been blessed with that time at Shanghai Lil's, then described the level of force necessary to create a sufficiently slick layer of sliding molecules that would be able to overcome the force of gravity bearing down upon each plate and bowl and saucer and paused a time or two, looking up and closing his eyes, as if calculating and then mumbling something to himself and then nodding his head with some hesitation and then with more certainty and finally, finally, the moment came.

He stepped back, way back, into a crouch so that he was holding onto the tablecloth and looking intently down the length of the table about to commit the mental aspects that were bouncing around in his fevered brow to kinetic motion and amaze us all. He did it, if that was what he had intended, and we loved it.

What he did was to slowly pull the tablecloth and the entire contents of the table off the end of the table into a pile on the floor, stepping backwards and making the long tail of the slow comet he held longer as the collection of dishes and detritus from the meal accumulated and was then covered in an instant as he threw the portion of the cloth he had been pulling on over the whole mess with a flourish, hoisting both hands into the air over his head in a triumphant gesture. "Ta Dah!" he said. Ta Dah indeed.

We had been roaring with laughter for some time by then and I could hardly breathe. What a show! What he was really doing was clearing the table in slow motion and all of the arranging of dishes and making us move back from the edge and the rest of it was just part of the act. He nursed the moment for all it was worth and once he had set up a steady tugging pull it was as inexorable as it was hilarious. When he was done and the deed was done, he gave us a P.T. Barnum bow and the applause was spontaneous and steady. From the doorway, the owner smiled and shook his head and then gestured to his staff who came forward and with a few quick motions picked the pile up by the corners of the cloth and carried it away.

I was impressed. I was in the presence of a real life magician who had the majority of all the things needed to be one for the ages, except for the magic – that part didn't happen. But the rest of it was wonderful! He had the patter and the gestures and a truly great sense of timing that made what he did, everything he did, mesmerizing. "The Old Tablecloth Trick" as it became known, was never repeated in my presence, but it was spoken of fondly and the performance itself ranked right up there with Stan Friduss's motorcycle streaking episode at Dade City but that is another story.

Men who race motorcycles are simply not like other men and are exceptional in some way just for doing it. Some of them are exceptional motorcycle racers as well. Sooner or later, if they persist at racing beyond the normal arc of most riders careers which is the: 'Can I do this?; ' I can do this!' ; "I can do this better than you;" "I can do this better than anyone;" "God that really hurt when I crashed;" Should I race again now that I am healed up?" "Yes, I can crash and come back";" Yes, I can win";" Yes, I can lose and still enjoy racing"; "This is pointless why am I doing it?" sort of curve, they may move on to the quest for salvation in racing that points the way to Zen.

Some never make the journey. Some never see the way. I have to tread lightly here not to be taken as uncharitable towards particular faiths, as this is not a religious text at all. I happen to be religious, but it wouldn't really matter because I see religion as part of the larger whole and that wholeness of things is what I call Zen so you can be Baptist or Muslim or Hindu or an agnostic Quantum Physicist for that matter and it doesn't change the truth of things as I see them one bit.

I point out, that's all, you can look away or deny if you care to, that's fine, but it is right there, and it is – well I don't have an adequate word to describe it or I wouldn't need to write a book to try to adequately convey what all it is. All I do here is to show it to you, over there, through the trees along the far edge of the lake playing off across the hills and then up onto the mountain side for just a moment or two as I drive Route 113 to Rod's house up in Maine to pick up a racing motorcycle fifty years after it was built and try to tell you that things are good for us if we notice.

Here is a list to consider that may help:

I believe –

1. Everything matters – every moment of every day is part of your life and you cannot ignore or neglect some in favor of others and expect the balance you seek in all things in the end. The only logical alternative to holding this view is that nothing matters, in which case there would be no point in racing because it would not matter if you rode well or not and you know in your heart, and in your soul, that it matters very much. The middle ground that some things matter and some don't is just your ego talking and you thinking that you matter so things you notice matter but things that happened to others don't matter because it wasn't you. Say that out loud to yourself and see if you can still believe it to be true.

2. Riding well is more important than winning because it is something that you have a degree of control over that permits you to speak to the forces of the universe that are in action that ordinarily overwhelm you and hold you back. On any given day, you may be the best rider on the track, but if you are on the slowest machine, you still may not win.

3. The fastest bike wins the race more often than the fastest rider. Sincerity is no measure of truth and courage is not a catalyst for speed.

4. Everything you do with racing; every moment of preparation and mechanical training and physical effort must be done like your life depends upon it because it does. Since you can't see the future, you can't predict what failure will commence the sequence of events that may prove fatal and your control of that moment may have slipped away from you before you recognized it so you must treat each moment as if that was its possible outcome.

    If you count on someone to do something for you, then you must trust them with your life, and that should not be done without serious consideration and sincere devotion to your safety. I have never forgiven Colin Chapman for Jimmy Clark's death. The steering broke on the Formula II car and sent him off the track to his doom, helpless to prevent it. Such an end for such a man was unforgivable.

5. Rules are not made to be broken, they are made to be considered as part of the problem which has been put before you to find within yourself the ability to excel and perform at a level that says to you, and to everyone, that you were as fast as you could possibly be.

6. Zen tradition teaches us to be slow and deliberate and to do just one thing at a time and do it completely. Zen racing is the opposite end of the continuum of activity that leads to enlightenment and tells us to do as many things as necessary all at once and do them all well. Zen meditation and discipline eliminates distractions and focuses consciousness on nothingness. Zen racing occupies the mind and body and spirit so completely that there is no place left in the mind for thoughts that are not about the survival of the moment, each moment, sealing it off from the distractions of the world and revealing, as mediation reveals, a simple truth – we are but a small part of a whole that occupies the universe completely and always has.

7.   Zen practitioners have rituals for many things, from eating to cleaning to meditation. Zen racers have rituals of their own, to prepare themselves for the moments to come when they no longer have the luxury of options. They still themselves before riding; put their leathers and helmet and boots and gloves on in a certain way, born of comfort and nervousness and repetition so that they are not bothered by silly things that might distract them from the business at hand. They do not deviate from this ritual once it is established by them because to do so would be to disrupt the karma of racing and that they do not want that. It is not superstition, it is worship, and they are not the same.

8.   The Zen Racer knows that time must be devoted to just sitting and letting thoughts come to him on their own. There is so much to think of and remember that unless he makes the effort to be still and let truths be revealed to him, he will neither hear nor see them. They come from everywhere and he must be ready to accept them.

     I saw two old friends talking with one another at Daytona and took their photograph. I did not see then what the picture revealed on closer inspection, which was that the wife of one of the friends was bathed in serene sunlight, loving her husband as she watched him speaking and listening to his friend and it was she who drank the deepest from the well of the moment while they were oblivious to her presence.

9.   Zen requires us to think of what is necessary and to eliminate the unnecessary from our lives. I used to have a list that I had made for loading up to go to the races that began, "Helmet, boots, leathers, license… " I would check things off from the list as I made ready until the day I realized that I knew what was necessary better than the list did because it was fixed in the past and I had acquired more knowledge in every moment since. It was not my memory that I needed, it was my conscious meditation about what was necessary and what was unnecessary.

10.   Zen tells us that it matters what we think as we do certain things, so that even the menial tasks that racing requires of us, to clean and repair and replace worn parts, should be done with

a certain mind set which does not begrudge the time taken from other things but sees the truth of them for what they are - stepping stone from where we are to where we want to be and we must make the journey ourselves or as much of it as we can, to arrive with a full appreciation of how far we have come.

11.   "Live Simply" is the hardest guide for a Zen Racer to follow because he knows so much of the complexity of the many interrelated forces in play when he races and what can be done about them that he tends to horde things that he sees as potentially useful. The shop of a Zen Racer may appear cluttered and over run with projects and things in various unorganized moments on their individual paths to completion but in the mind of their maker, all is well. The creation process has only been interrupted by something more urgent in a moment when a choice had to be made. It can be picked up again when the need and time for it to be done returns. To live simply as a racer then, requires resources, not just resourcefulness, and those who would follow the simple path must be able to pay the toll. Unlike spiritual Zen, which embraces the poverty of simplicity, racing Zen tells us that speed requires mechanical assistance and we must make what we can of what we have to acquire it. The Zen of that acquisition matters to the soul of the Zen Racer which sings when all has been done right.

12.   Life's greatest truths will come to the Zen Racer from racing. It may not be the only path to them, but it is the path of the true racer – someone who races because to do so brings forth a kindred spirit from within him that seeks, and can find, it's true home at speed.

I mean no offense to Zen masters by saying these things. I admire their teachings but confess that I do not especially understand their parochial nature when it comes to their insistence that only inactivity can reveal meaning to the mind that would otherwise be missed. I understand that their discipline and deprivations of things can have the effect they seek to achieve on the thoughts of their minds. I applaud them their success and enlightenment, and respect their teachings enough to do so with just one hand.

I am not one of them in the traditional sense because I follow a different path, one that I did not choose but which was chosen for me by the maker of my nature. It is my nature to ride the wind and go as fast as I can just for the going. It matters less to me if someone else rides next to me, or before me, or behind me than that we ride.

Having ridden and having placed myself beyond all reasonable limits of risk and the demands of judgment and balance and endurance, I find peace, and it is a peace so profound that I need no words to express it when it is upon me. I was called to a place by my life of all things together to do what I did and race and then, once it is over, if I have ridden well and the fruits of my labor have been sweet, then I know that I have the harmony I seek - That is the Zen of racing motorcycles.

55.

Zen After Crashing

EVERYTHING CHANGES AFTER YOU have a serious crash. If it is your first, then you have learned that it can happen. If it is anything other than your first, then you have learned that it can happen again despite the changes you've made since last time. Sometimes you have a memory of it, sometimes you don't, that depends on how it happened. I've had both, but I'm not sure if one is any different than the other in terms of getting back up to speed. If it were something else, some other activity that had hurt you, the decision to try it again would be different. If you survived, you have stories to tell your grandchildren now, if they will listen.

Some falls leave marks that don't go away. I still have a painful knee that doesn't work, but it's not bad compared to some injuries other riders have and still ride. There is a limit. For me that would be Bob Goodpaster, who fell at Gingerman one day and broke himself internally to the extent that a titanium plate and its associated hardware now holds him together. That's a game changer. Should he ride again, and fall, it would be like having a meat slicer inside you looking to get out. I interviewed him about that at Mid-Ohio as he was about to race again. He admitted that I was right about what would happen if he fell, but said he didn't think about that. Most of us ride without thinking about falling down, but it happens to everyone sooner or later. If I were in his condition, I would think about it.

Falling down is not unavoidable, you could go so slowly that it is just not possible, but then that wouldn't be racing, that would be something less, and why bother? You could try and be logical about it and extrapolate how many racing miles you have covered without crashing and then how many crashes you have had and now many bones that has cost you and so forth. I knew an AAMRR racer who had a spreadsheet of this before the days of computers and used it to explain to me that he was not due for another bad crash for another six races, therefore he could ride as hard as he wanted at Bridgehampton that weekend. When he asked me why I was asking him I explained that my plan was to die young and that racing was just a means to an end. I was kidding, but he took me seriously which paid off in a way as he was reluctant to come near me on the track.

If I had something in me that meant the likelihood that my next fall would be fatal, I would not race again. I do not have a death wish. Racing is not a psychotic episode, it is something else, something that can be truly beneficial and enlightening if done right, but there is the danger that you will fall too often and crash yourself out of the discipline before you get there. The odds are more in your favor than they once were, safety was not a word in use when I started racing. When I first raced I was required to have a jacket with leather sleeves and a helmet. I got a sparkly helmet at Western Auto and wore my letterman's jacket. Some guys wore football helmets. Real racers had the pudding bowl from England that stopped above your ears. None of them did any real good and we would have raced without them if they would have let us. It was well into the 70s before I had a conversation with an AMA official about wearing gloves. I never wore them, and didn't like them but learned to accommodate their necessity once it became a rule.

We have all sorts of equipment designed to minimize the effects of crashing. Back protectors, padded leathers, helmets, boots, all of them have been seriously developed to make falling as inconsequential as possible. They can only do so much, but what they do mostly is alter our expectation of what is about to happen when we are losing our motorcycle out from under us at a great speed. When I started racing, the expectation was that you would die if you fell off at speed.

Why wouldn't you think that? Lots of people did fall off and a good number of them died as a result. Mostly from head injuries, but there were any number of things that makes your body react badly to being smashed into solid things at great speeds. Leathers were just body bags to speed up the process of picking up a downed rider. Armco was the enemy and hay bales can only do so much. Air fence was decades in the future and for the most part you had to know that when you fell down you were going to be broken and could likely be killed. Still, we raced anyway.

Kenny Roberts and some of the California racers came around the pits at Loudon and tried to generate a rider's strike complaining that the track was not safe. We knew that already before we drove up there. I raced anyway, not as a daredevil, but as someone who only had the resources to make so many races and they had been spent already to bring me there. I wasn't going to waste them on a gesture. Rider caution or the lack of it was what prevented crashes in my opinion and if we made ourselves so safe that any amount of risk taking was acceptable, then guys would be throwing it away and expecting to get up from it unharmed. I'm happy it's a safer thing to do that it used to be, but it plays no part in why I do it.

We admire those that continue to race while broken, and I have done it, but it was foolish and I admit that now. I broke my collarbone, among other things, when another rider took my front wheel out trying to pass me on the outside and was unable to get it done before we got to the apex. It was all his fault and he said so later, but if I had known how it was going to turn out I would have done better at saying 'no' to being passed like that and he would have gone down instead of me. When I lost the front, my hands went with the bike in that first split second as things go bad and I went to the track helmet first, with the nearly inevitable result that the bottom of my full face helmet found my collarbone as it rolled me over, the clearly audible 'snap' being all too familiar from my football playing days telling me that I had broken my collarbone yet again. I had some other injuries, but nothing else broken, and the skin was mostly all there and since I had my sights set on the championship in my class that year, I decided that I would make the next race in a month.

The doctor said it was a simple break and if I kept myself still and didn't overdo it I would be back to normal activity is 8 to 12 weeks, depending how things went. There were no special devices to stimulate bone growth or any of that and the break was not so bad as to require pins or screws or any hardware. It did make it difficult to find a comfortable position for sleeping, however, which no one seemed to be very concerned about. Still, I managed. That was when I learned to like beer without being picky about which kind.

My job at the time was working as a roofer and since I could no longer carry the shingles up the ladder, it meant that I was nailing all day and trimming with a knife. I have to add that this was so long ago that we put nails into shingles with things we held in our hands and swung with force called hammers – nothing like the power nailers out there now. I managed that too, although I was pretty sure that a time or two I had moved the wrong way and undid all that nature was trying to do to mend me up to that point.

I had a difficult time getting the bike repaired, since I did the work myself, and had even more trouble getting it loaded into the van when it came time to go to the races. Funny how many things you do require some connection to your collarbone. The drive there was the easy part and I managed to get there early enough to get in a nap sitting behind the wheel. All was well enough through tech and some well wishers had stopped by to express their surprise at seeing me back so soon after 'it' had happened. The asshole that had knocked me down was there too, but kept his distance I noticed, which was just as well. I do not subscribe to the 'rubbin' is racin' foolishness, not on motorcycles. Motorcycle road racing when done properly should be a non-contact sport.

The part I had not anticipated as being difficult proved to be very nearly impossible – getting back into my leathers. They are always cold and stiff to begin with anyway and when we put them on we tend to do a few stretching moves that are partly for us, but mostly for them, to wake them up and get them going again. This was in the dark ages when leathers were nothing but leather and my Bates had taken a beating and kept me whole so I was not unhappy with them or how heavy they were. I knew guys who had the supple glove leather sort of suits but had also seen what they looked like after a crash and didn't want any part of that.

I managed to get suited up and got the bike started with a good deal of difficulty. No one used rollers then and the unspoken rule was if you couldn't start it yourself you probably shouldn't be riding it. FIM events were using dead motor grids in those days, which would have been a nightmare, so I was happy to face the problem alone in the pits rather than embarrass myself on the grid as everyone roared away. I got it fired up and paddled over to the line waiting to go out for practice. The time came quickly enough, and motors revved up, two stroke smoke abounded and we were sent back onto the track. Then the damnedest thing happened – I realized that I was not the same.

Always before, no matter how tired, or how preoccupied, or whatever else was going on in my life, it all melted away as soon as I was back on the track. Not this time. This time the 'I' was lower case 'me' and me was broken. Mechanically, physically, physiologically, I was broken. No matter how I tried to convince myself that it was temporary and the I could manage it with some adjustments here and there, the truth was that I was not the same and racing was not going to be the same either.

I put more of my weight on the seat and slid forward against the tank, letting the force under braking take its toll there. I didn't wrestle the clipons as I usually did but pushed down on the footpegs instead and found the effect different, but interestingly effective. Since I had changed, physically, I had to ride differently. Most of that went well enough and I was back up to a reasonable speed by the end of the session. But mentally? Well, that was going to take some work, and I was not used to that.

What was not going so well was my reaction to the proximity of other motorcycles in my little sphere of influence. My critical distance for what was 'too close' had changed and I was no longer comfortable shoulder to shoulder with someone in a turn, not that I had ever been all that comfortable. I would have to get used to the way things were now, I told myself, and managed two more practice sessions before the first race of the day. Then, things really got interesting.

56.

The Zen Of Gary Nixon

GARY NIXON SHOWED UP at the hotel room and did not wait in line like the rest of us to use the shower. We had all spent the day at the track at Indianapolis Raceway Park and Jeff Clark March had extended an invitation to come and take a shower to those of us who were camping out at the track. There were no showers there in those days and since I had spent the day in a leather suit in 90 degree temperatures the truth was I needed a shower.

It was irritating to all of us that Nixon did not wait his turn, or chip in like we did to help pay for the room but after I got to know him better we came to expect that. When he came out ten minutes later announcing that there was no more hot water, he was wrapped in the last dry towel and was carrying his clothes. He didn't have anything else to say, but just smirked his cocky 'better than you losers' smile at us and walked outside, not shutting the door behind him.

He was the image of a young James Cagney, self assured and more than confident in himself and what he could do; more so than anyone I had ever seen. I noticed that he had the scars to prove it too. Here and there, in odd places would be a dent in his freckled skin of different coloring that marked the place where a broken bone had been repaired or something had poked its way into him leaving its mark, or out of him.

I admired him. We all did. He didn't necessarily win anymore, but that wasn't what was special about him. He was there, elbowing his way into the buffet or leaving without paying his bill or clipping by you in practice when it meant nothing other than he was just taking the opportunity to show you something about yourself and about who the hell Gary Nixon was.

Begrudgingly, we had to sort of shake our heads about him. I had seen the leathers nailed up in his shop with all of its holes where he had gotten off in Japan and his bones came through. Eerily they matched the holes in his freckled skin and made you wince just thinking about it. He was tough; no that's not enough, he defined toughness.

He was not alone in that, there were others. Adrian told me about a British rider who literally pulled a pin out of his mending bone so he could ride, and he won every race he entered that day. Not smart, true, but he had done it and it certainly spoke about his determination and made the rest of us feel timid by comparison.

Dick Mann is another who can and has put pain on the back burner, as have a lot of racers. I tried racing with a broken collar bone once when I desperately could not see my way not to do it. I was not competitive. The next time I broke a collarbone I just went to the hospital.

Years after I has sat timidly with the boys on the floor of the motel and watched Nixon butt in line, I told him about that first impression he had made on the rest of us waiting in that room and he laughed about it. "Half the race is off the track," he had told me then, now an expert myself, and by then I understood what he meant.

As for our benefactor that day, Jeff was from back east somewhere and had the first conversion van I ever saw. I had struck up an acquaintance with him because on the little wing of his fairing that held the bubble where some guys had their name he had someone letter, "Who the Hell is Jeff Clark March?" which I thought so self-depreciating as to be the complete opposite of the Nixon persona he also possessed that I would encounter later.

He had a Chevy van that he used as a motorcycle hauler that was paneled and carpeted inside and very nice. When the bike wasn't in there, you would never have known that was what it was used for. He also had a big sweet dog with blue eyes that went everywhere with him. He rode with a shop from New Jersey called 'Motion Enterprises' who seemed to have good running machinery besides being a pleasant group of people that included Henri the Brush known far and wide as the man to have to paint your numbers on so they looked professional.

Bart Myers was a junior rider in that group and had a TR2B Yamaha that would finish 8th or so on most of the time and I heard later that he became a professor at Rutgers University. I was struggling with how to pass people and asked Bart about it and his advice was sound and sensible. "Don't bother with them," he told me, "you are already going faster than they are or you wouldn't have caught them. Just let them be somewhere you don't want to be and go on by." I had watched Bart and what struck me about his riding was how easily he seemed to go through the traffic of other riders that got in his way. Like a lot of riders of the time, he had that tidy tucked in style of the day and didn't do much of anything that took him off the seat or out past the centerline of the machine.

It was good advice and I listened. I finally had a bike that would pass people, which had been the problem when I started out, and now I needed more information. My first complaint; that my bike wasn't fast enough, had been taken care of by buying a Yamaha, now it was what I was doing, or not doing, that needed work. I was a novice in my third year of struggling to come to terms with what was required of me to be a racer and there were no rider schools in those days. You were welcomed to come and race if you wanted to or you could go back home and leave the racers alone. That was the extent of your AMA welcome.

Mostly AMA riders were dirt racers and apparently saw road racing as an interruption of what they thought racing was all about. There were a few exceptions, like Ron Grant, who rode for Suzuki, but they came from somewhere else. I did dirt track with the AMA eventually, as a way of chasing points to move up, and motocross as well when they made it a pro licensed event, and was surprised to see some of the same faces on and off the track at all of these venues. If you weren't an AMA club in those days you were nobody in the national sense, and while I joined the AFM to race in California and the AAMRR to race in the northeast, only the AMA went everywhere and that was what I thought I wanted to do. Blind ambition overrides intelligent judgment in young racers.

I rode for Speede Service, a shop in Carbondale, Illinois who was the Midwest distributor for CZ and when motocross was picked up by the AMA as a pro event I already had a license. The owner let me ride a new 250 CZ in the first Midwest pro event in Missouri on the condition I did not change anything, which meant I had to race it completely showroom stock. That meant non-folding footpegs that dug into the backs of your calves at every opportunity and levers on the handlebars fitted into welded brackets at impossible angles. Still, it was a fast bike and when I lined up for the start of the first professional AMA motocross in the Midwest next to some old man on a battered four stroke single I actually felt sorry for him.

Twenty minutes later, when the first moto was over, I had seen that old man plenty as he lapped me repeatedly on his BSA. Dick Mann was known to me but I had not recognized him in person beneath his goggles and get up. I had the good grace to go over and shake his hand afterward and he was kind enough to take it. I don't know where he had finished, but I knew it was way ahead of me and that I had a lot to learn about motocross. I would do it if I had to, but only if it would get me moved up to the next level so I could road race something bigger than a 250. I didn't like the dirt in my teeth or the lack of speed or the handlebars in my ribs but, if I had to, I would adjust.

I was desperate to be racing at the next national road race, no matter where it was or what it would cost me to get there. If I had to short track at Santa Fe, or Granite City, or half mile in Ohio or motocross in Missouri to get my license to ride big bikes at the road races then I would. Desperation is a poor mode for action, it leads to mixed results, some of which are later regretted.

Gary Nixon is gone now, and I miss his presence. His style was genuine and even though he was not an especially fast vintage racer, his own vintage was unmistakably valuable to have around. Likewise I have an appreciation for many of the riders of his era that I did not especially have when I only saw them as competitors. I wish there were some middle ground where admiration and friendship could be shared without the competition but that wouldn't be racing; that would be, well that would probably just be drinking!

Seeing Gary, visiting with him, you just knew you were going to miss him someday. It's the same sort of feeling I have about visiting abroad, whether I'm watching the sunset on the Rhine from the castles of Heidelberg, or watching it turn Paris from daylight to dark on the thousand steps down from Momartre. There is a twinge of regret with each passing moment that comes and goes and for those that stick out at us, and make us take special notice, it is often born of some premonition that it will be important someday, even if it isn't now. Listening to Gary was like that. It was his Zen.

I felt that way when I watched the royal wedding. I was up anyway and did not want to see another infomercial about how to get rich in real estate or make myself look like Cindy Crawford. Does anyone else notice she has a huge mole on her face? So I found myself having already walked the dog, fed the cat, and made coffee sitting in front of a magic box showing me pictures from across the world of a familiar place and I was interested.

I had spent a week in London some time ago and stayed at a cheap hotel in Piccadilly Circus which is across the mall and just up the hill from St. James Park. That was the green space next to the road lined with flags where the wedding party and the guests went to and from Buckingham palace and Westminster Abbey. My path into town each morning crossed that street just there where they were interviewing spectators about why they had come from Louisiana to watch and why they were wearing red hats - Curious, all of that, and amusing in its own way.

I fell in love with England on my first visit 40 years earlier, listening to the train conductor punch the tickets of all the riders and punctuating each punch with an adjective instead of repeating "thank you" or being so rude as to say nothing. He said, "Lovely; Brilliant; Smashing; Fabulous; Dazzling; Wonderful; Marvelous"… why the man was an encyclopedic thesaurus. They had tea everywhere, which I much prefer to coffee and tea drinkers got pots of the stuff with their meals while the coffee drinkers got tiny cups of it and had to wait for refills. Payback for all the times I sat with coffee drinkers here. Sure, they drove on the left hand side of the road, which seemed odd to me until I learned the reasons. If you met another traveler going in the opposite direction which hand would you rather have between you? Your sword hand, or your left hand? From a practical standpoint, the need for personal defense dictated the former, as a matter of etiquette it forbade the latter. The public use of the left hand was so frowned upon in polite society that those who were left handed had to apologize for using it each time or face retribution. I will not be so crude as to explain.

I like weddings of young people in love and did enjoy the ceremony. I had some fun with it and my remote control, switching between the different networks and comparing the commentary. "Catty" Katie Couric is thankfully now history herself and will be leaving CBS soon but she could not resist the opportunity to remind us of every negative thought she could dredge up to say. I suppose at one point it was fascinating to see someone who seemed so sweet be so vile but the new wore off of that some time ago and it was just sad. No, the wedding dress was not a copy of Grace Kelly's and yes we all knew that the groom's mother had died tragically after his father had divorced her and remarried a less attractive woman who will someday be queen but may not be called that. Fortunately, each network had a British translator working with the Americans, otherwise it was likely that the impression left by the millions of pounds spent would have been something less than desired.

As it was, it left a great impression. There is a proper way to do things and it does matter how people behave. I am democratic enough to feel a twinge of guilt at enjoying such carrying on by a small group whose station in life is imagined to be higher than everyone else's, but I must admit it has a certain fascination. *"Jolly good show he married a commoner; smashing for her."* Oh, it's all head shaking to us and we are so far from understanding it that it's revolting. We did that, actually, revolt I mean and did so pretty much for the same reason I feel odd now about enjoying it. The idea that some people are better than others does not sit well with Americans. To distinguish those that are better by birth as the Brits do, is only slightly more irritating than doing it with wealth as we do here in some Presbyterian kind of way and imagine the rich are the 'elect' of God, meaning they get to be rich while the poor Baptists just get better music.

None of this was any fault of the kids about to jump the broomstick, however, and there was no point in spoiling my enjoyment of their day by dwelling on it. He flies a rescue helicopter, which is not an easy thing and there is no faking it. She is lovely and knows how to act and seems to be very much her own person which is also good. Most importantly, they appear to be genuinely fond of one another and anyone who has ever been in love cannot resist wishing them well and hoping they actually get to live happily ever after. I know I do.

"I will", actually, is what they say in the Church of England as we all learned, and I noticed that she did not have to promise to "obey". It was here that the commentary of the various providers really showed their differences. NBC had the good sense and graciousness to remain silent and let events speak for themselves. The others could not resist pummeling us with factoids that sounded more like tabloid tidbits than appreciation for what was being witnessed. The real benefit to watching from here rather than being there was that you could choose your crowd. I did not want to be surrounded by negativity at such a positive moment and so chose to avoid it.

For those with some background in the presentation of things it had to be appreciated how very carefully the images shown the world from inside the abbey were selected, tracked, zoomed, panned and dissolved into one another. Surely you didn't think it accidental that an ethnically Asian choir boy was shown next to a Nordic youngster with blonde hair standing next to a black one flanked by a freckled faced Irish lad on the end with dark hair all singing in harmony. Men only, thank you very much. Trees in the church; the overhead view as if looking down from heaven; the perfect delivery of every line of every reading of scripture and sermon, all selected by the BBC and presented for us to follow along in the official "programme" published and made available to the common folk by the gracious permission of her Majesty the Queen.

Here we show images of our own vice president sleeping at a presidential address and think it newsworthy. The British may show such images in the tabloids, but not on the national broadcasting network. We have a national network too, of course, but our congress voted to cut off its funding. That makes an impression as well. By the time it was over the sun was up and I had things to do outside. I enjoyed visiting London in the spring so much that I decided while watching the royal wedding that I simply must go again. You don't think that might have been behind making such a production of it all do you? Oh, it's probably just my cynical American side coming out. I am going over again though.

Aintree is racing true vintage bikes still; while many clubs here and there have given up on the idea and have gone modern. Now if they will just hold an event in May while I'm there, then I can send my gear over and look for a ride so that I can work it in with the trip we've already planned to see the list of things we've never seen there yet, although we've been many times. If you've traveled much, you now how vary hard it becomes to feel at home somewhere.

That includes your home once you've returned to it because now you've seen the ocean or Niagara Falls or whatever it is that has no equal. None of those things are near your home as it turns out, which makes you wish your home was somewhere else. That's a road I've traveled, first with my parents as we bounced around, and later on my own as I raced the national circuit and tried to decide what spot would be best to make it easier to do that. I loved Boston and New England after having raced at Loudon in the spring, but when I got a job interview to teach high school in Brattleboro and drove up there in December to sit down and think about actually living there, I had to admit that it was not attractive. The locals were not all that keen on having me and my Southern ways either and there was some talk about it. But they were men and women of their word and they had extended the offer on which I had driven up from Florida to have a look and would stand by it.

It was grim and the smell of burning coal was in the gray air. None of the streets in town were on the level and I did not have some version of the apparently requisite four wheel drive propulsion on which to rely. Neither did I have sufficient layers of clothing to keep my core temperature above cadaverous and so it was that I thanked them, declined the offer to everyone's great relief, and turned myself around and headed south again, not stopping until I could drive comfortably with the windows down. I didn't get to stay, however, family ties press us all to be places we'd rather not be.

The Midwest is good for location if what you want to do is go to every race in America. I did, and so I used it as a place to begin from and found the trade off agreeable enough. Still, there is no ocean in the Midwest and the down home feeling you can get in any family sit down and eat with us restaurant is simply not available. California was extreme and I need not explain if you have lived there. If you haven't, but have visited, then you have just a bare idea, which should be enough. No, great weather cannot make up for all the rest of it and no again, it's not that great all the time.

I did enjoy Oregon and living on the coast really seemed to fill a niche in me, but in the time I was there I lived more in poverty than I ever cared to again and would not go back unless I would never have to try and make a living and live there at the same time. I'm not from there. The local people notice these things. They are not mean about it, it's just that there is only so much work to go around and their own kids are going to get the jobs first if possible. I get that; it's self preservation and while some would like to point a finger and say its 'unfair' I have to shake my head at that idea. If you have kids and they have grown up to the point that you hope they stop living with you, then you know what I mean.

Finally, I thought long and hard about being an ex-pat and nestling down in some part of Europe and living in blissful obscurity. I was fairly young when I first went and the young have ways of finding places for themselves and I found some. Other young people welcomed me and work was available and those with an education of any sort were preferred. I thought France lovely and Switzerland blissful, but the language hassle would have kept me out of them. England, however, was another matter. I could just wander around any town or village at all and feel at home in no time. They were cheery and would talk to you and seemed accommodating enough. They drank; and did it with a good deal of determination as if it was not just a pastime. "Oye! You! Whatchu think yer doin'?" was the worst I ever heard anyone say and it was a policeman expressing his displeasure at someone who had jumped the turnstile and disappeared into the tube.

Things are a good deal worse now, apparently, for which I am sadly disappointed, but I will keep a good thought about it and try and overlook the political upheaval that seems to be constantly stirring up some segment of the population to get them to rise up and claim their proper place in the scheme of things, whatever that might be.

I'm weary of the disadvantaged crying out for privilege; I might be more inclined to listen if it were equality for all they were after but that's not really it. They want payback for all the wrongs done to them over all the years of the past which translates into special status now. Well, special status is the status quo, so the only change they are advocating isn't one of doing away with privilege; they just want to sit in the cat bird seat and have their turn at the front of the queue.

So I watched the Royal Wedding and wished them well. It's been a while and they seem to be getting the hang of it all right. That they live in a world where Gary Nixon doesn't is troubling, but it was already unlikely that their paths would ever cross. I know their country has its problems and we do as well, still and all, when it's someone's wedding day; can't you put that aside for just a bit and wish them all the best? I do... er, I mean, "I will!"

57.

The Zen Of Relationships

ADRIAN BAKER AND I are related. We are related by experience not biology, but it's a bond that is closer than most. The relation is so close in fact that some might say we are twins in one respect, but it's clearly paternal, not identical and one of us is traveling through a space /time continuum so distinct from the other that Einstein would notice. Yes I know you were expecting me to say 'fraternal' but I'm not going to explain myself to make this easier for you, just suggest that speed is the common vicar of our relation and let it go at that. Yet there is a wall between us. I'll call it 'Adrian's Wall' because it is defensive and it keeps out more than the Scots.

He is a scientist and his heart beats in measured volumes of a carbon based organic mixture capable of analysis that would reveal its oxygenation and chemical make up at any given moment, including the ones in which we take the leap at Cadwell Park or take the turn behind the stables at Dade City. My own heart is not just a muscle, but a system of beliefs and feelings and desires that bundle around my consciousness and lend perception to what my senses are saying to me each moment, awake and asleep.

'I love this corner more than I hate that one' it may say while he thinks the latter is 12 degrees off camber and the former is an increasing radius crowned 9 percent similar to Druids or Sign Post Corner or whatever quaint label his world has given it. My heart races when I think about racing, his brain anticipates an increase in adrenaline and the consequential acceleration of his heart rate. He does not believe what I think possible. I do not find what he believes comforting. There is scientific evidence to support his position. What I know to be true is understood for reasons that are totally unscientific. Still, on the track together or far apart, we enjoy the experience mutually.

Back in 2003 when I was putting together "Vintage Motorcycle Racing / Start to Finish" Adrian was one of the few who understood what I was attempting. I thought there might be a number of others but I am wrong often enough about the future to make me question what it will be like so it did not especially upset me. I am not sure why so few people participated, but my mission was simply to offer the opportunity to be a part of something so I plowed ahead. I thought of it, paid for it, and published the book myself. While some in the organization I was working with as an official encouraged me, I got no more permission or access than anyone outside the group would have gotten. When I asked for contact information for their membership so that I could solicit submissions I was turned down on the grounds that it was 'confidential'. That being done, all I could do was attend as many races as possible and make as many contacts as I could to put the word out.

The part of racing that the book did not cover, or even suggest, was the mysterious hidden bit that proved later to be larger than any collection of photographs. Like the out of my depth experience of my first flying lap qualifier at Daytona on a TZ 750, the monster lurks in my subconscious to peer out at me from its dark corners, sometimes summoned, sometimes unbidden, but always present. My pretense that I was not totally terrified when I hit the banking at a speed too great for the bike I was riding and the equipment on hand was eradicated when the reality came back to me with a vengeance that it was otherwise. Once the suspension had collapsed and the spoke wheels were squatted down to their flexing point, the bike wandered across two lanes of the banking even though I held the clipons dead still. My only conscious thought through the beating I was taking was the distant warning that if I let up, the motor would seize and spit me off to certain death. It was real, not imagined, and experienced, not just recollected.

I had an image then of the writhing dragons I had seen in the Chinese New Year parades in San Francisco and recalled my curiosity what it might feel like to ride one. Now I knew. But, the terror I felt was brown gravy over caviar. Once I made myself ignore it, and the moments of what was occurring began to compile into a montage showing me a new raw experience, I quickly acquired a taste for it. What had seemed intolerable just a few moments before became quickly familiar and in turn, survivable.

The bike behaved a bit better the second time and I crossed the finish line still full on the throttle as I took the checker flag. On the cool down lap I took a breath and asked myself if I seriously intended to race this thing for two hundred miles if I made the field. No answer came to me immediately, rather a weighty back and forth considering all that had been sacrificed to make it possible and all I had said assuring everyone I could and would do it. Every groom has doubts and wonders whether his bride to be is really meant for Frankenstein.

I was still undecided when I pulled into the pits and coasted back to where the sponsor and a helper were waiting. I got off the machine and we put it on the stand. I turned the gas off and started to take my gloves off. As a long time habit I held out one hand to show myself that it wasn't shaking. To my surprise it was as steady as ever. Regardless of what I thought, my body was all right with it, even if my mind was still conflicted. Someone came over with a piece of paper that was the report from the speed trap on the back stretch – it showed just over 180 miles an hour. "Jesus Christ," the helper said and blanched.

The sponsor didn't know what to say but looked at me with an expression I was unable to read. "Too fast," I heard myself say, and wondered where such honesty had come from. Sometime between then and when the green flag for 200 miles of the same in a large company of others doing likewise waved two days later I found the will to race the thing and we finished after two bungled pit stops that poured more gas on me than in the tank. I didn't know where we finished and didn't especially care. Kenny Roberts and been favored to win but did not, neither did Agostini or Barry Sheene, or anyone else I can name. That's Daytona for you. On the trip home I was glad to be alive but knew that the arc of my racing career had reached its zenith. Somehow this was beyond me.

The trip home was long and lonesome. I did not tell myself I could do better like I always had before, and then start thinking about all the ways I could find more speed and improve my finish. No. I thought that the sky was the most beautiful shade of blue I had ever seen and turned up the radio when 'brown eyed girl' started to play because I just loved that song. I stopped for biscuits and gravy at a Waffle House and took my time, savoring every bite, pouring ketchup over the whole plate like I had when I was a child. It was dark when I came out and started for home and I knew it would be a long night.

In the U.K. they are noticeably tougher than we are here, even at Daytona. At the Isle of Man when riders fall and die, sometimes there is no opportunity to safely remove them so race officials just cover them with a sheet where they lay and let the race go on. Riders race by the corpse and make a mental note of its presence adding it to their list of landmarks that make their lap of thirty eight miles of track that is the island course. Americans are not in the same league when it comes to this sort of thing. We not only stop racing when a racer dies, we go ahead and remove the body. I know that scientifically it shouldn't matter what we do with them already being dead and all, but let's just say the Manx Marshalls and I differ when it comes to whether or not it matters in the grand scheme of things. In Zen practice, everything matters.

Adrian and I both have raced and currently own vintage T-20 Suzuki 250cc road racers. They were the fastest thing on the track when new, but that was in 1965. Our common opinion about them is that they handle horribly. We have also both ridden TZ350s, which are considerably better, but now have been pumped up by competitors to take the fat front forks from later model bikes and wider rims and all the rest so they are not actually what they used to be at all. Their power plants show the benefits of decades of development and the substitution of new shiny bits of metal for their inferior counterparts. It is scientifically understandable that such development is inexorable.

He came over for a visit last summer and spent several months traveling around the country using my lakeside cottage as a base.My blanching at a speed of 180 mph 30 years ago seems like a whimper now in the racing world. The qualifying speed at the MotoGP at Indianapolis he came to see was over 209 mph. These are not the bikes I rode, nor the ones he has ridden in the interim. These are machines with computer assisted traction control and braking sensors and chassis rigidity that we can barely imagine. I miss the old days, however, and think it less important that we make vintage motorcycles go faster than that we still make them go at all. What still interests me the most about it is not the mechanical aspects, but the larger experience itself.

Is it only money materialized? Is it just another form of extremely dangerous competition that some men seem to crave? Is it an intellectual enterprise? Is it mechanical masturbation? The old parable comes to mind of asking a man hitting himself in the head with a hammer why he is doing it and he answers, "Because it feels sooooo good when I quit." I used to wonder what it would feel like to quit, now I know that I will never know. I have taken time off from racing, but that is not quitting. Quitting is selling everything and taking up golf and that is just not going to happen for me. I have always had a motorcycle from the first moment I knew they existed and I could manage to get one. They set you free in a way that nothing else does. Anyway, I have questions that need answers; like why is it so easy for me to do what I can do what I can do out there on the track? This is not a scientific inquiry.

If Adrian and I were on our bikes going into a turn together and he was mentally calculating physics formulas and I was just feeling the experience and open to it, would it matter in terms of how fast each of us went? To find the answer, I think I should go back to England and have a go again and race my cold calculating friend with all my heart and soul and see. We both agree its fun to do, and we both find joy in the process, but I think it offers a chance to tap into something greater than ourselves and a universe limited by the laws of physics. Is his cat dead, or mine, or Schrodinger's?

He thinks the events of the future are a void ahead of us and we build our own bridges across time according to the rules of science by our conscious decisions. Neither luck nor fate plays a part in the results table for him. I think very different forces are at work. One of us may be correct, or neither one of us, but in racing that doesn't really matter does it? What matters is whose fastest on a given day at a given track.

The ultimate truth and validity of our belief systems won't be known until our existence comes to an end and then we may not be able to share the answer. If I go to my reward and he goes, well, I'm not sure exactly where physicists think they go, or even whether they think they go anywhere at all, is it worth the worry of trying to figure it out in advance? All of this may be too difficult to sort out with what is known and knowable but curious minds want to know and if something can be done to affect an outcome I certainly would care to hear it.

On the other hand it's a simple matter to suit up and twist the throttles on a couple of grand old bikes and have a go with one another around a circuit someplace so we should start there. Fair warning - I won't leave the kill switch off and I don't have Laura Ashley curtains in my transporter; It's bags of coal, axes and hammers for us in the bad boy's club.

58.

The End As A Beginning

ON JUNE 6, 1966 I came home from a summer duty visit to New Mexico to console my recently widowed grandmother and pay my respects. It was too late for that. I had been busy with my own cares finishing high school and had graduated as Roy had died a lingering death of lung cancer. I was alone in not participating in the bedside vigil that sent him on to a place where he would finally find the rest of his family. There was anger waiting for me when I arrived, and I had expected it, but no amount of charm made any difference.

I made the rounds, said "I'm sorry" a hundred times and having done so, made my way back to Illinois desperate to see a friendly face. One in particular came to mind as I drove through the warm desert night of west Texas and then across Indian Territory and on up through Missouri as the next day wore on. I wanted to see the girl that had been my true love all the years I had known one.

She knew I was coming, but I was going to surprise her and would get there a day early. It was not intentional, I had meant to become tired and stop and sleep, but things were on my mind that would not rest and so I just kept driving back to her, and home.

I went straight to her house when I got to town, like a homing pigeon after crossing the ocean. She was not there and her mother told me she had gone to the drive inn. She had a funny look on her face as she said it, but I thought she was just surprised to see me. No one was home at my house when I got there so I took a quick shower and changed and opened up the garage and pulled out the first motorcycle I came to.

I was wearing cut-off blue jeans, a tank top, and a pair of penny loafers without socks. The drive Inn was not far away and I rode slowly, enjoying the gloaming as I went, seeing the familiar back roads with new appreciation as I rode past the manicured greens and fairways of the country club and then on out past Betty Brown's place where her dad had killed himself in the barn and no one ever knew why.

I paid the fee without having to wait in a line which told me that the show was either not very good or had been playing too long. I found my friend Ernie Dees inside, sitting on his motorcycle and parked beside him as it was about to begin. There were previews and conversation and then a feature film about nothing that made an impression.

The car in front of us certainly did, however as it rocked around a good bit thanks to two eager inhabitants in the heat of some passionate mutual exploration. We commented about it and laughed good naturedly hoping they were enjoying themselves.

When the lights came up at intermission, we stood and stretched and were about to head off to refresh ourselves when a guy I didn't know got out of the car and held the door for a familiar looking blonde. It was her voice that caught my attention, I knew that giggle and laugh.

There was a moment then, when her face came up and our eyes met that I will never forget. It was really her and my heart was broken. She started to come over and say something but anything I had to say was already written on my face and I sat back down and pulled out the kick starter and turned on the key, realizing that tears were already filling my eyes. I got it started without looking up and rode the humps between the speaker poles over to the exit with increasing speed.

When I reached the highway, I was raging, and hurt, and eager to be as far away from this as I could get as quickly as I could get there. I was headed back into town, just two miles away and was soon laid out on the tank doing all she would do. I was seeing 100 on the speedometer when I passed the city limit sign and backed off a little but was still going way too fast blocks later when I went by the Dog 'N Suds and up and over the railroad tracks to the Big Four stop signs.

There was no way I could stop, but there was no traffic either so I just went on. I couldn't seem to make myself slow down. I was in trouble, big trouble, and coming apart inside and didn't know what to do about it. I just kept going faster. I saw the Carnegie library building coming up just as I passed the house where James Jones had lived and it registered vaguely that I had used his desk to do my homework on before realizing that such thoughts were out of place at a time like this. How would I know that? I had never had a time like this!

I turned north on Lincoln, heading toward home but not pro-cessing things well at all. I gave it full throttle and ran it through all six speeds, unable to stop myself. As the blocks rolled by the pattern of the elevation changes made by the grades of the crossing streets began to take on a life of its own and I was soon on a roller coaster ride of ups and downs as the streets intersected and humped up down.

It all became the back of a writhing dragon beneath me, trying to buck me off as I went past Ronnie Wilson's house. I could almost see it beneath the bricks under the street light there and was still looking for it when I ran out of road.

In the middle of a block, years before when the town fathers laid out the city streets, a three story red brick school house had been built sometime before the wars and it sat firmly in place surrounded by steel playground equipment worthy of battlement ratings. They were set in concrete. The yard they were in was covered with sharp white gravel and I was about to die.

The road curved away at the bridge and left only the school yard ahead of me and to reach it I would have had to get over the curb and between the power pole and its guy wire and the brick bridge abutment that hemmed me into the killing chute like a slaughterhouse ramp.

I was busily registering all this numbly and barely had time to look down at the speedometer and see that it said '90' and that was it.

I remember clearly what happened next like it was yesterday. The wheel hit the curb and the bike was yanked out of my hands by some unseen force. I went into the dense foliage of the late summer leaves of the ancient trees that rimmed the road and shaded the school like I had been shot from a cannon and immediately felt the whacking of branches and the rush of moving through them as the noise below me began to rise to a cacophony of metal being destroyed by brute force.

A full block away, on the other side of the building where the side street ran in front of the school's entrance there shone the single bare bulb of a street lamp. I did not see it until I landed heavily beneath it, flat on my back on the brick street. It was a killing blow. I did not move. I was not breathing. My eyes were open and I could see the light but nothing else.

Slowly sounds came to me as pieces and bits of shiny things came into and then passed out of my field of vision. I didn't recognize them at first and then realized they were the broken parts of what had been the motorcycle I was riding just a few moments before. Then I heard them.

My hearing returned to me with great suddenness and startling effect as the clanking, tearing, thrashing, thumping sounds of the steel and chrome and aluminum construction that had been the beautiful Suzuki X-6 was deconstructed by monkey bars and swing set chains and teeter totters. A wheel went by, dangling cables; a large black lump cart-wheeled drunkenly over me spewing liquid; another wheel followed and then it all began to pile up off somewhere out of my vision. Nothing hit me. I had been passed over.

The light began to dim and I realized that I was fading away. I did not hurt but it was uncomfortable not to be able to breathe. I heard a small bike approaching and then saw its headlight in the trees overhead and then heard Ernie's desperate pleading voice just before his face appeared and blocked out the light. I remember being irritated at having my last moments ruined this way but that was only beginning to register when he reached down and grabbed me by the waistband of my shorts and the front of my shirt and yanked me up to vertical in one motion asking over and over again if I was all right.

He began shaking me because I had not given him an answer and he apparently wanted one very badly. I caught my breath from his shaking and having it, held it a moment to enjoy the first one after thinking I had had my last one. "Are you all right?!" he repeated, close to my face now, still shaking me. " I will be," I answered, "if you will stop shaking me."

Ernie and I hugged one another a beat or two and then he stepped back and laughed that nervous laughter teenagers do when they don't know what else to do. I did too, but I didn't know why other than I felt like it. "Well, the bike ain't," he observed, looking around us, and I saw then that there was very little left that was not bent or broken and it was scattered all over the whole block from the teeter totters to the light pole with pieces everywhere in between.

We went through the drill of testing out my arms and legs and hands and things for movement like football players do and everything seemed to work. He was going through the motions of doing the things he had seen done and pretending that everything was going to be all right, but was very afraid that it wasn't.

Actually, it was unthinkable that anything would be all right. I had to be dead, this had to be a dream or I was about to explode somehow, we didn't know, so we just did things while we waited for reality to catch up to us again. We moved all the broken bits and junk over to the ditch beside the road and then looked around and after finding nothing else we would think of to do, he gave me a ride home on the back of his bike. I thanked him and he went on his way.

No one was home as I went in and then lay down on the couch. The house was quiet. I was suddenly very tired, and not so concerned any more that some girl I had loved once no longer loved me. That was unfair, I knew, but I also knew that I had nearly killed myself and I certainly didn't want that, convincing myself that nothing was worth that without much effort. I slept.

The next morning I woke up to the smell of frying bacon and my mother singing along with Hank William's "Hey Good Lookin'" as the radio of her '36 Ford played in her head. I was stiff and sore but seemed otherwise all right and went in to exchange greetings and welcome backs. She was still angry that I had not gone west when I should have to pay my respects to her father but that had faded some and she was glad enough to see me.

My brother was not so glad when he came in from the garage to complain that someone had taken his motorcycle in the night. I realized then that in my haste I had gotten the wrong one and it had been his that had been destroyed, not mine.

I told him we should talk about it after we ate and we did. He drove me down to the school yard in his Jeep and we loaded up the pieces of what had been an X-6 Suzuki six speed hustler. We walked around to be sure we had everything as if he was going to put it back together some day.

I stepped off the distance from the tire mark on the curb to the place under the streetlamp where Ernie had picked me up. It was 309 feet and I did it twice to be sure. I still had on the same clothes from the night before and made a comment about it and my brother started to give it renewed attention and made me tell him the whole thing again.

When I was finished, he protested. "There is not a scratch on you," he said finally, "what really happened?" "That's it, I swear," I told him, and after his best, 'you'd better not be lying to me' stare, he let it go, but I could see that he did not believe me. I added 'Scout's Honor,' but that was brushed aside as well.

I had trouble believing it myself for a long time. What force or power was so great that it could save a stupid kid from self destructive foolishness when he needed it the very most and why would it? I struggle with that still. No bruises appeared later on, no cuts or scrapes or broken bones ever surfaced. For that one moment in time I had been entirely invincible and it was when I needed it the very most. It was incredible.

I finally came to believe that it had to do with time. I had come home a day early and the mechanism of time was thrown off somehow and I missed a window or some twilight zone sort of thing happened.

I didn't believe that, not really. I did have a sense that it meant something important; that there was something I was supposed to do out there ahead of me in time and this had been an aberration that the master of time would just have to overlook to get me there.

I did give thanks in the traditional way and was sincere about it, and my gratitude has not flagged a bit. Still and all, if things like this can be done, and I am living proof that they can, then why isn't intervention more common?

I thought about that a good deal as well and decided that it probably goes on all the time and we just don't know enough to see it. I am sure, no I am absolutely certain, that things happen for a reason and that on that night, something saved me. I would never be able to complain after that about being unlucky. I live a charmed life. I don't know why I still live, and I'm not exactly sure what it is I am supposed to do with it but I am trying to find that out.

There are many around who will tell you they have the answer. They may have theirs; they don't have mine. First I have to know what the question is and I have to be able to state it in my own terms that come from my own experience. Once that is clarified, I can begin to work on what the answer might be. It is a work in progress.

59.

I Ride The Wind

*(a poem of long ago when there was no chicane at Daytona
and qualifying meant a flying lap alone.)*

"Onto the banking; Fifth;..Sixth; throttle wide open.
Tucking in, I feel the wind slip past me, around me.
The worry of the pit lane recedes behind me.
Excitement laces all before me.
The cream in my coffee.

I am one with the gas tank, my chest pressed hard against it.
Pushing back into the seat,the motor screams beneath me.
I slide my feet up to tiptoes on the pegs and feel
my knees pressing in against hard things.
I press back against them; harder.

I twist the throttle hard, holding it against the stop.
I keep my elbows in and arch my back
up to bring my helmet down
beneath the bubble
and I wait.

I am a diver falling through the air controlling
my posture to make my entry in that hard
moment of meeting the water as
Perfectly splashless as
Possible.

I am the pelican, having skimmed the waves
In formation then swooped and caught the
sunlight in the air while eyeing the waters
for my prey. Then, suddenly, folding up
I dart into the dark sea.

I am still. I watch the tach needle climb into the red.
I look side to side but don't dare move my head.
Concentration makes a ballet of my deed.
All other things now over –
I revel in the speed.

Behind me, long months of labor and effort
disappear in my wake like the turgid
tumblings of water behind a boat
about to plane up and rise
to its true calling

I am weary with the tiredness that comes from
sleepless nights and constant worry and work
to make all this possible; probable;then real.
A dream made true; a thing all new –
Finally, something I can feel.

I push back the regret of sacrificing others so that I
can have these moments for myself. It is selfish.
I know it. They say they don't mind – they do.
A few have had to let me go; not satisfied
with being second. Not for this.

I say they do not understand that there is nothing else;
Not love or money or glory or sunshine or starlight
or birthdays or waffles or lovers or anything –
not anything that comes even close
to this, just this, – " THIS".

Coming at me fast, somewhere ahead not very far away,
is the precise point where I must give it all up. Let off,
Sit up, Face the wind, Think, Hold on, Lean in,
Aim at the precise point, the exact spot
to turn away from such a selfish sin.

I try to not think about any of that, maybe later, but not now.
From here I hope to manage it all and try to juggle
enough things to make it be a "Win".
My mind races and hums along –
I ride the wind.

THE END

Acknowledgments

I THANK THE MANY who have helped me race and let me live when I might not have otherwise. Some supported me, some were indifferent, and some I annoyed. Still, I started young and was going through life and a career on the track at the same time as were many of those I have raced with over the decades. I always thought I would die young. That I have not, is a mystery.

I thank all the people who made this book possible. It began as a FaceBook post where I invited recollections and observations from those who had raced. I read them all and that they do not appear verbatim in the pages above has more to do with my publishers' legal department than my wish to acknowledge their contributions. This book was funded by a non-profit corporation as an effort to promote international good will and understanding through amateur competition and their board sees vintage racing as an avenue for that work for which I am grateful. I acknowledge my debt to them and will persist in their good works.

For all who race and all who love those that race and suffer from it I thank you. It is a madness of sorts, as you know already, but it is a fine madness and it makes a blaze of light where something less would probably have come in its stead but for racing. See you at the races.

CPSIA information can be obtained at www.ICGtesting.com
Printed in the USA
LVOW08s0610261114

415389LV00004B/5/P